India's 2004 Elections

India's 2004 Elections

Grass-roots and National Perspectives

Edited by

Ramashray Roy
Paul Wallace

SAGE Publications
New Delhi ■ Thousand Oaks ■ London

First published in 2007 by

Sage Publications India Pvt Ltd
B-42, Panchsheel Enclave
New Delhi 110 017
www.indiasage.com

Sage Publications Inc
2455 Teller Road
Thousand Oaks, California 91320

Sage Publications Ltd
1 Oliver's Yard, 55 City Road
London EC1Y 1SP

Published by Tejeshwar Singh for Sage Publications India Pvt Ltd, phototypeset in 11/13 pt Agaramond by Star Compugraphics Private Limited, Delhi and printed at Chaman Enterprises, New Delhi.

Library of Congress Cataloging-in-Publication Data

India's 2004 elections : grass-roots and national perspectives / edited by Ramashray Roy, Paul Wallace.
     p. cm.
Includes bibliographical references and index.
1. India. Parliament. Lok Sabha—Elections, 2004. 2. Elections—India. I. Roy, Ramashray. II. Wallace, Paul, 1931–

JQ292.I587   324.954'0531—dc22   2006   2006033222

ISBN: 10: 0-7619-3516-9 (HB)   10: 81-7829-668-3 (India-HB)
          13: 978-0-7619-3516-2 (HB)   13: 978-81-7829-668-5 (India-HB)

Sage Production Team: Aliya Rao, Roopa Sharma, Rajib Chatterjee, and Santosh Rawat

Joan Bondurant passed away in September 2006. She served as our teacher at the University of California, Berkeley and inspired us with her Gandhian approach to politics and non-violence.

Contents

List of Tables and Figures   ix

List of Abbreviations   xii

Preface   xv

Introduction: India Shining Trumped by Poverty   1
Paul Wallace

PART I: National, Theoretical, and Comparative

1. The Text and Context of the 2004 Lok Sabha Elections   9
   in India
   Ramashray Roy
2. Chaste Like Sita, Fierce Like Durga: Indian Women   34
   in Politics
   Sikata Banerjee
3. Contextualizing Religious, Caste and Regional Dynamics   58
   in Electoral Politics: Emerging Paradoxes
   Pramod Kumar
4. Of Hindus and their Nationalisms: Religion,   76
   Representation, and Democracy
   Jyotirindra Dasgupta
5. 'Jumbo Cabinets', Factionalism, and the Impact   116
   of Federalism: Comparing Coalition Governments
   in Kerala, Punjab, and Uttar Pradesh
   Virginia Van Dyke

PART II: Analytical State Studies

6. Gujarat after Godhra   151
   Ghanshyam Shah
7. Political Articulation and Policy Discourse in the 2004   180
   Elections in Andhra Pradesh
   Karli Srinivasulu

8. The New Alliance Made the Difference in Bihar   206
     Sanjay Kumar

9. Politics of Separatism in Assam   229
     Sandhya Goswami and *Monoj Kumar Nath*

10. Ethno-Regional Identity and Political Mobilization in   240
      Meghalaya: Democratic Discourse in a Tribal State
      Rajesh Dev

11. Validating Status Quo and Local Narratives in Orissa   267
      Mohammed Badrul Alam

12. CPI(M) Dominance and 'Other' Parties in West Bengal   291
      Amiya K. Chaudhuri

About the Editors and Contributors   320
Index   325

List of Tables and Figures

TABLES

1.1 Voter support for different political parties, 1999–2004 14
1.2 Caste group-wise votes for political parties, 1999–2004 16
1.3 Voter support (women) for different political parties 17
     and alliances, 1999–2004

2.1 Gender-wise breakdown of voter turnout in Indian 36
     general elections, 1952–2004
2.2 Representation of women in the Lok Sabha, 1957–2004 36
2.3 Gender-wise breakdown of individuals contesting 37
     general elections, 1957–2004

3.1 Vidhan Sabha elections in Andhra Pradesh 64
     (1994 and 2004)
3.2 Seats won by the Bharatiya Janata Party in parliament 68
     elections (1984–2004)
3.3 Party preference by social group 69
3.4 Performance of BJP and Congress in Gujarat Parliament 70
     and Vidhan Sabha elections
3.5 BSP vote support in Uttar Pradesh and Punjabe 72
     Legislativ Assembly

6.1 *Zilla* and *taluka panchayat* (direct) election results by 160
     party and district, 2000
6.2 Performance of the BJP and Congress in riot effected 162
     and unaffected constituencies in the 2002 Assembly
     and 2004 Lok Sabha elections
6.3 Performance of the BJP and Congress in ST reserved 171
     constituencies in different elections
6.4 Trend of party preference by various castes/communities 173

8.1   Bihar: Results of Lok Sabha elections, 1996–2004   210
8.2   Lok Sabha elections, 2004: Seats won and votes   211
      polled by alliances and parties
8.3   Region-wise analysis of Lok Sabha 2004   213
      election results
8.4   Community-wise opinion of Laloo Prasad Yadav   218
8.5   Class-wise opinion of Laloo Prasad Yadav   218
8.6   State of civic amenities and social conditions   219
8.7   Changes in economic condition during 1999–2004   220
8.8   Level of satisfaction with present economic conditions 220
8.9   Level of satisfaction with MPs of different   221
      political parties
8.10 Future expectations about economic conditions   222
8.11 Opinion regarding the country's image   222
8.12 Popularity of the various political alliances   223
8.13 Yadav and Muslim support for the RJD alliance   223
8.14 Voting pattern by economic class   224
8.15 Voting pattern by level of education   224
8.16 Voting pattern by age   225

9.1   Voter turnout in Lok Sabha elections, 1991–2004   231
9.2   Lok Sabha elections, Assam: Voting pattern within   235
      ST communities
9.3   Voting pattern in Lok Sabha elections in Kokrajhar,   236
      1991–2004
9.4   Voting pattern in Lok Sabha elections in the   238
      Autonomous districts, 1991–2004

10.1 Party-wise seats share in the Meghalaya Assembly,   252
      1972–2003
10.2 Party-wise performance in the Garo and Khasi-Jaintia   257
      areas, 1972–2003
10.3 Candidates returned to Parliament, 1997–2004   260

11.1 Orissa Assembly elections, 2000 and 2004   278
11.2 Orissa Lok Sabha elections, 1999 and 2004   278

12.1 Percentage of seats won by the Left Front in *Panchayat* 292
      elections, 1978–2003

12.2 Seats and percentage of votes won by political parties 303
in Assembly elections, 1967–2001

12.3 Seats and percentage of votes won by political parties 311
in Lok Sabha elections, 1996–2004

12.4 Percentage of votes won by LF in Parliamentary, 312
Assembly, and *panchayat* elections, 1998–2004

FIGURES

5.1 Vote share of political parties and fronts in the Kerala 134
Vidhan Sabha elections, 1977–2006

5.2 Vote share of political parties in the Punjab Vidhan 135
Sabha elections, 1967–2002

5.3 Vote share of political parties in the Uttar Pradesh 135
Vidhan Sabha elections, 1967–2002

6.1 Upper caste party preference in different elections 158
6.2 OBC party preference in different elections 166
6.3 Scheduled Castes' party preference in different elections 168
6.4 Scheduled Tribes' party preference in different elections 172
6.5 Muslims' party preference in different elections 175

List of Abbreviations

AATSU	All Assam Tribal Students Union
ABSU	All Bodo Student Union
ABVP	Akhil Bharatiya Vidyarthi Parishad
AGP	Asom Gana Parishad
AICC	All India Congress Committee
AIADMK	All India Anna Dravida Munnetra Kazhagam
AITC	All India Trinamul Congress
AKJSU	All Khasi–Jaintia Students Union
ALTVC	Area Local Tribal Village Council
APHLC	All Peoples Hills Leaders Conference
ARM	Alliance for the Reconstruction of Meghalaya
ASDC	Autonomous State Demand Committee
B. Cong	Bangla Congress
BAC	Bodoland Autonomous Council
BJD	Biju Janata Dal
BJP	Bharatiya Janata Party
BKS	Bharatiya Kisan Sangh
BLT	Bodo Liberation Tigers
BSP	Bahujan Samaj Party
BTAD	Bodoland Territorial Autonomous District
BTC	Bodoland Territorial Council
CAG	Comptroller and Auditor General
CITU	Center for Indian Trade Unions
CMRT	Closed Minimum Range Theory
CPI	Communist Party of India
CPI(M)	Communist Party of India (Marxist)
CPI(ML)	Communist Party of India (Marxist-Leninist)
DHD	Dima Halam Daogah
DHM	Democratic Hills Movement
DMK	Dravida Munnetra Kazhagam
EITU	Eastern India Tribal Union

FB	Forward Bloc
GKS	Gujarat Kshatriya Sabha
GNLF	Gorkha National Liberation Front
GSP	Gujarat Swatantra Party
HNF	Hynniewtrep National Front
HPU	Hill Peoples Union
HSPDP	Hill State Peoples Democratic Party
INC	Indian National Congress
IND	Independent Candidate
ITDP	Integrated Tribal Development Projects
JD	Janata Dal
JD(U)	Janata Dal (United)
JMM	Jharkhand Mukti Morcha
KBK Project	Kalahandi–Bolangir–Koraput Project
KHAM	Kshatriya, Harijan, Adivasi, and Muslim (alliance)
KHNAM	Khun Hynniewtrep National Awakening Movement
KLO	Kamtapur Liberation Organization
KPP	Krishak Praja Party
KSU	Khasi Students Union
LJNSP	Lok Jan Shakti Party
LS	Lok Sabha
MCC	Marxist Coordination Committee
MDP	Meghalaya Democratic Party
MLA	Member of Legislative Assembly
MP	Member of Parliament
MPLAD fund	Member of Parliament Local Area Development fund
MTYO	Meghalaya Tribal Youth Organization
MUF	Meghalaya United Front
MUPP	Meghalaya United Parliamentary Party
MWC	Minimum Winning Coalition
NCP	Nationalist Congress Party
NDA	National Democratic Alliance
NERISF	North Eastern Region Indigenous Students Federation
NERSU	North East Region Students Union
NSS	Nair Service Society
NSUI	National Students Union of India

OBC	Other Backward Castes
OGP	Orissa Gana Parishad
PDA	Progressive Democratic Alliance
PDF	People's Democratic Front
PDIC	Public Demands Implementation Convention
PDM	Peoples Democratic Movement
PKASH	Party of Patidars and Kshatriyas
PRAC	People's Rally Against Corruption
PTCA	Plains Tribal Council of India
PULF	Progressive United Left Front
PWD	Public Works Department
PWG	People's War Group
RJD	Rashtriya Janata Dal
RSP	Revolutionary Socialist Party
RSS	Rashtriya Swayamsevak Sangh
SC	Scheduled Castes
SFI	Students Federation of India
SHG	Self-help Groups
SJSS	Sanmilita Janagosthiya Sangram Samiti
SNDPY	Shree Narayana Dharma Paripalana Yogam
SSM	Samajik Sam-Rasata Manch
ST	Scheduled Tribes
SUC	Socialist Unity Center
TADA	Terrorist and Disruptive Activities (Prevention) Act
TADC	Tribal Autonomous District Council
TMC	Tamil Maanila Congress
UDP	United Democratic Party
UF	United Front
ULF	United Left Front
UMPF	United Meghalaya Parliamentary Forum
UP	Uttar Pradesh/United Provinces
UPA	United Progressive Alliance
UPDS	United People's Democratic Solidarity
URMCA	United Reservation Movement Council of Assam
VHP	Vishwa Hindu Parishad
WODC	Western Orissa Development Council
YDF	Youth Democratic Front

Preface

We continue in this volume our efforts to understand the working of the world's largest democracy through the telescope of elections in India. This volume, the third in our election series with Sage Publications, India, covers the election process and related phenomena at the national and state levels. We consciously decided to restrict the scope of this volume to several selected states and to specific subjects relevant on an all-India basis. Accordingly, our contributors provide their interpretations of the 2004 elections in a manner that provides provocative depth and analysis rather than a cookbook approach only dealing with results.

Our appreciation is extended to the numerous individuals and institutions that assisted in the research and preparation of this and the preceding volumes. In particular, we are indebted to Sage Publications India. Tejeshwar Singh, Managing Director of Sage India, has been the one constant persona in an ever-changing cast of talented personnel. Even he, after 25 years, has relinquished that post for the new role of Chairman of the Board of Directors. Debjani Majumdar Dutta, then Acquisitions Editor, encouraged us to undertake this third election study with special topics to be included with the state studies. Her successor in this project, Dr Sugata Ghosh, Senior Manager, Commissioning subsequently authorized publication of the manuscript. Ashok R. Chandran, Deputy Commissioning Editor, ably shepherded the project through its editorial phases. Careful proof-reading by the Sage staff resulted in the polishing and accuracy that is a characteristic of all three election books. The professionalism of all concerned along with their patience and humanity enabled a complex process to proceed with marked success.

Each of the contributors is indebted to their university and research institutions. In particular, the Centre for the Study of Developing Societies provided invaluable data from its election surveys. As always, the Election Commission is the source of most of the official elections results. Many individuals also contributed with valuable suggestions, critiques, and information. Each of the contributors could compile a lengthy list. Strenuous efforts have been made by all concerned to be accurate and scholarly.

Ramashray Roy and Paul Wallace

Introduction:
India Shining Trumped by Poverty

PAUL WALLACE

India's electoral politics continues to be full of surprises. Prime Minister Atal Behari Vajpayee led his Bharatiya Janata Party (BJP) and coalition to an early election in May 2004 on the basis of economic progress that they labeled 'India Shining.' Thus the economy and governance became issues in a manner that is unusual for a polity more accustomed to personalities, electoral waves based on transitory phenomena, religious identity passions such as *Hindutva*, caste, tribal, and minority concerns. India Shining met its match in the Congress party-led coalition emphasis on attacking poverty.

Economic themes dominated the national dialog in 2004, but votes are cast for individual members of Parliament, and the same variables differ as they operate in each state. Thus, two approaches are followed in this volume even more than in the two previous volumes in this election series from Sage Publications.[1] One set of chapters in this volume focusing on the national level, are comparative, or on themes that transcend individual states. A second set continues the earlier focus on state politics, with special attention to tribal politics. Taken together, the three volumes provide a rich panorama of electoral politics and social change at the national and state levels in India from independence in 1947 through the elections of 2004.

Macro electoral trends as emphasized in the two earlier volumes continued in the 21st century. Two outstanding facts of the May 2004 parliamentary elections are that, as predicted in the previous volume,[2] Congress finally entered the coalition political game in full measure and, second, the regional parties continue to develop political muscle. They cumulatively now command a majority of the popular votes, a significant degree of veto power within any governing coalition over its continuance and are the major party or a vital part of the ruling coalition in most states. The Congress's 2004 vote total of 26.2 percent added to the BJP's total of 21.5 percent is 47.7 percent. Thus, India's two major parties together received less than half of the total votes. In 1999, together, they totaled 52.05 percent of the total votes—28.3 percent for the Congress party and 23.75 percent for the BJP.[3]

Macro trends do inform us about particular patterns such as the transformation over time from dominant one-party to coalition politics. Nevertheless, while they may provide us with some general characteristics, they don't convey the complexity of electoral politics in India. Diversity, rather than uniformity, marks Indian politics as reflected in an increasingly decentralized democratic federal political system embracing over one billion people. India's economy and society also span a spectrum ranging from subsistence to highly modernized agriculture, back-breaking physical labor to world-class information technology, and from age-old social structures and practices to 21st century modernity and its accompanying problems.

Consequently, this volume, as well the earlier ones, does not attempt to provide a formula or rigid categories that the contributors must follow. No one size fits all! Politically relevant data in India comes in different sizes, is expressed differently at different points in time, and consequently is subject to various kinds of interpretations. A rising part of the social strata applauds change, while receding or status quo elements may bitterly fight it. 'India Shining' vs continuing poverty illustrates differences that proved to be politically relevant in the elections.

In Part I, Ramashray Roy examines and analyzes these developments resulting in the surprising victory of the United Progressive Alliance (UPA) over the National Democratic Alliance (NDA). In particular, he emphasizes that the election 'highlights the growing distance between what the people need' and what the parties 'are able to provide despite their high sounding rhetoric.' Accordingly, he questions the ability of the Congress-led coalition to achieve its egalitarian promises.

Women's electoral participation and leadership is becoming more notable with a corresponding increase in scholarly attention. Sikata Banerjee examines this trend in the context of the 'cultural, economic, and political parameters limiting many Indian women's access to political power.' She provides an insightful and provocative cultural metaphor.

Pramod Kumar's concern is with the political consequences of the changes to a competitive liberal market economy, to coalition governance, and to a 'polarized socio-cultural' politics. These, he argues, result in paradoxes that make it difficult to neatly categorize political parties in economic, communal and caste terms, especially in regard to their positions while in power as contrasted with their role in the opposition. He concludes, 'Ideological filters have become convenient labels ... for what is otherwise a blatantly legislative power game.'

Jyotirindra Dasgupta provides a more optimistic, longitudinal perspective in an elaborately constructed essay on religion and nationalism. He builds an edifice extending from the stirrings of nationalism in Bengal to contemporary Hinduism and nationalism. 'Allegiance is a political creation,' he states, which is recognized in the construction of a 'composite nationalism' in India. Citizens therefore have multiple identities, e.g., village, caste, Bengali, Indian—from which to draw. Electoral politics tend to moderate the parties in power as, 'cultural nationalism as advocated by Hindu nationalists is too aggressively combative ....'

Conventional wisdom suggests that since coalitions have to aggregate many interests and leaders, they result in jumbo cabinets and enhanced factionalism. Virginia Van Dyke examines coalition and cabinet formation in Punjab, Kerala, and Uttar Pradesh. Existing literature has largely been based on western European cases. India's federalism and marked differences between states provide a rich arena for comparison and fresh analysis.

Part II consists of seven state studies, each with a theme that provides depth to the electoral context. Gujarat is conditioned by the 2002 communal carnage as well as 'three decades of constructing *Hindutva* ideology and action,' according to Ghanshyam Shah.

Nonetheless, 'polarization is not total' with a large part of the state free from direct communal violence and some resistance to the *Hindutva* agenda. Gujarat's challenge, Shah concludes, is to 'build unity among all castes and classes' and 'spur economic growth with its Swadeshi model.'

Andhra Pradesh provided an electoral surprise with the defeat of the incumbent Telegu Desam Party (TDP) and its economic reforms by the Congress party. TDP's populism led by a charismatic cinema star gave way to Chief Minister Chandrababu Naidu's economic policy orientations. Success over a period of nine years could not be maintained within the electoral discourse that became a plebiscitary election. A former TDP leader, K. Chandrasekhar Rao, effectively raised the Telangana regional issue. The Congress, allied with Rao and his regional party, also benefited by an alliance with the left against the Naidu-led TDP–BJP alliance.

Alliance politics also highlighted the Lok Sabha elections in Bihar in 2004 and the Assembly elections the following year. These two elections had opposite results. In 2004, Laloo Prasad Yadav and his allies, including the Congress party, continued their long-term dominance of Bihar. But they lost in February 2005 to Nitish Kumar's Janata Dal (U) in alliance with the BJP. In addition to alliance politics, Sanjay Kumar concludes, 'After 15 years of RJD rule,' Biharis 'do want some development to take place in the state.'

Complex tribal politics is the theme of Sandhya Goswami and Monoj Kumar Nath's chapter on separatist politics in Assam as also the succeeding chapter on Meghalaya by Rajesh Dev. Electoral politics led to the 'ethnicization of politics' in Assam and 'explosion of ethnicities' as many formerly passive groups are brought into the political arena. Accommodating this diversity with its 'fragmentation of the political party space' provides the contemporary challenge. Similarly, in Meghalaya, 'groups and clusters that emerge as a result of the cascading politicization of ethnic identities have merely resulted in the shallow ethnicization of politics where justification of claims and their legitimization can take place only on ethnic terms.' At the same time, there is the possibility that 'greater democratic visibility and political accountability' can be pursued.

Orissa also has a significant tribal population that the ruling BJP accommodates through various development projects resulting in 'small yet significant support from the tribal bloc.' More importantly for the continuance of BJP dominance in Orissa since 1999 is the organizational support provided by the Hindu organizations known collectively as the Sangh Parivar. Effective united leadership under Naveen Patnaik contrasted with the Congress leadership's struggles enabled the BJP to deviate from the national trend as well as the anti-incumbency factor.

West Bengal clearly is the outstanding case—unique in India—in its long-term dominance by one political group. The Communist Party of India (Marxist) (CPI[M])-led left alliance has ruled West Bengal since 1977 at both the Lok Sabha and Assembly levels without succumbing to the anti-incumbency factor, including in the 2004 Lok Sabha elections. Amiya K. Chaudhuri examines the development of CPI(M)'s hegemony during these three decades. Particularly important are their strong party and front organizations as contrasted with 'the absence of any viable alternative non-Marxist coalition.' Also important are the CPI(M)-directed land reforms, its relationship to rural self-governance, maintenance of law and order and electoral and political management.

India's politics is described and analyzed in this volume, and the preceding two published by Sage in this series, in greater depth and scope than any comparable set of scholarly studies. One-party dominant politics has been replaced by two national coalitions led respectively by the Congress and the BJP. The question of the tail wagging the elephant[4] in terms of the importance of regional parties at the national and state levels can be significant at almost any time. Electoral politics has ensured that compromise is essential to maintaining national parties as well as coalitions at the state level. Extremist rhetoric based on religion, caste and even secularism is moderated by the compulsions of electoral politics as filtered through India's diversity. Thus, the Congress and BJP-led coalitions are not incompatible ideological formations[5] but competitors in India's federalist, democratic political system.

NOTES

1. Ramashray Roy and Paul Wallace, *Indian Politics and the 1998 Elections: Regionalism, Hindutva and State Politics* (New Delhi: Sage Publications, 1999); Paul Wallace and Ramashray Roy, *India's 1999 Elections and 20th Century Politics* (New Delhi: Sage Publications, 2003).
2. Wallace and Roy, *India's 1999 Elections*, p. 8.
3. Election Commission of India—General Elections, 1999 (13th Lok Sabha), Vol. 1, *National and State Abstracts and Detailed Results*, pp. 49–56.
4. Paul Wallace, 'Introduction: India's 1998 Election—Hindutva, the Tail Wags the Elephant, and Pokhran', in Roy and Wallace, *Indian Politics in the 1998 Election*, op. cit., p. 17.
5. For a contrasting conclusion, see Baldev Raj Nayar, 'India in 2004', *Asian Survey*, Vol. XLV, No. 1 (January–February 2005), p. 78.

PART I

National, Theoretical, and Comparative

CHAPTER 1

The Text and Context of the 2004 Lok Sabha Elections in India

RAMASHRAY ROY

Exit Poll: It is their exit and our poll.

—Kapil Sibal, Congress MP and Minister in the UPA Government.

When Atal Behari Vajpayee announced the holding of a fresh election much before the term of his government expired, it surprised many politically informed and interested persons. It is reported that he was not at all in favor of having an early poll and was determined to continue till the five-year term came to an end. As a matter of fact, he had several times expressed his intention to complete his term. But then the Modi government in Gujarat won the State elections held after the infamous Godhra carnage involving atrocities including arson, pillage and murder, allegedly by Rashtriya Swamsevak Sangh (RSS) supporters and the Vishwa Hindu Parishad (VHP), and it changed things. It gave a lot of confidence to several of the partners in the ruling coalition of the certainty of the return to power by the National Democratic Alliance (NDA). Pressure began to mount on Vajpayee to hold an early elections. Much against his earlier judgment he gave in and a fresh election was announced. The electoral die thus was cast and the election was held in April–May 2004.

The first Parliamentary election in the 21st century has come and gone. It, however, produced a major upset in the Indian political universe insofar as it shook the basis of the carefully constructed and assiduously guarded edifice of a ruling coalition, the NDA, under Bharatiya Janata Party (BJP) Prime Minister Atal Behari Vajpayee. The coalition comprised of 22 middling and small parties, and was able to pull on for a little over four years. But then it decided to go to the electoral battlefront and measure its strength against other political combines. The reason for this premature opening of the electoral battle was the over-confidence in its certain victory with increased strength in Parliament.[1] However, its confidence was shattered by the 'fickle' voters who inflicted on it a big shock of unexpected defeat at the polls. It forced Vajpayee to ruefully comment that he could never understand the mood of the voter. A new coalition, the United Progressive Alliance (UPA), under the prime ministership of Dr Manmohan Singh of the Indian National Congress (INC) as a major partner, took over the reigns of governance.

Only five years ago, the BJP had the fortune of emerging as the largest party in Parliament by winning 182 of the 339 seats it contested. By contrast, its national rival, the Congress party registered its lowest ever seat tally of 114 of the 453 seats it contested. Its share of popular vote, 28.3 percent, was higher than the BJP's 23.8 percent due to the larger number of seats it contested. However, Congress's share of parliamentary seats plummeted.

Despite its unexpected defeat in the 2004 election, the BJP did well in its traditional strongholds of Madhya Pradesh, Rajasthan, and Chhattisgarh. It also made substantial gains in Karnataka, but slipped a little along with its close ally, the Shiv Sena, in Maharashtra. BJP's biggest losses have been registered in Uttar Pradesh (UP), Bihar, Jharkhand, Delhi, Haryana and, of all the states, Gujarat. Some of its heavyweight cabinet ministers have been humbled, among them Murli Manohar Joshi, Yashwant Sinha, and Saheb Singh Verma as well as the erstwhile speaker of Parliament, the Shiv Sena's Manohar Joshi.

The rise of the BJP as a major party at the national level has been slow but steady since its appearance in the political firmament of India as a serious and determined contender for power in 1950. In the 1952 election to the Lok Sabha it could capture only three of the 94 seats it contested. But since then, it has been steadily improving its position going, however, through the process of ups and downs.[2] Since 1989, the BJP made advances on the national stage partly through raising its vote share incrementally, but even more through its success in striking alliances in every region with parties big and small. However, in the 2004 election, three of its senior partners in key states suffered a spectacular debacle—Jayalalitha's AIADMK (All India Anna Dravida Munnetra Kazhagam) in Tamil Nadu, Chandrababu Naidu's Telegu Desam Party (TDP) in Andhra Pradesh and Mamata Banerjee's Trinamul Congress (TMC) in West Bengal. Besides, a critical ally—the Janata Dal (United) (JD[U]), fared poorly in Bihar. The heavy losses that the NDA constituents suffered at the 2004 polls could not be compensated by the exceedingly better performance of two of its allies, the Biju Janata Dal (BJD) in Orissa and the Shiromani Akali Dal (SAD) in Punjab, for the big losses in the south and in the east.[3]

The other side of the coin is the improvement of the Congress party's performance in comparison to 1999 and the impressive performance of its key alliance partners in Tamil Nadu, Andhra Pradesh, Bihar, Jharkhand, and Maharashtra. However, it failed totally in Kerala. The Congress had the distinction of ruling over the subcontinent as a dominant party. Nonetheless, it had been suffering a steady decline since 1967. It suffered a big jolt in 1977 after two years of a harsh and oppressive regime under the National Emergency declared by Prime Minister, Mrs Indira Gandhi, in 1975.[4] It recovered in 1980 and maintained its position with considerable improvement, but began to lose ground till it reached its lowest point in 1999 when it could win only 114 Lok Sabha seats. Recovering in the 2004 election, it went beyond its own expectations capturing 145 of the 417 seats it contested. The Congress joined several parties, the Rashtriya Janata Dal (RJD), the Dravida Munnetra Kazhagam (DMK), the left parties, the National Congress Party of Sharad Pawar and others. This alliance enabled it to form a ruling coalition under Dr Manmohan Singh as the prime minister.

There is no doubt that the BJP combine was self-assured of its victory at the polls. But its electoral performance was much below what had been in 1999. On top of this, its key alliance partners, barring a few exceptions, did worse.[5] As a result, the NDA could not muster enough numerical strength in the Lok Sabha to form a government. It is against this background that the question why in just a span of less then five years, it lost vital support among the electorate and, as a consequence, failed to emerge again as a ruling coalition. It is true that some of its key alliance partners did not do well. However, this should not detract from the fact that the BJP's own performance was not satisfactory. This raises, therefore, the important question about the factors that can be said to be responsible for this decline. Why did the BJP lose its power base so soon? Or, why did some of its alliance partners, too, suffer heavy losses? Are these two separate questions calling for two different answers? Or, is there a common factor that can account for both the situations? Needless to say that elections in different states took place in varied conditions that have been building up over time to create a particular mood in each state. However different these immediate factors may have been in the various states, all of them point to one distinguishing common factor—the mood of the electorate.

It must be accepted that the term 'mood' is a nebulous element that assumes different meanings in different psychological states. Also, it is characterized by a variation in density signifying the strength of mood; it may be very strong or very weak, prone to change depending on the stimulus received from the environment. Whatever may be the conditions in which a particular mood is formed, there is one particular mood that we are concerned with here: it is the mood of the voter that refers to the phenomenon of legitimacy of a particular regime. It does not need to be emphasized that it is the sense of legitimacy, and variations in it, that determine electoral outcome. Given this, it is natural to assume that the loss of the BJP and some of its key alliance partners must have been caused by a significant drop in their legitimacy in the eyes of the voters. If this is true, then we must ask how we should account for this loss. This loss was caused both by the operation of some short-term as well as long-term factors. The exploration, therefore, of what these factors were and how they affect the political fortune of the BJP and its alliance partners must receive our attention. What should be added is that insofar as the term 'factor' is concerned, it is the same in the case of the BJP and its defeated alliance partners. The immediate contextual factors, however, may be different in each state.

But before we discuss these factors, it needs to be pointed out that the electoral situation in which the 2004 Lok Sabha polls took place was quite distinct in different states. The demise of the one-party dominance system meant the emergence of different patterns of party competition in different states. The reason for the fall of the Congress party from its pre-eminence is also responsible for the fragmentation of the Congress-dominated national party system underlining the growing politicization of social cleavages along regional lines since the late 1960s due to the increasing centralization of the Congress party and Congress government.[6] The fall of Congress is also due to the insensitivity of Congress governments at the national level towards regional economic development.[7] There are several factors that account for the differential patterns of party competition in different states.

The divergent state patterns of electoral competition present a variegated picture of electoral competition. This underlines the fact that diverse trends operate in different states indicating that when Congress dominance began to wilt, it reflected the decline in its social support base. If, as Chhibber and Petrocik argue, the Congress party is a coalition of state parties joined together in the venture of capturing power at the national and state levels,[8] it follows that when the Congress lost its pre-eminent position and as politicization of state-based forces grew in intensity, the social bases from which the Congress drew its support began to move away to regional or state parties. This gave rise to differential patterns of party competition in different states. Anthony Heath and Yogendra Yadav argue that as a consequence of the changing social support base of the Congress party, the nature of party competition also changes. For example, the Congress draws on different social groups when it is in competition with the BJP than it does when it is in competition with the Left Front (LF).[9]

On the basis of the nature of party competition, Heath and Yadav identify five main groupings where the nature of party competition and the pattern of electoral outcomes vary. In the first group are Delhi, Rajasthan, Madhya Pradesh, Himachal Pradesh, and Gujarat where the 1990s witnessed a direct contest between the Congress and the BJP. The second group comprises those states where two-party competition between the Congress and the LF can be witnessed. These states are West Bengal, Kerala, and Tripura. The third group includes a number of states where the main contenders are the Congress and a regional party. States such as Andhra Pradesh, Assam, Goa, Meghalaya, Pondicherry, Punjab, and Tamil Nadu are included in this group. There are states, such as Haryana, Maharashtra, Karnataka, and Orissa where the BJP, in alliance with local parties, is a serious contender for power. This comprises the fourth group. And the last group includes two states, Bihar and UP, where the Congress has lately been reduced to the status of a minor party.[10]

It is this variegated pattern of party competition that has a great implication for the national party system, in general, and the major contenders for power at the national level, in particular. If the balance of forces operating at the state level is, for some reason, disturbed it reflects on the electoral strength of the two major contenders, the Congress and the BJP. This could be ascertained on the basis of survey data relating to both the 1999 and 2004 elections.[11]

Table 1.1
Voter support for different political parties, 1999–2004

	Voter Support			
	1999		2004	
Parties	Total	%	Total	%
Congress and allies	3,070	36.5	8,881	39.8
BJP and allies	3,272	38.9	8,729	39.3
Left	660	7.8	1,530	6.9
BSP	255	3.1	635	2.8
Others	1,152	13.7	2,522	11.2
Total	8,409	100.0	22,297	100.0

Source: Data Unit, Center for the Study of Developing Societies, Delhi.

We can discern, as Table 1.1 underlines, a major shift in the electoral choice of voters as reflected in sampled voters, between 1999 and 2004. The gain of the Congress and its allies is obvious; it shows a 3 percent shift in voters' electoral preference in favor of the Congress between these two elections. In contrast, the BJP and its allies show only a slight increase (0.4 percent) between 1999 and 2004. Other parties and party groups show some change only minimally except for other parties including the Socialist Party, which register a 2 percent loss in their support base.

In the case of different caste groups and their support for different parties, we see an interesting picture emerging from the survey data (see Table 1.2). The Congress and its allies improved their position among Scheduled Caste (SC) voters (from 40 percent in 1999 to 43.9 percent in 2004), as did the BJP and its alliance (from 25 percent in 1999 to 27.3 percent in 2004). In all other cases, we can see a slightly improved position for the Congress and its allies. They received sizeable support from non-Scheduled and Backward Communities, that is mostly *savarna* Hindus, recording an increase of slightly more than 9 percent in 2004 over 1999. This is indicative of the fact that the BJP and its allies lost support in those higher castes that are considered to be a reliable support base for the BJP. Where the Congress and its allies suffered great loss was among the Scheduled Tribes (ST) who shifted their support to the extent of about 9 percent between 1999 and 2004. By the same token, the loss of the Congress and its allies meant a gain for the BJP and its allies recording a 9 percent gain among the STs. Most surprisingly, women respondents seem to be much more stable in their electoral choice, registering only a slight degree of decline in their voting preference for both the major parties. As Table 1.3 shows, the only party that shows an increase in women support is the Bahujan Samaj Party (BSP).

The overall picture that emerges is that while the Congress and its allies, despite a slight loss in their combined votes, did, in fact, register a big gain of 69 Lok Sabha seats. By contrast, the BJP and its allies lost only 2.3 percent of vote support as compared to the 1999 election, but they lost as many as 89 seats in the 2004 Lok Sabha elections. The heaviest loss was suffered by the BJP itself: 44 seats as a result of a loss of about 2 percent of the votes polled. The second in line were TDP (a loss of 13 seats), JD(U) (a loss of 13 seats) and AIADMK (a loss of 10 seats) and its alliance partner, the TMC (a loss of 6 seats). While the AIADMK did not win a single Lok Sabha seat in Tamil Nadu, the TMC was able to retain at least two seats.

This general picture in itself needs to be explained in terms of causative factors, both short- and long-term. We must also add to it the peculiar situation created by the demise of Congress dominance itself. The decline in the Congress party led, at the same time, to two factors. The combination of these two factors, as we shall see shortly,

Table 1.2

Caste group-wise votes for political parties, 1999–2004

Caste Groups	Year	Congress and Allies		BJP and Allies		Left		BSP		Others		Total	
		Total	%	Total	%	Total	%	Total	%	Total	%	Total	%
SC	1999	621	40.0	387	25.0	162	10.5	183	11.5	193	100.0	1,546	100.0
	2004	1,577	43.9	977	27.3	357	9.9	432	12.0	250	7.0	3,594	100.0
ST	1999	324	45.2	214	31.8	48	7.8	1	1.6	85	3.3	672	100.0
	2004	1,257	34.7	1,450	40.0	225	6.2	10	0.3	688	20.8	3,630	100.0
OBC	1999	1,275	38.5	1,319	39.5	206	6.2	53	1.6	481	14.4	334	100.0
	2004	3,118	41.0	3,081	40.5	469	6.0	130	1.7	823	10.8	7,621	100.0
Others	1999	815	30.0	1,285	48.2	216	7.0	18	0.7	383	14.1	2,717	100.0
	2004	2,961	39.2	3,258	43.0	496	6.5	631	8.0	97	10.5	7,575	100.0
Total	1999	3,035		3,205		632		255		1,142		5,269	
	2004	8,913	39.7	8,766	39.2	1,547	6.9	1,203	2.8	1,858	11.4	22,420	100.0

Source: Survey Data, Data Unit, Center for the Study of Developing Societies, Delhi.

Table 1.3

Voter support (women) for different political parties and alliances, 1999–2004

| | Voter Support | | | |
| | 1999 | | 2004 | |
Parties	Total	%	Total	%
Congress and allies	1,572	39.4	3,883	37.8
BJP and allies	1,469	36.8	3,670	35.0
Left	332	8.3	927	8.9
BSP	98	2.5	550	5.3
Others	572	13.2	1,442	13.8
Total	4,043	100.0	10,472	100.0

Source: Data Unit, Center for the Study of Developing Societies, Delhi.

acts to delay, if not altogether prevent, the emergence at the national level of an alternating two-party system. Additionally, it also makes unavoidable the forging of alliances with regional and personal parties operating at the state level with a view to capturing the seat of power at Delhi. This necessity provides the opportunity to smaller parties to wield power disproportionate to their strength in the Lok Sabha. They enjoy almost a god-like power to make a coalition possible or unmake it if the coalition fails to satisfy them. As their existence becomes vital to the success of a coalition, their continued existence is guaranteed insofar as they can get enough compensation for their small size in terms of electoral benefits in their local bailiwick. This situation also has a serious ramification for the durability of the coalition since any change in their electoral fortune is bound to have serious repercussions for the coalition.

The varying patterns of party competition in the states as well as the continued existence of small parties of different varieties, combine to have a great influence on the electoral fortune of the major national parties, such as the Congress and the BJP. Moreover, it is also tied to the performance of the party or a coalition of parties that comes to power at the state level. It is these factors that lend a distinctive characteristic to the environment in which the parties fight electoral battles with each other for acquiring control of governmental power at the national level. The combination of these factors are both the reflection of as well as a contributing factor to the operation of a secular, long-term factor that impinges on the process of the making or breaking of a particular ruling coalition. This long-term factor is the determinant of the immediate causes that produce a particular electoral outcome at any time; it is also the outcome of the dynamic interplay of short-term factors.

As indicated earlier, the legitimacy of the ruling party or coalition depends, to a large extent, on the internal dynamics of the ruling coalition itself. The fact is that the need to form coalitions through alliances among different parties arose in India much earlier. However, it was for the first time that a ruling coalition at the national level with Atal Behari Vajpayee at its head, could survive for almost a full term. But this does not in any way detract from the fact that Vajpayee had to face a lot of problems in managing the coalition. As a matter of fact, he had to face these problems as a result of the differences in ideology, orientation, perspective and perception of the importance of one's own political role in the political arena; these factors were the source of growing difficulties within the NDA. These differences reached such a high pitch that eight of the NDA constituents parted company almost towards the end of the tenure of the Vajpayee regime in search of greener pastures elsewhere. Despite these difficulties, the NDA coalition continued its troubled existence but lost the initiative and dynamism in pushing through the much-needed programs of overcoming the growing economic difficulties of several sections of Indian society.

Two factors explain why, despite continued difficulties in effectively running a coalition of 22 disparate political groups, the ruling coalition could stay in power for so long. One of these factors is the painful and extremely humiliating political experience of Vajpayee who could not survive beyond 13 days the first time he became the prime minister. The resulting election saw the BJP win 179 Lok Sabha seats. More than 12 parties joined the BJP to form a ruling coalition and Vajpayee was sworn in as prime minister on March 19, 1998. But the ministry had to quit after a year due to difficulties caused by unreasonable demands, particularly by two of its alliance partners, Mamata Banerjee (with seven members) and Jayalalitha (with 18 members). While Ms Banerjee could be pacified, Ms Jayalalitha's demand for the removal of the DMK government and dropping of court cases against her or be soft-pedaled, could not have reasonably been met. At the initiative of Subramanian Swami, the arch turncoat in Indian politics, Jayalalitha met with Mrs Sonia Gandhi, the Congress President, over a cup of tea on April 14, 1999. In the afternoon of the same day, Jayalalitha met the President of India and informed him that her party no longer supported the BJP-led coalition. In the ensuing vote for confidence that Vajpayee sought in the Lok Sabha, the members of Parliament voted against his ministry—260 for and 270 against. The election that followed gave a verdict that led to the formation of the NDA as a ruling coalition in 1999.

The second is the long-term factor that has developed as a result of the cumulation of several elements that defined the situational context in which the ruling coalition functioned. Add to it the personal style of Vajpayee's functioning. He had developed this style over his long political career marked by a slow but sure rise in the party hierarchy. It is during his rise that he adopted a mild but indeterminate style. Thus the second factor refers to the long process of political development in Indian politics, particularly the party system, which came to be characterized by the fragmentation of the mostly regional or local political parties. This combined with the personal style of Vajpayee's functioning to produce the long-term secular tendency.

Impelled by this bitter experience, Vajpayee was determined to make the coalition experience a success. Since the coalition comprised 22 alliance partners with sharply divergent views on economic and political questions, differences were bound to surface from time to time. This made it necessary to adopt a strategy of adjustment and compromise in a situation where any one coalition partner could bring the coalition crashing down if it felt ignored and unrewarded for its support to the coalition. What also contributed to the policy of adjustment and compromise was the manner which Vajpayee developed in the course of his rise in the party hierarchy and political eminence. As Khare puts it, a man, who for all his adult life, made a political career by using his golden tongue, could hardly be expected to indulge in the luxury of consistency and conviction.[12] The result was that on several occasions Vajpayee had to take back what he announced publicly, presenting numerous examples of flip and flop.[13]

Firmness in the determination of policies and programs for the promotion of the welfare of the largest section of society that suffered many deprivations and indignities was *sine qua non*. However, it was likely to endanger the very existence of the coalition. Faced with this fateful situation, firmness can easily be sacrificed at the altar of expedience. The reflection of this phenomenon in the case of Vajpayee was the lack of firmness and indecision. As Khare notes:

> There were only two occasions in his tenure as the Prime Minister when Vajpayee stood firmly by his convictions; first during the Kargil conflict when he refused President Bill Clinton's *demarche* to come to Washington to work out a ceasefire with Nawaz Sharif and, second, when he refused to fire his Principal Secretary, Brajesh Mishra, despite combined pressure from the RSS–L.K. Advani faction in the wake of Tehelka re-evaluations.[14]

Vajpayee's determination to ensure continuity of the coalition for the full term, along with his personality trait emphasizing indecision and lack of firmness, combined to make the NDA coalition rich in rhetoric but very poor in performance. As Subramanian notes, 'With the kind of coalition represented by the ruling alliance, it would seem that Vajpayee has set himself a *status quo* objective—how to proceed for five years showing a lot of activity with no real action.' Subramanian cites one very revealing example of how Vajpayee's mind worked. As he notes: 'And there was the expectation a government fresh from electoral success would bring into action a strong tone of governance. But the trends that I saw during (the first fortnight) were worrisome.' Subramanian refers to a cabinet meeting to fix the pricing formula for certain types of fertilizers involving heavy subsidies: 'I had felt that they would keep under check the fiscal deficit by scaling down subsidies. I instead found a generous finance minister who was more than willing to declare a heavy new dose of fertilizer subsidy, not to speak of a cut or a roll back.'

The finance minister was encouraged by the prime minister, 'on the grounds that farmer's interests were involved and that they could not afford to be too strict.' Subramanian reminded him that 'it was not so much the question of the farmers but more of subjugation to the large private fertiliser manufacturers, and that there were powerful vested interests working to keep the level of subsidies high. At this, the prime minister, in a now familiar gesture, shut his eyes and with a shake of the head declared that 'we will not tolerate vested interests, we will root out all vested interests.'[15]

This sharply underlines the wide divergence between what the ruling sub-coalition promised and what it, in fact, realized. The grandiose BJP election slogan 'India Shining,' was supposed to be the unfailing *mantra* that could bring sure success. But the claim of 'India Shining' was supported only by the creation of an agency for issues as 'National Disinvestments,' success in the Kargil war, and such other slogans that were quite peripheral to the existence of the common man who has progressively been harassed by the deteriorating conditions of an assured livelihood. The persistence of drought conditions in many parts of the country, the mounting rate of suicides among the farmers unable to provide the subsistence needs of their families, an increasing army of the unemployed, the pursuit of policies that reduced the livelihood of ordinary people—all these factors took away the shine and luster from the slogans 'India Shining,' and 'Feel Good.' The BJP's effort to achieve what it could not do through governance, and tried to with the help of grand high sounding slogans, did not succeed with the voters.

The best example of peripheralization of the problems of the ordinary man is represented by Chandrababu Naidu, the erstwhile chief minister of Andhra Pradesh. Naidu largely ignored the problems faced by the common man. Instead, he put at the center of his programs such issues as cyber revolution, the challenges posed by biodiversity and the problem posed by the need to modernize agriculture. But these programs could not be stomached by the starving farmers, unemployed youths and a countryside ravaged by drought and destruction by the Naxalites. It is true that Naidu did raise the question of investment in agriculture since it was incapable of supporting the poor farmer. He did raise the question of the future of small land holdings, but ignored those sections of society who suffered distress and disaster because of small landholdings. He spoke of the need to expand employment opportunities but left the currently unemployed to fend for themselves.

These paradoxes characterize the performance of Naidu's government. However, the media hype of Naidu's model developmental strategy was instrumental in Naidu's losing sight of the real, immediate problems facing the state and its people. What also contributed to Naidu's neglect of the real problems was the seal of approval that the World Bank put on Naidu's development model. Persistence of these paradoxes was fateful to the Naidu government in the sense that government policies, both at the national and the state levels, were divorced from the actual hopes, aspirations and frustrations that constitute the basic elements of everyday life of the common man. However, when the conduct of the government focuses on problems that have little or no relevance for the real, immediate situations of the people, then there is obviously no relationship between what the people need and what the rulers propose to do. Both the NDA and the Naidu government are prime examples of this. As a result, these policies were not germane to solving the people's problems in any real sense of the term.

There existed a wide gap between what needed to be done and what, in fact, was being done. The worsening life conditions of the people in Andhra Pradesh required that something must be done to ameliorate their condition, not simply as a matter of necessity but, in fact, for providing some relief to the people. However, what was being done by the Naidu government had no immediate relevance for the mounting problems of the people of Andhra Pradesh. Nonetheless, it was being advertised and praised as a model of development worth emulating by other states. Keeping this in mind, the scale of Naidu's defeat may be massive, but it is by no means poignant, as Shiva Vishwanathan seems to think. His argument centers round his perception that Naidu's idea of cyber development 'pluralized development beyond the linear bureaucratic imagination.'[16]

It is true that Naidu chose to deviate from the traditional approach to promoting the welfare of the poor. For example, N.T. Rama Rao (NTR) had initiated three programs: (*a*) rice at Rs 2 per kilogram, (*b*) the Janata Cloth Scheme, and (*c*) subsidized power supply to the farm sector. Naidu deviated sharply from these policies and instead brought about a new distinct policy orientation in state politics. He put emphasis on empowering the people by promoting the formation of several self-help groups with a view to encouraging the people to participate in the management of certain important functions such as education, water use, and protection of the forest wealth. However, these programs were no substitute for instant relief to the poor and the helpless in the state.[17] The sacrifice of immediate relief to the poor for promoting self-help is reflected in the consistent neglect of the Telangana region, a chronically drought-prone area, and increasing difficulties of farmers resulting in more than 100 suicides during his regime. The Telangana issue has had an active presence for more than three decades. However, in the last three years it picked up momentum and assumed electoral significance. This was due to the efforts of K. Chandra Shekhar Rao, a former TDP leader,[18] who formed the Telangana Rashtra Samithi and made it into an organization for expressing the demands of the people in the Telangana region.

Naidu is not, by any means, an exceptional case illustrating the great divide between the people and the ruling power. He constitutes merely a single instance of a generic case. As we have seen, the NDA came to power riding on the horse of an ensemble of promises, all of which aimed at assuring the *demos* of a good life, a life that the previous ruling coalitions also promised but thoughtlessly ignored. As the NDA performance shows, it never conformed to its claims of opening a 'democratic' alliance committed to promoting the well-being of the people. If democracy has anything in abundance, it has leaders. 'Today we more or less take it for granted,' observes Voegelin, 'that our society is swarming with leaders, left and right, who supply substance to the human automaton.'[19] It is true that the *demos* are the basis of what we know as representative democracy. However, the fact cannot be gainsaid that it is the representative who is the mainstay of democratic politics. It is the representative who wields 'tremendous power inasmuch as he necessarily picks and chooses between competing demands, factors these demands through the ideological prism of the political party of which he or she is a member, or indeed manipulates mass claims for partisan political ends.'[20]

It is this situation that creates a paradox, for ultimately the representative acquires autonomy from those he or she represents. It is in this paradox that we can discern the phenomenon that 'pervades modern politics and are still increasing in importance, the origin of the artificiality of modern politics as engendered through propaganda, education, re-education, enforced political myth, and so on, as well as through the general treatment of human beings as functional units in private enterprise and public planning.'[21] As a consequence, 'representatives do not only register the will of the people; they are rather engaged in the determining that will and thereby of the identity of the community.'[22] But the process of determining even goes beyond this. It is the ruling power that defines what kinds of socio-economic programs and policies the political system must seek to implement so that it can become possible for individuals to shape their own development by satisfying their ordinary life needs involved with the pursuit of wealth, power, and prestige. And we should also keep in mind the fact that in his modern *avatar* (incarnation) the individual is primarily a *homo economicus* (economic man) who, as an entrepreneur, engages himself in the act of provisioning for satisfying his ordinary life-needs along with that of his nearest kith and kin. It is, therefore, the pursuit of economic goals that is supposed to hold the key to man's felicity, his personality development and the onward journey of civilization on the path of progress.[23]

The primacy of the pursuit of economic goals enables the government to determine what kind of economic programs must be pursued so that the values inherent in a liberal perspective on man and his world may be expeditiously realized. As such, the responsibility of determining the substance as well as direction of economic policies and programs, supervising the process of their realization and most importantly, influencing through its policies, the pattern of distribution in society, devolves on the shoulder of the ruling power. It is through the discharge of this crucial function that the government assumes the authority and power to determine economic life and relations of the individual. It is as a result of this determination that the government shapes and forms the identity of the community. It is against this background that we can appreciate why in modern politics human beings are treated as merely functional units in private enterprise and public planning on the one hand, and why, on the other, the divide between the people and the public authorities comes into being and persists.

It is the combination of these two factors, that is, the erosion of the sovereignty of the *demos* and the rise of the behemoth state that has grown all-powerful and progressively enlarged the field of its operation and assumed the responsibility of reordering the patterns of the life of the people in a situation of the fragmentation of the party system, that created a situation in which a large degree of incongruity had occurred between electoral policy and policy outcomes. The Indian Constitution has committed the state to foster what Granville Austin calls 'social revolution.'[24] The Constitution combines in itself both substantive goals that the society as a whole must seek to realize and the procedural rules for articulating, defining and realizing these goals. This combination, it must be emphasized, is not at all fully compatible. Two incompatibilities need to be pointed out here. In the first place, the Constitution embodies procedural rules that are supposed to endure in the face of the ongoing changes in society and regulate both the direction and content of these changes. The substantive goals, on the other hand, are meant to initiate a process of change; this process may not be easily accommodated within the confines of the prescribed procedural rules.

This is because, as Jasay points out,

> Constitutional rules are not Moses' fables. They are not made in heaven, and even if they were, men on earth would soon unmake them. It is the strange supposition that politics goes on within constitutional constraints, but that the constraints themselves are somehow above politics, determining it without being determined by it like any other product of collective decision-making. This is why no constitution is a fixed one. As values change, and views of how the world works and the social force associated with these views change, constitutions also change. Either their letter is amended or their spirit (their 'intent') is reinterpreted.[25]

This in itself exercises a great influence in defining what the goals of social revolution should mean and what should be the manner of implementing these goals after they have been filled with specific content. This becomes especially significant in a situation of a non-unanimous, collective decision-making system. This is so because a non-unanimous, collective decision-making system indicates the frequent change in a party or a coalition. As a result of this, different

ruling coalitions with entirely different ideological perspectives, interest and partisan ends define the content and direction of policies and
programs of social revolution. And since these policies are couched
in such ambiguous terms as welfare, humanity, progress—terms which
are all twistable whenever there is a change in the constitution of
the ruling coalition, these terms, too, change in their content without any change in the label itself. It is for this reason that the goals of
social revolution change and, as a result, produce incompatibility between the content given it by one regime from that given by another.
Additionally, there also exists incompatibility between different
strands of the social revolutionary goals of the political order. If the
goal of preserving national unity and integrity collides with fundamental rights, so do fundamental rights with social justice.

Second, all social revolutionary goals are essentially re-distributive.
They involve the fact that some decide for all. The few that constitute
the ruling coalition 'makes choice[s] over what domain, over what kind
of alternatives collective choice should be exercised, by what rules
and what shall be left over for individuals to decide for themselves.'[26]
Once this question has been settled, choice must be made as to the
proportion of material resources that must be pre-empted through
fiscal means, such as taxes, revenues, and so on, and taken away from
material resources available to each individual. This decision fixes
the proportion of material resources meant for public rather than
private purposes.

No matter what decisions are made through adopting alternatives
relating both to the domain from which material resources are to be
mobilized or the proportion of these resources that must be mobilized
for public purposes, what counts is that the ultimate burden of all
these decisions has to be borne by the individual. And to the extent
that the individual has to bear this burden, it virtually amounts to
forcing the individual to do what he would not freely do, and to for-
bear from what would be chosen if left to himself. What happens is
that the state takes a lion's share of individually earned and owned resources and uses them in collective ways[27] that the individual would
not have chosen.[28] All of this seems, in more or less some obscure

manner, legitimate.[29] And if these decisions do not seem legitimate, we will have no occasion to obey the commands of the state in this regard.[30]

The promise of fostering social revolution through the mobilization of private resources for public uses has certain important ramifications. In the first place, one of the ramifications is the phenomenon of free riders who have no hesitation in getting certain services without paying anything in return. This adds to the pressure on the political process for more services. As a result, the state acquires more and more functions and resources to perform these functions. The state therefore becomes unlimited. The second ramification has to do with the accentuated competition between political parties for capturing power. In order to leave behind their rivals, they tend to promise more and more services at low cost or, alternatively, completely free.

The third ramification pertains to the severing of the link between costs, natural and moral, and the benefits the programs of social revolution create. What causes this is the fact that the usefulness of these programs is judged not with the help of any rational calculation but conjecturally by their potential success that can assure the pre-eminence of the ruling coalition. What really prompts the adoption of a particular substantive program is that parties are in competition with each other for occupying the power positions of society by winning the support of the people. They do so by spending more on such welfare programs whose political value usually outweigh their economic costs. As such, the link between the cost of welfare programs and the benefits that accrue to the people is snapped and expenditure mounts to horrendous proportions.[31] The amalgamations of these factors lead not only to financial irresponsibility but also to political irresponsibility.

This situation produces three adverse consequences for the working of democratic politics. In the first place, the promise of social revolution pushes people's aspirations to ever-higher pitches resulting in the processing of excessive demands in the political process, which it is incapable of satisfying. The other side of the coin is the stiff resistance by those sections of the population that are adversely affected by the active fostering of social revolution. Resistance to the state grows in magnitude and the government has to spend a lot of energy and resources to keep resistance within manageable limits. This also contributes to the growing incapacity of the government to perform well on the development front. A decline in the government's capacity to perform well creates a widespread feeling of what Max Scheler calls *resentment*, the seething and bubbling discontentment of the people against the rulers. Second, the growing competition among political parties for capturing the power apparatus of the society makes power the driving force in politics. Finally, the politicization of traditional socio-cultural referents of identity formation occurs because politics then assumes the responsibility of deciding who gets what, and when. And since what is to be distributed is very scarce, the mobilization of ethnic and other traditional socio-cultural referents of identity formation as a political resource is bound to take place. As Kanchan Chandra has shown in what she calls 'the patronage state,' elected officials of the state gain the resources that they can distribute. These resources are state-owned and for the elected functionaries of the state to distribute. As a result of this, ethnic divisions in society get reinforced, politicizing caste and communal groups.[32]

When parties have to rely on power for making their existence meaningful, other mundane concerns, such as the welfare of the people, assume secondary importance. The result is that 'powerful party bureaucracy and political élites, preoccupied as they are with the consolidation of power in Indian society (shrug off) the very same masses which ... brought them to power. (U)nresponsive party, amoral and power hungry party leaderships who (are) completely impervious to the fact that they have failed miserably to represent the needs of the peoples.'[33] It is not, therefore, surprising that we find a very large degree of incongruity that 'has grown in the political system between the electoral process unable to produce the mandate to rule and the governmental and the inter-party process that have become subject to such pressures and interests which often undermine the very principle of democratic representations.'[34] The manifestation of this incongruity is decisively reflected in the growing inability of the government to implement the mandate in the face of the structural resistance it meets from within the system and from the outside by people who feel their aspirations are frustrated in the process.[35]

When policy outcomes deviate from the election mandate, there is on the one hand, the quick turnover in ruling coalition, and considerable decline in the retention capability of political parties, on the other. Since the direct impact of the incongruency between electoral mandates is felt directly at the constituency level, the voters express their discontent against party candidates seeking re-election. The retention capacity has, as a result, decisively gone down in the 1990s. As Sanjay Kumar notes, a party may seem to be very popular at the national level but it may not be the sole criteria [*sic*] to win elections at the constituency level.[36] He further notes that during the last three Lok Sabha elections (that is, 1996, 1998, and 1999) the BJP renominated nearly 80 percent of its sitting MPs, but nearly two-thirds of those renominated won the elections while others lost. In the case of the Congress, more than 50 percent of renominated candidates lost the elections.[37] This underlines the fact that 'democracy in India is increasingly playing second fiddle to its own spectacle. We celebrate its scale but do not talk about the process that must keep it open and accountable after elections are over.'[38]

This is amply demonstrated by the preceding discussion which highlights the growing distance between what the people need and want and what the rulers of different hues and colors are able to provide despite their high-sounding rhetoric. They have promised, over the years, to give to the people the much-awaited comfortable living and a dignified life. However, as the promise of bringing the pie from the sky down to earth remains unfulfilled, the progressively escalating expectations of the people put severe limitations on the capacity of both the economic and the political system to deliver the goods. Two things happen simultaneously. In the first place, the financial burden on the state increases enormously, but the people do not get benefits commensurate to the financial contributions they make to the state coffers. It tremendously widens the gap between costs and benefits. Meanwhile, frustrated expectations of the people accumulate and go on simmering till they can express them in their electoral act of 'driving out the rascals.' Second, political parties, given their aspiration of capturing seats of power, set in motion a process of outbidding one another with a view to increasing voter support. This itself contributes to the escalation of expectation—either to be frustrated later or to be only partially satisfied. The combination of these two factors leads to a situation where it becomes very difficult either to sustain a coalition composed of diverse ideological parties or to have a longer tenure in the government.

What is also important in this connection is that the Congress-led UPA government made tall promises to remove poverty and meet the needs of the poor, a tradition that the Congress inherited from Indira Gandhi when she was prime minister. However, in doing so the ruling coalition invites a severe financial crunch making it necessary for it to only dilly-dally in fulfilling its populist slogans. This, again underlines the crucial fact of the unreality of politics that has become the dominant trend in political life and relations in India. Thus, every election that is held to elect the rulers of the country repeats the same phenomenon over and over again. This, however, is dubbed by politicians and scholars alike as progress, rather than as the great irony of Indian politics.

NOTES

1. This over-confidence was the product of the victory of the BJP in the elections to the Gujarat Assembly despite the communal carnage in Godhra in Gujarat in 2002.
2. In 1957, for example, it won only four seats, improved its share of seats to 14 in 1962, 35 in 1967, but came down in 1971 to 22; and although it fought the parliamentary election in 1977, it formed part of an alliance as a member of the LD. The number of seats won by the LD in 1997 was 295. However, it is not possible to separate the individual share of the Jana Sangh as it was called then. It went blank in 1980, winning only two seats in 1984. However, from then on, it recorded steady upward gain in seats: 120 in 1991, 161 in 1996, 179 in 1998, and 182 in 1999.
3. As Vandita Mishra notes: 'An arrogant government convinced of its own invincibility was shown the door', in 'Only on a Saturday', *Indian Express*, June 30, 2004.
4. The case of the Congress defeat in the 1977 parliamentary election is somewhat unusual in the sense that the Congress upset was due to the harsh regime of a national Emergency that was imposed on the country in 1975 by the then prime minister, Mrs Indira Gandhi, with a view to propping up her sagging political fortune. It was a very harsh regime in the sense that it meant authoritarian rule

without any constitutional or political restraints. Arbitrary measures included media censorship, political arrests without due process, perpetrating numerous atrocities in the country, and letting loose a regime of fear—all these factors made a deep impact on the psyche of the people. The anger was expressed in the 1977 polls with the result that the Indira Gandhi Congress could win only 154 seats out of 543 parliamentary seats.

5. It must be kept in mind that voters do not represent merely an 'echo chamber,' as V.O. Key characterized them. As a matter of fact, voters have their own preference scale embedded in their psyche and points to what is referred to as *homo-politicus* selectivity. The voter does receive stimulus from his environment, but then he does not receive it as it seems to others. The voter himself interprets the stimulus he receives in terms of his own life world and living experience.

6. For a useful discussion on this, see E. Sridharan, 'The Fragmentation of the Indian Party System', in Zoya Hasan (ed.), *Parties and Party Politics in India* (New Delhi: Oxford University Press, 2002), p. 492.

7. K.S. Krishnaswamy, T.S. Gulati, and A. Vaidyanathan, 'Economic Aspects of Federalism in India', in Nirmal Mukarjee and Balveer Arora (eds), *Federalism in India* (New Delhi: Vikas Publishing House Pvt. Ltd., 1992), pp. 180–84.

8. Pradeep K. Chhibber and John R. Petrocik argue that the Congress has depended upon a definite social base, one that varies from state to state. As they put it:

> The Congress emerges as a party that represents not national but local interests. It is not a center party nor, is it a party of consensus. It is a collection of state based factions linked not by common constituency but by elites who cooperate in the pursuit of office. The Congress is not a heterogeneous party in the normal sense of that concept. It is a heterogeneous pre-election coalition of substantially homogenous parties, which are rooted in salient local conflicts.

'Social cleavages, Elections and the Indian Party system', in Richard Sisson and Ramashray Roy (eds), *Democracy and Dominance in Indian Politics* (New Delhi: Sage Publications, 1990), I, pp. 105–22.

9. 'The United Colours of Congress: Social Profile of Congress Voters 1996 and 1998', *Economic and Political Weekly*, Vols XXIV–XXV, 34–35 (August 22 and September 3, 1999), reprinted in Zoya Hasan, op. cit., p. 109.

10. Ibid. See also Sridharan, op. cit.

11. The survey data refers to post-poll surveys in 1999 and 2004 conducted by the Center for the Study of Developing Societies, Delhi. I am grateful to their data unit for making this information available to me. The total sample size for the 1999 survey was 9,418, and for the 2004 survey it was 27,189.

12. Harish Khare, *The Hindu*, May 14, 2004.

13. A young political science graduate, a computer buff, developed a scale of Verbal and Rhetorical Consistency. Measured on this scale, Vajpayee is reported to have flip-flopped 683 times in the six years that he was prime minister. There was a 3 percent margin of error. *The Hindu*, May 14, 2004.

14. Khare, op. cit.

15. T.S.R. Subramanian, *Journeys through Babudom and Netaland* (New Delhi: Rupa and Co., 2004), p. 298. Subramanian, an IAS officer, was Cabinet Secretary when Vajpayee formed his government in 1998.

16. Shiva Vishwanathan, 'Election Riddles: The Search for a New Political Paradigm', *The Times of India* (Delhi edition), June 19, 2004.

17. On this point, see P. Sainath, 'Chandrababu: Image and Reality', *The Hindu*, July 18, 2004.

18. Four years ago, Rao, a three-term MLA, wanted a cabinet berth but was given the Deputy Speaker's post. He quit in anger and floated the Telangana Rashtra Samithi (TRS). The TRS is seeking separate statehood for Telangana. It was this four-year-old party that whipped up emotions in the region to the highest pitch and was able to halt Naidu's attempted third term in office.

19. Eric Voegelin, *History of Political Ideas*, Vol. VIII: *Crisis and the Apocalypse of Man*. David Walsh (ed.) (Columbia: University of Missouri Press, 1999), p. 62.

20. Neera Chandhoke, 'Crisis of Representative Democracy', *The Hindu*, June 19, 2004.

21. Voegelin, op. cit., p. 61.

22. Chandhoke, op. cit.

23. There is a vast literature available on this point. See, however, Charles Taylor, 'Growth, Legitimacy and Modern Identity', *Praxis International*, Vol. 1, No. 2, July 1981.

24. Social revolution consists of different strands. These strands relate to the preservation of national unity and integrity, protection and promotion of fundamental rights and the promotion of economic growth along with justice. See Granville Austin, *Working a Democratic Constitution: Indian Experience* (New Delhi: Oxford University Press, 2004), p. 6.

25. Anthony de Jasay, *Against Politics: On Government, Anarchy, and Order* (London: Routledge, 1997), pp. 136–37.

26. Ibid.

27. It is interesting to note in this regard that one estimate shows that out of the total expenditure on welfare programs in India, only 10 out of 100 paise go to the really needy persons. Partha J. Shah and H.B. Saumya, 'Who Pays for Welfare Programs', in *Sarvekshana*, Vol. XIV, No. 46 (January–March 1991), pp. 5–7 and 5–8.

28. de Jassay, op. cit., p. 1.

29. Ibid.

30. This unavoidably raises the question of the link that we identity between society and state. The question calls for an answer, but it is not possible to do so here. However, see de Jassay, op. cit., pp. 1–2.

31. A study by the National Council of Applied Economic Research, New Delhi, estimates that the total expenditure at present stands at more than Rs 33,000 crore in India. Another recent study shows that if the program of providing

100 days of employment to needy people in the rural and urban areas to which the UPA government is committed is ever implemented, it alone will cost more than Rs 208,000 crore (Rs 2,080 million). See Bibek Oberoi, 'Rs 208,000 Crore Riddle', *The Indian Express*, October 23, 2004.

32. Kanchan Chandra, *Why Ethnic Parties Succeed: Patronage and Head Counts in India* (Cambridge: Cambridge University Press, 2004), p. 4.

33. Chandhoke, op. cit.

34. D.L. Sheth, 'The Crisis of Political Authority', in Rajendra Vora and Suhas Palshikar (eds), *Indian Democracy: Meaning and Practices* (New Delhi: Sage Publications, 2004), p. 58.

35. Ibid., p. 56.

36. Sanjay Kumar 'Increasing Fluidity in Electoral Contests', in Vora and Palshikar, op. cit., p. 369.

37. Ibid., pp. 370–72.

38. Vandita Mishra, op. cit.

CHAPTER 2

Chaste Like Sita, Fierce Like Durga: Indian Women in Politics

SIKATA BANERJEE

In the wake of the 2004 general elections in India, there have been a plethora of scholarly and not-so scholarly discussions concerning the various facets of electoral politics and bargaining. One aspect of the elections did not provide much grist for the psephological mill as it has not changed since independence, nor is it seen by the mainstream journalistic and scholarly gaze to be an exciting part of India's present electoral terrain: the participation of Indian women in politics. Although marginalized by conventional scholarship and media, women's electoral participation and political leadership is being slowly brought to the foreground by many feminist leaders, activists, and scholars.

This process of foregrounding began with the activities of leaders involved in the independence struggle. Sarojini Naidu in her 1930 presidential address to the All India Women's Conference stated:

> We are not week [*sic*], timid, meek women. We hold the courageous Savitri as our ideal; we know how Sita defied those who entertained suspicion of her ability to keep her chastity. We possess the spirit of creative energy to legislate for the morale of the world ... women have always been by the side of men in Council and in the fields of battle ....[1]

Naidu's speech introduces two themes surrounding women's political participation that still resonate within the modern polity. She draws on female mythic figures to energize women's activist presence and implicitly her speech is sanguine that once India receives independence, women in India will at last, politically, seize their rightful space. Indeed the visible presence of women in various facets of political activism support Naidu's strong statement. In colonial times, women were enthusiastic and effective participants in the national liberation movement. They even took up arms against colonial administrators. After Independence, the vibrant autonomous women's movement[2] as well as female participation in unions, protests and demonstrations emphasize Naidu's point that Indian women are not timid or weak. Nor can it be denied that individual women such as Indira Gandhi, Mamata Banerjee, Uma Bharti, Sadhvi Rithambhara, and Jayalalitha have achieved considerable public, political power.

But such an optimistic assessment of women's lived experience in all spheres of activity, not just electoral politics, is only one strand in the complicated tapestry that is Indian women's lives. The optimism pervading Naidu's speech was completely shattered by *Towards Equality*, the 1975 report published by the Committee on the Status of Women appointed by Indira Gandhi. According to this report, Indian women had been losing ground in terms of literacy, labor force participation and other socio–economic indicators since Independence. The most shocking statistics provided by this document was its report that due to deliberate negligence, foeticide, and infanticide, the number of women per 1,000 men had been declining over time in India. This trend continues today.[3] One path that may provide a means of increasing the status of women in India is participation in electoral politics.

As Table 2.2 indicates Indian women have not achieved a high level of representation in the Lok Sabha. Why is it that an important female presence in national liberation, at the grass roots in both left- and right-wing parties, as well as strong role models such as Indira Gandhi and Mamata Banerjee has not translated into a substantial female presence in the national parliament of India? This fact is even more interesting when (as Table 2.1 emphasizes) we realize that female voter turn out while lower than male, is still quite high. So women are political activists and they vote, so why are they not running for (see Table 2.3) and/or getting elected to office?

Table 2.1
Gender-wise breakdown of voter turnout in Indian general elections, 1952–2004

Year	Male	Female	Overall
1952	n.a.	n.a.	61.20
1957	n.a.	n.a.	62.20
1962	63.31	46.63	55.42
1967	66.73	55.48	61.33
1971	60.90	49.11	55.29
1977	65.63	54.91	60.49
1980	62.16	51.22	56.92
1984	68.18	58.60	63.56
1989	66.13	57.32	61.95
1991	61.58	51.35	56.93
1996	62.06	53.41	57.94
1998	65.72	57.88	61.97
1999	63.97	55.64	59.99
2004	61.66	53.30	57.65

Note: Retrieved on October 30, 2006, from www.eci.gov.in/miscellaneous_statistics/votingpercentage_loksabha.asp

Table 2.2
Representation of women in the Lok Sabha, 1957–2004

Year	Total Seats	Men Elected	Women Elected	Women in Lok Sabha (%)
1957	494	467	27	5.5
1962	494	459	35	7.0
1967	520	490	30	5.7
1971	520	499	21	4.0
1977	542	523	19	3.5
1980	542	514	28	5.1
1984	542	500	42	7.7
1989	529	502	27	5.1
1991	521	492	39	7.5
1996	543	504	39	7.2
1998	543	500	43	8.0
1999	543	489	51	9.4
2004	543	498	45	8.3

Note: Retrieved on October 30, 2006, from http://in.rediff.com/election/2004/mar/18kbkwom.htm

Table 2.3

Gender-wise breakdown of individuals contesting general elections, 1957–2004

Year	Total No. of Contestants	Men Contesting	Women Contesting	% of Women
1957	1,518	1,473	45	3.0
1962	1,985	1,915	70	3.5
1967	2,369	2,302	67	2.8
1971	2,784	2,698	86	3.1
1977	2,439	2,369	70	2.9
1980	4,620	4,478	142	3.0
1984	5,574	5,406	164	3.0
1989	6,160	5,962	198	3.2
1991	8,699	8,374	325	3.7
1996	13,952	13,353	599	4.3
1998	4,750	4,476	274	5.8
1999	4,618	4,335	283	6.1
2004	5,435	5,080	355	6.5

Note: Retrieved on October 30, 2006, from http://in.rediff.com/election/2004/mar/18kbkwom.htm

Dominant, heteronormative, social constructions of womanhood not only provide ideals of femininity but also encourage women to model their behavior on these visions of femininity and such cultural expectations shed light on some aspects of the gender gap as well as the meaning of political representation for women.[4] Naidu's invocation of the mythic figures of Sita and Savitri provides an important point of departure for such an examination. It cannot be denied that Sita and Savitri are dynamic and powerful female images. But simultaneously, in the popular realm, the power of their mythic status lies in the notion of *pativrata* or extreme devotion to one's husband. The manner in which such devotion is interpreted in Hindu, Indian society is a wife's complete capitulation to her husband's wishes. Alongside the *pativrata* idea of wifehood, powerful male figures such as Mahatma Gandhi and Swami Vivekananda, made the notion of the self-sacrificing, Hindu mother politically salient.

These notions of wifehood and motherhood need not imply a shy, retiring, woman. According to popular Hindu mythology, Sita lived in exile for 14 years and fended off the advances of Ravana by using her intelligence; Savitri succeeded in getting her husband back from the dead and the popular Jijabai, the mother of Hindu warrior Shivaji, offers a heroic model of motherhood which includes knowledge of martial strategy. But, all these models emphasize that a woman's power derives from devotion to a man, i.e., husband or son, and also that a powerful woman is a chaste woman (a complete erasure of a woman's sexuality). Indeed a diminishing or loss of chastity is directly related to her increasing disempowerment[5] (N. Banerjee 2003 and S. Banerjee 2005).

This chapter will argue that while these heteronormative ideas of chastity, wifehood, and motherhood may be used by individual women to electoral advantage, at a general level these notions complicate and limit women's access to electoral power. Specifically familial obligations and expectations of modesty and virtue limit freedom of mobility, especially within spaces—usually all-male—necessary for informal networking and political bargaining. I will discuss this argument by looking at some successful politicians, the experience of women in some *panchayat*s in Maharashtra, and the women in two Hindu nationalist organizations: Rashtriya Sevika Samiti (henceforth Samiti) and the Sadhvi Shakti Parishad (henceforth Parishad).

I will begin by examining the manner in which these latter organizations have disseminated and politically used ideas of wifehood and motherhood, since they provide the strongest interpretation of these socially salient ideas of womanhood. The Samiti and Parishad assume a form of Hindu nationalism that is strongly contested by self-styled secular parties such as the Congress, Janata Dal, CPI, and CPM and indeed such ideological differences (related to the issue of Hindu dominance and minority rights) are vast. However, I will argue that in terms of their imagining of women as wives and heroic mothers, with chastity being an important pre-condition for women entering the public sphere of politics, these organizations are not radically separate from other political parties.

A note of clarification about the background of my argument is in order before I begin. The mythic icons I emphasize as well as the notions of wifehood and motherhood are embedded in a Hindu context. This Hindu contexualization by no means implies that cultural images and process of other communities in India are similar or unimportant, but rather reflects my expertise and work. I will leave the discussion of the intersection of women's electoral and political participation and Islamic, Buddhist, Sikh, or Christian cultural values to those better suited for such work. Further, given the hegemony of Hinduism in India and given that socially powerful figures such as Gandhi and Vivekananda drew on explicit Hindu images even women who did not identify as Hindu were forced to face the power of such constructs.

CHASTITY, WIFEHOOD, AND MOTHERHOOD

Sarkar[6] argues that as Indian men felt effeminized in the public sphere under an imperial gaze which condemned them as cowards (read weak and effeminate), they responded by asserting their manhood in the 'inner world' or the domestic sphere. One impact of this masculinization was the creation of a chaste wife, devoted to her husband and children. Politically, these ideas informed many of the reform movements of the nineteenth century.[7, 8]

An important political manifestation of this image was in the words of Swami Vivekananda. Vivekananda held a rather ambiguous position towards women. On the one hand, he extolled the virtues of historical figures such as the Rani of Jhansi and even celebrated various women of his time—Sister Nivedita and Sarala Debi—who had transcended traditional gender roles to enter the public sphere as nationalists. Yet, on the other hand 'wife' and 'mother'[9] were held up as potent images in his interpretation of women's role in the nation: 'The height of a woman's ambition is to be like Sita . . . the patient, the all-suffering, the ever-faithful, the ever-pure wife'[10] and 'Now the ideal woman, in India, is the mother, the mother first, and the mother last. The word woman calls up to the mind of the Hindu, motherhood.'[11]

The valorization of such images led him to ignore actual women when he was organizing the Ramakrishna Mission as a training ground for monks dedicated to nation-building. Women, because of their potential for seducing a monk away from a path of spiritual righteousness, were to be kept under strict surveillance in the religious organization.[12] All dedicated followers of the Ramakrishna Order were to be monks who had embraced celibacy and accepted the wearing of the saffron robe (as did Vivekananda) of Hindu holy men. In this

narrative of male celibacy, the sexuality of women becomes a perceived threat. Thus, it became necessary for women not to enter the
Ramakrishna monasteries. Further, because of their primary roles as
mothers and wives, 'woman-making education' was to be kept separate from 'man-making' education and to include only a rudimentary
introduction to religion, arts, and science, with an emphasis on 'housekeeping, cooking, sewing, hygiene .... It is not good to let them touch
novels and fictions.'[13] Likewise, women ascetics, skilled in such arts,
could be trained as educators of women in separate institutions. Wife
(pure and chaste), heroic mother, and celibate female ascetic represented the entirety of women's role in the nation. We may note that
female sexuality has been erased, and it can be inferred that women
who do embody markers of femininity—jewelry, make-up, colorful
clothing—thus enhancing their sexual nature are not deemed as appropriate participants in the nationalist struggle.

This notion was echoed in Gandhi's vision of women:

> [A Woman] would prove her satihood not by mounting the funeral pyre
> at her husband's death, but ... by her ... sacrifice, self-negation and dedica-
> tion to the service of her husband, his family, and the country and by
> completely identifying herself with her husband (she would) learn to
> identify herself with the whole world.[14]

When in 1925 the Bengal Congress Committee organized women
sex workers, 'Gandhi was almost hysterical with rage' for 'No woman
who was not "chaste in thought, word and deed" was to be allowed
into his movement.'[15] While Gandhi emphasized the necessity for all
members of his Sabarmati ashram to be chaste and celibate, leading
the life of a *brahmacharin*, like Vivekananda he viewed women's sexuality as being specially dangerous to dedicated political work and as
such women were viewed with suspicion unless they had removed all
signs of their sexuality and femininity.[16] Revolutionary, terrorist movements of the 1920s and 1930s attracted many women (Preetilata
Wadedar, Kamala Dasgupta, Shanti Ghosh), but even as women
picked up arms against the British colonial presence, chastity became
a pre-condition for their revolutionary involvement. So deeply did
male activists fear female sexuality that it 'was an iron rule for the revolu-
tionaries that they should stay away from women.'[17] So as women joined

men as comrade in arms, they were held to high standards of chastity and any deviation was seen as politically dangerous.

In modern India, the two major women's organizations affiliated with the Hindu nationalism, Sadhvi Shakti Parishad and Rashtriya Sevika Samiti have politically energized this chaste notion of women in skillful ways.

RASHTRIYA SEVIKA SAMITI

In April 1998, I attended a large meeting of the Samiti in Mumbai, India. The Mumbai meeting took place in a local school. At the back of the room where we met, a large poster depicted a beautiful woman imposed onto a map of India. This was the Devi Ashtabhuja or the eight-armed goddess, embodying the Indian nation. Later, a *pracharika* (or celibate activist) of the Samiti explained the icons held aloft by each arm: the fire symbolizing purity; the *japmala* (a Hindu prayer beads), national responsibility; the sword, martial resistance to the enemy; the upraised hand, a blessing; the saffron flag, Hindu culture; the Gita, knowledge; the bell, a call to an awareness of the purity of life; and the lotus, the burgeoning purity of the new Hindu nation among the filth of cultural decline. The lion by her side represented control and martial power.[18] I watched young girls brandish wooden daggers and practice martial arts.

My visit to the Samiti *shakha* was coordinated by Kamalatai, Hematai, and Sheelatai, three older women who had been involved in the Samiti for many years. All three were strong and articulate middle class women dedicated to the Samiti.[19] The girls ranged in age from 11 to 22. All were in school, ambitious, and self-confident. I spoke to a young married woman who had just begun a Master's program in Education. She informed me that all was going well because her husband and in-laws approved of her decision to study, and further, she made sure that her household duties were not neglected. A group of young girls, gathered around us to listen. They too, referred to the necessity of privileging the roles of wife and mother over all other roles a middle class woman can choose to play in contemporary Indian society.

In speaking with these girls and women, it was unclear whether they were really inspired by the ideology of maternal glory disseminated by the Samiti or if they had shrewdly grasped the circulation of power relations in middle class Hindu families, where women can only win the right to education or a career by not disrupting gender stereotypes too radically. Put another way, are they really convinced of the Samiti's ideology of heroic mother in the Hindu nation or do they accept that getting up early to cook meals and wash clothes, before they go to work or university is the price they pay for their choice—for some it may not be a choice but an economic compulsion—to join a changing modern India. Indeed, it does not matter. The Samiti provides them with a language to order and accommodate social, gendered change.

The Samiti *pracharika* of the Delhi office lives by herself, actively organizing and coordinating the work of the Samiti. Radhaji's political activism is justified by an explicit rejection of her sexual nature through voluntary celibacy and modest dress. According to Radhaji, weekly *shakha*s or meetings along with the annual camps form the foundation of the Samiti's work among young women. In these arenas young women participate in physical exercise, learn about Hindu myths, and join in group discussions. When I asked her about the topics of discussion, she looked at me and asked, 'What do Canadian women speak of?' I answered, 'They discuss juggling home and work, being mothers and workers.' 'Then Canadian women,' answered Radha, 'are not so different from us.'[20] It became clear that negotiating home and work within the boundaries of traditional Hindu ideas of wifehood and motherhood forms a vital part of the Samiti's discourse. The Samiti orders and disseminates its vision of female participation in Hindutva against a changing socio-economic context through the skillful use of historic female figures.

The Samiti's depiction of powerful women can be emphasized by their textual treatment of Jijabai (1598–1674), mother of celebrated Hindu warrior Shivaji. The Jijabai of the Samiti's narrative was mortified by her husband's subordination to a Muslim ruler and in addition she decried the declining martial prowess and pride of Hindus.[21] She prayed to the goddess Bhavani for a son, who would fulfill Hindu

India's need for leadership. Bhavani answered her prayer. Thus, we have two feminine images, the goddess and Jijabai, the mother, moulding the perfect Hindu warrior, Shivaji, ready to defend communal honor. Shivaji's father, Shahaji, according to the Samiti's narrative, had no influence on Shivaji's education. Indeed, it seems to be implied that as Jijabai was contemptuous of Shahaji's capitulation to the Islamic rulers, she moved Shivaji away from his father so that he could be exposed to good Hindu training. Thus, according to the Samiti's reading, Shivaji's patriotism, martial ability, and administrative skills derived from his mother's, not his father's training. However, the Samiti's Jijabai never disrespected her husband nor did she deviate from the roles of dutiful daughter-in-law or ideal wife. Indeed the Samiti's texts[22] underline that wives and mothers should be strong women able to negotiate their way in a public world of economic decision-making and political action.

But feminine power is only acceptable if chastity and virtue remain important norms. The Samiti by no means advocates that women remain at home sheltered and powerless; indeed its privileging of icons such as Jijabai, Shivaji's heroic mother; the warrior queen Lakshmibai, and the powerful queen of Indore, Ahilyabai, emphasizes strength and action. However, all three icons never transgressed the boundaries of chastity and virtue. The Samiti women I met over years: the women at the 1998 *shakha*, Radhaji the Delhi *pracharika*, Hemaji the lawyer, Sitaji who stayed at home but maintained a lively interest in politics and an active involvement in weekly *shakha*s, and Sheilaji the college professor, were strong articulate women, traveling alone and actively spreading the message of the Samiti. But their lives, in their perception, remain anchored in a context that valorizes asexual, chaste, women who are responsible for the honor of their body, family, and nation.

Indeed, these three sites are embedded in an endless loop wherein a chaste wife and mother (whether she be warrior, administrator, or leader) represents a strong family which in turn represents a powerful and honorable nation worthy of protection which is represented by a strong yet chaste woman. These ideals are echoed in the narratives of the VHP's (Vishal Hindu Parishad) Sadhvi Shakti Parishad.

SADHVI SHAKTI PARISHAD

On a cool winter's day in February, I met Sadhvi Uma. She lives in a modestly furnished room in the VHP's sizeable compound in New Delhi. Dressed in saffron robes, her salt and pepper hair tied back, and devoid of any jewelry, she welcomed me warmly. Once I had been given tea, I asked her about the Sadhvi Shakti Parishad (literally, the Association of Sadhvi Power). She spoke at length about the Parishad and its goals. This association was formed in 1998 under the aegis of the VHP and at the moment has 1,000 members. According to the Sadhvi, women *sadhvis* or *sants* (ascetics) who have taken a vow of celibacy and eschewed a householder's life to preach Hindu values form the basis of this group. The *sadhvis* know the basics of Ayurveda, practice meditation, and are well-versed in various Hindu rituals. They reach out to young women, and impress on them the importance of self-reliance, independence, resistance to westernization, and the necessity for celebrating woman as mother.[23] I asked her about the saffron robes. She answered, 'The saffron robes of the *sadhvis* emphasize detachment. Celibacy is necessary as family detracts from following the true path of nation-building. We must focus on social activism. *Sadhvis* should not just pray but be active in society.'[24] Then she went on to emphasize that a woman should be modest, be ready to sacrifice and take on the mantle of a dutiful wife because a woman's husband forms the core of her strength.

A Sadhvi Shakti Parishad publication titled *The Power of Motherhood*, a collection of essays penned by important Parishad activists and ideologues outlines the manner in which *sadhvis* are intersecting the landscape of *Hindutva*.[25]

The Sadhvi Shakti Parishad: An Introduction, authored by Sadhvi Kamlesh Bharati outlines some ideological trajectories that are pursued and elaborated in other essays found in the volume. In this essay, Sadhvi Bharati claims, 'Therefore, woman in the form of *Prakriti* (nature) is the main foundation of society.'[26] However,

As time passed, men created institutions that have destroyed this image of women .... They have limited her greatness ... if we make her only a mother or a wife, then her personality's most important part does not blossom .... After independence when educated women resisted, they joined a so-called westernized women's liberation movement that killed the Indian family.[27]

Alongside, this misguided westernized women's movement, Indian leaders bedazzled by western materialism focused on economic growth, ignoring the country's spiritual evolution. Remember, argues the Sadhvi, 'A country's strength lies not in sky scrapers, roads, big schemes, nice clothes but in their citizen's character, especially their women's decency, their cultures ....'[28] Simultaneously, because of this neglect of Indian (read Hindu) spiritual development, '... crores [one crore equals 10 million] of rejected Hindus became Christians and Mussalman and we ... Hindus stayed dreaming in our ashrams. As a result, hundreds of Hindus were killed in Kashmir, and the numbers of Hindus declined in Assam, Manipur, Kerala, Mizoram, Bengal, Bihar.'[29] Given this national situation, 'The Sadhvi Shakti Parishad was created to reinvigorate the traditional power/respect of Indian women ....'[30]

The essay clearly links a woman's body (modesty) and her role as cultural (and biological) reproducer to the health of a nation. If women do not perform their cultural role in a proper manner, then the family suffers, and by extension the nation. Feminism, an alien westernized construct is demonized as the enemy of the Hindu family. Sexism in Indian society is not denied, but is linked to the degradation of Hindu culture. The Sadhvi does not clarify where the forces responsible for the degradation of Hindu culture lie, but it is possible to infer the following chain of reasoning from her observations: exposure to western ideals lead many Indians to privilege materialism, and consequently women become wanton, retreating from their role as mother (read cultural and biological reproducer), causing the Hindu family and the nation to falter. Thus, by reinvigorating Hindu womanhood, the Parishad will resist this decline.

It is also interesting to note that she argues that a woman will not blossom if she is seen 'only as mother and wife.' Presumably, given the title of the monograph and the Parishad's focus on motherhood, the Sadhvi is not rejecting women's role as wife and mother, but rather, proposing the models of heroic mother (i.e., Jijabai) and/or chaste but powerful wife (later essays mention Savitri who snatches her husband from the clutches of Yama, lord of death because of her devotion) as the ideals to be emulated. Therefore, it is possible to deviate from these models and be a bad mother and wife. The reasons for such deviation may either lie in the influence of westernization or the failure of Hindu society to train women in the values expressed by the lives of Jijabai and Savitri. Women's failure to undertake their cultural duty is also linked to the decline of the Hindu nation measured by conversion and death at the hands of Islamic militants (i.e., Kashmir).

There are also articles that analyze sexual harassment, assault, and women's legal rights: 'Contemporary Women's Problems and their Solutions;'[31] 'Protection of Women's Rights;'[32] and 'The Oppression of Women and Some Ways to Resist.'[33] The second essay is actually written by a woman lawyer who provides a devastating critique of the Indian legal and judicial system's inept handling of sexual assault.

However, lest such views be construed as too radical or confrontational, women's problems including sexism and dowry deaths are blamed by one author on women themselves and the demon of westernization.[34] There are also several essays extolling the virtues of *pativrata*.[35]

Further, these ideas of woman/womanhood are validated by boxed sayings—proverbs outlined by bolded borders—inserted after essays and photographs in this monograph. For example, 'It does not look good for women from respectable families to daily sit out on the balcony, look at unknown men through windows, and to laugh without any reason.'[36] The ideology of *pativrata* coupled with admonishments against perceived 'uncontrolled' behavior capable of enflaming male passions provide an effective counterfoil to any social anxiety stemming from fear of the radical disruption of gender roles—marked by articles on sexual harassment, sexual assault as well as the entrance of women onto the political stage—within the Parishad's vision of the Hindu nation.

Sarojini Naidu's reference to Sita and Savitri, the notion of female chastity reverberating in the words and ideas of Vivekananda, Gandhi, and anti-colonial armed resistance movements as well as the Parishad and Samiti's skillful use of heroic wives and mothers, underline the broad reach of these ideas in the Indian polity. I will discuss the implications of these ideas for women politicians by discussing their lived experiences at the national, state, and *panchayat* levels.

CHASTITY AND WOMEN POLITICIANS

Madhu Kishwar[37] writes of Sarojtai Kashikar who was elected to the Legislative Assembly (1991–95) of Maharashtra on a Shetkari Sanghatana ticket. However, her frequent trips to Mumbai had to be carefully planned. She did not feel 'safe' living in the hostel accommodations provided for MLAs (Member of Legislative Assembly) in Mumbai and she told Kishwar that she had to be very careful of her reputation because to be seen chatting and socializing with her male colleagues was to be interpreted as 'unchaste' and 'forward'. Her young brother-in-law had to remain by her side at all times to protect her virtue.

One wonders how an Assembly member is to conduct business and advocate for her district if she cannot be seen talking and negotiating with male members without a chaperone. In the same article Kishwar writes of female members of a rural, Maharashtra *panchayat* who explained to her that an important part of the process of negotiating services and benefits for their village was socializing with government officials. Again, the specter of 'immodesty' and 'lack of chastity' emerges if women *panchayat* members have to spend time, alone, drinking tea and talking with male, government officials. The other aspect of trips away from home is that entry into the political sphere does not mean that others are ready to take over a woman's responsibility at home. Indeed, as Sarojtai Kashikar indicated if her sister-in-law had not been willing to take over her household duties and if her sons were not teenagers, a political career would not have been possible for her.

This dilemma, in feminist theorizing, is seen as the 'double shift' or 'double burden' wherein women can enter the public sphere of economic and political activity only if they continue their work in the house. Thus in actuality, by entering the public world, women increase their workday. Therefore, it is easier for unmarried women with no children or married women with older children and a supportive husband to succeed in electoral politics. These conditions, by definition, decrease the number of women able to run for political

office considerably. So the idea of the double shift and ideas of chastity limit women's movements and access to power in a political culture where deals are made in social situations, frequently involving alcohol; no woman politician, however powerful, could risk being seen in this milieu without severe damage to her reputation.[38, 39]

Indeed Uma Bharti of the BJP was driven to a suicide attempt when some of her male BJP colleagues, suspicious of her power, spread rumors about her 'inappropriate' liaison with another colleague.[40] As Uma Bharti herself says, 'Women rarely manage to come forward and when they try to do so, their own colleagues brand them as loose-characters. Therefore, I believe that women will come into politics only if a reservation policy is implemented. My own entry into politics was in a large part a result of my rare luck; …'[41] Bharti is referring to the bill that has been discussed and debated several times, but never passed: a one-third reservation of parliamentary seats for women. *Manushi*'s[42] published interview with women MPs (members of parliament) from the BJP, Congress, Janata Dal, and CPI indicate that despite ideological differences these MPs were agreed on the barriers that prevent women's entry into politics and the need for a bill supporting reservation.

The importance of chastity in a woman politician's life is illustrated by the manner in which several important women politicians are socially constructed. The fiery Mamata Banerjee who challenged entrenched Communist Party power in West Bengal by forming her own political party is addressed as '*Didi*' or elder sister. She is unmarried without children and she is always dressed in very simple saris which do not emphasize her sexuality. Jayalalitha of Tamil Nadu is seen as '*Amma*' or mother by her followers. Uma Bharti, styles herself as a female ascetic or *sadhvi* by wearing saffron robes and remaining celibate. Mayawati of Uttar Pradesh is an unmarried woman. The late Rajamata Vijayaraje Scindia and Sonia Gandhi are constructed as the respectable, white-clad widows. Even female politicians who are married emphasize their chaste, *pativrata* status. Mother, older sister, widow, respectable married women all of these images shape the image of women politicians and construct ideas of women's 'proper and chaste' behavior.

Madhu Kishwar[43] refers to the idea of non-consort goddesses, i.e., Durga or Kali, in India who show the fierce face of femininity. So it is possible for women in India to appeal to such mythic female representations of power as well as the tradition of the heroic mother or powerful wife, within their political role. But appeals to potential female power have to be embedded within politically salient notions of chastity and the double burden carried by most married, Indian women who have children. The earlier sections have discussed the idea of chastity, I now turn to barriers to entry into electoral politics created by the double shift and its impact on the lived experiences of Indian women. This argument is illustrated by the lives of women *panchayat* members in the state of Maharashtra.

WOMEN AND *PANCHAYATS* IN MAHARASHTRA

In 1992 and 1993, constitutional amendments strengthened local government councils (or *panchayats*) at the village level and created quotas for women's participation not only as general councilors but also as council presidents and vice-presidents. *Gram panchayats* are a basic unit of de-centralized decision-making in rural India. *Panchayats* are elected by and accountable to the *gram sabhas* or village councils that are comprised of the adult electorate of a village. Although, the budget of the *panchayat* does include funds from taxation, the bulk of its financial resources come from state and central government grants. Members of the *panchayat* debate how the money will be used and hence do have access to considerable economic power. A *gram sevak* who is a government employee signs the checks with the *sarpanch* (or head of the *panchayat*, elected by *panchayat* members).[44]

Maharashtra was one of the few states that allowed reserved seats for women in the *panchayats* before the constitutional amendments were passed, as well as being the first to elect all-women *panchayats* after the amendments were passed. One of the few studies done on these all-women *panchayats,* very clearly emphasize the barriers that the double shift poses to women in politics, 'When one woman wanted to attend a training camp on Panchayati Raj, her husband asked,

"And who will make the chapattis?.'"[45] Pramila Danadavate of the Janata Dal narrates a similar reaction when a bill advocating the reservation of one-third of the Lok Sabha seats for women was debated in Parliament, 'The male members joke about this issue but basically they feel threatened. Chandrasekhar has said, "What is the necessity of these 181 women [one-third of the 543] seats in the Lok Sabha?" Others ask in jest: "Who will make our food?"'[46]

This is not a unique complaint, but as this 1998 study shows, most women were expected to carry out their time-consuming household duties while in office. This is why age became an important criterion in selecting women candidates, 'D'Lima points out that the average age of women in local government is 45 years. Older women, she says are allowed greater mobility, face less sexual slander, do not have the workload of young women, or can assign their workload to their daughters-in-law.'[47]

The presence of all-women *panchayat*s provides a vital and important image of women in political spaces. But what does this mean? Are women taken seriously as political beings? Do such *panchayat*s actually enhance women's lives? There are no simple answers to these questions. Sometimes, the social picture appears quite bleak as the following conversation with a *gram sevak* about the *gram sabha* indicates:

> '"Who attends the gram sabha?" we ask (note: 'we' refers to the researchers who contributed to Datta)'[48]
> "Everyone," he says.
> "Everyone?"
> "Yes, everyone."
> "Do the men attend?" we specify.
> "Yes."
> "The women?"
> 'No, no.'"

This conversation needs no explanation, and one wonders at how many levels of political and electoral activity it is assumed that politicians and political activists have male bodies. Thus, making women invisible.

The marginalization of women in the political machine is narrated by many women MPs. Margaret Alva of the Congress party recounts her effort to get a woman (who had a successful background as a member of a *gram panchayat* and who was willing to finance her own campaign) accepted as a contestant in a Uttar Pradesh Legislative Assembly election, 'I went to the Congress president, to the members of the so-called selection committee, I went to as many people as I could. "Yes, yes her name is there," they said ... in the end what do they do? They get a man ....'[49]

Uma Bharti of the BJP offers a reason for this reluctance to support a woman candidate, 'The society fosters the belief that women are incapable of taking their own decisions and our laws reinforce this.'[50] Pramila Dandavate of the Janata Dal, offers a similar reason for the dearth of women in politics, 'the lack of funding for those whose families are not willing (or able) to support them; criminalization of politics; rampant character assassination of women in politics; and the burden of household duties.'[51] In keeping with this rather bleak picture, many authors argue that actually women just become the pawns in the hands of male, upper caste villagers and if women do indeed try to challenge certain areas of gender exploitation, they face severe consequences, sometimes even bodily harm.[52]

Others argue that women on *panchayat*s are able to meet women's practical needs but not their strategic needs.[53] Practical needs are rooted in the gendered division of labor, i.e., the fact that women are responsible for cooking (including gathering fuel), fetching drinking water, and looking after children. Women on *panchayat*s have been successful in lobbying for better access to fuel, water, and even child care as such lobbying shores up social views of 'women's work.' But, they run into the backlash described by the feminist scholars mentioned above when they venture into the areas of strategic needs, i.e., needs rooted in the circulation of gendered power in family and society which includes challenging the incidence of domestic violence, violence deriving from the dowry system, equal wages for equal pay, and resisting rape. Such challenges require a deconstruction of the manner in which male power is sustained by the Indian cultural, social, and economic systems and also a dismantling of the notions of chastity and double burden integral to this process.

CONCLUSION

Political parties have attempted to redress the shamefully low percentage of women in politics through constitutional amendments requiring quotas of women in the *panchayats* as well as the hotly debated one-third reservation of women in Parliament. As the brief discussion of women in *panchayats* indicates, quotas do not necessarily force people to accept women as legitimate politicians and/or challenge structures of society that enforce the notion of chastity and double shift that limit women's access to politics in the first place. The autonomous women's movement[54] in India[55] has been very active in resisting structural ideas of womanhood linked to notions of chastity and women's role as wife and mother which has facilitated domestic violence and sexual harassment in schools and work places and created a very low social awareness of rape.

However, it has a very interesting relationship with electoral politics. The Institute of Democratic and Electoral Assistance's report on India states that none of the 39 women members of the 1991–96 Lok Sabha entered electoral politics through the women's movement (I would argue this is true of women members of most Lok Sabhas) nor has the autonomous women's movement made a great effort to push for women's electoral presence.[56] The many groups comprising the autonomous women's movement are suspicious of organized politics in India. They believe that structural barriers make resistance to the types of issues integral to women's lives impossible within this system. Further, like Sarojini Naidu, many women MPs simplify and erase the diversity within the women's movement by seeing them as 'elite', 'westernized women' with no knowledge of the 'real' India and women who by speaking of women's oppression deny women's strength and agency.[57]

This interpretation of the diverse and fragmented women's movement akin to the one found in the Samiti and Parishad's discourse, tends to be quite prevalent in India. However, it seems to me that as long as India remains a democracy, women's entry into electoral politics is one important avenue for women to reach for political power. But, there should be no automatic assumption that just an increase in female bodies in legislative assemblies will mean political policies that will enhance women's lives or even that legislators will admit the existence of patriarchy. Such a perspective assumes that women are united politically just because of their gender identity. Women parliamentarians by virtue of their gender do not necessarily accept that Indian society is patriarchal nor do they automatically support policies seen as feminist which include effective resistance to violence against women, implementation of pay equity, protection of women's property rights, divorce legislation that will not discriminate against women, and so on. Even given this complication and the obstacles described in this chapter, increasing the presence of women in legislative bodies remains one tactic among several that feminists can use to resist the trends identified by the *Towards Equality Report*.

The benefits of lobbying for female electoral presence flows from the dichotomy of needs identified above: strategic and practical. These two categories are not mutually exclusive and indeed recognition of practical needs can facilitate a realization of and/or resistance against structural barriers that shape strategic needs. For example, any political and policy decision-making surrounding women's access to fuel and water (a practical need) can possibly spark a discussion around why women are solely responsible for gathering fuel and water? This discussion in turn can enable the excavation of ideas of womanhood and the role of women in society. Further, participation in discussion and policy making can increase women's self-confidence which is an important pre-condition for using political power obtained through elected office in effective ways.

Obviously, discussions and realizations do not necessarily lead to change nor can we expect that actions rooted in such potentially disturbing actions will be met with no resistance. But, still the potential for discussion and possibly action contained in women's participation in electoral politics foreground this strategy as a valuable weapon among the many (legal action, protests/demonstration, conscience-raising through public theater, opening crisis centers for women surviving rape and domestic violence) women in India must draw on to resist a sexist society.

However, given my argument, it becomes clear that the ability to use electoral politics strategically is an option that is closed to many women. The hegemonic Hindu cultural norms shaping ideas of womanhood can primarily be exploited by women like Mamata Banerjee, Jayalalitha, Rajmata Vijayraje Scindia, Sonia Gandhi, Margaret Alva, Uma Bharati, and Mrinal Gore, because their path to political power has been ameliorated by class, caste, educational, and/ or family advantage. The strategic political use of images such as chaste wife, heroic mother, asexual elder sister comes at a price that women who do not have access to societal advantages will not be able to pay. This price spans a range of possibilities beginning with the economic ability to pay for housekeeping or child care to wielding charismatic authority (bestowed by membership in a royal or politically prominent family or being associated with a beloved film star) that enhances the political affect of exploiting iconic female images.[58] Further, it is also important to note that such societal advantages benefit women at all levels of political activity ranging from the *panchayat* to the Lok Sabha.

Having said this, it must be emphasized that a clear implication of my argument is that even such advantages would not easily protect a woman's political legitimacy and efficacy if she were perceived to be challenging norms of chastity and purity underlying Hindu hetero-normative ideals of womanhood. However, this is not to deny that many women leaders/politicians have effectively and adroitly used such ideals to negotiate the Indian political terrain and manufacture an impressive political profile. But such prominence and success must not lead to a simplistic individualist analysis that celebrates equal opportunity without acknowledging the cultural, economic, and political parameters limiting many Indian women's access to political power.

NOTES

1. Kumud Sharma, *Power vs. Represntation: Feminist Dilemmas, Ambivalent State and the Debate on Reservation for Women in India* (New Delhi: Center for Women's Development Studies, 1998), Occasional Paper No. 28.
2. Radha Kumar, *The History of Doing: An Illustrated Account of the Movements for Women's Rights and Feminism in India, 1800–1900* (New York and London: Verso, 1993) and Nivedita Menon, 'Introduction', in Nivedita Menon (ed.), *Gender and Politics* (New Delhi: Oxford University Press, 1999), pp. 1–35.

3. Rajeshwari Sunder Rajan, *The Scandal of the State: Women Law and Citizenship in Postcolonial India* (Durham, NC: Duke University Press, 2003) and Nirmala Banerjee, 'Between the Devil and the Deep Sea: Shrinking Options for Women in Contemporary India', in K. Kapadia (ed.), *The Violence of Development: The Politics of Gender, Identity and Social Inequities in India* (London: Zed Press, 2003), pp. 43–68.

4. Even when Hindu society perceives women to be impure because they are sexually aggressive, this perception of 'anti-social' behavior occurs within norms of heterosexuality. Queer or lesbian women do not exist in the dominant, Hindu imagination.

5. Nirmala Banerjee 2003, op.cit., and Sikata Banerjee, *Make Me a Man! Masculinity, Hinduism and Nationalism in India* (Albany, NY: State University of New York Press, 2005).

6. Tanika Sarkar, *Hindu Wife, Hindu Nation: Community, Religion and Cultural Nationalism* (Bloomington: Indiana University Press, 2001).

7. Anshu Malhotra, *Gender, Caste, and Religions Identities: Restructuring Class* in *Colonial Punjab* (New Delhi: Oxford University Press, 2002).

8. 'However, it is important to remember that even within the limits of this regulated "inner world", many nineteenth century women like Pandita Ramabai, Swarnakumari Debi, Sarala Ghosal, Rashsundari Debi remained articulate, critical, and very aware of the limits of patriarchy' (Kumar 1993 and Sarkar 2001).

9. Vivekananda, *Our Women* (Calcutta: Advaita Ashram, 2000).

10. Ibid., pp. 11–12.

11. Ibid., pp. 26–27.

12. Indira Chowdhury, *The Fragile Hero and Visile History: Gender and Politics of Culture in Colonial Bengal* (New Delhi: Oxford University Press, 2001), p. 134.

13. Vivekananda, op. cit., p. 37.

14. Gandhi cited in Kumar 1993, op. cit., p. 85.

15. Kumar 1993, op. cit., p. 83.

16. Ibid., p. 83.

17. Dutt cited in Kumar 1993, ibid., p. 85.

18. Personal Interview, New Delhi, February 2002.

19. All names have been changed to preserve anonymity.

20. Personal Interview, New Delhi, February 15, 2002.

21. Rashtriya Sevika Samiti, *Empowerment Pragmatic* (Nagpur: India Sevika Prakasan).

22. Ibid.

23. Personal Interview, New Delhi, February 8, 2002.

24. Ibid.

25. This text was in Hindi and has been translated by the author.

26. Kamlesh Bharati, 'Sadhvi Shakti Parishad: An Introduction', in *The Power of Motherhood* (New Delhi: Vishwa Hindu Parishad, 2000), pp. 11–13.

27. Ibid., p. 11.

28. Ibid.
29. Ibid.
30. Ibid.
31. Manju Sharma, 'Contemporary Women's Problems and their Solutions', in *The Power of Motherhood* (New Delhi: Vishwa Hindu Parishad, 2000).
32. Sandhya Bajaj, 'Protection of Women's Rights', in *The Power of Motherhood* (New Delhi: Vishwa Hindu Parishad, 2000), pp. 64–65.
33. Santosh Khanna, 'The Oppression of Women and Some Ways to Resist', in *The Power of Motherhood* (New Delhi: Vishwa Hindu Parishad, 2000), pp. 66–72.
34. Sharma 2000, op. cit., p. 63.
35. Abdhyashand Giri, 'The Glory of Pativrata Women', in *The Power of Motherhood* (New Delhi: Vishwa Hindu Parishad, 2000), pp. 31–33.
36. Bharati 2000, op. cit., p. 13.
37. Madhu Kishwar, 'Women's Marginal Role in Politics', in *Manushi* 97 (1997). Internet Version not paginated. Retrieved January 27, 2005 from http.//freespeech.org/manushi/97/politics.html.
38. Ibid.
39. I have personally experienced these limiting notions of chastity when as a Ph.D student I went, alone, to interview several MLAs. A substantial portion of these MLAs at the end of the interview made inappropriate, even lewd, proposals. After several unpleasant encounters, I hired a male assistant to accompany me. Since then I have not interviewed a man alone, either an assistant or my husband accompanies me.
40. Madhu Kishwar 1997, op. cit.
41. Meenakshi Nath, 'Cutting across Party Lines: Women Members of Parliament Explain their Stand on Reservation Quotas', in *Manushi* 96 (1996), pp. 7–16.
42. Ibid.
43. Madhu Kishwar, 'Indian Politics: Encourages Durgas, Snubs Women', in *Manushi* 111 (1999). Internet Version not Paginated. Retrieved on January 27, 2005 from http://freespeech.org/manushi/111/women-pol.html.
44. Bishakha Datta, *'And Who Will Make the Chapatis?' A Study of All. Women Panchayats in Maharashtra* (Kolkata: Stree, 1998).
45. Ibid., p. 125.
46. Nath 1996, op. cit.
47. Datta 1998, op. cit.
48. Ibid.
49. Nath 1996, op. cit., p. 8.
50. Ibid., p. 10.
51. Ibid., p. 14.
52. S. Anadhi, 'Grassroots Women in Governance: A Case Study of Panchayat Raj Institutions in Tamil Nadu', in K. Kapadia (ed.), *The Violence of Development: The Politics of Gender, Identity and Social Inequities in India* (London: Zed Press, 2003), pp. 425–58 and Shail Mayaram, 'New Modes of Violence:

The Backlach against Women in the Panchayat System', in K. Kapadia (ed.), *The Violence of Development*, pp. 393–424 and Seemanthini Niranjana, 'Exploring Gender Inflection within Panchayat Raj Institutions: Women's Politicization in Andhra Pradesh', in K. Kapadia (ed.), *The Violence of Development*, pp. 352–92.

53. Datta 1998, op. cit.

54. By autonomous women's movement I mean the various non-governmental, women's groups that have emerged in India since the 1970s. The women involved in these groups tend to reject political party affiliation and emphasize their independence of any political machine (see Kumar 1993 for an excellent discussion of these groups).

55. Kumar 1993 and Menon 1999, op. cit.

56. Shirin Rai, 'Caste, Class and Gender: Women in Parliament in India', Retrieved on February 2, 2005 from http.//www.den.int.women/parl/Studiesya.html.

57. Kumar 1993, op. cit.

58. For example, Vijayraje Scindia belonged to the royal family of Gwalior, Sonia Gandhi draws on the Nehru dynastic glory, Jayalalitha was the ersatz wife of an immensely popular actor turned politician MGR; and Mrinal Gore, who has been an MP from Maharashtra also belongs to a politically prominent family.

CHAPTER 3

Contextualizing Religious, Caste and Regional Dynamics in Electoral Politics: Emerging Paradoxes

Pramod Kumar

Indian politics is confronted with a new set of issues and challenges posed by the dynamic process of development. This is reflected in the qualitative shift from a command to a competitive liberal market economy,[1] from one-party dominance to coalition of parties,[2] from nation-building to representation of polarized socio-cultural reality into politics.[3] These shifts have brought to the surface certain paradoxes as reflected in the electoral process.

The paradox in electoral promises and mandate of governments, in threat from and need of democratic institutions, in ideological monotheism and ideological pluralism has been reflective of the Indian electoral system since the mid-1960s. As a result, it may not be possible to evolve neat categories of political analysis for labeling political parties as pro- and anti-economic reforms, communal and non-communal, casteist and non-casteist. In fact, the two national political parties, the Bharatiya Janata Party (BJP) and the Indian National Congress (INC), while in power favor economic reforms, but oppose reforms at the time of elections. Similarly, both parties have compromised with communal persuasions. For instance, the Congress has been accused of being anti-Sikh and branded as communal in elections in Punjab, whereas elsewhere in India, the Bharatiya Janata Party has been labeled as communal by the Congress-led front. Therefore, it would be appropriate to analyze the 2004 elections in an historical context and as a process rather than through often misleading labels, pronounce-ments of political parties and their shifting coalition partners.

Historically, the state-led nation-building project has provided the necessary conditions for the existence of divergent phenomena and also the emergence of paradoxes in electoral politics in India. The nation-building project attempted to bridge the gap between organized interest groups and people without means with a well entrenched mid-dle class.[4] The Congress which has been the main protagonist of the nation-building project claimed in its manifesto for the 2004 parlia-mentary elections, the creation of the middle class as its main achieve-ment without integrating marginalized sections into the market and decision-making system. This strata, in collaborative arrangement with the organized interest groups, became the custodians of the state while the nation consisting of people without means looked the other way.[5] These poorer sections of society are reduced to mere victims, benefi-ciaries, clients and recipients. In this dichotomous relationship, the state is seen as 'dole giver' and the nation the 'dole receiver'. In other words, a patron–client relationship defines the boundary conditions for electoral discourse.

The relationship uncovers itself in a variety of ways. Political leaders mediate between the state and the electorate through:

(i)   policies, whereby subsidies are given as doles for poverty alle-viation, debt redemption, augmentation of income;

(ii)   facilitating access to schemes, government services and pro-tection from crime and violence. For providing access to doles, the discretion available with government functionar-ies, enlarges the scope of political patronage. For instance, to have access to these doles, the poor need ration cards, identity proof and a residential certificate which are to be provided by the functionaries, often mediated by political leaders;

(iii) application of ideological filters at the level of policies and their implementation. Non-secular categories like caste, reli-gion and region and secular categories like *aam admi* (common man) are used to acquire legitimacy for their polit-ical claims.

This complex interaction between *aam admi* and electoral politics is dynamic in nature and has been undergoing a change. The transformation agenda within the nation-building project dominates Indian electoral politics.

PROMISES AND PERFORMANCE: FROM GAP TO PARADOX

The paradox between the transformational discourse and economic reforms agenda has shaped electoral politics in India. This discourse occupied a large space in electoral politics until the 1980s. Populist slogans like '*garibi hatao*,' 'land to the tiller,' 'social justice for all,' 'anti-corruption,' and 'fight against authoritarianism' have been raised for election purposes. The theme of elections has undergone a change with successive political leaders. Under India's first Prime Minister, Jawaharlal Nehru, it was social justice for all, expressed in various forms like 'land to the tiller.' In the 1971 parliamentary elections, Congress leader Mrs Indira Gandhi won with the slogan '*garibi hatao*' (poverty eradication) and under the non-Congress leadership in the 1977 parliamentary elections, it was restoration of democracy and anti-authoritarianism.

All these slogans, along with the promise of building a socialist society, remained the hallmark of Indian politics. The Congress promised what Nehru called the socialistic pattern of society by following a policy of industrialization with increased government ownership so as to command the heights of the economy. The state took upon itself the task of building infrastructure like dams, steel plants, oil refineries, and machine tool factories. In fact, these were essential for the fast growth of private industries. Indian industrialists were unwilling and unable to undertake the construction and management of these capital-intensive heavy industries.

In other words, the national political leadership sought to realize the goal of socialism by creating a large industrial and agricultural base and by developing science and technology. This process of industrialization and even the policy of nationalization were used for increasing production and not as a means of attaining social justice.

Another populist slogan, that of land reforms, was used to create a vision of equality. Land reforms and the way they were implemented transformed big land owners from a class solely dependent on land and feudal privileges to a class of rural entrepreneurs. These rural entrepreneurs, no doubt, retained substantial interest in land, but made considerable investment in transport, warehouses and rice mills. All these measures threw up a class of privileged people who were gripped by a kind of 'scarcity psychology.' On the other hand, the same process multiplied and marginalized the poor sections of the population.

However, after the mid-1980s, this discourse was not as dominant as it was in the earlier phase. The slogan of justice for all was replaced by justice for backward castes, Dalits, and minorities. It provided hope to the downtrodden without providing any concrete gains. The Mandal Commission itself acknowledged it.

When a backward class candidate becomes collector or a superintendent of police, the material benefits accruing from his position are limited to the members of his family only. But the psychological spin-off of this phenomenon is tremendous; the entire community of that backward class candidate feels socially elevated.[6]

The Mandal Commission had little to do with equality and social justice. It focused on a strategy of co-option by multiplying caste cleavages and attempting to achieve a balance of group interests. This, in a limited way, provided continuity to the discourse on transformational politics.

In the 1990s the emphasis was shifted from the public sector-administering of prices, subsidies, control of wages and poverty to structural reforms with a veneer of liberal non-regulatory state.[7] The major initiative for economic reforms was taken during the tenure of Prime Minister Rajiv Gandhi. Within months after taking office, the prime minister announced new policies to accelerate India's slow industrial growth—liberalizing imports, providing new economic incentives for exports, permitting the import of technologies, encouraging foreign investment through joint ventures, reducing taxes, and de-regulating the economy so as to make it more competitive.[8]

Thereafter, a near consensus on economic reforms package among the major political parties and actors was built, notwithstanding the occasional noises relating to *swadeshi*. For instance, the Congress and the BJP election manifestos for 2004 on economic reforms reinforced each other. The BJP highlighted its commitment to:

> further broadening and deepening the economic reforms based on a self-reliant approach, sustained double-digit GDP growth rate to achieve complete eradication of poverty and unemployment, end of regional and social disparities and bridging the urban–rural divide.[9]

The Congress manifesto asserts that,

> The Congress would broaden and deepen economic reforms. The overriding objectives would be to attain and sustain year after year a 8–10% rate of economic growth and to spread this growth over all sectors, particularly agriculture and industry … aimed at local level economic and social transformation that directly benefit the poor in rural and urban India, bringing prosperity to the 6 lakh-odd villages of India and improving the living conditions of the urban poor.[10]

The space vacated by slogans like '*garibi hatao*' was allowed to go unattended with symbolic references in election manifestos. The dichotomy between electoral promises and the mandate of governance became pronounced. Earlier, electoral promises used to be in line with the ideological commitment of the government. Now with the adoption of economic reforms, electoral promises were in contradiction with the government's mandate.

In elections, political parties ideologically support economic reforms but find it difficult to politically popularize them. This is because the content of economic reforms is to reduce employment in the public sector without creating corresponding employment in the private sector, to encourage people to participate in self-help groups and launch small businesses in the face of intense competition. Nor can political parties tell the people to mind their own health and give subsidies to private hospitals and, above all, in the name of building their stakes, 'motivate' them to pay for life-saving services even if they do not have the opportunities to earn a livelihood.

It is important to note there has been a wide gap between electoral promises and government performance in both the phases, that is, 1947–77 and 1977 onwards. The difference is that in the earlier phase, the electoral promises were ideologically in convergence with the mandate of the government, whereas in the latter phase the electoral promises and the government's mandate were ideologically divergent. The reasons identified for this crisis of non-performance range from structural causes to political behavior of leaders. However, in the first phase it became manifest in the form of a leadership crisis, whereas in the second phase it took the form of a crisis of trust in leadership.

The 2004 elections have empirically shown that the legitimacy of the government in power declines faster due to the mismatch between the electoral promises and the stark realities of the new economic policies. The National Democratic Alliance (NDA), particularly the BJP, made implementation of economic reforms a major poll plank in the 2004 elections. The campaign was labeled 'India Shining.' Congress raised issues relating to 'aam aadmi' (common man) and branded the as anti-poor. The mismatch between the electoral mandate of the 1999 elections and the performance of the BJP-led government contributed to its poor electoral performance in the 2004 parliamentary elections. It won 138 seats with a 22.16 percent vote share.

Further, this paradox between electoral promises and government performance can be captured clearly from two case studies—Andhra Pradesh and Punjab. Andhra Pradesh was considered the best governed state with shifting emphasis from state as provider of services to being merely a facilitator. In the 1994 elections, the Telegu Desam Party (TDP) won by opposing the economic reforms of the Congress. A decade later, in 2004, the Congress launched itself onto a pro-poor bandwagon and against economic reforms to defeat the TDP-led by Chandrababu Naidu government (see Table 3.1).[11]

The Congress made electoral promises like

> free electricity for agriculture, subsidies on crop loans, more funds for irrigation projects, relief package to the families of suicide victims, loans to women self-help groups at 3 per cent interest per annum, and the

sanction of a revolving fund to all DWACRA groups which completed six months, 2.5 lakh jobs for the youth by lifting the ban on recruitment in government service, enhancement of old-age pension, and revival of the subsidised cloth scheme. [12]

Table 3.1
Vidhan Sabha elections in Andhra Pradesh (1994 and 2004)

	1994			2004			
	Seats Contested	Seats Won	% of Votes Polled	Seats Contested	Seats Won	% of Votes Polled	Loss or Gain % Increase in Seats Won
Congress	294	26	33.85	234	185	38.56	611.54
TDP	251	216	44.14	267	47	37.59	−78.24
Left	37	34	6.35	26	15	3.37	−56.0
BJP	280	3	3.89	27	2	2.63	−33.34
TRS	–	–	–	54	26	6.68	–
Others	2,357	15	11.78	1,288	19	11.17	26.67

Source: Statistical report on general election to the Legislative Assembly of Andhra Pradesh (various years).

Chandrababu Naidu opined that

the Congress was making fantastic promises that could not be implemented by anyone in power and that it was resorting to populist promises to deceive the voters. He said international financial agencies, such as the World Bank, would not approve free electricity to the agriculture sector and that would mean the stoppage of loans to the state. The Congress immediately termed the TDP government as anti-farmer and pro-World Bank. [13]

The results of the elections were dismal for the TDP and the Congress won the elections. The first step the Congress government took after coming to power was to announce free electricity for the farmers as was promised in its election manifesto.

In Punjab, the Congress demonstrated this paradox between electoral promises and government mandate in a blatant manner as it was caught between Assembly elections (2002) followed by parliamentary elections (2004). In the 2002 Assembly elections, it promised free electricity to farmers, removal of octroi and registered a victory over its major opponent, the Akali Dal. The election manifesto committee was chaired by Dr Manmohan Singh, the present Prime Minister of India.[14]

After coming to power it backtracked from its electoral promises and announced a number of initiatives for introducing economic reforms. Consequently, it did poorly in 2004 parliamentary election. Learning lessons from its defeat, the Congress government announced sops like free electricity to farmers in the wake of the forthcoming Assembly elections in early 2007. Interestingly, these sops were opposed by Prime Minister Manmohan Singh. The Chief Minister, Captain Amarinder Singh, reminded the prime minister that he had chaired the election manifesto committee which made these promises in the 2002 elections.

The patron–client relationship is carefully nurtured by offering doles in the name of subsistence subsidies to the electorate. Doles have been used as a poverty-alleviating and vote catching device. People without means constitute the backbone of Indian electoral politics.

> There are more illiterates, rural-based people, Scheduled Castes and OBCs who comprise voters today than earlier …. In 1996, over the average polling of 58 per cent there were 1 per cent more OBCs voting as against merely 2 per cent less than the upper castes; that is 59 per cent OBCs voted as against 56 per cent upper castes. It becomes more pronounced if we look at the Scheduled Castes who are 2 per cent above the average, that is, about 60 per cent of them voted as against 56 per cent upper castes.[15]

It is this reality that sustains the paradoxical response of the political parties not only in terms of electoral promises, but also in their performance. The politics of populism became more pronounced with the introduction of economic reforms. Political parties, in order to compete with each other, promise doles. Consequently, it has liberated political parties from the burden of adopting political positions based on transformational politics.

THREAT AND NEED PARADOX OF DEMOCRACY

The interaction of the state-led nation-building project with the path of development produced shifts in political discourse from a transformational thrust to the consolidation of sectional interests. It also brought about a shift from the need of democratic institutions to meet a perceived threat from these same institutions leading to institutional collapse in the 1980s.[16] As a result, participatory institutions were either made defunct or ineffective and consequently led to the decreased power of liberal democratic institutions and their leadership.

There has been centralization of authority and de-institutionalization of governance in the midst of popular revolts in Gujarat; the mass movement in Bihar spearheaded by Jayaprakash Narayan leading to the imposition of internal emergency in 1977. This process of de-institutionalization was attributed to the then Prime Minister, Indira Gandhi, by some political analysts. Myron Weiner opined that 'in Mrs Gandhi's view, these institutions—state Congress organizations with local leaders independent of the Centre, a hostile opposition, a critical press and an independent judiciary—had impeded the movement towards a modern, socialist, equalitarian social and economic order.'[17] The structural and historical causes were not analyzed and reflected available political options and choices. The issue of de-institutionalization was identified as a principle reason for the non-performance and collapse of democratic political processes.[18] No doubt there has been gradual de-democratization and whittling down of the basic rights of the people and abdication of the basic obligation of the system leading to the downgrading the most precious facet of the democratic system—legitimacy. Retrospectively, it can be conceptualized as a cyclical process and can be termed as a threat and need paradox of Indian democracy.

The institutional collapse which was caused by the threat perception of these leaders was selectively reversed. Having curtailed the democratic functioning of various institutions, these leaders frequently misused the paramilitary forces to overcome the crises. The 1980s saw the revival of law enforcing agencies with an overactive police; as a result, the heroes of the 1980s were the supercops. The 1990s produced an 'overactive judiciary' which took upon itself most of the functions of the state, including the moral and ethical role of the non-state institutions. The Chief Election Commissioner shared the glory of performing the role of reforming the system single-handedly.

This selected restoration of institutional framework did not restore the secular institutional culture.[19] However, competitive electoral politics became activated leading to the decline of one-party dominance. In order to mobilize regional electoral constituencies based on caste, language, tribal and religious considerations, competing political parties built bridges with ideologically divergent groups. This 'bridge politics' blurred ideological differences. For instance, the party responsible for atrocities against Sikhs in 1984 was being wooed by all secularists, and parties known for their communal outbursts were in alliance with former socialists and liberal democrats.

POLITICS OF IDEOLOGICAL MONOTHEISM AND MULTICULTURAL SECULARISM

This seeming paradox contributed to a shift from one variety of ideological monotheism to another and to the negation of forces of ideological pluralism. Nehruvian institutional secularism was replaced by ideological monotheism having its basis in unified conception of indigenous (Hindu) nationhood, thus negating the policies of appeasement of minorities and in opposition to secular nationhood terming it as pseudo-secularism. On the other hand regional, caste, and tribal groups became mobilized for the expansion of electoral constituencies.

The monocultural secular nation-building project, in interaction with multicultural social reality, led to the subversion of the rights of various cultural and linguistic groups. This provided a context to the strengthening of communal assertions and currency to caste groupings as electoral capital.

There are at least three crucial events in this chronology; the Shah Bano-Muslim Women's Act affair of 1985–86, the BJP's defection in 1990 from

the United Front government of V.P. Singh, and the ongoing Mandir–
Masjid saga …. By overturning the Shah Bano decision in the widely
publicized case, available and explicable to a nation-wide audience, the
Rajiv Gandhi Government gave apparent credence to the widespread
and long-held charge against the Congress that the substance of its secularism was 'pseudo-secularism,' communally divisive 'vote bank politics',
and 'pampering' Muslims in order to get their votes.[20]

COMMUNAL MONOLITHS AS VOTE BANKS

The Ram Janmabhumi movement consolidated the Hindu majority
vote bank and consequently the BJP increased its electoral tally in
Parliament from two seats in 1984 to 182 seats in the 1999 elections.
As a ploy to fragment and weaken the Hindu vote bank, a caste-based
political co-option strategy in the form of the Mandal Commission
was unleashed.

As Table 3.2 shows, the BJP won two seats in the 1984 elections
with an 8 percent vote share. It increased its tally by winning 85 seats
in 1989, 120 seats in 1991, 161 seats in 1996, 182 seats in 1998, and
1999 and 138 seats in 2004.

Table 3.2

Seats won by the Bharatiya Janata Party in parliament elections (1984–2004)

Year	Seats Contested	Seats Won	% of Votes Polled	% of Seats Won Out of Contested Seats
1984	224	2	7.74	1
1989	225	85	11.36	38
1991	468	120	20.11	26
1996	471	161	20.29	35
1998	388	182	25.59	47
1999	339	182	23.75	54
2004	364	138	22.16	38

Source: Statistical report on general elections to the Lok Sabha (various years).

Political mobilization of backward castes found expression in parties like the Rashtriya Janata Dal, Janata Dal, Samajwadi Party, Samata
Party, and other regional parties. Dalit politics also emerged as a

powerful force and found articulation through the Bahujan Samaj Party. The participation of Dalits in elections increased.

In 1996 parliamentary elections the percentage of SC [Scheduled Caste] voter turnout was 89.2 per cent as against the national average of 87.3 per cent in the case of upper castes. This trend continued in the 1998 elections where voter turnout of the SCs and the upper castes was 93 per cent and 91.9 per cent respectively. In 1971 SC voter turnout was 78.7 per cent (CSDS data unit, CSDS Delhi).[21]

In the initial years of post-Independence India, the dominant political discourse was secular in its thrust and was not consistent with areas governed by caste or religious domains. Whereas since the mid-1980s, the dominant political discourse increasingly became consistent with a communal, sectarian, and caste-based cultural reservoir. The political parties transformed this reservoir into electoral capital (see Table 3.3). Therefore, to label electoral battles between political parties as communal versus non-communal is a misnomer.

Table 3.3

Party preference by social group

	Congress — NCP	BJP	N
Upper castes	33	60	161
Patidars	18	75	158
OBCs	55	40	230
Dalits	67	23*	89
Adivasis	46	48	172
Muslims	60	20*	79

Source: National Election Study 2004; weighted data set.
Note: 1. *The Sample size for Dalits and Muslims voting for the BJP is too small to be statistically significant.
2. N = Number of respondents.

Political formations in Punjab labeled the Congress as communal as it was seen to be responsible for Operation Bluestar at the Sikh religious shrine, the Golden Temple at Amritsar, and anti-Sikh riots following the assassination of Prime Minister Indira Gandhi. Similarly, the BJP could be labeled communal as being allegedly responsible for the communal carnage in Gujarat. In the 2004 parliamentary elections and even in the 2002 Assembly elections in Gujarat, the BJP could consolidate the Hindu vote and win with massive margins.

In the 2002 Gujarat Assembly elections, 154 out of 182 constituencies were affected by communal riots, and the BJP could win in 127 (Table 3.4). Can communal riots influence people's response to political parties?

Table 3.4

Performance of BJP and Congress in Gujarat Parliament
and Vidhan Sabha elections

	Lok Sabha				Vidhan Sabha			
	1999		2004		1998		2002	
	BJP	Congress	BJP	Congress	BJP	Congress	BJP	Congress
Seats contested	26	26	26	25	182	179	182	180
Seats won	20	6	14	12	117	53	127	51
% of vote	52.48	45.41	47.37	43.86	44.81	34.85	49.85	39.28

Sources: 1. Statistical report on general election to the Legislative Assembly of Gujarat (various years).
2. Statistical report on general elections to the Lok Sabha (various years).

In fact, the results do not validate the thesis that the riot-hit constituencies, or even those with high rioting, had BJP as the sole claimant. Gandhinagar and Dessa were among the worst affected by riots yet they returned Congress candidates. Thus, the Congress has won in a significant number of constituencies (12 percent) which witnessed a high degree of riots and others which had moderate riots (24 percent). On the other hand, among the riot-free constituencies, more seats went to the BJP than to the Congress (more than 60 percent), even in the proclaimed anti-incumbency heartland of Saurashtra. In other words, the BJP won irrespective of the presence or extent of riots in Gujarat, whereas it could win more than 60 percent of the constituencies which had no rioting or low rioting. The Congress, on the other hand, did win seats in the heavily and moderately riot-hit constituencies.[22]

The Gujarat elections have produced a major shift from one variety of ideological monotheism to another, that is from the minority religious group to the majority religious group—from nationalization of *Hindutva* to regionalization of *Hindutva*. The nurturing of regional sentiments and aspirations around *Hindutva* is a unique experiment which has serious implications for the nation-building project. It has not only reversed the secular nation-building project launched at the time of Independence, but has also distorted the RSS concept of nationalization of *Hindutva*. The whole tenor of electoral mobilization in Gujarat was a clever blend of Gaurav of Gujarat[23] and *Hindutva* identity. Providing a saffron garb to regional aspirations cannot be explained as a consequence of post-Godhra developments. In fact, the Godhra episode and the riots that followed are the products of an ideological fermentation carefully nurtured by the Vishwa Hindu Parishad (VHP) and the BJP.

The massive response to regionalization of the *Hindutva* ideology and regional leadership can be understood in the backdrop of globalization. The process of globalization has undermined the concept of a nation. Having compromised on economic sovereignty, countries like India and Pakistan have surrendered their political sovereignty, as maintenance of domestic peace has been pushed into the realm of global political-decision making and diktats. It is in this context that President Pervez Musharraf raised the question of Gujarat riots at the United Nations and the '*Mian Musharraf*' symbolism gained currency in the Gujarat elections. The process of globalization provided an impetus to the son-of-the-soil movement, particularly in Gujarat, which has a long history of communalizing the job market.

In the 2004 parliament elections, Congress could win in 12 out of 26 Lok Sabha seats as compared to the six seats it won in the 1999 elections. The Congress was leading in 92 of the 182 Assembly segments as compared to 51 in the 2002 elections. The moot question is that in less than 15 months, is it possible that anti-incumbency could become a potent factor overriding communal polarization? Or did the defensive response of the Congress under the leadership of former RSS activist Shanker Singh Vaghela provide the electorates a choice between soft and hard communalism?[24]

CASTE AS A POLITICAL CAPITAL

Caste as a political capital has found varied responses blended in regional flavors covering a vast political spectrum. The content of the emerging Dalit identity includes an assertion of de facto recog-nition of their rights, occupational mobility, status parity and parallel religious symbols. The local cultural context has shaped Dalit response to political parties. For instance, the Bahujan Samaj Party (BSP) found a positive response in Uttar Pradesh (UP), whereas in Punjab, with the highest percentage of Dalit population in the country, it found a nominal response. To illustrate, the BSP vote share in UP increased from 11 percent in 1993 to 23 percent in 2002.[25] Both in Punjab and UP the initial response was to identify with the BSP as there was a low degree of representation of the SCs. But in Punjab there is a trend to move away from the BSP.

Table 3.5

BSP vote support in Uttar Pradesh and Punjab Legislative Assembly

	Uttar Pradesh			Punjab		
	2002	1996	1993	2002	1997	1992
Seats contested	401	296	164	100	67	105
Seats won	98	67	67	0	1	9
% of vote	23.06	19.4	11.12	5.69	7.48	16.32

Sources: 1. Statistical report on general election to the Legislative Assembly of Uttar Pradesh (various years).

        2. Statistical report on general election to the Legislative Assembly of Punjab (various years).

Why could the BSP not make electoral inroads in Punjab which has been known for its liberal ritualistic religious practices in relation to caste? Both Sikhism and the Arya Samaj have liberated the Dalits from the stringent purity–pollution based behavioral patterns. For instance, equality in religious gatherings, establishment of common kitchen and the institution of *langar* were initiated to overcome caste-based superior and inferior relationships. Not only this, offering of *Karah Prasad* by any one, irrespective of his caste, was a symbolic departure from the notion that forbade food sharing by the upper and lower castes.[26]

Interestingly, in Punjab, Dalit assertion has usurped the idea of purity to present itself as a competing identity. Notions of honor, re-venge and levirate marriages (*chaddar* system) that were considered exclusive to peasant groups are now being adopted by the Dalits. [27]

For the Dalits, it meant preventing 'pollution' of their exclusive identity. At the individual level, the Dalits are resentful of being unable to protect their women from what they now perceive as transgression of their manhood and identity. Sharing the common cultural reservoir to acquire social parity without getting assimilated into the hierarchical system provided them with a greater political bargaining capacity without becoming hostage of a particular Dalit party.

Further, the ideological content of the BSP has been unable to capture the regional, cultural and economic specificities of Punjab. The purity–pollution and *Manuwad* that are the BSP's main ideological planks do not find expression in the socio-cultural domain of Punjab in its fundamental form as it exists in UP. Therefore, it would be appropriate to see the impact of globalization and regional dimension on the communal and caste-based political formations and their electoral performance.

To sum up, the above analysis shows that the promises and performance of political parties may not be analyzed in terms of gap, but as a paradox. Further, the crisis of leadership has acquired a systemic form leading to a crisis of trust in politics and political leadership. Ideological filters have become convenient labels for acquiring legitimacy for what is otherwise a blatantly legislative power game.

NOTES

1. Robert E.B. Lucas and Gustav F. Papanek (eds), *The Indian Economy: Recent Development and Future Prospects* (New Delhi: Oxford University Press, 1988).
2. E. Sridharan, 'Electoral Coalition 2004 General Elections', *Economic and Political Weekly*, Vol. 39, No. 51, December 18, 2004, pp. 5418–25. Paul R. Brass, 'India, Myron Weiner and the Political Science of Development', *Economic and Political Weekly*, Vol. 37, No. 29, July 20, 2002, pp. 3026–40.
3. Robert W. Stern, *Changing India: Bourgeois Revolution on the Subcontinent* (Cambridge: Cambridge University Press, 2003).
4. 'A nation which had two-thirds of its people under the poverty line at independence is now a nation with two-thirds of its population above the poverty line in the half century since independence. The middle class of India is the proud creation of the Congress.' *Lok Sabha Elections 2004: Manifesto of the Indian National Congress.*

5. Pushpendra, 'Dalit Assertion Through Electoral Politics', *Economic and Political Weekly*, Vol. 34, No. 36, September 4, 1999, p. 2611.

6. B.P. Mandal, *Report of the Backward Classes Commission* (New Delhi: Government of India, 1980), Vol. I, p. 57.

7. To quote, P.N. Dhar, the then advisor to Prime Minister Rajiv Gandhi:

> The broad purpose of policy changes now is to move away from directives, regulations and controls to a greater role for market incentives and to indirect policy instruments as against direct physical controls. Greater importance is now being attached to productivity, competitiveness and technological modernisation with a view to promoting more rapid growth of manufactured exports. Similarly, quantitative limits on imports are being replaced by tariffs to expose domestic industry to a reasonable amount of external competition. Some more items have also been added to the open general licence.

P.N. Dhar, 'The Indian Economy: Past Performance and Current Issues', in Robert E.B. Lucas and Gustav F. Papanek (eds), *The Indian Economy: Recent Development and Future Prospects* (New Delhi: Oxford University Press, 1988), p. 15.

8. Myron Weiner, *The Indian Paradox: Essays in Indian Politics* (New Delhi: Sage Publications, 1989), p. 297.

9. *Bharatiya Janata Party: Vision Document—2004*, p. 2.

10. *Lok Sabha Elections 2004: Manifesto of the Indian National Congress*, p. 8.

11. He undertook a 1,500 km-long *padayatra* across Andhra Pradesh in May 2003. During his campaign, he called Chandrababu Naidu an agent of the World Bank and alleged that the reforms pursued by the TDP government had landed the state in a debt trap and resulted in underdevelopment. He charged huge loans taken from international agencies had been spent on unproductive sectors, and much of it had been pocketed by Telugu Desam functionaries. K.C. Suri, 'Andhra Pradesh: Fall of the CEO in Arena of Democracy', *Economic and Political Weekly*, Vol. 39, No. 51, December 18, 2004, p. 5494.

12. Ibid., p. 5495.

13. Ibid.

14. *Punjab Congress Election Manifesto, 2002*

15. Javed Alam, 'What is Happening Inside Indian Democracy', *Economic and Political Weekly*, Vol. 34, No. 37, September 11, 1999, p. 2654.

16. Pramod Kumar, 'Flaws in the System', *The Hindustan Times* (Chandigarh), June 30, 1999.

17. Myron Weiner, op. cit., p. 269.

18. To quote, Rajni Kothari, 'among other things, I have focused on what I believe to be the principle malaise, namely the erosion of institutions and the challenge of both "restoring political process (by which I have meant restoring political institutions) and reinstitutionalising the political terrain in terms of processes

and interactions that emerge from the grassroots upwards to macro "political structures."' Rajni Kothari, 'Fragments of a Discourse: Towards Conceptualization', in T.V. Sathyamurthy (ed.), *State and Nation in the Context of Social Change* (New Delhi: Oxford University Press, 1994), Vol. 1, p. 42.

19. Paul R. Brass, op. cit., p. 3027.

20. Robert W. Stern, op. cit., pp. 185–86.

21. Pushpendra, op. cit., p. 2609

22. Pramod Kumar, 'Ideology Overrides Anti-incumbency', *The Hindustan Times* (Chandigarh), December 24, 2002.

23. The Gaurav of Gujarat means pride of Gujarat. The Chief Minister of Gujarat on August 12, 2000 said, 'I am determined to take out the yatra and tell the world the Gaurav Gatha [Story of Pride] of five crore [50 million] people in the state. It is not the story of Godhra, Narora Patia or Gulmarg. Gujarat was not a state of murderers and rapists as the pseudosecularists, fanatic and power-hungry Congress leaders are attempting to project.' *India: Modi Determined to Take out Gaurav Yatra in Gujarat*, http:/www.rediff. com, August 12, 2002.

24. The BJP was ahead of the Congress by 7 percent votes in LS polls of 1999. Winning 12 seats in 2004 from six in 1999 was a great boost to the Congress, which was terribly demoralized after the 2002 verdict. Then and now, the Congress has been clueless about countering the religio-communal propaganda and mobilization of the BJP. Priyavadan Patel, 'Gujarat: Anti-Incumbency Begins', *Economic and Political Weekly*, Vol. 39, No. 51, December 18, 2004, p. 5475.

25. A.K. Verma, 'Uttar Pradesh: Caste and Political Mobilisation,' *Economic and Political Weekly*, Vol. 39, No. 51, December 18, 2004, pp. 5463–66.

26. Pramod Kumar, 'Checking Caste Antagonism to Prevent Violence', *The Hindustan Times* (Chandigarh), August 13, 2003.

27. Pramod Kumar and Rainuka Dagar, 'Gender in Dalit Identity Construction in Punjab,' in Harish K. Puri (ed.), *Dalit in Regional Context* (Jaipur: Rawat Publication, 2004), p. 279. Livirate marriage, a customary practice of Punjabi peasantry in which a window is 'married' to her deceased husband's brother of other male relative by performing a specific ritual. The patriarchal family thus retains land, assets and children within its fold, while also providing legitimate protection and space to the widow. Levirate marriages are now also being practised by Dalits in Punjab, claiming parity with the Jat peasantry by providing protection to 'family honor.'

CHAPTER 4

Of Hindus and their Nationalisms: Religion, Representation, and Democracy

JYOTIRINDRA DASGUPTA

Brands normally refer to proprietary products or blends that consumers in the marketplace can easily identify and differentiate from others. Some forms of religious nationalism in South Asia, bearing Hindu, Muslim or other labels, may assume a brand quality that may be easy to miss in both popular and academic discussions.[1] The complex relation between religious communities in India and specific nationalist formulations claiming to speak for them is frequently misunderstood by observers. How do Hindus, for example, prefer to express their ideas of nationalism? How can we distinguish them from particular versions of nationalism claimed by organized groups as authentic brands of Hindu nationalism?[2] No matter what some leaders advocate as authentic community perspectives or how observers choose to brand them with particularistic implications, the issue of representational legitimacy of specific nationalist claims may pose serious problems. The dilemmas of voice, differentiated representation of interests and legitimacy of nationalism claims extend to all the major religious communities of India, though the problems in the Hindu case would seem to be rather more intractable.

This essay explores major variations of nationalist orientations or nationalisms associated with specific religion-based communities in modern India. What accounts for such variations? Greater attention for our purpose will be given to variations in nationalist formulations among Hindus at selected *historical moments* and in *different cultural areas*. There is an interesting lineage of contending elaboration of nationalist ideas by leaders and intellectuals of Hindu origin in different moments of Indian history. Where does the recently-branded form of Hindu nationalism fit in? How do we locate its competitive place and relative importance in the multicultural political space? One important purpose of this work is to treat the nationalist ideology and practice systems associated with religious identities and their organized political expressions in the context of developing public spaces.[3] In doing so, we intended to trace the relevant evolutionary phases of nationalist formulations. We ask if there is a pattern of *cumulative trends* since the early colonial era. Why did some formulations gain wider and deeper support than their competition? What was the role of the institutional system during the colonial and the post-colonial time? Did democratic institutions of representation encourage moderate methods? What was the role of sub-political and international factors in influencing the goals and methods of nationalist movements and organizations in recent times?[4] Tracing the tracks of these developments will necessarily require a long view of relevant history, throwing light on the relative place and prospects of competing nationalisms claiming to represent Hindu community interests and perspectives.

COMMUNITY, RELIGION, AND SOURCES OF COHESION

Communities categorized by religion are not easy to define in the Indian context. Census categories like Hindu, Muslim, and others offer more classificatory convenience than clarification of religious boundary, or significance of membership or shared values. The recent census figures indicate the Hindu and Muslim population of India to be approximately 80 and 13 percent of the total respectively.[5] These numbers are arguable. The Hindu proportion would substantially decline if some of the scheduled castes and tribes are allowed to opt for other categories. A disaggregated analysis will reveal the danger of drawing inference regarding coherence or solidarity associated with any major religious community. Relative schism, solidarity, inclusion, exclusion, and other processes within these communities change over time in ways that census mechanisms in India can rarely respond to.

All religious communities and cultures may look more united and integrated from outside than from inside.[6] What baffles the social and political observers of the Hindu community in particular is the difficulty to detect the bonds that would indicate the boundaries and degrees of identifiable cohesion in practice. However, from inside the community, as it were, most practitioners rarely find the issue very puzzling or even interesting. It is not readily apparent to them as to why integral sacred order, authoritative as well as disciplining texts, and codified practice are strictly necessary for the pursuit of religious life or spiritual conduct. It is this difference of perception that is specifically distressing for observers deeply socialized in the Abrahamic religious cultures.[7]

One of the most valuable dividends of differences in Indian society and culture is that no uniform story can be expected to reliably account for the origin and development of nationalist values, objectives, and practice. As opportunities for public communication emerged in widely separated parts of the country at different moments of modern political transition, different patterns of programs, practices and even institutional forms evolved. Regional political inheritances and initiatives, though necessarily divergent, frequently led to compatible courses. The beginnings of pre-nationalist patriotic sentiments in pre-colonial Maratha lands by late 16th century onwards, for example, revealed several concurrent elements of regional coordination including the integrating impulse promoted by Hindu saints. C.A. Bayly narrates how ideological movements, common language development and local political promotion of a sense of identity, led to the growth of a sense of patriotism in western India.[8] This pre-colonial process of political development was strongly aided by bhakti devotional movement that demonstrated a remarkable 'capacity for fusing and amalgamating regions and communities ...' and helped diminish differences between competing Hindu cults as well as among caste formations in the region.[9]

The Hindu components of inspiration and inducement, however, did not prevent the newly emerging space in western India from including local Muslims. Despite many shifts in the political fortune of the rulers of this region the growth of the patriotic tradition continued through the 19th century. Gradually, a case for transcending local ties and networks gained ground in many regions of the country.[10] A sense of patriotic sentiments across regions soon became prominent.[11] Most visibly, during the Rebellion of 1857, the idea of Hindustan as a larger space of affinity for Hindus and Muslims attained a special significance. However, the transition was marked by many difficult moments. Eventually, expanding colonial order provided a new set of challenges as well as opportunities for the development of sentiments of inter-regional unity. It also offered new possibilities for connecting religious community issues with nationalist formulations.

NATIONALIST FORMULATIONS AND RELIGION: FORMATIVE DISCOURSE

More than political oppression, it was the gross misrecognition of indigenous religion, society, and culture that challenged the educated leaders of the community to offer appropriate response.[12] Limited growth in literacy, communication and public space by the beginning of the 19th century in the metropolitan cities offered new opportunities for both internal examination of the major religious communities and energetic response in public action. The scope of the latter was obviously constrained by British authoritarian rule. Regional language media and communication, however, offered a relatively better source of opinion formation and opposition. Fortunately for the major metropolitan cites, educational development and media formation provided the initial resources for public response. Calcutta, Bombay, and Madras began nationalist response patterns that soon caught on in other areas.

It is interesting to note some of the regional differences revealed in the response patterns that may be partly traced to the variation in pre-colonial political lineages connected with these areas. If the new leaders shared Hindu religious identification, their nationalist sensibilities did not develop along any uniform or deliberately designed course of Hindu nationalism. In different ways and using their own regional language and historical inheritance, they sought to devise and compose various modes of nationalist sensibility to nurture collective strength and honor. Their cultivation of social solidarity and associational expressions in public space generally lacked aggressive ethno-national chauvinism. This augured well for laying the ground for an inter-regional development of a federative culture that eventually strengthened the foundation of a multicultural post-colonial order. A brief exploration of the beginnings in Bengal may offer an example of why a particular source of religious initiative need not necessarily lead to exclusionary nationalism.[13]

Nationalist sentiments inspiring Hindu religious and social reform movements in Bengal had the benefit of an unusually gifted leadership. These leaders demonstrated a creative ability to combine selected streams of modern knowledge with what they valued in their indigenous tradition. Radically different styles and voices of eminent scholars like Rammohun Roy (1772–1833) and Iswar Chandra Vidyasagar (1829–91) appealed to different segments of people in Bengal, and elsewhere. Rammohun's incredible command of multiple Asian and European languages, religious texts, and political and cultural discourses commanded national and international admiration.[14] Iswar Chandra Vidyasagar offered a very different blend of Sanskritic, Bengali, and European idioms to contribute a 'national cosmopolitan' discourse staying close to the traditional social and religious domain.[15] Both Rammohun and Iswar Chandra came from Brahman families, the former endowed with wealth and aristocratic background while the latter grew up in a desperate situation of poverty and hardship.[16]

Rammohun offered innovative principles and programs designed to prepare his society to challenge the established order of things and seek rational courses of reform. His familiarity with the ideas and events of contemporary Western countries in addition to proximate colonial sources of knowledge helped him to see certain collective possibilities for the people of India. He had an uncanny sense of the prospective emergence of Indian nationalism and independence. He was confident that the learning capacity of the Indian people when added to the future development of resources and vast population size would enable the country to rival the British Empire in approximately hundred years.[17] According to him, colonial connection and experience were initially required for preparing the country for 'reclaiming her political independence.'[18] The sense of political community that he envisaged clearly included people belonging to all religious groups. When he organized protest action in Bengal, for example, in the case of the petition against the Jury Act of 1827, the signatories included Hindus and Muslims equally affected by the Act.[19] The idea of membership of an ideal political community, as his references to the 'English ... nation' governed by 'civil and political liberty' suggested, also implied democratic governance ensuring 'free inquiry into literary and religious subjects.'[20] All his active involvements in constitutional and reform movements and practical contributions to associational and media developments bear testimony to the political fact that his concern for these liberal national norms was more than philosophical.[21]

How did the public dialog and libertarian assumptions contributing to national norms deal with the issue of uneven participation of different religious communities in the emerging public space? Around Rammohun Roy's time, Muslims and Hindus enjoyed an approximate parity of numbers in the cultural region of Bengal.[22] These two communities might have good reasons to recall the centuries of Muslim rule that preceded the colonial take over in significantly different ways. Did this differential recall pose serious problems for new nationalist formulation? Or did centuries of living together in all parts of Bengal create enough inter-community understanding and learning making for positive effects on the emerging discourses? As for the person and reformer Rammohun Roy, the positive effects were deeply impressed in his life, work, and even appearance. In dress, manner, diet, scriptural scholarship, and communicative competence he appeared to be closer to Muslim culture than that of his own.[23] He read Islamic texts in Arabic, and published some of his important works and periodicals in Persian.[24] His proficiency in Islamic knowledge and cultures earned him the admiring designation of a *Zabardast Maulavi* from Muslim scholars.[25] Given his strong preoccupation with Hindu religious reform and social renovation one may forget that a major source of his reformist inspiration was Islam. Another source was the basic principles of Christianity. It should not surprise any observer to notice that Rammohun's analysis of prior Muslim rule or his attitude to Muslim people and culture of his own time was marked by a 'fraternal' lack of prejudice.[26] There were times, when he admitted that Muslim social conduct was superior to that of the Hindus.[27] These, of course, were more than matters of personal attitude.

His active campaigns in the public space reflected these attitudes that aided the development of a cosmopolitan nationalist discourse without any exclusionary religious commitment.[28]

How did such inclusionary attitudes fare in the growing public space marked by the emerging associations including the Brahmo Samaj and its successors? Rammohun's experiments in associational organization for reform oriented discourse and action in the form of Atmiya Sabha (1815) and Brahmo Samaj (1828) gave rise to a group process that opened new possibilities of social movement and public action.[29] Though ostensibly designed to renovate the structure of Hindu religion and society, these small beginnings paved the road for large-scale civic engagement and nationalist construction. As a reform movement that called attention to the need to purify Hinduism by rejecting icon worship and restoring reverence for the original notion of one formless God, its contribution was much wider than originally expected.[30] The logic of religious restoration was evidently employed to legitimize a call for rejecting voices of unreason, abysmal ritual systems, moral degeneration and immoral practices. But its emancipatory social role in history should deserve greater attention. Unfortunately, the Hindu religious aspect has misled many observers to gloss over the general social and political significance of such reform in its proper range and depth.[31]

One indication of the extensive range of such reform-oriented actions was clearly indicated in a foundational statement of the Brahmo Samaj in 1830. The facilities provided by it were supposed to be used for public meetings open to 'all sorts of and descriptions of people without distinction ....'[32] There was a strict prohibition of any disrespect for anything that is sacred to any religious community.[33] The new institution was not designed for exclusive promotion of a new religion. It was intended to be a universal forum for rational understanding and fraternization open to people loyal to any religious system. The reform movement, as it proceeded through many organizational transitions and transformation, including redefinition of its religious content, steadfastly promoted public debate and justification of faith, morals, and social practice. A succession of intellectuals trained in European and Indian languages sought to challenge the foundations of customary, ritualistic, and superstitious aspects of religion and society.

Their immediate adversary was the customary Brahman authority hiding behind the 'dark curtain' of Sanskritic language, usurping the use of Hindu texts as one of their sacred prerogatives.[34] But their interventions in the growing media and active campaigns were also directed to other adversaries lacking the benefit of reason, including condescending Christian missionary propaganda and even some of their textual sources. This was designed as a way of building self-confidence for a revitalized social collectivity including renovated Hindus and people of all religious persuasions.[35]

SOCIAL PREPARATION AND POLITICAL MOBILIZATION

From the very inception of the reform associations, the leaders made determined efforts to widen the social base of membership and support structure of these organizations. Nobody expected the small beginnings led by highly educated upper caste leaders to make rapid strides of a revolutionary social dimension. Given the context of time and place, their gradual moves to include the participation of lower caste and non-Hindu groups in the Brahmo religious services indeed marked a radical point of departure.[36] The abolition of hereditary restrictions of access to religious texts or assembly was a major step in the direction of social egalitarianism.[37] Despite some ambiguities regarding the reformist organization's practical strategies of struggle against the injustice of caste, rank and wealth distinctions, Rammohun and most of his successors never compromised their basic egalitarian perspective. Judged in the context of the deep-seated privilege and prejudice guiding both the colonial ruling authorities and the conservative gatekeepers of Hindu and other traditional religious systems, the reformist words and actions set a surprisingly radical social direction. In fact, as early as 1828, a clear case was made that '… the evils of caste were a national liability …,' and that such sectarian loyalties among Hindus 'deprived them entirely of patriotic feeling.'[38]

Religious reform thus symbolized a bold design for comprehensive reform to prepare the people for collective 'political advantage' and social gain.[39] All the modes of public protest and action connected with social, moral, educational, judicial, political, and even economic reform were directed to generate positive sentiments for a national collectivity with an autonomous capacity to develop and prosper. Later generations of reformers operating in the 19th century expanded the base of social support, widened the reach of their print media and made a stronger bid for rational, liberal thought and practice. Aksay Kumar Datta's role as the editor of the *Tattobodhini Patrika*, offered a new pillar of strength to rational discourses. Uncritical reverence for religious text was forsaken and the focus was on social and moral responsibility. The preference for universalism henceforth 'looked as much to modern science as it did to the authoritative Sanskritic tradition.'[40] Aksay Kumar's historical exploration of relatively large Hindu religious sects (*sampradaya*) based on unorthodox practices rejecting authority that even appealed to non-Hindu communities in some areas, indicated the importance of egalitarian and rebellious social formations in Indian history.[41] The importance of such explorations and discourses suggesting the fallibility of sacred texts and iconic authorities cannot be overestimated from the perspective of nurturing liberal consciousness. If isolated, ritualized and compartmentalized life was the basic source of weakness of traditional religious society in India, these reformist enterprises in the realm of thought and practice promised new possibilities of solidarity.[42]

Gradual expansion of public dialogs concerning religion, society, and politics made possible by the increasing impact of the Bengali language media and publications opened new avenues. If the English language dialogs gained greater limelight, it was the systematic cultivation of Bengali language that dramatically extended the social and participative base of the new public. Iswar Chandra Vidayasagar played a key role in developing Bengali language resources to effectively communicate the urgency of collective efforts for social reform for public action. His modest social background and indigenous style offered a contrast to many of his reformist colleagues. Combining Sanskrit scholarship with European and national knowledge he succeeded in making the case for a culturally acceptable mode of universalism in a Bengali idiom that brought him closer to the people. His public action on behalf of Hindu widows in the middle of the 19th century indicated a skilled capacity to use Hindu scriptural knowledge against the privileged gatekeepers of conventional authority in Hindu society.

If there were some moments of intellectual ambiguity in his balancing of old text with the rational reformist purpose, the margins of pragmatic necessity probably called for it. His 'vernacularizing' strategy of public action was directed to a diligent 'rhetoric of improvement.'[43]

If Debendranath Tagore and Aksay Kumar Datta were deeply involved in esoteric religious and philosophical dialogs, Iswar Chandra Vidyasagar's active engagements were more pragmatic. It was a dedicated sense of moral righteousness that drove him to use his teaching position and access to the media and publishing fields to engage in extensive public service and constructive action. His important role in school and language reform to spread education conducted in Bengali medium left a profound mark on the development of Bengali culture and sense of civic efficacy. Generations of Bengalis have deeply benefited from his school books beginning from elementary levels to higher order text books, biographies, translation from Sanskrit, English, and other languages, civic discourses and other works.[44] Language reform and literary creations of extensive range transformed Bengal's cultural resources serving Hindu, Muslim, and other religious communities. At the same time, his contributions inspired similar constructive enterprises elsewhere in the country. Iswar Chandra's unassuming personal *pandit* (Sanskrit scholar) style brought him closer to the poorer classes and facilitated his programs for educational deepening and social mobilization.[45]

Dynamic developments in language, education and communication in Bengal gradually revealed certain limitations of the reformist associations and their leadership. The unity of the Brahmo Samaj leadership gave way to new waves of dissent and pressures for incorporation of lower caste and class support. From outside, orthodox Hindu associations and their public campaigns were persistently promoting a conservative brand of nationalist agenda. Their participation in the growing public space offered strong competition to their Christian missionary and Hindu reformist rivals. The passionate attachment of the Dharma Sabha and its publications to the goal of 'Hindu self-determination in religious matters' carried clear signals for future political mobilization on a wider scale.[46] But their intense loyalty to traditional Hindu social codes, structures and authorities were hardly exciting material for popular mobilization cutting across

social segments and classes. From inside the Brahmo Samaj organization, the struggle against tradition and ritual relentlessly pushed
for structural changes in leadership as well as society. By 1866, the
pressures of the younger leaders of the Samaj forced the older ones to
retreat. A more dynamic movement under the stewardship of Keshab
Chandra Sen (1838–84) followed. It led to an ideological and organizational transition that also marked the beginning of a national
coordination of reform movements.

The new leadership in Bengal boldly broadened the base of religious ideology by advocating a stronger case for egalitarian universalism than what the prior leadership was prepared to concede. They
waged a concerted attack on the caste system. Their advocacy of female and working class education, support for widow remarriage,
campaign against polygamy, promotion of inexpensive publications
for popular education and public welfare activities added new dimensions to religious initiative for national development.[47] They also
reached for a national extension to Bombay, Madras, and the North
Western Provinces by the 1860s. The formation of Hindu reform associations in different parts of India, including the Prarthana Samaj,
and Brahmo Samaj in western and southern India respectively, symbolized a turning point.[48]

In western India, Madhav Govind Ranade (1842–1901) led a group
of eminent intellectuals and social workers that set a new standard
for connecting social preparation with political mobilization.[49] A number of organizations including the Prarthana Samaj, Poona Sarvajanik
Sabha and Indian Social Conference prepared the ground for an
institutional base for active social work and public action.[50] Their
diligent contribution to social and religious reform, investigation of
economic conditions of living, and public processes involving political education and mobilization provided valuable resources for liberal
nationalism. The religious roots of Ranade's social and political reform
were selectively based on Hindu texts in a manner amenable to the
needs for gradual social transformation.[51] The integrative lineages of
the Maratha tradition were prominently recalled to strengthen collective
bonds to serve the evolving norms of nationalism. The regional patriotic
tradition and intense pride in common culture made the Maharashtrian
reform movements politically more confident than their counterparts

in Bengal. Ranade and his associated organizations enjoyed broader support from the relatively lower caste formations.[52] The martial prestige of the numerous Maratha–Kunbi caste members served as a valuable symbolic capital for strengthening the drive for national mobilization.

Ranade and his associates' deep concern for the condition of the poor peasants and practical prospects of agrarian revenue reform considerably aided constructive preparation for nationalism. Their organized attempts to press for such reform were facilitated by systematic economic investigations of agricultural system and carefully prepared reports advocating administrative action. Active popular involvement to expedite reform in this field was energetically induced by a number of newspapers and publications carrying radical messages.[53] The Sarvajanik Sabha's most dramatic constructive role was probably the 'direct help it rendered during the great famine of 1876–77.'[54] This is when it carried a major responsibility for the massive relief operations and also to secure concessions for the peasants and other victims of catastrophe in the region.

Extension of popular support resulting from expanding involvement with the issues connected with mass poverty, agrarian productive structures or with the special problems of the drought prone areas of Deccan also raised some difficult questions. Ranade and his colleague's modest egalitarian assumptions did not satisfy the growing number of radical leaders of Maharashtra who wanted to mobilize the lowest caste groups and depressed classes to seek liberty on their own terms. They were more interested in their own programs to pursue legal equality and access to administrative jobs than in sharing the reformist platform of the Sabha or similar organizations.[55] Low caste exponents of radical emancipatory programs, like Jotirao Phule (1827–90), opened new awareness of campaigns and constructive programs for realizing rights and amenities for the depressed classes, women, and children from the poorest families.[56] At the same time, the claims of the Hindu reform spokesmen to either speak for their own religious community or multi-religion national platform were strongly contested.

Unlike many Hindu reform leaders in other parts of India, Ranade himself was a strong advocate of wider intra-Hindu and Hindu–Muslim common cause for developing a composite national community.[57] His identification with the Hindu religious community was inspired by a strong rejection of revivalist trends. In fact, his critical approach to religion was connected with his nationalist mission of 'collective growth' which involved a 'great struggle against our own weak selves' within the Hindu and Muslim communities.[58] Both these communities required urgent inward attention to reduce the incidence of social stratification, oppression of women and indifference to civic spirit and public action.[59] His long involvement in the national enterprise of the Social Conference was deeply informed by a rejection of segmental separatism. A sprit of 'elastic expansiveness' was promoted by the social activism of the Conference leaders who also tried to induce the political leaders of the Indian National Congress (INC) (founded in 1885) to do the same.[60] In fact, Ranade's illustrious followers, including Gopal Krishna Gokhale and others, helped build a long tradition of composite political culture that provided strong support for democratic nationalism before and after independence in India.[61]

EVOCATIVE SENTIMENTS AND PARTISAN CONTAGION

The liberal legacy, as nurtured by the leaders of Hindu origin discussed so far, was by no means either a homogenous or harmonious composition.[62] As its span covered different cultural areas of the country, it tended to include adaptative practices and strategic concessions to expand the popular base. The dialogic mode was increasingly supplemented by the use of more exciting emotional appeal generated by the growing body of works in the fields of literature, music, drama, and other arts. While the evocative appeal of such cultural products tremendously aided the nationalist cause, they also raised some delicate religious issues. Ranade's cautious pursuit of reason did not prevent him from using the popularity of Hindu devotional poets in Maharashtrian history.[63] Even earlier in Bengal, Brahmo reformers used the public forums provided by religious fairs and festivals to popularize patriotic themes and songs in large-scale gatherings of people. Some of these as well as other Bengali patriotic songs of that time transcended regional barriers. The spirit and content of these songs, despite their religious origin or regional source, were designed for wider appeal.[64] Even when a song like 'Bande Mataram' raised questions regarding religious bias, its significant role in national mobilization across regions was hard to dispute.[65] Two dramatic examples of such songs transcending narrow boundaries were written in Bengali by Rabindranath Tagore. Eventually, one became the national anthem of India and the other, of Bangladesh.[66] The growing popularity of novels and other literary works in regional languages succeeded in disseminating nationalist sentiments among literate circles. Dramatic adaptations of these works extended the reach of their popularity.[67] But the references to historical events or religious symbols in these works often alienated members of particular religious communities. For example, some historical novels in 19th-century Bengal written by nationally prominent authors of Hindu origin were criticized for their bias against Muslim characters or episodes of history. Bankimchandra Chatterjee's works in this genre raised many questions. Did his negative references intend to offend Muslims as persons, or some of their historical or fictional roles in oppressive systems or corrupt practices?[68] How does one separate the literary contribution of his novels from the issues of ideological inclinations? How did the nascent nationalist movement receive or utilize the contributions of his pioneering literary work?[69] His prolific writings on religious themes connected with Hindu history and discourses always made it easy for many observers to read more particularistic than universal messages in his works.[70] Some of his own texts, however, clearly record his support for a universalistic notion of religion that 'conceives divinity in human terms.'[71] His political idea of selfless popular commitment, as depicted and dramatized in his fiction works, inspired many anti-colonial movements across different regions. Different segments of nationalist actors derived different lessons from his works. Radical nationalist groups used the militant activist messages against colonial targets without, in many cases, a sense of how their utilization of Hindu symbols would alienate other religious communities.[72] Moderate nationalists relied more on the evocative value of the themes of emancipatory calling and national dedications in the same works. When Rabindranath Tagore composed the tune for 'Bande Mataram' and introduced the song to a session of the

Indian National Congress, he obviously assumed its compatibility with his own sense of impartial solidarity.[73]

Like Bankimchandra, literary authors in other parts of India also felt deeply distressed by the degeneration of social conditions within their own religious communities. Their critical and sensitive gaze often moved them to use literary devices to explore possible alternatives. When a great Urdu poet like Hali (1837–1914) regretted the degrading conditions in his own Muslim society, his mood was one of examining the internal causes rather than blaming external factors. It is interesting that similar internal critiques also became a part of Gujarati, Bengali, Hindi, and other poetic traditions.[74] The patriotic sentiments expressed in these critiques were more in tune with the liberal themes of diligently preparing the society for freedom rather than engaging in premature action. The converging impact of these literary works on the development of nationalist discourse has not always been appreciated in the political analysis of those critical decades following 1857. The symbolic significance of Hali's Urdu poetry lamenting how community failings '… have brought disgrace to Mother India today' may not be apparent to observers who lack a sensitivity to the history of cultural sharing across religions and regions in India.[75] The case for cultural convergence of nationalist sentiments, however, had to contend with two major adversaries. One of them, the colonial authority, had no good reason to welcome national unity to displace alien rule. The other was a partisan drive within the nation to make a bid for exclusive power in the name of religion.[76] Before the end of the 19th century some frankly partisan associations were increasingly calling attention to the issue of the political rights and relative advantages, if not privileges, of religious communities in the political order.[77] By 1885, when the Indian National Congress was founded as a united platform to pursue a composite course of nationalist movement, the leaders were not always sure about the intensity of the partisan challenges.[78] Some of the most important founding leaders belonged to a Zoroastrian religious community that was very small in size but big in terms of socio-economic status, self-esteem and national pride.[79] They had little difficulty in collaborating with their Hindu or other colleagues. The Christian leaders also felt the same way. It is significant that the first four presidents of the Congress organization were a Hindu, Zoroastrian, Muslim, and a Christian.[80]

In a multicultural society, however, majority culture, religion, or any other identific mark may tend to be privileged since inclusive nationalism approximates political power.[81] Some Muslim associations believed that the public interest of Hindus and Muslims are necessarily divergent. Syed Ahmed Khan, the leader of the Aligarh educational movement, regarded the establishment of the Indian National Congress as a threat to the 'Muslim community' or 'nationality.'[82] He refused to believe that different communities in India could live together in a system of representative government. The latter, according to him, requires 'the highest degree of homogeneity.'[83] His description of 'different nationalities' in India included categories like 'the Muslims, the Marathas, the Brahmins ..., the Sudras, the Sikhs, the Bengalis, the Madrasis ...' and others.[84] He warned that the democratic objectives of the Congress attempting to bring these groups into a multicultural political system were 'fraught with dangers and suffering for all the nationalities of India, specially for the Muslims.'[85] He also reminded the Congress leaders that Muslim are a 'highly united minority' who are 'traditionally ... prone to take the sword in hand when the majority oppresses them.'[86]

What made him so sure about either the homogeneity of the Muslim religious community or its unity of political purpose to resist any national alliance against the colonial rulers at that moment (1880s) of history? His own conceptualization of Muslim nationality was complicated by his limited perspective anchored in the area later known as the United Provinces and the Urdu-speaking community.[87] This involved a basic insensitivity to the majority of his coreligionists spread over extensive language areas in Bengal, Punjab, and other regions. His reference to Bengali speakers as a separate nationality was surprising because a majority were Muslims. The latter, in fact, outnumbered the Muslims in his own area. Was it a case of unconscious admission of stratification among Muslims so that Urdu-speaking Muslims of north India were out to claim a cultural privilege setting them apart from lower status Muslims elsewhere in the country?

Syed Ahmed Khan's modernist reputation also raised the issue of the relative authority of the self-appointed westernized Muslim leaders versus that of the traditionally educated clerics to certify such ranking. This issue was important because there were major differences in outlook between these two sources of Muslim voice.

The idea of 'special unity' of minority voice, as claimed by the Aligarh movement of Syed Ahmed Khan in the United Provinces (UP), was actually a carefully crafted product marketed by a regional political group. The brand of Muslim interest that it sought to promote was contested even in the limited UP region by competing forces within the religious community. A small group of landowners and administrators claiming to speak for the entire regional, if not national, religious community was more articulate than persuasive in its claim of community representation. Some of the clerics of the Deoband school encouraged Muslim participation in the Congress or other inclusionary movements extending beyond the region.[88] Judging by the criteria appropriate to that moment of history, the Muslim response was not discouraging for those competing movements.[89] The definition of Muslim interest, as articulated by the exclusivist leaders of the UP region at that time, was a product of rhetoric of lost privileges of the Muslim élite enjoyed during the Muslim and early colonial periods of rule.[90]

If the proclaimed unity of interest of the Muslim religious community across regions did not exist, it could be created by political organizations. A national marketing of the Aligarh brand of religious nationalism was neither easy nor immediately realizable. The deep-seated social heterogeneity and language diversity of the Indian Muslim community were not readily compatible with the call for homogenized Muslim nationalism. It took nearly two decades to begin to sell the Aligarh idea of a Muslim 'nation' to the members of their religious community in other parts of India.[91] In fact, the first significant opportunity was offered by the colonial regime. By the middle of 1906, official signals encouraged the Aligarh leaders to seek support from Muslim notables from other regions to build a national platform. The basic purpose was to gain colonial protection of a favored system of representation of Muslims whereby they would obtain a larger than proportionate share because of '... their political importance, and ... the contribution which they made to the defense of the empire.'[92]

By the end of 1906, the Muslim League was established in Bengal, led by wealthy notables who 'selected themselves, and were mainly from north India, and UP in particular.'[93] The colonial authorities, however, enthusiastically welcomed the 'representative character' of such notables including financial sponsors of the League like Prince Agha Khan and the Nawab of Arcot.[94] They were happy to concede the principle of separate electorates for Muslims for the sake of a 'fair share' of representation in legislative councils of very limited franchise and power. The composition of the Muslim deputation of leaders advocating such 'fair share' was interesting. Out of 35 members of this group, UP with seven million Muslims had eleven while Bengal (East and West) with more than 25 million Muslims had only one member. The transactions of the deputation and of the founding session of the Muslim League also demonstrated how the UP-based leadership ignored important issues affecting Bengali Muslims. The issue of the Partition of Bengal was uppermost in the minds of Bengal Muslims since at least 1905. Their concerns did not matter in the agenda despite the fact that they comprised the single largest bloc of Muslim population in the country.[95]

The politics of religious identity of the Muslim community and its definition of collective interest was reduced to a pact of convenience between a few conservative northern notables and the British rulers. The issue of representation boiled down to an official endorsement of the privileged segments' interest, status, and power. Lower-status groups within the community, including the poorer classes, and large cultural segments from Bengal and Assam, without the benefit of northern aristocratic lineage, did not command attention except when political arithmetic needed their numbers. No wonder, even with the protection granted by the system of exclusive representation and other official modes of encouragement, the national role of the League remained less than conspicuous until the late 1930s, if not the 1940s.[96] Meanwhile, Muslim electoral and popular politics remained active at the provincial and local levels, mainly drawing upon resources of regional origin and unconnected with the League's brand of exclusivist religious nationalism.

The Muslim League's failure to make headway in the Muslim-majority provinces for more than three decades did not strengthen its claim to represent its religious community. The results of the countrywide elections in 1937 left it with 'only 109 of the 482 seats reserved for Muslims.'[97] It was now time to approach the Muslim people to seek their voice—in their own, diverse languages—rather than to appropriate it by an assumed mandate to speak for them. While re-organizing the Muslim League to give it a popular base, Mohammed Ali Jinnah (1876–1948) introduced organizational reforms and plans for a mass campaign.[98] These processes gained unexpected support from the impact of the World War II in 1939 and a conjuncture of other events in the following years to strengthen the League's drive to divide the country.[99]

The short route to success in achieving a Muslim state by the catastrophic politics of Partition also extracted a price in several installments, imposing untold suffering on members of the religious community. The creation of Pakistan in 1947 as a Muslim homeland also meant that nearly 40 million community members were left behind. The implications of this partition of the Muslim community, in addition to that of the country, carry many tragic signals. Jinnah had no doubt about how to read them. He clearly stated in 1941 that 'in order to liberate seven crores of Muslims where they were in majority he was willing to perform the last ceremony of martyrdom if necessary and let two crores of Muslims be smashed.'[100] Unfortunately, the extent of sacrifice turned out to be much larger by the fateful movement in 1947 because of the final deals to divide Punjab and Bengal. However, almost overnight there were ethnic redefinitions in the new Muslim nation that cast deep shadows on the future of Muslim nationalism.[101] In less than three decades, the new state of Pakistan was partitioned in 1971 when the Bengali-speaking majority decided to secede and form the state of Bangladesh. This was a desperate move to use cultural nationalism to escape from ethnic oppression, economic domination, and military atrocity perpetrated by a privileged combination of minority groups with better access to ruling resources.[102] The partisan contagion driven by competing collective identities now seemed to be poised for new modes of public contention.

RELIGION, REPRESENTATION, AND IDENTITY PROCESS IN PUBLIC SPACE

Religious nationalism with exclusive claims to represent a community has good reasons to resent the standard norms of public communication in a reasonably open political system.[103] To the extent such an order permits some opposition to the ruling authorities, it encourages groups within religious communities, or outside, to make competing claims undermining exclusivism. The founding claims of Muslim nationalism before the formation of the state of Pakistan offered a mobilizing rhetoric to gain statehood. But the very first session of the Pakistan Constituent Assembly in 1948 demonstrated the capacity of the members to use the debates to substantially contest a nationalist claim concerning the choice of official language. There was a demand for making Bengali a language of the Constituent Assembly along with Urdu and English.[104] The demand was rejected. At the time, however, Bengali was spoken by nearly 55 percent of Pakistan's population followed by the next, numerous (28 percent) group of Punjabi speakers. Urdu as native speech accounted for a little more than 7 percent.[105]

Urdu's symbolic value for Muslim nationalism was assumed to be more important than its numerical base. Jinnah affirmed this value in 1944 when he claimed '… we are a nation with our distinctive culture and civilization, language and literature, art …' and a long list of other marks of differentiation.[106] Bengali Muslims' rejection of such homogenizing rhetoric so soon after the formation of the Muslim state, infuriated Jinnah. He warned them in 1948 saying that '… the State Language of Pakistan is going to be URDU and no other language. Anyone who really tries to mislead you is really the enemy of Pakistan.'[107] He died that year and the nascent public space in the country encountered severe problems in settling for a structured civil order. Meanwhile, widespread popular Bengali language and cultural protest movements led to violent repression by the state. These acts of repression, including brutal police action killing several people in East Pakistan on February 21, 1952, were interpreted as West Pakistani attempts to impose Urdu on Bengali Muslims.[108] By 1954, both Bengali and Urdu were recognized as state languages by the Constituent Assembly of Pakistan. But the delays and breakdowns of the constitutional system and the failure of the civil government considerably weakened the prospect of a negotiated conciliation of the major ethnic or cultural components.[109] Military domination made matters worse. The delayed national elections of 1970 in Pakistan provided an opportunity for a liberal alternative to authoritarian exclusionary identity of Muslim nationalism. Bengali Muslim leaders won an absolute majority.[110] If they were allowed access to power, the history of Pakistan and of Muslim religious nationalism might have been dramatically different. At the very least, the 1970 democratic elections proved that a clear majority of the Muslim state's citizens were willing to go for a turn of nationalism that could admit plural modes of connecting faith and freedom.[111]

One virtue of the public space, if allowed to function openly and fairly, is that it serves as an impartial merciless site for scrutiny of claims of group representation and arbitrary equation of identities. It sensitizes citizens engaged in a democratic order to recognize the group or community representation as a complex process and not a consummate product for possession or exclusive entitlement. Representation may be properly conceptualized as a '... *differentiated relationship* among political actors engaged in a process extending over space and time.'[112] Group differences based on religion, language, ethnicity, race, or class are as real as the possibility that they can also cut across each other. Members of each group, again, are likely to have significant and changing difference of interests, opinions, ideological positions, or ethical preferences.

In a developing society endowed with multicultural complexity, these differences, intersections and shifting connections would make it impossible for any single representative to speak for any group or to claim the role of a sole spokesman of a community. Individuals reflecting so many aspects and linkages would necessarily call for a separation between the representative and the constituents.[113] The process of representation in such a situation can be understood as ways of mediation 'among members of a constituency, between the constituency and the representative, and between representatives in a decision-making body.'[114] A complex understanding of how the constituents connect with each other and authorize their representatives in ways such that accountability can be ensured would be necessary for evaluating the quality of representation. It is this kind of differentiated understanding that can clarify the limits of the claims of nationalist leaders, movements or organizations to speak for communities and their constituents. The authoritarian implications of exclusive religious nationalism using Muslims, Hindu, Sikh or any other symbols obviously dread such a pluralist sense of fluid relations. Their strategies of sacred solidarity require a deliberate act of transforming plurality into monolithic unity to permit arbitrary exclusions.[115]

The concept of representation as a process seemed to be a part of the disposition and development of the INC as an institutional expression of inclusionary nationalism. A number of regional associations came together to build this unifying organization in 1885. Ever since, inter-regional and cross-group collaboration have been some of its most prominent concerns. This must have been the oldest and eventually the largest political experiment of multicultural nationalism in world history. From the beginning, it demonstrated a clear commitment to representative institutions and respect for pluralism. These political values '... remained central in Congress thinking through the drafting of India's constitution after Independence in 1947.'[116] As early as 1888, it adopted a rule that no resolution was to be allowed to which the Hindu or Muslim 'delegates as a body object, unanimously or nearly unanimously.'[117] This was a way of conveying assurance to religious minority groups that their interests would be protected and their perspectives institutionally acknowledged. Founding leaders like Naoroji, or his liberal successors like Gokhale, were eager to make sure that only common programs conveying political aspirations should be pursued by the Congress organization. Their sense of difference-sensitivity made them acutely aware of the divisive effects of social reform issues in the country. The second session of the Congress accepted the rule that it '... must confine itself to questions in which the entire nation has direct participation ....'[118] Social reform issues were distinguished from political representation issues and the former were supposed to be attended by other organizations. Even national-level enterprises favored by liberal leaders like

Ranade were strongly discouraged from using the organizational facilities of the Congress in order to maximize the common platform of national political representation. But as the Congress progressively succeeded in gaining popular support, it became increasingly difficult to resist the evocative popular appeal of emotional symbols of solidarity for mass mobilization.

When the nationalist movement witnessed extensive use of religious symbols in its campaigns to resist the colonial plan to partition Bengal, it posed a number of problems for composite concepts of nationalism. In a country where the use of religion in politics could be divisive, was its use necessarily incompatible with the norm of composite nationalism? If most people in the country were Hindu, would it be proper for Hindu Congress leaders to use Hindu symbols to mobilize popular support to resist colonial rule? Is the religious association of the symbol more important than its wider cultural sharing across religions as, for example, in the case of the 'mother' symbol we have discussed before? When the Deoband school and other Muslim institutional leaders used religious arguments to support a common nationalist movement, was the composite norm strengthened?[119] These are difficult questions to answer. Deep religious commitments and political uses for mobilization by Gandhi and Khan Abdul Gaffar Khan, and at the same time their profound contributions to composite nationalism, to take a few examples, may offer some positive signals.[120] Evidently, in a multicultural society it was hard to avoid the use of symbolic resources for mobilization—particularly at a level of communication where the modes of access to the masses were fairly underdeveloped. The colonial regime had left the public at a level of illiteracy as high as 94 percent in 1911, and it severely hindered political channels of persuasion.[121] It is equally important to note that the instrumental use of religious appeal frequently contributed to mobilization for the common cause of anti-colonial struggle and political amity among religious groups. In fact, effective use of religious symbolism was frequently made to mobilize peasants to secure their rights through organized struggle. Swami Sahajanand, one of the most successful organizers of peasant movements in the 1930s, was a Hindu religious activist who made extensive use of religious symbolism and traditional ties. His effectiveness in utilizing these means of mass mobilization served well the ends pursued by the Kisan Sabha, its close relation with Congress, and also building bridges between peasants of different religious affinity.[122]

The saffron robe was less relevant than the use of religion as a mass mobilizing resource in the agrarian sector to socially deepen the foundation of nationalism and to steer it to a radical turn. From the 1920s onward, the rise of organized interest representation in the public space on the part of industrial workers, peasants, women, students, and other groups helped expand the institutional support base of composite nationalism. The Left forces within and outside Congress, including socialists and communists, through the 1930s and later added a more energetic and determined enterprise to build class-based alliances across religious or regional affinities. In fact, some established Congress' leaders at regional levels often failed to lend support to peasant alliances across religious lines when such efforts, for example, were initiated by a Muslim party like the Krishak Praja Party (KPP) in Bengal. The Kisan Sabha, however, was willing to go along.[123] Many such regional initiatives in the crucial 1930s indicate that the political space of composite nationalism reflected a much larger set of movements and leaders than what was subsumed in the Congress organization or ideology alone.

Fortunately for India, the catastrophic events leading to the partition and its aftermath did not privilege the role of religious nationalism during the making of the Constitution. The continuity of the Congress' dominance of the nationalist movement and its majority in the Constituent Assembly ensured an amicable incorporation of the basic principles of composite nationalism in the law of the nation. Secular protection of all religions without enshrining any religion as legally official was guaranteed by the state. Given the wide variation of meaning and use of the word secular, it was just as well that this term was initially (in 1950) left out. Its delayed inclusion in the Preamble in 1976 did not add anything new. Basically, the Constitution offers impartiality to religion and the fundamental right to freedom of religion to safeguard liberty of belief, faith and worship.[124] Judicial interpretations have strongly affirmed secularism as the fundamental law of the land. The right of interpretation has also given the judiciary a wide span of authority. How this authority has been used has raised many important issues, particularly those pertaining to occasional judicial impatience with cultural differences.[125] In fact, a deeper political problem may lie with some of the ideological inclinations of the major advocates of notions of secularism. There was a pervasive fear of 'separatism' after Independence in the Congress party and its leaders, including Nehru. Without going into the complexity of nuances and contexts, they wanted to direct national unity against '… communalism, provincialism, and casteism.'[126] There were times when uncritical rigidity in treating these problems could, and indeed did, impair the relevant difference-sensitivity that multicultural nationalism with a democratic base calls for. This was evident even before Independence in their rigidly negative attitude to Muslim nationalist politics.[127] After gaining national power, Nehru and his ruling party strongly resented regional demands for autonomy despite their endorsement of the regional principle of reorganization since the 1920s. Only a number of determined movements by regional political groups in different areas and over many years made them gradually concede political autonomy. The resulting polity produced a culturally differentiated state reasonably assuring many linguistic communities. It also led to the emergence of a number of states with majority status for non-Hindu religious communities and some with tribal preponderance.[128]

DEMOCRACY AND DIFFERENTIAL NATIONALISM: REVERSAL, REITERATION, AND RENEWAL

The founding parents of the Constitution of India were not expected to precisely foresee the gradual transition to a federalizing system under the auspices of a changing political leadership and party alignments. By leaving enough flexibility in the basic law, however, they ensured its adaptability to incorporate processes of regional affirmation and party pluralization in the formative decades of national development. The growing regional authorization of the nation following the states' reorganization, and the regularity of civic engagement in multiple layers of elections and other public processes, endowed the democratic system with an institutional value transcending particular parties or leaders.[129] The collaborative enterprise involved in the system added strength to differential nationalism as a developing process, just as the latter rendered critical support to it. But this mutuality has been far from seamless. The gathering strength of an exclusivist brand of cultural nationalism claiming to represent Hindu interests and perspectives posed strong challenges to the virtuous circle implied in that mutuality between democracy and nationalism. How serious a competition to the long tradition of composite nationalism can be expected from a homogenizing version of Hindu nationalism in a multicultural country like India? Does it pose grave threats to democracy? If it is legitimate for minority religious communities to have their parties claiming to represent them in the democratic system, why should communitarian representation for Hindus be treated differently?[130] More practically, now that parties seeking to represent Hindu interests, opinions, and perspectives have actively participated in public space, the record should yield some answers to these questions.

As our earlier discussion of the reformist beginning of composite Indian nationalism showed, the Hindu social origin of the leaders did not preclude them from seeking to represent common perspectives across religions, for political movements. It is not surprising that later narrower interpretations of Hindu interest with an emphasis on exclusionary mobilization were also articulated in the public space. Ideas of Hinduness or *Hindutva*, Hindu glory or even romantic notions of superiority were circulated from the last quarter of the 19th century.[131] Unlike the common perspectives of reformers from different parts of the country that were nationally aggregated in organizations like the Indian National Congress, the particularist perspectives tended to be more regionally nurtured. Even when the latter gained a large popular following, as in the case of the Arya Samaj in north India, their political expressions needed wider platforms like the Congress, where they were also likely to face strong internal competition. In fact, the religious inspiration of the Samaj ideas were used by social and political activists in many different ways, including exclusionary and inclusionary perspectives on social and political relations.[132] How creative individuals could successfully use Arya Samaj values that are normally regarded as particularist in exactly opposite ways was exemplified in the works of Premchand, one of the greatest Indian literary writers.

Here was a writer who '… fought relentlessly against all religious fanaticism and attacked it mercilessly,' and he had no problem in combining Samaj and Gandhian ideas to conduct '… his constant vigil against Hindu orthodoxy….'[133]

It is interesting that despite all the organizational movements to mobilize forces of exclusivist Hindu nationalism for nearly a century, their representation was almost invisible in the Constituent Assembly of India. The strident voices of the Hindu Mahasabha since 1914 and the Rashtriya Swayamsevak Sangh (RSS) since 1925 proclaiming the virtues and visions of *Hindutva* did not succeed in delivering a single elected Hindu voice in the Assembly to draft the country's constitution. Two Mahasabha leaders became members on Congress tickets and a third represented a princely state.[134] Why did Hindus turn away from religious leaders at a critical time in the country's history? Despite V.D. Savarkar's notion of Hinduness and common culture, the RSS emphasis on exclusive organizational mobilization, or even Shyama Prasad Mookerjee's and Jana Sangh's efforts after the 1950s to combine a broader 'middle-class liberalism' with 'Hindu traditionalism' to attract Hindu support, the response from the constituents was extremely weak.[135] The political fortune of Hindu cultural nationalism did not shine for about another decade even after the new party, the Bharatiya Janata Party (BJP), was formed in 1980. Until 1989, the party and its previous incarnations never crossed the 10 percent mark of the national vote. After 1991, the vote gradually climbed from about 20 percent in 1996 to approximately 22 percent of the national vote for the Lok Sabha in 2004. From two seats in 1984, it moved to 182 in 1998 and 1999, though in 2004 it had to settle for 138.[136]

How did it gain such support? What role did cultural or religious nationalism play in this process of expansion of popular support? When the Congress party, after Independence, was strong and stable the BJP's predecessors remained weak. The 1967 crisis of the Congress system offered an opportunity to Opposition parties to make profitable alliances. Ever since, the BJP made a series of co-operative moves with parties of very different, including secular, ideological persuasions that yielded tempting dividends including phases of stable national power. While such doses of political pragmatism did not please its spiritual mentors in the RSS, the BJP also had programs to satisfy them as well as its own appetite for cultural combat and conquest. Thus began organized campaigns to resist religious conversion and to support the Vishwa Hindu Parishad's (VHP) move to re-convert the Dalits to the Hindu faith. Given the strong negative sentiments about religious conversion in Hindu society, the BJP found convenient constituents to politically represent in the public space. Issues such as Muslim personal law involving the question of a uniform civil code, the Ram Janmabhumi campaigns relating to what the VHP perceived as the case for destroying the Babri Masjid (mosque) and secessionist insurgency in Kashmir offered opportunities for Hindu vote consolidation. Issues of illegal Muslim immigration in the eastern and northeastern parts of the country also came in handy. Organized campaigns to pursue these issues demonstrated converging, if not orchestrated, movements of the BJP, VHP, RSS, and other allied organizations.[137] The combined support for a political party and subpolitical organizations prodding, serving, and profiting from it offered strong competition to the Congress as well as an umbrella for fragmented Opposition forces of secular persuasion in the 1980s and the following decade. The BJP's rise to national power by the end of that decade was hard to avoid—at least until early 2004 when it lost and its secular opponents, in a surprising combination, won.

The leaders of Hindu nationalism have claimed that their populist movements substantially accounted for the BJP's access to power, just as the neglect of *Hindutva* issues was the cause of its electoral reverse in 2004.[138] How reliable are such claims? As detailed analysis of the recent Indian elections clearly show 'a good deal of the electoral outcome can be accounted for by simple mechanics of the electoral system: seat–votes disproportionality and the arithmetic of alliances.'[139] The prudence of alliance worked well for the BJP in 1999, just as it did for the Congress party in 2004. No sweeping philosophical judgments need to be made regarding assured public mandates for either side or cause. On the other hand, one may reasonably assume that the critical role played consistently by secular parties in the BJP alliances should convey a consoling message for the forces of composite nationalism. India's pluralization of parties for national governance should call more attention to them as important agents for building the foundation of composite nationalism. These parties have proved to be durable and collaborative when called upon to respond to critical national need for group co-ordination.

The record of governance during the BJP rule preceding the 2004 elections suggested that the party was apparently willing to compromise its Hinduness issues in the interest of broader unity. Prime Minister Atal Bihari Vajpayee and his National Democratic Alliance pursued a moderate course with a fairly impressive record of economic reform and management. The impression that Vajpayee conveyed recalled the centrist fascination and style of his mentor, Shyama Prasad Mookerjee, whose manners were too liberal for the RSS taste. His relations with Pakistan were more positive than those of some of his secular predecessors. But the quality of governance was less important for the RSS–VHP combine. They wanted temple action. However, even hardline leaders like L.K. Advani seemed to veer more to political consolidation of power than moving to a Hindu state. For a time it looked like the combative communal programs might lose. The Gujarat massacre of 2002 demonstrated otherwise. The party won several important state elections in 2003, though it lost the national one in 2004. But the processes of political representation are less important for the organizational leaders of the RSS–VHP type because they operate at a sub-political level where accountability and difference-sensitivity are non-issues. India's multicultural democracy, however, requires a high degree of transparency regarding the processes of public authorization and accountability. Nearly six decades of operation of civic representation has conveyed a continuity of institutional assurance to different groups based on a variety of ties that the polity can ignore only at its peril. The beauty of this inter-group assurance is that it does not call for affective solidarity based on faith or common belief.[140] All it calls for is a sense of political belonging to a political system. Hindu or non-Hindu identity is unnecessary and irrelevant for the political community to cohere or prosper. Citizens can draw on repertoires of identity available to them.[141] Allegiance is a political creation. The builders of composite nationalism in India did not ignore these simple facts and thus made it compatible with a federalizing form of democracy. Cultural or religious nationalism, as advocated by Hindu nationalists, is too sociologically innocent, aggressively combative and politically short-sighted to worry about such compatibility.

NOTES

1. The notion of brand here refers to a distinction between a specific form of manufactured product and the wider generic category that admits a much wider variety. Branding, however, may refer to disapproval of the observers. Popular references to nationalism provide many examples.
2. For example, the Bharatiya Janata Party (BJP) in recent history as a political party and Viswa Hindu Parishad (VHP) as an activist group.
3. The importance of selecting public action for a democratic context is discussed in general theoretical terms in Seyla Benhabib, *The Claims of Culture*, 'Equality and Diversity in the Global Era' (Princeton: Princeton University Press, 2002), p. 18.
4. The notion of sub-political groups may refer to social and cultural pressure groups that exert influence on openly political organizations.
5. Figures are for 2001 (unadjusted); the adjusted ones are 81.4 and 12.4 respectively. For details see Ashis Bose, 'Beyond Hindu–Muslim Growth Rates', *Economic and Political Weekly*, Vol. XL, No. 5, January 29–February 4, 2005, p. 370.
6. For an analysis of the conceptual distinction between the perspective of social observer and that of a social agent, see Seyla Benhabib, *The Claims of Culture*, op. cit., p. 5.
7. See Axel Michaels, *Hinduism, Past and Present*, translated by Barbara Harshav (Princeton: Princeton University Press, 2004), pp. 3–5.
8. C.A. Bayly, *Origins of Nationality in South Asia*, 'Patriotism and Ethical Government in the Making of Modern India' (New Delhi: Oxford University Press, 1998), p. 21.
9. Ibid., p. 23.
10. For details, with reference to 'Orissa,' 'Gujarat,' and 'Tamil Nadu' examples, see, ibid., pp. 73 ff.
11. Patriotism here refers to a positive sentiment for an assumed political community based on laws, institutions, and social communication. Affinities of blood, race, religion and other kinds are not required. See for one definition, ibid., p. 11.
12. Savage attacks from evangelical and utilitarian sources were quite common during the beginning of colonial rule. For examples, see Dermot Killingley, 'Modernity, Reform, and Revival', in Gavin Flood (ed.), *The Blackwell Companion*

to Hinduism (Oxford: Blackwell Publishing, 2003), p. 513. For an analysis of the problems of misrecognition and its relation to the notions of injustice, see for example, Patchen Markell, *Bound by Recognition* (Princeton: Princeton University Press, 2003), pp. 15 ff.

13. This is a difficult task, given the theoretical tendency to assume polarity between civic and ethnic nationalism. See Yael Tamir, 'Theoretical Difficulties in the Study of Nationalism', in Ronald Beiner (ed.), *Theorizing Nationalism* (Albany, NY: State University of New York Press, 1999), p. 70 ff.

14. For a general work elaborating these aspects, see S. Cromwell Crawford, *Ram Mohun Roy, Social, Political, and Religious Reform in 19th Century India* (New York: Paragon House Publishers, 1987), esp. Part 1.

15. See Brian A. Hatcher, *Idioms of Improvement, Vidyasagar and Cultural Encounter in Bengal* (New Delhi: Oxford University Press, 1996), pp. 2, 7–19, for a perceptive account using Bengali sources.

16. For a description of Rammohun as a 'man of means', see S. Cromwell Crawford, op. cit., p. 16, with details of involvement in land holding, business, and other activities. Like Rammohun, Iswar Chandra was 'not a child of Calcutta.' Unlike the former, however, he grew up in a family that experienced considerable poverty and hardship. See Brian A. Hatcher, op.cit., pp. 41 ff. Iswar Chandra provided a graphic portrait of his father's encounter with poverty and hunger in his autobiography *Vidyasagarcharit*, included in P.K. Patra (ed.), *Vidyasagar Rachanabali* (collected works of Vidyasagar) (Calcutta: Patra's Publication, 1992) (in Bengali), esp. pp. 410–12 (Vol. 1).

17. See Rammohun's letter of August 19, 1828 to J. Crawford cited in S. Cromwell Crawford, op. cit., p. 133.

18. This is included in a statement quoted in ibid., p. 133.

19. The Jury Act of 1827 was a measure 'by which the Christians, including native converts could not be tried by a Hindu or Musalman juror, but any Hindu or Musalman could be tried by Europeans or native Christians.' R.C. Majumdar (ed.), *British Paramountcy and Indian Renaissance*, Part II (Bombay: Bharatiya Vidya Bhavan, third edition, 1991), p. 437.

20. S. Cromwell Crawford, op. cit., p. 130.

21. For negative views asserting his lack of 'nationalist sentiments' see, for example, Thomas Pantham, 'The Socio-religious and Political thought of Ram Mohun Roy', in Thomas Pantham and Kenneth L. Deutsch (eds), *Political Thought in Modern India* (New Delhi: Sage Publications, 1986), p. 48.

22. Towards the later part of his century, Muslims gained an advantage in numbers: '... by 1900 Muslims outnumbered Hindus by 10 percent ....' See J.H. Broomfield, *Elite Conflict in a Plural Society* (Berkeley: University of California Press, 1968), p. 5.

23. S. Cromwell Crawford, op. cit., p. 6.

24. See ibid., pp. 100 ff.

25. Maulavi Abdul Karim, 'Rammohun, the Pioneer of Modern India', in Sajal Basu (ed.), *Rammohun Roy* (Calcutta: Sujan Publications, 2003), pp. 102–3.
26. See Ramananda Chattopadhyay, 'Rammohun Roy and Modern India', in Sajal Basu, op. cit., p. 50.
27. Ibid., pp. 50–51.
28. Some of these campaigns are discussed in S. Cromwell Crawford, op. cit., pp. 147–56.
29. Brahmo Samaj originally began as Brahmo Sabha.
30. For a recent analysis of the religious dimension of such reform with reference to Rammohun's contribution and its relation to Vedanta, see Brian A. Hatcher, 'Contemporary Hindu Thought', in Robin Rinehart (ed.), *Contemporary Hinduism, Ritual, Culture, and Practice* (Santa Barbara: ABC Clio, 2004), pp. 187–204.
31. An innocent remark like '… with the Brahmo Samaj, we have the beginnings of a sense of a Hindu national identity …' may, unfortunately put a premium on the 'Hindu' more than the 'national' aspect. See Gavin Flood, *Introduction to Hinduism* (Cambridge University Press, 1996), p. 254.
32. This refers to the specification of purpose in the trust deed of the property (January 8, 1830) dedicated for the Samaj operation. See Cromwell Crawford, op. cit., p. 91.
33. Ibid., p. 91.
34. See Wilhelm Halbfass, *India and Europe* (Albany, NY: State University of New York Press, 1988), pp. 204–6. He refers to Rammohun's ideas.
35. See ibid., for one example of Rammohun's reference to Muslim, Christian, and Sikh communities as possible sources of inspiration for the Hindus (p. 206).
36. This process picked up a bolder pace in the second phase of organizational development under Debendranath Tagore's leadership. Cormwell Crawford, op. cit., pp. 88–90.
37. The traditional restrictions refer to qualifications or *adhikara* appropriated by the highest case group to enjoy access to religious texts or congregation.
38. Ibid., p. 98, the author's statements are based on Rammohun's ideas expressed in 1828.
39. Ibid., p. 28.
40. For a detailed treatment see, Brain A. Hatcher, *Idioms of Improvement*, op. cit., pp. 220–30. The cited passage is on p. 230.
41. See Aksay Kumar Datta, *Bharatbarshiya Upasak Sampradaya* (Calcutta: Karuna Prakashani, 1987, originally published in 1870–82: 2 volumes), (in Bengali) Vol. 1, esp. pp. 113–14 for a note on sects that are based on rejection of authority, and internal caste stratification. Many of these sects extended their influence far beyond Bengal.
42. For an analysis of the tradition of isolation and its relation to ritual and privilege, see Wilhelm Halbfass, op. cit., pp. 172–85.

43. For an extensive discussion of Iswar Chandra's 'vernacularist' role, see Brian A. Hatcher, *Idioms of Improvement*, op. cit., pp. 86 ff.

44. See ibid., esp. pp. 138–88 for an excellent treatment of educational enterprise and its impact. For a collection of his school level and other works, see P.K. Patra (ed.), *Vidyasagar Rachanavali*, op. cit., esp. pp. 9 ff. (Vol. 1) (in Bengali).

45. Rabindranath Tagore thought that Iswar Chandra's utter simplicity in his personal dress, manner, and indigenous Bengali style carried a rebellious sense of national esteem. See his 'Vidyasagar Charit', in Rabindranath Tagore, *Ravindra Rachanavali*, centenary edition (Calcutta: West Bengal Government, 1961, Vol. 11, essays), pp. 347–48 (originally published in 1895).

46. The Dharma Sabha (Association for Religion) was founded in 1929. Its periodical, *Samachar Chandrika*, offered a strong voice of traditional Hindu society presented in a modern way. For the related movements and the media, see Brian K. Pennington, *Was Hinduism Invented? Britons, Indians, and the Colonial Construction of Religion* (New York: Oxford University Press, 2005), esp. pp. 164–65 for the citation and generally, pp. 139–65.

47. For a survey of the Samaj transition, see R.C. Majumdar (ed.), *British Paramountcy and Indian Renaissance*, op. cit., pp. 101–6.

48. See ibid., pp. 106–7.

49. For a short account of Ranade's political and social theory and practice along with selections from his works, see William Theodore De Bary (ed.), *Sources of Indian Tradition* (New York: Columbia University Press, 1964), Vol. 2, pp. 128–42. Ranade's academic accomplishments and judicial experience are described in Richard P. Tucker, *Ranade and The Roots of Indian Nationalism* (Bombay: Popular Prakashan, 1977).

50. The Prarthana Samaj (Prayer Society) was founded in 1867, the Sabha in 1867 as a peoples' association, and the Indian Social Conference in 1887.

51. For a discussion of Ranade's 'method of tradition' and its bearing on gradualist reform, see Rajendra Vora, 'Two Strands of Indian Liberalism: The Ideas of Ranade and Phule', in Thomas Panthan and Kenneth L. Deutsch (eds), *Political Thought in Modern India*, op. cit., pp. 103 ff.

52. For a brief comparison of the relative social base and reach of reform associations in eastern and western India of that time, see D.S. Sarma, *Hinduism Through the Ages* (Bombay: Bharatiya Vidya Bhavan, 1967), pp. 82–83.

53. See C.A. Bayly, *Origins of Nationality in South Asia*, op. cit., p. 106.

54. R.C. Majumdar (ed.), *British Paramountcy and Indian Renaissance*, Part II, op. cit., p. 522.

55. For a discussion of such radical liberal approach, see Rajendra Vora in Panthan and Deutsch, op. cit., p. 107.

56. R.C. Majumdar (ed.), *British Paramountcy and Indian Renaissance*, Part II, op. cit., p. 265. Also see Rosalind O' Hanlon, *Caste, Conflict and Ideology* (Cambridge: Cambridge University Press, 1985) for a comprehensive treatment of Phule's role.

57. See, for example, Ranade's speech to the Indian Social Conference of 1899 where he said 'Every effort on the part of either Hindus or Mahomedans to regard their interests as separated and distinct ... and not to heal up the wounds inflicted by mutual hatred of caste and creed, must be deprecated on all hands.' De Bary, *Sources of Indian Tradition*, op. cit., Vol. 2, pp. 136–37.

58. Ibid., p. 137.

59. Ibid., pp. 137–38.

60. Ibid., p. 137.

61. For an account of the relevant linkages of leaders and movements serving this political culture, see B.R. Nanda, *Gokhale, The Indian Moderates and the British Raj* (New Delhi: Oxford University Press, 1998), esp. pp. 40 ff.

62. We assume that the deliberative requirements and the negotiating compulsions in a multicultural setting need a special order of difference sensitivity in such a liberal discourse. See, for example, Seyla Benhabib, *The Claims of Culture*, op. cit., pp. 12–16.

63. For example, the objects of worship like Rama (for Ramdas), Krishna (for Eknath), and others. See D.S. Sharma, *Hinduism Through the Ages*, op. cit., p. 84.

64. One of the earliest patriotic songs, composed by the first Indian member of the Indian Civil Service of the colonial era Satyendranath Tagore, for Hindu *mela* (fair) in 1868, became a Bengali classic. Its theme was India's unity and glory. See Shyamali Basu, 'Swadeshi Gaan ebam Thakur Parivar' (National Songs and the Tagore Family) in *Sambad Bichitra*, August 1, 2005, p. 14 (in Bengali).

65. 'Bande Mataram,' a song written by Bankimchandra Chatterjee, using a blend of Sanskrit and Bengali languages, to invoke the glory of the mother or the motherland was written sometime between 1874 and 1876. It was probably the most popular patriotic song during the nationalist movement. It has the official status of a national song. Its controversial reception among many Muslim leaders is well known. Supportive literature from Muslim sources also exist. See Rezaul Karim, 'In the Eyes of a Non-Hindu', in Bhabatosh Chatterjee (ed.), *Bankimchandra Chatterjee*, Essays in Perspective (New Delhi: Sahitya Akademi, 1994), pp. 177–81.

66. The first one, 'Jana Gana Mana ...' (minds of all people ...) was sung by Rabindranath Tagore at the Calcutta session of the Indian National Congress in 1911 and published in a Brahmo Samaj journal in 1912. The second, '*Amar Sonar Bangla ...*' (my golden Bengal ...) was sung in 1905 in a Calcutta meeting to oppose the Partition of Bengal. See Rabindranath Tagore, *Swadeshchinta* (Calcutta: Granthalaya, 1988 edition), pp. 82–83, 111–12 for song texts and notes (in Bengali).

67. For example, Bankimchandra Chatterjee's novels were adapted for theater in Bengal from 1877 onwards. Many of them later were also adapted for indigenous Bengali theater (*Jatra*) that is immensely popular in small towns and rural areas reaching the poorest segments of population.

68. See note 65, for example. A careful textual analysis indicating Bankimchandra's equal rejection of Hindu and Muslim social shortcoming and oppressiveness can be found in Jiban Mukhopadhya, *Anandamath O Bharatiya Jatiyatabad* (the role of Anandamath, a novel by Bankimchandra that includes the song '*Bande Mataram*', in Indian nationalism) (Calcutta: Orient Book Emporium, 1983), esp. pp. 179–88 (in Bengali).

69. According to an eminent Hindi writer, Indian '… freedom was built on the initiative of Bankimchandra' whose work inspired '… the minds and hearts of the masses and infused into them the love of the motherland … and Indian culture.' Vishnu Prabhakar, 'The Great Predecessor', in Bhabatosh Chatterjee (ed.), op. cit., p. 171.

70. See ibid., for an interesting collection of essays covering a wide range of authors and perspectives from different regions of India.

71. The citation is from R.K. Das Gupta, 'A Religion of Man', in ibid., p. 197. Bankimchandra says, 'the religion of man is what the human essence can be identified with,' *Bankim Rachanabali* (collected works of Bankimchandra Chatterjee) (Calcutta: Sahitya Samsad, 1954), Vol. 2, p. 695 (in Bengali).

72. The deep impact of patriotic spirit promoted by literature, music, drama, and other arts became particularly prominent from the time of the Swadeshi movement (1903–08) and its aftermath. The impact of the movements on the arts was equally significant. See, for example, Bipan Chandra et al., *India's Struggle for Independence* (New Delhi: Penguin Books, 1989), esp. pp. 124–31.

73. For more than a century, this song has been sung and recorded in many different versions. The most recent versions in audio and music video recordings for television were initiated by a popular composer, A.R. Rahman ('*Vande Mataram*': Bombay, Sony Music, 1997). Most popular recordings in this decade have been contributed by a Muslim (A.R. Rahman) and a Christian (Yesudas) musician.

74. See Sisir Kumar Das, *A History of Indian Literature* (New Delhi: Sahitya Akademi, 1991), Vol. 8, p. 157, for examples like Narmad (Gujarati), Hemchandra (Bengali), and Bharatendu (Hindi).

75. Ibid., p. 158.

76. Partisan movements pursuing exclusive power derived direct or indirect sustenance from Hindu associations like the Arya Samaj (1857) mainly in North India, Muslim associations like the Central National Mohammedan Association (1877) in Bengal and a series of organizations led by Syed Ahmad Khan beginning in 1864 through 1893 leading to the Mohammedan Anglo-Oriental Defense Association in North India.

77. Syed Amir Ali, the leader of the Muslim association in Bengal (cited earlier) said the urgent need of the Muslims is to catch up with the advantages enjoyed by the Hindu Community, ibid., p. 87.

78. Like all new organizations, the initial leaders needed learning time in a vast country like India where the communication system had only recently developed.

Some of the perplexities are indicated in B.B. Majumdar and B.P. Majumdar, *Congress and Congressmen in the Pre-Gandhian Era, 1885–1917* (Calcutta: Firma K.L. Mukhopadhyay, 1967), esp. pp. 80–98.

79. The reference is to the Parsi community of western India.

80. Ibid., p. 98. Between 1885 and 1917, there were 27 Presidents. Of them, 16 were Hindus, three Muslims, three Zoroastrian, and five Christians (p. 135).

81. For a theoretical discussion of such privileging, see Will Kymlicka, *Politics in the Vernacular*, 'Nationalism, Multiculturalism, and Citizenship' (Oxford: Oxford University Press, 2001), pp. 27–28.

82. De Bary, *Sources*, op. cit., pp. 194–95.

83. Ibid., p. 194.

84. Ibid., p. 195.

85. Ibid.

86. Ibid.

87. Formally known as North West Provinces, the United Provinces (UP) became Uttar Pradesh (UP) after Independence.

88. See Majumdar and Majumdar, op. cit., p. 89.

89. For example, in the 1888 session held in the United Provinces, there were 1,248 delegates, of whom Muslims accounted for nearly 18 percent (the corresponding figure for 1887 was 13 percent). See ibid., p. 98.

90. For an example of disproportionate advantage enjoyed by the Muslim administrative élite in the judicial and executive services of this province it may be noted that in 1886, given the Muslim proportion of 13.4 percent in the province, they held 45.1 percent of these posts. In other parts of the country they held less than a proportional share of such positions. See B.B. Misra, *Indian Middle Classes* (London: Oxford University Press, 1961), p. 388.

91. The idea of a Muslim 'nation' originated in the United Provinces and not in the provinces with Muslim majority. For an interesting analysis, see Asma Barlas, *Democracy, Nationalism and Communalism, The Colonial Legacy in South Asia* (Boulder: Westview Press, 1995), p. 151.

92. P. Hardy, *The Muslims of British India* (Cambridge, Cambridge University Press, 1972), pp. 154–55. These ideas were a part of an address submitted to the colonial authority by a Muslim deputation (October 1, 1906).

93. Judith M. Brown, *Modern India, The Origins of an Asian Democracy* (Oxford: Oxford University Press, 1994), p. 191.

94. Ibid., p. 165.

95. Ibid.

96. See Judith M. Brown, op. cit., p. 192.

97. Hardy, op. cit., p. 224. These elections were held under the Government of India Act of 1935. Congress success in these elections allowed it to form governments in seven and later eight provinces. In fact, 'the League fared worse than Congress in Muslim majority areas, where it failed to win most Muslim reserved seats.' See David Ludden, *India and South Asia* (Oxford: One World, 2002) p. 223.

98. Ibid., pp. 223–24.

99. The critical importance of the combination of events in the decade preceding the partition is analyzed by Mushirul Hasan in his introduction to his edited volume, *India's Partition, Process, Strategy and Mobilization* (New Delhi: Oxford University Press, 1994), esp. pp. 5 ff.

100. Speech at Kanpur on March 30, 1941, cited in A.G. Noorani (ed.), *The Muslims of India, A Documentary Record* (New Delhi: Oxford University Press, 2003), p. 3. (Italics in the text as it appears in the introduction: a crore equals 10 million.)

101. See an account of such redefinition by Hamza Alavi, 'Politics of Ethnicity in India and Pakistan', in Hamza Alavi and John Harris (eds), *South Asia* (New York: Monthly Review Press, 1989), esp. pp. 238–46.

102. Concerning Punjabi dominance, Hamza Alavi noted that they 'were the new bearers of privilege, the "true Muslims" for whom Pakistan was created.' Ibid., p. 239. On the language and culture based Bengali nationalism and its development in Pakistan, see Badruddin Umar, *Language Movement in East Bengal* (Dhaka: Jatiya Grontha Prakashan, 2000), esp. pp. 83 ff.

103. For a discussion of the role of public communication in an open political system, see Iris Marion Young, *Inclusion and Democracy* (Oxford: Oxford University Press, 2000), pp. 168 ff.

104. B. Umar, *Language Movement in East Bengal*, op. cit., p. 46.

105. See Jyotirindra Dasgupta, 'Official Language Problems and Policies in South Asia', in Thomas A Sebeok (ed.), *Current Trends in Linguistics* (The Hague: Mouton, 1969), p. 581. Figures are based on Census of Pakistan, 1.71, 1951. Even in Pakistan after 1971 reorganization, the proportion of Urdu speakers (as mother tongue) remained less than 8 percent (Punjabi: 48 percent) according to the 1981 census. See Sahiba Mansoor, *Punjabi, Urdu, and English in Pakistan* (Lahore: Vanguard, 1993), p. 3.

106. Partha Sarathi Gupta (ed.), *Towards Freedom, Documents on the Movement for Independence in India, 1943–1944*, Part III, p. 3248 (M.A. Jinnah to M.K. Gandhi, September 17, 1944); emphasis follows the citation.

107. Cited in Keith Callard, *Pakistan, A Political Study* (London: Allen and Unwin, 1957), p. 182.

108. For an account of police violence and popular reaction see, B. Umar, *Language*, op. cit., pp. 109 ff.

109. See Charles H. Kennedy, 'Constitutional and Political Change in Pakistan: The Military-Governance Paradigm', in Rafique Dossani and Henry S. Rowen (eds), *Prospects for Peace in South Asia* (Stanford: Stanford University Press, 2005), pp. 37–74.

110. See ibid., p. 40.

111. The Awami League continued its pursuit of nationalism transcending religious barriers following the formation of Bangladesh. It also drew a distinction between Bengali cultural identity and Bangladeshi state identity putting

a premium on the former. See Kabir Chaudhuri, 'Bangali Jatiyatabad,' (Bengali nationalism), in Amir Hossain Amu (ed.), *Swadhinatar Rajat Jayanti Smarakgrantha* (Silver Jubilee Commemorative Volume of Independence) (Dhaka: Bangladesh Awami League, 1997), pp. 23–36, esp. p. 34 (in Bengali).

112. Iris M. Young, *Inclusion and Democracy*, op. cit., p. 123; emphasis in the original text.

113. See ibid., pp. 127 ff., for highly useful conceptual distinctions and analysis particularly relevant to the problems of democratic representation in developing multicultural societies.

114. Ibid., p. 129.

115. See ibid., pp. 122 ff., for a relevant conceptual analysis.

116. J.R. McLane, *Indian Nationalism and the Early Congress* (Princeton: Princeton University Press, 1977), pp. 94–94.

117. A.M. Zaidi (ed.), *The Muslim School of Congress: The Political Ideas of Muslim Congress Leaders from Mr. B. Tayyabji to Maulana A.K. Azad, 1885–1947* (New Delhi: Indian Institute of Applied Political Research, 1987), p. 40.

118. Bipan Chandra et al., *India's Struggle for Independence* (New Delhi: Penguin, 1989), p. 76.

119. See Ziya-ul-Hasan Faruqi, *The Deoband School and the Demand for Pakistan* (Bombay: Asia Publishing, 1963), p. 43. Also M. Mujeeb, *The Indian Muslims* (Montreal: McGill University Press, 1967), p. 435, where he states how a *fatwa* from a Muslim organization had 'reinforced' the Non-cooperation movement resolution of the Congress organization.

120. The role of the Congress in the Khilafat movement (1919–24) may raise serious questions about its involvement in religious politics despite its anti-colonial intent. Could it be that it actually helped Muslims turn away from a '… secular understanding of politics …?' Hamza Alavi, 'Ironies of History: Contradictions of the Khilafat Movement', in Mushirul Hasan (ed.), *Islam, Communities and the Nation* (Delhi: Manohar, 1988), p. 54.

121. 'Overall literacy … did not exceed … six percent …' (1911); David Ludden, *India and South Asia* (Oxford: One World, 2002), p. 162.

122. See Gyanendra Pandey, 'Peasant Revolt and Indian Nationalism: The Peasant Movement in Awadh, 1919–22', in R. Guha and G. Chakravorty Spivak (eds), *Selected Subaltern Studies* (New York: Oxford University Press, 1988), esp. pp. 258 ff.

123. See Gautam Chattopadhyay, *Bengal Electoral Politics and Freedom Struggle, 1862–1947* (New Delhi: Indian Council of Historical Research, 1984), p. 139. The complex role of the KPP as a popular rival of Muslim League and later co-operating with it, is analyzed by Taj Ul-Islam Hashmi, *Pakistan as a Peasant Utopia, The Communalization of Class Politics in East Bengal, 1920–1947* (Boulder: Westview Press, 1992), pp. 176 ff.

124. For details see, Durga Das Basu, *Introduction to the Constitution of India* (New Delhi: Prentice-Hall of India, 1999), esp. pp. 27 and 111 ff.

125. See, for example, Sanghamitra Padhy, 'Secularism and Justice, A Review of India Supreme Court Judgments', in *Economic and Political Weekly*, November 20, 2004, pp. 5027–32.

126. Nehru's letter to chief ministers, July 16 and August 1, 1953, cited in Granville Austin, *Working a Democratic Constitution, The Indian Experience* (New Delhi: Oxford University Press, 1999), p. 149.

127. For a discussion of Nehru's failure to negotiate with Muslim communitarian voices, see Akeel Bilgrami, 'Secularism, nationalism, and Modernity', in Rajeev Bhargava (ed.), *Secularism and Its Critics* (New Delhi: Oxford University Press, 1998), esp. pp. 395–96. Communalism as a dismissive term may make one miss negotiable values in communitarianism.

128. For example, three states in the northeast with Christian, one in the north-west with Sikh, and another with Muslim majority (Mizoram, Nagaland, Meghalaya, Punjab, Jammu and Kashmir respectively). Large states with tribal preponderance are Jharkhand and Chhattisgarh.

129. For elaboration and examples, see Jyotirindra Dasgupta, 'India's Federal Design and Multicultural National Construction', in Atul Kohli (ed.), *The Success of India's Democracy* (Cambridge: Cambridge University Press, 2001), esp. pp. 58 ff.

130. The reference is to parties claiming to represent Sikh, Muslim, or other commu-nities. Does the Mizo National Front represent Christian interest or tribal interest? Are caste based parties communitarian or communal? What definitions should apply?

131. See a discussion of Chandranath Basu's ideas in his work titled *Hindutva* (in Bengali, 1913) in Chetan Bhatt, *Hindu Nationalism: Origins, Ideologies and Modern Myths* (Oxford: Berg, 2001), pp. 25–26.

132. Simple branding of the Arya Samaj in terms of ethnic nationalism or Hindu nationalism normally ignores the plurality of directions that Samaj members in practice have followed for more than a century. See an interesting discussion in John Zavos, *The Emergence of Hindu Nationalism in India* (New Delhi: Oxford University Press, 2000), pp. 6–7.

133. Sisir Kumar Das, *A History of Indian Literature, 1911–56* (New Delhi, 1995), p. 356. Compare the normal expectations about the Arya Samaj members that are likely to be generated by academic writing like, '[the Arya Samaj]... became one of the first crucibles of Hindu nationalism' as in Christophe Jaffrelot, *The Hindu Nationalist Movement in India* (New York: Columbia University Press), p. 17.

134. The two were Shyama Prasad Mookerjee and M.R. Jayakar; the third, N.B. Khare lost his seat in 1948. The generous move of the Congress also brought in a number of minority members in addition to those already elected to make the representation more reasonable. See Granville Austin, *The Indian Constitution: Cornerstone of a Nation* (New Delhi: Oxford University Press, 1999 edition), pp. 13–15.

135. For Mookerjee's different direction and his leadership, see B.D. Graham, 'The Leadership and Organization of the Jana Sangh, 1951 to 1967', in Zoya Hassan (ed.), *Parties and Party Politics in India* (New Delhi: Oxford University Press, 2002), esp. pp. 154–58.

136. See Partha S. Ghosh, 'The Bharatiya Janata Party: Hindu Nationalism and the Compulsions of Pluralism', in Subrata K. Mitra et al. (eds), *Political Parties in South Asia* (Westport, CT: Praeger, 2004), pp. 58–63.

137. For a brief analysis of the growth path of the BJP, see Robert L. Hardgrave, Jr., 'Hindu Nationalism and the BJP: Transforming Religion and Politics in India', in R. Dossani and H.S. Rowen (eds), *Prospects for Peace in South Asia*, op. cit., esp. pp. 193 ff.

138. The RSS chief K.S. Sudershan claimed that the combined Hindu nationalist movements (noted earlier) accounted for the BJP success in gaining national power. See K.S. Sudershan, 'Interview' in *India Today*, April 4, 2005, pp. 80–81, (Indian edition).

139. Yogendra Yadav, 'The Elusive Mandate of 2004', in *Economic and Political Weekly*, December 18–24, 2004, p. 5383.

140. For a theoretical discussion clarifying relevant concepts and issues, see Arash Abizadeh, 'Does Liberal Democracy Presuppose a Cultural Nation? Four Arguments', in *American Political Science Review*, Vol. 96, No. 3, September 2002, pp. 507–8.

141. See Rogers M. Smith, 'Identities, Interests, and the Future of Political Science', in *Perspectives on Politics*, Vol. 2, No. 2, June 2004, pp. 309–10.

CHAPTER 5

'Jumbo Cabinets,' Factionalism, and the Impact of Federalism: Comparing Coalition Governments in Kerala, Punjab, and Uttar Pradesh*

Virginia Van Dyke

The literature on coalition governments has been based for the most part on the Western European case where certain assumptions and research designs make sense. Suzanne Huber Rudolph has described how her survey research design came head to head with Indian conditions when carefully crafted questions intended to probe *individual* values and opinions were in fact answered by a consensus arrived at through an impromptu 'committee' composed of family and even local élites.[1] Similarly, types of questions generated by the literature on coalition governments, again based largely on the experience of Western European multiparty democracies concerning the way coalition governments are formed and function, do not elicit very useful information from Indian politicians or political party workers.

Expected conventions such as quantifiable 'rounds' of talks to hammer out policy agreements, an actual document outlining a common minimum program, a co-ordination committee that meets, and institutional requirements regarding transparency and participation—all common in most European countries—are generally absent from

* This chapter draws on the first stage of an on-going research project comparing coalition cabinets in Indian states funded by the American Institute of Indian Studies.

Indian politics. My own research has confirmed this distinction, as questions that assumed or explored these anticipated practices were met with bewilderment or outright exasperation. Moreover, the literature on coalitions tells us very little about how coalitions actually function in India—envisaging neither extreme volatility, coalitions among ideologically diverse parties (and the apparent impossibility of coalitions among seemingly compatible parties), nor minority governments/surplus majority governments.

The most recent state-level elections in India, held in April–May 2006, highlight just how prevalent this political development has become. Out of five states, coalition governments, or minority governments supported from the outside, emerged in each. With the end of one-party dominance, and the concomitant increase in the numbers and importance of regional parties, coalition government has become an established trend in India, and an unsurprising one, many argue, given the heterogeneity of Indian society. Beginning with the general elections in 1989, no one party has been able to win a majority at the Center in six ensuing elections; with elections held in quick succession in 1996, 1998, and 1999. Coalition governments at the state level have a much longer history, first emerging after the elections in 1967 when Congress lost control in a number of states.

Indian coalitions have been shown to be 'far more short-lived than their Western counterparts,'[2] and are predicted to continue to be 'unstable.'[3] However, there are notable exceptions. The most recent NDA coalition at the Center fell short of lasting its full five years only because of misguided optimism by the government, which called for early elections that led to its entirely unpredicted defeat. At the state level, many coalitions are fractious and unstable, while a lesser number are quite stable. In the tiny state of Goa, for example, seven cabinets took office from 1989 to 1994 whose life-span varied from 48 hours to 2.4 months. Yet, in Kerala, two fronts alternate in power with each expecting to last a full term once elected.

For the purposes of generating theory, India does seem to be exceptional, as the Indian political system differs from that of Western European, multiparty democracies in a number of important aspects. India has factional rather than unitary parties, operating in a 'patronage-democracy' within a federal system. Parties which are opposed to each other at the state level, may form coalitions together at the Center, while Indian states themselves demonstrate a great diversity in the configuration of their political party systems, ranging from a two-party system to a multiplicity of parties.[4]

In analyzing the formation and duration of Indian coalitions it is essential to account for these differences. I will argue that volatility in the Indian case often stems from factionalism, federalism and the patronage, and thereby 'opportunistic,' structure of the system. In India, state-level cabinets often meet a precipitous end due to factional splits or Central government intervention/manipulation. Moreover, the lack of conformity to one of the hoariest of theories in coalition theory, that of the minimum winning coalition (MWC), with the emergence of surplus majority or 'jumbo cabinets' is also due to re-quirements of survival, most specifically the need for politicians in power to include faction leaders, from their own party or others, within their government to protect themselves from factional splits, thereby creating surplus majority governments or its mirror image, minority governments. The goal is then to include as many coalition partners as can possibly be accommodated.[5]

It is certainly true that the empirical evidence from Western European coalitions may also fail to conform to theory. Extreme volatility does occur in European coalition cabinets with Italy providing the consummate example. Moreover, Scandinavian countries often have minority governments, while 'grand coalitions' across the ideological spectrum occur, as in the most recent coalition in Germany. One of the central concerns of coalition literature is that of predicting or ex-plaining the duration of a coalition government. Yet, none of the theories put forth which examine 'structural attributes' of the given political system 'have explained more than 20 percent to 30 percent of the variation in governmental or coalition duration.'[6]

Responding to this inability to construct a grand theory, Frandreis et al. have advocated combining this type of approach with stochastic models, that is, an attempt to theorize the type of random and unpre-dictable event which they believe often leads to premature cabinet termination.[7] Brass responds to this, as well, by urging a combination of 'quantitative analysis and case studies' to 'improve our explanatory capacities,'[8] while Luebbert argues for a 'partial theory' approach which takes into account the structure of a given political system which includes the 'opportunities' and constraints that configure the choices made by politicians.[9]

This study proposes to explore these specific opportunities and constraints by analyzing the creation and functioning of coalitions in three states with very different political party structures and histories—Punjab, Kerala, and Uttar Pradesh. It will place those political developments within the context of theories which attempt to explain the likely composition of a coalition cabinet the reasons behind the formation of minority or surplus majority cabinets and the reasons for stability or lack thereof. In so doing, this chapter asks what the unique situation in India contributes to the comparative literature on coalitions, while also adding to a more nuanced understanding of a new development in Indian politics, which will persist for the foreseeable future.

The state of Kerala has developed a two-front system in which relatively stable coalitions of parties compete in a manner similar to a two-party system, while in the most recent state government in Punjab, two parties which are in opposition in ideological terms governed in a coalition which lasted its full term. A further anomaly in Punjab was that while the Shiromani Akali Dal, the *formateur* party, had a clear majority on its own, it still invited a party with much fewer seats, the Bharatiya Janata Party, to be a coalition partner. On the other hand, politics in Uttar Pradesh have been characterized by extremely unstable, opportunistic alliances containing, at times, unlikely combinations of parties.

By comparing states rather than focusing on coalitions at the Center this study will control to some degree two explanations that have been given for cabinet instability: political culture and the electoral system. Both Sridharan,[10] in his important study of Indian coalitions, and Luebbert,[11] in a study of European coalitions, argue that the proportional representation electoral system contributes stability in that the number of seats won by a political party varies less from election to election. However, in the first past-the-post method of elections used in India, a small change in the voting percentage can mean a big change in terms of seats, which may encourage a type of brinks-manship behavior among politicians who may believe that big risks can pay off in terms of big gains. Stability, however, does vary from state to state. Without discounting this argument, what will be argued here is that the stability of a party's base of support, that is, the degree of party institutionalization, the interaction of the interests of parties at the Center and state levels, and the ability of the formateur party to encompass a MWC of not just parties but crucial individuals within parties are key explanations of longevity.

FACTIONAL POLITICS AND MINIMUM WINNING COALITIONS

Indian political parties are characterized by factions. Moreover, coalitions are often formed and broken through party splits and mer-gers. Part of the political strategy is to engineer such splits through various types of bribes, including proffered cabinet berths. Party loyalty and discipline are non-existent to the point that party leaders often sequester their members prior to important votes, possibly even taking them to another city; a tactic that cell phones have made much less efficacious.[12] Individuals seeking opportunities for dispensing patron-age such as ministerial berths and appointed positions in government-owned corporations or other types of institutions are only constrained by the anti-defection law, which proscribes individuals from changing parties freely in response to incentives offered. For this reason, it is common for Indian coalition cabinets to have members, the so-called jumbo cabinets, to accommodate individuals, often faction leaders.

Discarding the assumption of parties as unitary actors, calls into question the 'size principle' first set out by Riker in 1962, that the most likely, and durable, coalition government is a minimum winning combination of parties.[13] The logic behind this is that fewer the mem-bers, fewer are the divisions made in the spoils of cabinet posts. This argument was further elaborated by Axelrod and De Swann[14] who suggested that the most likely coalition would be minimal winning, but among parties ideologically connected to cut down on the costs of negotiation. These have been labeled closed minimal range theories (CMRT) or policy distance theories. De Swann offers a number of 'suggest[ed] hypotheses' of why excess majority cabinets may occur, two of which anticipate the argument made here: the concern that one of the coalition parties may not remain with the government, or the concern that not all members of a party will vote with the government.[15] Dodd argues that a MWC is the ideal, but lays out certain conditions under which minority or majority coalitions may form based on two main variables: 'information uncertainty' and 'generalized a priori willingness to bargain.'[16] So, political party leaders are expected to value MWCs, while other formulations are considered to be second-best alternatives necessary under certain situations. However, in India, coalitions are often oversized due to the inclusion of more small parties than needed to protect against parties pulling out of the government. It is also the case the 'excess' parties are included in the government because their vote transfer capability through a seat sharing arrangement was crucial for the ruling party in elections.[17]

Once the MWC argument is expanded to include faction leaders who might defect, along with sufficient parties to ensure the persistence of a majority, the MWC argument becomes consistent with excess majority cabinets; Indian political party leaders are motivated to include as many supporters as possible. The difficulty with this argument in terms of political strategy is that even MLAs who are ministers may pull out of the coalition if there is a potentially better offer such as becoming chief minister, as Lachman Singh Gill did in the first Jana Sangh/Akali Dal coalition in Punjab. As Chandra argues, rather than seeing a government as oversized, it makes sense to see parties as divided into competing MWCs, each vying for position; expecting defectors once in a position of authority.[18]

Minority governments can be seen in the same light of factional splits, as this development is often the result of a split. Strom argues that minority governments tend to form when it is not advantageous to be in the government in terms of impacting policy, but yet anti-incumbency sentiment is strong.[19] Given that Mehta argues that in India, '[t]he probability of a sitting member of Parliament getting

re-elected is close to 50 percent, lower than for any established democracy,'[20] there is a clear incentive for parties to choose to offer support
to a government from the outside, particularly if ideological differences prohibit participation in government. For example, in the current Central government, the Left parties are supporting the Congress
minority government at the Center from the outside to separate themselves from policy decisions, as well as due to considerations of the
political configuration in their own states where they are in opposition
to the Congress. Further, as will be discussed later, supporting a minority government from the outside may be a preliminary step within a
strategy of bringing down the government at a later date. The Congress
and the RJD, for example, both support the current government in
UP from the outside, but could withdraw this support at any time.

Further, as parties in India often lack an identifiable ideology, or a
set of policy positions, with the exception of the Communist parties
and to some extent the Hindu nationalist BJP, it is not useful to
analyze coalitions in terms of their degree of ideological or policy
preference 'connectedness' for the most part, although there are exceptions to this such as in Kerala. For the most part, voters are often un-
concerned about policies articulated by parties, nor do they read the
quickly hammered out party manifestos. As India is a 'patronage-
democracy,'[21] access to the state is crucial; which party is in power
and in a position to dispense patronage is more important than policy
statements or ideology.[22]

This makes it difficult to place Indian coalitions within the context of theories which argue that the actions of decision makers are
motivated by considerations of desired policy outcomes. For example,
Vanberg and Martin argue that the time involved in putting together
a coalition after an election varies; an extended length of time, which
can be months in certain European countries, reflects difficult-to-
negotiate ideological or policy differences which can predict possible
cabinet instability.[23] This explanation does not resonate with the Indian
case where coalitions may be put together in one or two meetings
with only a few party élites present. Policy differences are often not
the major issue of possible dissension (although of course policy disputes are not entirely absent). Often, the largest party in the coalition

does not even consult its coalition partners on important policy issues. Moreover, there may be no mechanism for such consultation outside of *ad hoc* creations for specific situations.[24]

COALITION GOVERNMENTS AND FEDERALISM

As Dua (1979) and Kashyap (1974) have exhaustively documented, the Central government has intervened in state-level governments with the ability to engineer the latter's demise, if desired, in a number of different ways: by manipulating factions or coalition partners—often through the office of the governor, by controlling access to resources or by simply dismissing the government by applying Article 356.[25] State-level coalitions, then, cannot be analyzed in isolation from the impact of the Central government. However, with the advent of co-alition governments at the Center, the parameters within which the Central government can maneuver have been attenuated, as it is de-pendent on regional parties to stay in power.[26]

Many of the parties involved in coalitions at the Center have a presence in only one state and are only interested in state-level politics. The *formateur* party at the Center, be it the BJP or Congress, has an interest, then, in supporting its coalition partners at the state level through resource allocation and political assistance in order to main-tain the coalition at the Center; that is, if the demands are not too exorbitant. The state-level party has an interest in participating in the coalition at the Center in order to gain these benefits. The precipit-ous withdrawal of Jayalalitha, autocratic party head of the AIADMK, from the BJP-led coalition at the Center in 1999 provides an example of this interaction. As leader of a party that controlled a few, albeit crucial, MPs, Jayalalitha demanded that the government dismiss a rival party from power in her home state of Tamil Nadu, as well as protect her from pending court cases involving corruption. Her with-drawal, when she was not satisfied on these issues, caused the govern-ment to fall. She then attempted to support a Congress-led coalition, but unfortunately she had miscalculated and that possible eventuality did not develop.

Coalitions in Punjab; the Impact of Factionalism and State–Center Relations

The arguments, just made on the importance of a surplus majority government to protect from defectors, along with the importance of support from the Central government, may be illustrated by the situation in Punjab. From 1998 to 2003, there were co-terminous coalitions in both the state of Punjab and the Center between the BJP and the Shiromani Akali Dal (SAD). SAD included the BJP in its cabinet at the state level in order to ensure that opposing factions within the SAD did not gain sufficient support to bring the government down. It also participated in the coalition at the Center, in fact it was one of the few regional parties to support the BJP in its first attempt to form a government in 1996. In return, the BJP stood behind the ruling faction of the SAD, incorporated a member of this faction from among the Akali Dal MPs as a minister in the Central government,[27] protested allegations of corruption directed at the chief minister and his family, contributed funds toward celebrating the tercentennial of the establishment of the Khalsa,[28] but notably did not address any of the policy issues historically identified with or articulated by the SAD. But one important factor in why the state-level coalition lasted its full term was the insurance against factional conflict provided by the BJP's unswerving support of the Badal government, in spite of the defection of a major Akali leader and the efforts by his faction to bring the government down.[29] This was the first time an Akali Dal government had lasted its full five years.

Since the state's re-organization in 1966, Punjab has had an essentially two-party system within which anti-Congress coalitions have been put together on four occasions. While the Akali Dal has come to represent largely rural Jat Sikhs, the BJP is supported by urban Hindus. So the parties coincide with a rural–urban as well as communal divide, with then 'complementary electoral bases.'[30]

Prior to 1966, Congress was able to dominate electorally, with the Akali Dal actually merging with the Congress on two separate occasions. Brass argues that it was able to create this situation as it 'maintain[ed] an intercommunal coalition' by giving tickets and cabinet berths to large numbers of Sikhs, while finding a compromise on contentious issues.[31] Since the redrawing of the states boundaries in 1966, however, which changed the communal make-up of the state, a two-party system has emerged. But even so, until the era of militancy, the Akalis had only been able to come to power with the support of the Jana Sangh. Although, it has been argued that since they are both communal parties they are able to work well together,[32] there are basic differences in interests and proposed policies. For example, during the lengthy and acrimonious agitation for a separate Sikh majority state led by the Akali, couched in the language of a Punjabi-speaking state, the Jana Sangh allied with the Arya Samaj and the RSS to lobby against this and for a 'Maha Punjab.'[33] In order to oppose this movement, many Hindus gave their language as Hindi, rather than Punjabi, to census enumerators in response to encouragement by the Jana Sangh and Arya Samaj which created resentment among the Sikh community. Moreover, the 1971 coalition between the two parties fell apart at least partially over a dispute over the status of newly established universities including the issue of creating a 'separate University after the name of Swami Dayananda [founder of the Arya Samaj] ... in the interests of Hindi and Hindu culture.'[34] Moreover, the RSS has always claimed that Sikhs are part of the larger Hindu community, in opposition to Sikh assertion that the Sikhs are a separate nation, although the RSS position has recently been modified in the interests of the political alignment with the SAD.

It is the case, however, that the Akali Dal and the BJP are not competing for the same constituency base and so, unlike in UP where coalition partners are trying to poach each other's supporters, it does give a certain stability. Also, unlike the Akalis' competition with Congress, politicians do not regularly move back and forth between the two parties. However, both the Congress and the Akali Dal are made up of factional groups which maneuver for power and which make alliances outside the party to boost their own position. Congress's position at the Center has enabled it to both pull down and support factions within non-Congress coalitions.

The 'Popular United Front' was the first coalition in Punjab, created after the Congress failed to win a majority in 1967. It combined all the non-Congress parties, among which the largest was SAD followed by the Bharatiya Jana Sangh (BJS). Due to the very small majority held by the United Front, both it and the Congress tried to attract defectors to bolster their position. Ultimately, Congress was successful in splitting the Akali Dal by propping up a minority headed by an Akali defector, Lachman Singh Gill.[35] Over time, Congress was itself split on the issue of continuing to support this minority government—one argument was that the Congress was interested in supporting Gill to divide the Akali Dal in the interests of competing in the Shiromani Gurudwara Prabandhak Committee (SGPC) elections; that is, the elections to a board that manages the historic Sikh *gurudwaras*. Congress's chances of doing well in those elections would be increased if the Akalis were split. It was the Congress party central leadership that continued to back Gill, while the state-level party was split along factional lines on the question of maintaining support. Rarewala, a state-level Congress party legislative leader, was hoping to be the chief minister (CM).[36] In fact, he had initially argued for a coalition ministry between the Akalis and Congress.[37] That government lasted only 10 months before it fell and President's Rule was imposed.

In the 1969 mid-term elections, the Akali Dal and the BJS formed a coalition under the same chief minister who had headed the United Front of 1969. Balramji Dass Tandon of the BJS was deputy CM and Sant Fateh Singh was President of the Akali Dal. Congress had won 38 seats to the Akalis' 43, but immediately began losing numbers as Congress members defected to the winning party. Meanwhile, Sant Fateh Singh found his position undermined as a prominent leader undertook a fast-unto-death over the status of Chandigarh. The Sant undertook a similar vow, but then gave up the fast in the context of promises from the Central government that ultimately did not yield any clear concessions that would justify, to some, abandoning the fast.

There was then a factional split in the Akali Dal as the CM supported a candidate for the Rajya Sabha who was not the Akali's official candidate, but reportedly of another action instigated by Congress. Gurnam Singh was expelled from the party and resigned as chief minister and Prakash Singh Badal became CM in 1971 with the support of the Jana Sangh. The Badal ministry itself ultimately fell as the Jana Sangh members who originally supported Badal left the ministry and he dissolved the ministry in the face of increasing defections and to counter the Gurnam Singh threat.[38] The next coalition ministry was composed of a pre-poll coalition of the CPI(M), the Akali Dal and the Janata Party, of which the latter included the Jana Sangh, after the Congress ministry led by Giani Zail Singh was dismissed by the Janata Party-led government at the Center. This government was later dismissed when Congress returned to power in 1980.

As illustrated earlier, factional politics are crucial to understanding these developments. The Jana Sangh did not back just the Akali Dal, but certain factions within it. Moreover, Congress's desire to split the Akali Dal with an eye on the SGPC elections was repeated in 1979, when the Congress supported the militant leader Sant Jarnail Singh Bhindranwale's candidates for elections to the SGPC. He in turn supported the Congress candidates in the 1980 Assembly election, thereby giving a fillip to militant politics.

From 1980 to 1996, there were no alliances between the Jana Sangh (now the BJP) and the Akalis. After Operation Bluestar, the assassination of Indira Gandhi and the Punjab Accord signed by Rajiv Gandhi and Sant Longowal, the Akali Dal came to power on its own for the first time; although a tacit Congress–Akali arrangement has been alleged. However, factional politics continued to play a crucial role in the longevity of the Akali Dal government. The Akali Dal (Longowal) won the elections in spite of a boycott by the militants. But the politically powerful Prakash Singh Badal stayed out of the ministry, and a separate group of dissident Akalis turned the Barnala government into a minority government by withdrawing support. Darshan Singh Ragi, acting Jathedar of the Akal Takht, undertook the ultimately unsuccessful task of uniting all the factions; the division of which he saw as a plot by the Center to keep the government weak. In the end, President's Rule was imposed by the Congress party at the Center on the charge that militancy was not being contained.

Immediately after the return of electoral politics in Punjab in 1992, Congress came to power in the face of a boycott by the Akali Dal factions and militant groups. The Akal Takht Jathedar, Manjit Singh, was involved in trying to bring all the factions together. The Badal faction stayed resolutely out of this reconciliation, which it rightly saw as an attempt to attenuate its position, ultimately proving itself as the largest faction. In the 1996 general elections, the Akalis had a seat-sharing agreement with the Bahujan Samaj Party (BSP). This experiment was not viewed as successful since the Akalis transferred votes to the BSP, but the BSP was not able to transfer votes to the Akali Dal.[39] Still, the Badal faction of the Akali Dal won a decisive victory in the face of opposition by two other factions—the Akali Dal (Panthic) and the Akali Dal (Amritsar).

During the 1997 Assembly elections, the Akali Dal and the BJP had a seat sharing agreement. Twenty-four seats were allotted to the BJP, urban seats that the Akalis on their own would not have expected to win, out of which the BJP won 18. The Akalis won 75 out of 94 contested. Given that there are 117 seats, the Akalis had a clear majority. Still according to a prominent politician from the BJP, it was Badal who insisted on the BJP joining the government, in fact stating that he would not take the oath of office until the BJP agreed to be part of the government.

The BJP-led coalition at the Center, which came back to power in 1998, wanted this coalition to work. So how in fact did it function? What benefit did the Akalis reap from this? The Akali Dal has long-standing grievances that have pitted them against the Central government. The most important of these are: the status of Chandigarh, disputes over river water allocation and the inclusion of some Punjabi-speaking areas in Punjab. Moreover, there were issues of more contemporary origin: the Akalis reportedly wanted some seats allocated to them outside of Punjab and wanted Udham Singh Nagar district in the Terai area of UP left out of the new state of Uttaranchal, as there was a concern that land reforms there would adversely impact the large number of Sikhs living there.[40] The Akalis were not even allowed to raise the first three issues and received no assurance on the other two.[41]

Clearly, what the Akalis did gain was a stable state government that lasted its full term. The Akalis were also part of the coalition at the Center and had a minister in the government. While there is disagreement over whether or not Badal's government was actually at risk from factional splits, it was the case that the long-time president of the SGPC and leader of a faction, Gurcharan Singh Tohra, left the Badal government with other dissidents who then actively worked to bring down the government.

As an extension of a long-term factional rivalry, Badal was allegedly trying to gain a foothold in SGPC and to sideline Tohra, who had an alliance with the Akal Takht Jathedar, Bhai Ranjit Singh.[42] Further issues involved the transfer of pro-Tohra administrators from Tohra's home district, in response to Tohra's suggestion that Badal should not be CM and president of the party at the same time.[43] In this context, Tohra was also criticizing the BJP for not responding to political demands concerning the state.

The complaints of dissidents allied with Tohra included the issue of one man–one post, and the belief that Badal was trying too hard to project his own son. Five of Tohra's supporters quit the ministry, including Mahesh Inder Singh Grewal and Manjit Singh Calcutta. No one joined them in their efforts to bring down the government because the BJP stood so resolutely with the Badal faction. Tohra's group then formed the Sarb Hind Shiromani Akali Dal on May 30, 1999, which failed to win any seats in the general and Assembly elections in 1999 and 2002, but were able to take away support from the Akali Dal—to Congress's advantage. The factions reunited in time for the 2004 general elections.

Why would the Akalis adopt this strategy, particularly since Congress was weak at this point and unable to fulfill the role of pulling down the government? It has been argued that after a decade of militancy in the state, in which the normal political process completely broke down, the Akali Dal needed to participate in national politics in order to legitimize itself as a mainstream party that did not support terrorism, that is, a nationalist party, not 'anti-national.' The BJP on the other hand wanted to establish itself as not hostile to religious minorities. Further, both parties had an interest in smoothing over relations between Sikhs and Hindus.[44] Pramod Kumar suggests that the impetus for the coalition was 'political,' 'not merely electoral.'[45] Ashutosh Kumar points out that the Akali Dal government gained 'legitimacy' with Hindus by inviting the BJP to join the government in 1997, as virtually only Sikhs vote for the Akali Dal.[46] This assertion fits with the argument of Laver and Shepsle that an oversize cabinet may reflect the need to include excess parties in order to have a 'credible proposal for a government.'[47] These are valid and important arguments. However, the key to the explanation remains factional politics.

UTTAR PRADESH AND UNLIKELY
COALITION PARTNERS

Politics in Uttar Pradesh has been typified by unstable coalitions since 1989. Further, the actual functioning of the coalitions has been characterized by violence or the threat of violence, while MLAs are kept 'in line' through threat of legal maneuvers. An example of the first phenomenon is the 'guest house incident' when Mayawati and some followers were surrounded in a guest house by Mulayam Singh's followers and threatened with dire consequences if she chose to withdraw from the Samata Party–BSP coalition. An example of the second is that of the case of Raghuraj Pratap Singh—Raja Bhaiya—an independent MLA who was imprisoned under TADA following withdrawal of his support to the Mayawati-led government.[48]

Uttar Pradesh has moved from a one-party dominant system to a two-party system with the rise of backward caste-based parties that coalesced around Charan Singh, to the current four-party configuration of the BJP, Samajwadi Party, BSP, and Congress. They all vie for power within certain constraints, including decisions on which is the non-coalitional party, based on personal animosity. All the parties attempt to gain support at each other's expense, in contrast to the situation in Punjab. There the BJP, Samajwadi Party and even the Dalit-based BSP court the Thakur (high caste) vote and the BJP tries to win Dalit votes. In the first coalition between the BSP and Samajwadi Party, for example, from April 1993 to March 1995, the BSP pulled out because the SP was gaining strength (by virtue of having the best 'organization') through defections from the BSP as well as decisive wins in the *panchayat* elections. The competition between the two parties was especially intense over the Muslim vote.[49]

THE BJP–BSP COALITION OF 2002

Elections to the UP Assembly in 2002, with a BJP government in power, threw up a very fractured verdict. Out of 401 seats, the

Samajwadi Party won 143, the BSP won 98, the BJP won 88, the Congress won 25, and Ajit Singh's Rashtriya Lok Dal (RLD) won 14. The BJP considered this a humiliating defeat and insisted 'that it would sit in the Opposition . . . rather than support BSP leader Mayawati's attempt to form a government.'[50]

Ultimately, though, the BJP decided to support Mayawati as chief minister in forming a government as no other configuration was suggesting itself. This coalition lasted in the state from March 2002 to October, while at the same time there was a BJP-led coalition at the Center which did not include the BSP. Although the party leaders in the Central government were convinced that the coalition in the state was beneficial for the party's long-term prospects and insisted on it many leaders at the state level were equally convinced that the coalition was decimating the BJP's strength in UP. The BJP had an understanding with the BSP that it would support the party's leader, Mayawati, as chief minister, and the two parties would then contest the up-coming general elections together.[51] Since Mayawati was believed to be able to transfer the votes of her supporters to another party at will, BJP strategists calculated that the support lost to them due to Mayawati's anti-upper caste actions and rhetoric would be more than made up by this transfer of Dalits votes.

The BJP's tactical concerns were how to grow out of its limited support base which was largely confined to upper castes and some backward castes. This, then, seemed a necessary compromise. As one BJP minister in the Central government argued, they were likely to alienate and lose some supporters through the coalition, but would make up for this by adding much more.[52]

Many of the state-level party workers and leaders disagreed, most notably former chief minister and the then BJP president, Rajnath Singh. There was a legacy of coalitions between the BJP and BSP from June to October 1995 and from March to September 1997. Those opposed to this new alliance drew on memories from this experience; expressing concern about Mayawati's mercurial manner of operating, her policies of directing benefits toward her party's supporters at the expense of her coalition partner's and her rhetorical attacks on upper castes, who form the main constituency of the BJP. Mayawati was accused by BJP supporters of transferring upper caste officers in the administration, harassing Dalits who were not BSP supporters,[53] BJP members 'being given relatively junior positions in the government'[54]— all of which undermined the BJP.

There was a concern that the BJP was losing its aura of being a party with a difference and becoming known as a party which would join hands with anyone and do anything for power—exactly the accusation it used to direct at the Congress. Ajit Singh pulled his party members out expecting the government to fall. A number of dissident BJP MLAs had tried to pull the government down earlier; they were restrained by the party with difficulty. The state and national level decision-makers in the party were able to maintain their support to the erstwhile government, but this precipitated conflict within the BJP and between the coalition partners.

Mayawati pulled out of the coalition abruptly and for no clear reason—certainly it shocked the BJP. The speculated reasons were allegations of corruption, for example, the Taj Corridor scandal, but Mayawati could definitely have protected herself from criminal cases better when in power. According to Grofman and Roozendaal's proposed hypotheses, parties will terminate a government when they (a) 'expect electoral gains', (b) expect a better allocation of ministries, and (c) expect better policy outcomes.[55] Several reasons have been suggested for Mayawati's decision, the first of which fits with the above hypotheses. It appears that she expected fresh elections and hoped to improve her position, rather than the unlikely development of the BJP supporting Mulayam Singh's government. Second, there was some concern about alienating Muslim voters through an alliance with the BJP. Finally, it has been suggested that the BJP was demanding what she considered an inordinate number of seats in the upcoming general elections which pushed her away from the option of a seat-sharing agreement and the then, current coalition arrangement.[56]

One of the assumptions in the literature on coalition politics is that all parties have the same interests—maximizing power and positioning themselves for the next election, or in the case of policy-based theories, attempting to push through their chosen policies. In India's federal system, there are parties that have national reach or aspirations and state-based parties with interests that function at different levels;

hence the national-level decision-making structure of the former type of party may see matters quite differently from the state level.

These short-term fragile coalitions may not appear to make sense for a number of reasons: the costs involved in creating and maintaining the coalition, the potential to alienate supporters by joining hands with an ideologically opposed party or by precipitating new elections by pulling a government down. Luebbert argues that intrigue in coalition formation is exaggerated as 'politicians generally want and expect to work with each other for years to come.'[57]

As Mershon argues, however, élites can manipulate costs to keep them low; this is part of her explanation as to why coalitions in Italy are of such short duration. On some occasions, very little investment has gone into coalition formation in terms of creating institutions to manage issues.[58] Further, certain leaders command such personal loyalty that whether they join or leave a coalition has no impact on their support—that is, parties, or factions within a party, do not assume that voters will punish them for bringing down a government 'prematurely'.[59] Meanwhile, the opportunity of being part of government, even if short-lived, in order to become part of the patronage system is an incentive.[60]

The BJP–BSP coalition met this description largely because no one expected it to last very long. No co-ordination committee was created. Several party leaders from the BJP would meet with Mayawati herself on an *ad hoc* basis to deal with issues that arose. No protocol was established for regular co-ordination and no MCP (Minimum Common Program) was hammered out. In fact, one party leader stated that the BJP had learned from this experience and the next time it would establish a formal program. While BJP's alliance with the BSP may alienate some of its supporters, Mayawati's supporters are not put off by her strategies; they are, instead, impressed by her power in making and breaking governments.

KERALA: COUNTER EXAMPLE OF STABILITY

Coalitions are unstable because no party knows what percentage of the vote they have.[61]

Kerala's exceptionalism crops up in many areas: high literacy rates, an equitable gender ratio, successful movements against multinationals and a large dam project. Kerala is also exceptional in the stability of its political system. Beginning with the government installed after the elections of 1982, each of the subsequent governments—all of which were coalitions—lasted their full tenure. The 2006 Assembly elections confirmed the pattern unique to Kerala of the communist-led front, the Left Democrate Front (LDF), alternating with the Congress-led front, the United Democratic Front (UDF), in forming the govenment. Further, the large swings in vote share of the major parties from election to election, common in other states, typically do not occur in Kerala. Dating from 1977, 'most elections have been decided by a gap of two to four percentage points.'[62] According to an exit poll published by the Center for the Study of Developing Societies, 75–80 percent of Kerala's voters are firm supporters of one front or the other.[63] Hardgrave also argues that, 'Kerala reflects a salience of party identity rare in India.'[64]

Figures 5.1, 5.2, and 5.3 compare vote shares of the major parties in Assembly elections in Kerala, Punjab, and Uttar Pradesh. As is immediately apparent, parties in Kerala maintain their support base much more consistently.

Figure 5.1

Vote share of political parties and fronts
in the Kerala Vidhan Sabha elections, 1977–2006

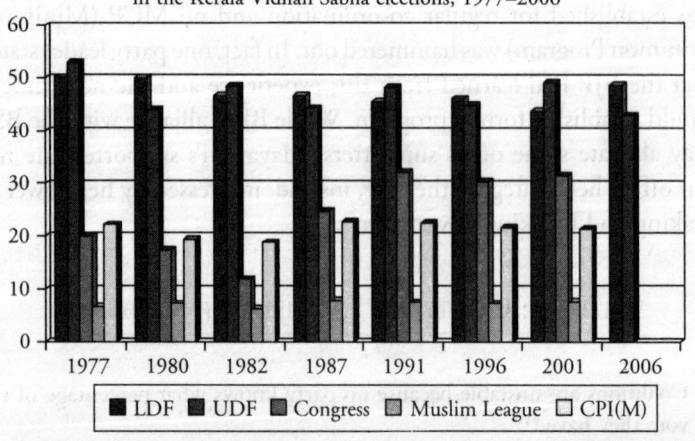

Figure 5.2

Vote share of political parties in the Punjab Vidhan Sabha elections, 1967–2002

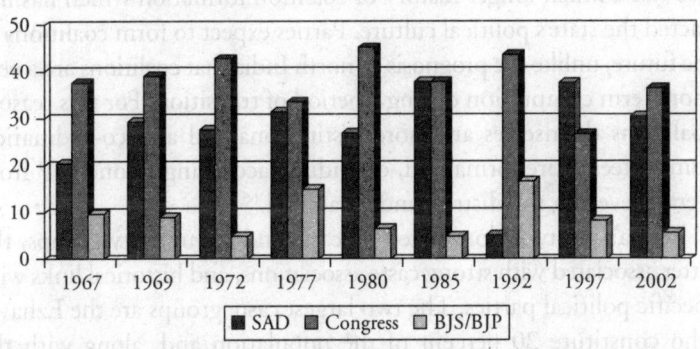

Figure 5.3

Vote share of political parties in the
Uttar Pradesh Vidhan Sabha elections, 1967–2002

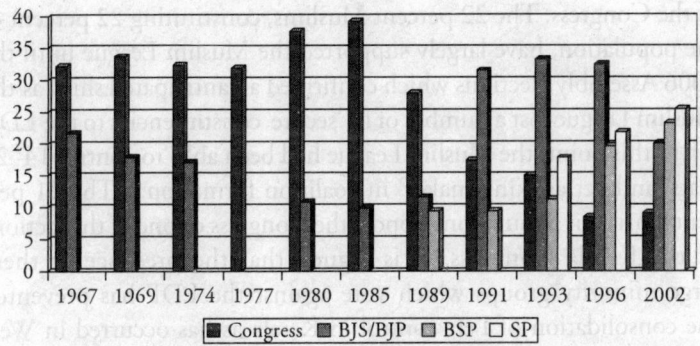

Source: Data drawn from: 'Political Parties and Elections in Indian States: 1990–2003',
reprint from *Journal of Indian School of Political Economy*, Vol. XV, Nos 1&2,
January–June 2003; with the exception of the results from 2006 Assembly
Elections in Kerala, drawn from 'UDF unseated, LDF gets 2/3 Major-ity', *The
Deccan Herald*, May 12, 2006.

STABLE BASE OF SUPPORT OR PARTY INSTITUTIONALIZATION

The striking difference in stability between Kerala's coalition governments and that of many other Indian states[65] can be explained by a political party system which is characterized by partisan politics, by institutionalized parties and by parties with a constituency defined not only by caste and community but by geographic location. Kerala also has a much longer history of coalition formation which has impacted the state's political culture. Parties expect to form coalitions in the future, unlike the prognosis in north India that coalitions are a very short-term compulsion during a period of transition. For this reason, coalitions themselves are more institutionalized and co-ordination committees more formalized, extending, according to one MP from Kerala, even to the district and local level.[66]

Kerala's polity is dominated by caste and community groups, the latter associated with strong caste associations, and historical links with specific political parties. The two largest caste groups are the Ezhavas who constitute 20 percent of the population and, along with the scheduled castes (10 percent), form the base of the Communist Parties, and the Nairs who comprise 15 percent of the population and who initially supported the Praja Socialist Party, but later became supporters of the Congress. The 22 percent Muslims, constituting 22 percent of the population, have largely supported the Muslim League until the 2006 Assembly elections which confirmed an anticipated shift, as the Muslim League lost a number of its 'secure' constituencies to the LDF. Up to this point, the Muslim League had been able 'to control 14–20 seats' and act as 'king-maker' in coalition formation.[67] The 21 percent Christian population support the Congress or one of the factions of the Kerala Congress. It is argued that the presence of these large minority groups which vote against the LDF has prevented the consolidation of Left control in Kerala as has occurred in West Bengal.[68] Moreover, the institutionalization of a two-front competition has limited the success of the BJP which has yet to 'open its account' in Kerala, in spite of the presence of a number of RSS *shakha*s which would be expected to correlate with the presence of a Hindu nationalist party.[69]

Brass has argued that the degree of party institutionalization 'dwarfs the importance of all other independent variables' in explaining the longevity of a coalition government. That is, when parties are assured of a certain degree of support they are able to 'maintain internal cohesion' as would-be defectors or political opportunists are less likely to desert a party that is more likely to guarantee their success in elections.[70] Further, such consolidated parties bargain with each other assuming each represents a given level of support. [71] This is in contrast to the situation in UP, where political strategists are not sure which parties will be viable opponents in the next election which leads to opportunistic and seemingly short-sighted behavior.

The institutionalized nature of the political party system in Kerala stems from politicized caste and community movements that emerged during the colonial period. By World War I, 'the major communities . . . were organized, and were engaged in collective activities to advance their communal and secular interests.'[72] This is in contrast to north India, where large-scale mobilization around caste happened much later. Ambedkar's demand for separate electorates for Untouchables was outflanked by Gandhi's insistence on maintaining a unified community, encompassing 'at least' all Hindus. But in the Princely state of Travancore, later incorporated into Kerala, Ezhavas, specific Christian groups and Muslims demanded and were granted reservations in representation and government service in 1932 and 1936 respectively, solidifying the communities as political interest groups.

Low caste Ezhavas were first organized by the Shree Narayana Dharma Paripalana Yogam (SNDPY), founded in 1903. Through this organization, the Ezhavas demanded access to government schools along with an end to humiliating and discriminatory practices, the latter which included exclusion from temples, certain roads and the prohibition of a certain type of dress and behavior. Because of their agitations, in 1935, the Temple Entry Proclamation assured entry to temples for Untouchables.

Movements for greater opportunities and social power coalesced around demands for government jobs and access to education among the high caste Malayalam-speaking Nairs. Nairs formed the Nair Service Society in 1914, in the context of competition with Tamil-speaking Brahmans, and Christians; along with tremendous social turmoil in the break-up of the large matrilineal estates that had characterized economic and social relations within the caste.

Catholics formed the All Kerala Catholic Congress in 1918, while the Dalit Pulayas organized the Pulaya Maha Sabha. Community lines divided the nascent nationalist movement as the Mappila revolts of the Muslims of Malabar ending in 1921 evidenced a complicated mix of resistance around tenancy and nationalist issues which took on a communal coloring, as many landlords were Hindu and many tenants Muslim.[73]

How is this different from the pattern elsewhere? In the example of Punjab, colonial-era revival and reform movements consolidated community identities, and beginning in 1925, the Shiromani Akali Dal became identified with Sikh nationalism. However, factional politics enabled Sikh politicians to move back and forth from the Congress to the Akali Dal; in many cases prominent families have members in each party. Scheduled caste assertiveness is just beginning in Punjab. In Uttar Pradesh, the Congress was able to be the catch-all or rainbow party, as the mobilization of middle and lower caste groups and the competition to represent these groups emerged decades after Independence.

COALITION GOVERNMENT AND CENTER–STATE RELATIONS IN KERALA

Unique in Kerala, almost all the post-linguistic reorganization governments have been coalitions. Parties have struggled to find a winning combination in a fractured constituency, in contrast to the one-party dominant system that initially prevailed in much of the rest of India. The role of the Central government with regard to Kerala has taken some finesse in managing. Rather than the familiar pattern at the state-level of the Congress versus a regional party, or a competition between two regional parties with the Congress allying with one or the other as in Tamil Nadu, the Congress finds itself allied with parties at the state-level that it could not ally with at the Center, specifically the Muslim League, most often the second largest party in the UDF. On the other hand, the Congress has taken the support of Communist parties at the Center, while opposing them at the state level, with the exception of the alliance between Congress (R) and the CPI in 1970, and the short-term alliance between A.K. Anthony's Congress faction, Congress (S), ('the Communist Party of Anthony')[74] which ultimately joined the UDF.

The Congress party at the Center has played the role of patching up factional politics within the state-level party, by urging co-operation in seat adjustments, along with finding places for adversaries in factional fights at the Center. On the other hand, Indira Gandhi's government was directly involved in pulling down the first Communist government led by the CPI(M).

In 1957, Kerala installed the first elected Communist government anywhere in the world. There was, however, widespread opposition to the party and its policies. Agitations were launched by the Nairs, Christians, and Muslims, as part of a 'liberation struggle,' led by Mannath Padmanubhan of the Nair Service Society (NSS) and an activist priest, Father Vokakkan. The Central government decided, after the movement became violent, that the CPI-led government had lost the faith of the people, imposing President's Rule without testing this assertion on the floor of the House. The following elections installed a Congress-led coalition which precipitated a 'congressization crisis,' Dua's term for the process of converting a partially Congress cabinet into an entirely Congress cabinet. The Congress party at the Center offered the non-Congress CM the post of Governor of Punjab. Once a Congress CM was installed, defections created a Congress majority government, which then fell in a factional split between the Ezhavas and Christian–Nair-led factions.[75]

President's Rule was imposed again after the mid-term elections of 1965. The CPI(M) won the largest number of seats, 40 to Congress's 36, which included a considerable number of candidates who were elected from their jail cells. Following the split in the Communist Party and the fall-out from the 1962 war, with the CPI(M) appearing to be less than virulent in condemning the Chinese, the Central government imposed and then extended President's Rule for two full years, from 1965 to 1967, claiming no party was in a position to form a government, directly keeping the Communists out of power.[76]

In 1967, a seven-party front came to power incorporating both the CPI and the CPI(M). This government fell due to differences among them, including disagreement as to whether the purpose of being in government was to further a revolution or to provide progressive governance, besides disagreements over whether a Communist Party should co-operate with the Congress. It managed, however, to set the stage for the system of fronts to follow.[77] By the 1980 elections, the fronts established the pattern that has to some degree persisted, with the Communist parties as part of the same front, although there has been a proliferation of parties through splits; the remnants of splits are then absorbed by one of the two fronts. The ideological polarization is not perfect, with small communist/socialist parties in the UDF, and Kerala Congress factions in the LDF. Moreover, the LDF was criticized for allowing the IFDP, a former member of the BJP-led NDA, to merge its way into the coalition for the 2006 Assembly elections.

Factional fighting continues. In the 2006 Assembly elections, the Congress bore the brunt electorally when veteran leader and former chief minister K. Karunakaran left the party, largely over opposition to his efforts to gain seats for his son and daughter. He then founded his own party, affiliating it with the LDF, leading to the nemesis of his long political career with the Congress. He was forced to return to the UDF for the Assembly elections when the LDF refused to ally with him after working with his party in *panchayat* elections and by-elections, but the split and the ignominious return impacted the election results.

In spite of factionalism, voters think of the political competition as revolving around two ideologically distinct fronts with known policies for contentious issues, such as actions of the police. Although the fronts are generally closely matched in vote share, the margin of victory is such that bringing down the government by engineering defections by the opposition is not viable.

CONCLUSION

Luebbert argues that any grand theory that purports to account for all aspects of coalition politics across political systems would be at such an 'abstract' level as to render it 'superficial'.[78] He urges rather for the development of a 'partial theory' that explains the behavior of party leaders within the variability of a particular system. In line with this approach, I have attempted to draw out the specificities of the

Indian political system, that is, federalism, factionalism and the patronage nature of the system, to explain some of the anomalous developments that occur. These include extreme volatility in the case of Uttar Pradesh, a seemingly extraneous coalition partner added to the government in Punjab and a counter example of relative stability in Kerala. In so doing, I have suggested that relaxing the assumption that coalitions are made up of unified parties, along with modifying the definition of a MWC, would make this concept more useful. Further research may indicate cross-country commonalities within the category of patronage democracies.[79]

I have argued that jumbo cabinets such as in Punjab are related to both factional politics, that is, the necessity of protection from the likelihood of a party splitting, federalism and the patronage nature of the party system. Governments need to include sufficient faction members with control over patronage to have adequate cushion to detour major defections. Further, support from the government at the Center is essential in the case of instability at the state level in preserving the state government.

The stability of the support base of political parties, following cleavages within society, explains much of the stability of coalition governments in Kerala, frequent factional splits notwithstanding. Unlike the situation in Uttar Pradesh, where newly emergent parties are vying for the support of caste groups which have only recently become assertive, a much earlier mobilization of caste groups, including former Untouchables, solidified the support of 'vote banks' with specific parties much earlier. Moreover, the support of Scheduled Castes for the Communist parties, along with some Backward Castes and Muslims, also became linked to partisan politics and ideology.

Rapid turn-over of governments can be associated with efforts by the Central government to remove a challenger at the state level, that is, to federalism, but also to decisions made by state-level party leaders. Such volatility may appear counter-productive as rapid changes of government come with costs, including (a) potentially alienating voters and (b) potentially alienating future coalition partners, since, to borrow a phrase from game theory, coalition formation can be treated as an iterative game where expected repeat meetings set up the possibility for retaliation and in so doing, should also encourage co-operation.

Further, policy implementation becomes extremely difficult in the face of changes of government. There are, however, a number of reasons why behavior that results in premature cabinet termination may be rational, as is illustrated in the volatile situation in Uttar Pradesh.

Mershon, in attempting to explain why Italian cabinets typically last only a short duration, but the same parties tend to come together repeatedly, argues that political leaders have the ability to lower their costs in government formation and dissolution. This is clearly the case in the Uttar Pradesh situation, where little effort has gone into co-ordinating policy or the mechanics of functioning.

There are several conditions that would appear to limit arbitrary or capricious decisions by politicians; (*a*) the expectation of working with the same party leaders from other parties in the future and (*b*) a requirement that agreements between party leaders be subjected to a vote by the entire cabinet. Neither of these apply to the situation in Uttar Pradesh. The risk of alienating present, and thereby probable future, coalition partners is not seriously considered since most party leaders operate on the assumption that the next electoral results are uncertain,[80] that the next coalition (if any) is an unknown, and the ability to poach the other party's MLAs is the strategy.

The risk of alienating voters is also not a major consideration; since, in India's patronage democracy, voters typically do not 'punish' parties for pulling down governments; nor do they punish parties for lack of policy implementation. In fact, the incentive is there for a government to be formed no matter how unstable, so that politicians can take advantage of manipulating the levers of patronage.

NOTES

1. Susanne Hoeber Rudolph, 'The Imperialism of Categories: Situating Knowledge in a Globalizing World', *Perspectives on Politics*, Vol. 3, No. 1 (2005), p. 5.

2. Paul R. Brass, 'Party Systems and Government Stability in Indian States', *The American Political Science Review*, Vol. 71, No. 4 (December 1977), p. 1388.

3. E. Sridharan, 'Principles, Power and Coalition Politics in India: Lessons from Theory, Comparison and Recent History', in D.D. Khanna and Gert W. Kueck (eds), *Principles, Power and Politics* (New Delhi: Macmillan India Limited, 1999), pp. 271–72.

4. The following authors have discussed the differences between the Indian political system and that of Western democracies:

   Paul R. Brass, 'Party Systems and Government Stability in Indian States', *The American Political Science Review*, Vol. 71, No. 4 (December 1977) and 'Coalition Politics in North India', *The American Political Science Review*, Vol. 62, No. 4 (December 1968), pp. 1174–91; E. Sridharan, 'Principles, Power and Coalition Politics in India: Lessons from Theory, Comparison and Recent History', in D.D. Khanna and Gert W. Kueck (eds), *Principles, Power and Politics* (New Delhi: Macmillan India Limited, 1999); Bruce Bueno de Mesquita, 'Need for Achievement and Competitiveness as Determinants of Political Party Success in Elections and Coalitions', *The American Political Science Review*, Vol. 68, No. 3 (September 1974), pp. 1207–20; Andrew Wyatt, 'The Limitations on Coalition Politics in India: The Case of Electoral Alliances in Uttar Pradesh', *The Journal of Commonwealth and Comparative Politics* (July 1999).

5. I am grateful to Paul R. Brass for this point.

6. John P. Frandreis, Dennis W. Gleiber, and Eric C. Browne, 'The Study of Cabinet Dissolutions in Parliamentary Democracies', *Legislative Studies Quarterly*, Vol. 11, No. 4 (November 1986), p. 620.

7. Frandreis et al., ibid.

8. Brass, n. 2, p. 1385.

9. Gregory M. Luebbert, 'Coalition Theory and Government Formation in Multiparty Democracies', *Comparative Politics*, Vol. 15, No. 2 (January 1983), p. 245.

10. Sridharan, n. 3, pp. 279–80. Sridharan does argue, however, that the single member district plurality system used in India does not have the destabilizing impact in states, such as Kerala, where partisan politics prevails over opportunism (pp. 284–85).

11. Gregory M. Luebbert, *Comparative Democracy: Policymaking and Governing Coalitions in Europe and Israel* (New York: Columbia University Press, 1986), pp. 50, 53–54. Luebbert argues that his theories do not apply in political systems that do not use proportional representation (p. 249).

12. To take just one example, as the Karnataka governing coalition appeared to be in danger of falling, the BJP flew its MLAs to Chennai while rebel Janata Dal (Secular) legislators 'were also being shifted out to Goa.' 'Karnataka Crisis: BJP MLAs flown to Chennai', *Rediff*, January 21, 2006.

13. William Riker, *The Theory of Political Coalitions* (New Haven: Yale University Press, 1962).

14. Robert Axelrod, *Conflict of Interest: A Theory of Divergent Goals with Applications to Politics* (Chicago: Markham Publishing Company, 1970); Abram De Swaan, *Coalition Theory and Cabinet Formation: A Study of Formal Theories of Coalition Formation Applied to Nine European Parliaments After 1918* (Amsterdam: Elseview Scientific Publishing Company, 1973).

15. Lawrence C. Dodd, *Coalitions in Parliamentary Government* (Princeton: Princeton University Press, 1967), p. 81.

16. Lueberrt, 'Coalition Theory', n. 9 pp. 237–38; Lawrence C. Dodd, ibid., pp. 67–70.

17. Shridharam, n. 3, p. 275.

18. *Economic and Political Weekly* (December 18), p. 107.

19. Kaare Strom, *Minority Government and Majority Rule* (Cambridge: Cambridge University Press, 1990) as cited in Carol Mershon, 'The Costs of Coalition: Coalition Theories and Italian Governments', *The American Political Science Review*, Vol. 90, No. 3 (September 1996), p. 537.

20. Pratap Bhanu Mehta, 'Constraints on Electoral Mobilization', Kanchan Chander, *Why Ethnic Parties Succeed: Patronage and Ethnic Head Counts in India* (Cambridge: Cambridge University Press, 2004), p. 5399.

21. Kanchan Chandra, *Why Ethnic Parties Succeed*, n. 18.

22. The language used by constituents reflects this understanding of politics. In village-level interviews, the phrase is often used that it is 'our government' in power or 'their government' in power depending on the party's association with particular caste groups.

23. Lanny W. Martin and Georg Vanberg, 'Notes and Comments: Wasting Time? The Impact of Ideology and Size on Delay in Coalition Formation', *British Journal of Political Science*, Vol. 33 (2003), pp. 323–44.

24. Still, however, the presence of coalition partners may make certain policies untenable, as the BJP's coalition partners in the NDA forced the BJP to put its most controversial issues on 'the back burner.'

25. B.D. Dua's extensive data on President's Rule in *Presidential Rule in India: 1950–74* (New Delhi: S. Chand and Company, 1979) and Subhash Kashyap, *The Politics of Power: Defections and State Politics in India* (Delhi: National, 1974).

26. For example, in the 2004 general elections, the DMK's move from the NDA to the UPA created the conditions for the establishment of the Congress-led minority government.

27. For a discussion of Akali Dal faction leaders lobbying the Central government for a Ministry see, Gobind Thukral, 'Badal Against Tohra man in Cabinet', *The Tribune* (January 17, 1999).

28. Praveen Swami, 'RSS Forays into Punjab', *Frontline*, Vol. 17, Issue 11 (May 27–June 9, 2000).

29. Interviews with politicians in Punjab, August 2005.

30. Ashutosh Kumar, 'Electoral Politics in Punjab: 1966–2004', *Journal of Punjab Studies*, Vol. 12, No. 1 (Spring 2005), p. 111.

31. Paul R. Brass, *Language, Religion and Politics in North India* (Cambridge: Cambridge University Press, 1975), pp. 358–89.

32. Kashyap, *The Politics of Power*, n. 25, pp. 441–42.

33. Kumar, n. 30, p. 114.

34. Kashyap, op. cit., p. 437. Although, as Kashrap points out, there 'were pure and simple calculations of the politics of power.'

35. Interviews with politicians in Punjab, August 2005.
36. Kashyap, op. cit., pp. 420–21. Rarewala led one state-level Congress faction, while Prabodh Chandra and Giani Zail Singh led another and opposed Rarewala's efforts to become CM.
37. J.S. Grewal, *The New Cambridge History of India: The Sikhs of the Punjab* (Cambridge: Cambridge University Press, 1994), p. 207.
38. Interview with politician in Chandigarh, August 2006.
39. Interview with politician in Chandigarh, August 2005.
40. Gobind Thukral, n. 27, *The Tribune* (January 17, 1977). One Akali politician, Mr Dhindsa, argued that the Akalis would refuse to join the Council of Ministers at the Center, if necessary, over this issue. *The Tribune* also reported on September 13, 1998, in 'Coalition to Set up Coordination Panels', that Mr Badal had promised his party would support the BJP 'even in the "worst case scenario."'
41. More symbolic issues were adopted by the NDA. For example, on August 2, 2005, the NDA walked out of Parliament in protest over the blocking of a new report on the anti-Sikh riots of 1984. This, though, stood to benefit the entire NDA as it was very embarrassing for the Congress.
42. P.P.S. Gill, 'Badal Tightens Grip on SGPC', *The Tribune* (December 20, 2005).
43. Jagtar Singh, 'Akalis Crisis Boils Over: 5 Tohra Men Quit Badal Cabinet', *The Indian Express* (December 15, 1998).
44. Pramod Kumar, 'Punjab: Changing Political Agenda', in Ramashray Roy and Paul Wallace (eds), *Indian Politics and the 1998 Election: Regionalism, Hindutva, and State Politics* (New Delhi: Sage Publications, 1999), p. 301.
45. Pramod Kumar, ibid.
46. Ashutosh Kumar, 'Electoral Politics in Punjab: Study of Akali Dal', *Economic and Political Weekly* (April 3–10, 2004), pp. 1518–19.
47. Michael Laver and Kenneth Shepsle, 'Coalitions and Cabinet Government', *American Political Science Review*, Vol. 84, No. 3 (September 1990), p. 885.
48. He was immediately released from jail when Mulayam Singh Yadav became chief minister, demonstrating the political underpinnings of a supposedly 'terrorist case,' but this was action was overruled by the Supreme Court.
49. Ian Duncan, 'New Political Equations in North India', *Asian Survey*, Vol. XXXVII, No. 10 (October 1997), pp. 989–94.
50. Purnima S. Tripathi, 'The Drubbing of its Life', *Frontline*, Vol. 19, Issue 5 (March 2–15, 2002).
51. Interview with politician in New Delhi, August 2005.
52. Interview with politician in New Delhi, August 7, 2004.
53. Interview with dissadent BJP member in Lucknow, August 2004.
54. Purnima S. Tripathi, 'Coalition Troubles', *Frontline*, Vol. 19, Issue 23, (November 9–22, 2002).
55. Bernard Frofman and Peter Van Roozendaal, 'Toward a Theoretical Explanation of Premature Cabinet Termination', *European Journal of Political Research*, 26 (1994), pp. 155–70.

56. Interview with politician in Lucknow, August 22, 2005.
57. Luebbert, 'Coalition Theory and Government Formation in Multiparty Democracies', n. 9, p. 242.
58. Mershon, n. 19, pp. 534–54.
59. I am grateful to Yogendra Yadav of CSDS for making this point during a conversation in Delhi, on September 23, 2004.
60. Paul R. Brass made this point during a personal conversation.
61. Paraphrase of statement by politician in personal interview, New Delhi, August 16, 2005.
62. Sanjay Kumar, Rajeeva L. Karandikar, Gopa Kumar and Yogendra Yadav, 'Left Democratic Front set for a big win in Kerala', *The Hindu*, April 13, 2006. Also available at: http://www.lokniti.org/opinionpollsurveys.htm.
63. Kumar et al., ibid.
64. Robert L. Hardgrave, Jr., 'The Kerala Communists', in Paul R. Brass and Marcus F. Franda (eds), *Radical Politics in South Asia* (Cambridge: MIT Press, 1973), p. 143.
65. The Left Front governments of West Bengal and Tripura are also relatively stable, but are outside the focus of this study.
66. Interview with a politician from Kerala in New Delhi, August 2005.
67. Steven Wilkinson, *Votes and Violence* (Cambridge: Cambridge University Press, 2004), pp. 182–83. See also, R. Krishnakumar, 'A Minority Power Crisis', *Frontline*, Vol. 21, Issue 10 (May 8–21, 2004), for a discussion of the shift away from the Muslim League.
68. CSDS, 'Kerala: Small Swing, Big Sweep', *Frontline*, Vol. 18, Issue 11 (May 26–June 8, 2001).
69. There have been clashes between RSS members and CPI(M) supporters and, according to Varkey, some in Kerala who do not otherwise support the RSS, saw it as a counterweight to Marxist 'intimidation and violence.' Ouseph Varkey, 'The Rise and Decline of the Left and Democratic Front in Kerala', in John R. Wood (ed.), *State Politics in Contemporary Indian: Crisis or Continuity* (Boulder and London: Westview Press, 1984), n. 63, p. 137.
70. Brass, n. 2, p. 1396.
71. Sridharan, n. 3, pp. 284–85.
72. K.C. Alexander, 'Caste Mobilization and Caste Consciousness: The Emergence of Agrarian Movements in Kerala and Tamil Nadu', in Francine R. Frankel and M.S.A. Rao (eds), *Dominance and State Power in Modern India: Decline of a Social Order* (New Delhi: Oxford University Press, 1989), p. 371.
73. Alexander, ibid, pp. 373–74.
74. Term belongs to C.M. Stephen and is quoted in Varkey, op. cit., p. 113.
75. Dua, n. 25, pp. 188–93.
76. Dua, ibid., pp. 204–10.
77. The Congress was accussed of pulling this government down also by the CPI(M), although Dua argues there is little evidence for this. Dua, ibid., p. 308.

78. Luebbert, 'Coalition Theory', n. 9, pp. 240–41.
79. As argued by Chandra in a different context, n. 18, pp. 6–7.
80. Politicians in Uttar Pradesh sometimes assert that certain parties will not even be a consideration after the next election. Therefore, working with them during the present situation is just not necessary.

PART II

Analytical State Studies

CHAPTER 6

Gujarat after Godhra

GHANSHYAM SHAH

Gujarat and India have been in a volcano of communal strife since the late 1980s with the Ram Janmabhumi movement. Gujarat has played a leading role in the mobilization of Hindu emotions against Muslims. For the Sangh Parivar, it has become a laboratory of their *Hindutva* ideology and actions. In this milieu, the ghastly incident of February 27, 2002 occurred—causing the death of 56 passengers traveling in compartment S-6 of the Sabarmati Express. Most of the victims were Ram *sevak*s returning from Ayodhya. Before the tragedy, some Ram *sevak*s had a tussle with Muslim vendors on the railway platform at Godhra. The media and political leaders of all hues immediately assumed that the incident was due to the conflict between Hindus and Muslims. It was condemned as a barbarous act by all political parties, religious organizations (including the All India Muslim Personal Board) and many public figures of both communities. Wasting no time, the chief minister and home minister of Gujarat declared that it was a 'pre-planned, violent act of terrorism.' The home minister and defence minister of the Union government pointed to the 'ISI hand' (Pakistan's Secret Service) in the carnage. However, the district collector of Godhra, in her statement relayed on the 27th on Doordarshan (Government of India TV channel) and radio, observed that 'the incident was not pre-planned, it was an accident.'

After three years, the committee appointed by Union government observed that the fire was an accident. It rejected the theory of conspiracy. The damage had been done, however, and soon after the Godhra incident, stray stabbings took place in Vadodara, Ahmedabad, and

Anand. From February 28 large-scale looting, torching, and killing of Muslims began in several parts of urban and rural Gujarat. The violence continued intermittently for nearly nine months. More than 2,000 people—women, children, and males (about 80 percent of whom were Muslims) were killed and property worth several million was destroyed or looted. Around 250 mosques, *dargah*s, *madrassa*s, and other religious places of the minority community were damaged or completely destroyed.[1] Godhra and its aftermath have a far-reaching impact on Gujarat's public life. This chapter endeavors to assess its impact in general and on the political arena in particular.

It is difficult to say whether the Godhra carnage was an accident or a 'pre-planned' conspiracy; if it was a conspiracy, then by whom? It is, however, certain that the successive, selective violent aftermath of Godhra's frightful event was not spontaneous. It was a continuation of the process of building of militant *Hindutva*. It involved considerable planning, co-ordination and state patronage. Among others, the leaders of the Sangh Parivar were active and in the forefront of mobilization of Hindu mobs for violence against Muslims. Their involvement was geared with the following objectives:

- to preserve and strengthen their political power in the forthcoming elections;
- to unite different castes as Hindus;
- to polarize Gujarati society on religious lines—between the majority community of Hindus and minorities;
- to replicate the Gujarat experiment in other parts of the country; and,
- to establish a de facto—in fact for some both de jure and de facto—Hindu *rashtra* and marginalize minority religious communities.

How many of their objectives have they attained? This chapter, confined to Gujarat, will address only the first three objectives. The scenario of post-Godhra Gujarat, it is argued here is not an aberration. It is part of an on-going process of communal politics encouraged by the Sangh Parivar.

COMMUNAL RIOTS AND ELECTORAL MOBILIZATION

Violent conflict in the form of riots between two communities in Gujarat is not confined only to Hindus and Muslims. In the 1950s, there were a number of clashes between the Adivasis—particularly Bhils—and upper-caste Hindus—the landed and money-lending classes in the eastern part of the state. They still continue intermittently in some parts, such as Bharuch district. Armed fighting, leading to killing, is not uncommon between Rajputs and Patidars in Saurashtra, between Patidars and Bareeyas (Kshatriyas) in central Gujarat, and between Dalits and Darbars (Rajputs, Thakores, and Bareeyas) as well as Dalits and Patidars in many parts of Gujarat. In all such cases, the state curbed them, though more often than not in favor of the dominant classes. Such clashes have largely remained localized except in the case of Dalits and caste Hindus and Adivasis and upper-caste Hindus in the 1980s. But Hindu–Muslim riots in the 20th century have acquired a character different from other riots. They hinge on religious nationalism. In the post-Independence period, communal politics of all varieties, irrespective of religion, breeds and nurtures communal animosity.

It is over-simplification to say that the BJP and Sangh Parivar are solely responsible for the creation of conflict between Hindus and Muslims. They have certainly manipulated the conflict for political purposes. A well-conceived theory that riots breed insecurity both in the majority and minority communities is wildly shared by their cadres and ideologues. In such a situation, people close their ranks against 'others' and communal consciousness flourishes. This is a sure way to polarize society on religious lines and take advantage of the passions of the majority community in expanding political support for their projects. All major riots in Gujarat since the mid-1960s have been followed by the arousal of high pitched emotions by the champions of *Hindutva*. The campaign is accompanied by propaganda—construction and deconstruction of 'fact' and systematic dissemination of anti-Muslim and anti-Christian material through informal chats; printed literature such a leaflets, pamphlets, articles and letters to editors in newspapers and journals; and now, cassettes as well as videos.

The visibility of the Jana Sangh (earlier *avatar* of the BJP) and the RSS in Gujarat politics was closely linked with the Indo-Pak war of 1961 and communal tension in Saurashtra, a region bordering Pakistan. According to official figures there were as many as 2,938 instances of communal violence between 1960 and 1969 in Gujarat. The Indo-Pakistan war in 1965 further aggravated tensions, and provided fertile ground for rumor-mongers. The death of then chief minister Balwantrai Mehta, when Pakistan shot down his plane, strengthened anti-Pakistani sentiments among the urban middle class. More often than not, anti-Pakistan sentiments were transformed into hatred against local Muslims. Communal speeches of the RSS and Jana Sangh leaders added fuel to the prevailing communal tension. For the first time, the Jana Sangh won the municipal elections in Botad in Saurashtra in 1965. It then won an Assembly seat in the 1967 elections from Rajkot. In 1968, the RSS organized a rally which was attended by 1,615 volunteers from different districts of Gujarat. Addressing it, M.S. Golwalkar emphasized that only Hindus were secular because they had tolerated all nature of suffering at the hands of various 'others'. He pleaded for the making of a '*Hindu Rashtra*,' a concept on which there had already been extensive discussions in the Gujarati press. The major thrust of the debate was that Muslims had destroyed Hindu culture and now enjoyed special favors in the country.

A counter-view of this position hardly appeared in the media or in any public forum. In the following year, the Jana Sangh played a leading role in retaliating against the protests by Gujarati Muslims against the attack on the Al-Aqsa mosque in early 1969. Balraj Madhok, a Jana Sangh leader, addressed a number of meetings in Gujarat that year where he criticized Muslims for raising a hue and cry over a mosque, which was thousands of miles away from India. He asserted that the same people did not utter a word when Pakistan attacked the Dwarka temple during the Indo-Pakistan war. 'Do you think that Hindus have no feelings for their religion?' Madhok asked. Some religious leaders and Jana Sanghis formed the 'Hindu Dharma Raksha Samiti' (committee to defend Hindu religion) in Ahmedabad in 1968 and the journal *Vishwa Hindu Samachar* was launched. The committee played a very important role in mobilizing anti-Muslim feelings in the city before the 1969 communal riots. A procession was taken out and slogans like, 'Protect Hindu Dharma, and let the irreligious perish' were shouted. Tension between the two communities culminated in large-scale communal riots in September–October 1969 which spread to cities like Vadodara and towns like Anand, Modasa, Godhra, and others. The Jan Sangh and RSS workers were actively involved in the riots either by provoking the people, taking the initiative in leading mobs or simply by providing money or materials to the rioters.[2] The Jana Sangh fielded five candidates in the 1971 Lok Sabha elections and 100 candidates in the 1972 state Assembly elections. It could not compete effectively with the '*Garibi hatao*' slogan of Mrs Gandhi who dominated the elections, and nor did it have an appropriate organizational network to fight elections. All its Lok Sabha candidates lost their deposits. It won three Assembly seats and gained 9 percent of the votes polled.

A lull with respect to communal riots prevailed in the 1970s. Gujarat witnessed the *Nav Nirman* student movement which focused on issues of corruption and price rise. The Jana Sangh and particularly its students' front, the Akhil Bharatiya Vidyarthi Parishad (ABVP), participated actively in the movement. As the movement was loose in its organization and vague in ideology, the ABVP successfully spread its influence among a section of upper-caste students on the issue of corruption and under-played the issue of price rise and scarcity. They were in the forefront in the demand for dissolution of the state Assembly and surrounded the MLAs. After the dissolution of the state Assembly, the Jana Sangh forged an alliance with the Janata Morcha in order to defeat the Congress. The party contested 40 seats and won 18 in the 1975 elections. The party joined the coalition government of the Janata Morcha and three of its members became ministers, which facilitated the further spread of the party. The Parivar then joined with other groups in protest against the Emergency. It is their claim that the RSS, Jana Sangh and ABVP together constituted the largest single bloc in the anti-Emergency movement.[3] Their participation in the popular movement helped the party to broaden its base among the urban middle class in Ahmedabad, Vadodara, and Rajkot (Shah 1977).[4]

The Jana Sangh became the Bhartiya Janata Party (BJP) in 1980. It contested 127 Assembly seats and won nine. Its votes went up to

14 percent. Its performance in the 1985 elections was not impressive. It won 11 seats, but played a significant role, particularly in 1985, in converting the anti-reservation agitation into communal riots.[5] During this period, the issue of Pakistani infiltrators across Gujarat's border was highlighted. Repeated allegations and concocted stories that the Muslims in Gujarat were hand-in-glove with the infiltrators were circulated, leading to communal riots. The tension between Hindus and Muslims was at a high emotional peak in the late 1980s on the issue of Ram Janmabhumi. In 1989, the Sangh Parivar organized the *Ramshila Pujan*, a campaign aimed at collecting foundation bricks for the future temple in Ayodhya. Religious sentiments were fanned by the recital of *bhajan*s, slogans, legends, myths, movies, and rituals. This religious fervor was used for political purposes to broaden the base of the BJP and to recruit volunteers for *kar seva* (labor for religious activities) in Ayodhya. Bricks for the Ram *mandir* were collected from villages as a token of solidarity. The Sangh Parivar circulated news-stories and video films showing the 'bravery and sacrifice' of the *kar sevak*s in the face of 'brutal repression' by the Uttar Pradesh State Reserve Police. Further, in order to gear passions to a high pitch, Hindus were told: 'The blood of the innocents shed in Ayodhya should not be allowed to go waste.' Communal clashes followed.

L.K. Advani began his dramatic *rath yatra* from Somnath in Saurashtra in September 1990, and several mini *rath yatra*s were organized by the BJP to spread the message of Ayodhya. *Trishul*s (trident), saffron flags and caps, stickers declaring, 'Say with pride that I am a Hindu', and slogans swearing by Ram that the temple would be constructed at the same place, appeared in cities and towns and captured the public imagination for Hindu unity and nationalism. During the *rath yatra*, communal riots occurred at 26 places, killing 99 persons between September 1 and November 20, 1990. Repeated communal clashes, high-pitched campaigns for *Hindutva* and the issue of the construction of Ram *mandir* at Ayodhya helped the BJP a great deal in the 1991 Lok Sabha elections. It won 20 out of 26 seats in the Lok Sabha.[6]

The next phase of the campaign for the demolition of Babri Masjid and construction of Ram *mandir* at Ayodhya was set in November 1992. Several hundreds of *kar sevak*s from various castes, including the OBCs, Dalits, and tribals, were deputed from Gujarat for Ayodhya. The Sangh Parivar called for a *Dharma Yudha* (holy war) on December 6, 1992, and projected the cause as a matter of do or die in Ayodhya. In December 1992, the VHP not only published posters but also placed advertisements in the newspapers appealing people to prepare for a holy war for the construction of the Ram *mandir*. Walls were painted with slogans to encourage Hindu militancy, calling for a *Dharma Yudha* and abusing Muslims. '*Garva se Kaho Hum Hindu hai*' (say with pride that I am Hindu), '*Ek Do Babri Masjid Tod Do*' (demolish a few Babri mosques), and '*Muslim Babar ki Aulad*' (Muslims are progenies of Babar, who was an invader). Following the demolition of the masjid, communal riots took place on a large scale in different parts of Gujarat. They were most intensive in Surat, continuing inter-mittently for nearly six months and claimed more than 200 lives. It may be noted that south Gujarat in general and Surat in particular was free from communal riots in 1969 and 1980s. Till 1992, the Congress had majority Assembly seats from this area. But in the sub-sequent elections Congress was wiped out both in the district *panchayat* and City Corporation.

In the 1995 election the BJP raised the slogan to build a Gujarat free from *bhay* (fear), *bhukh* (hunger), and *bhrastachar* (corruption). This slogan, coupled with *Hindutva* sentiments, clicked in the public mind. It won 121 out of 182 seats with 42 percent votes in the state Assembly. For the first time the party won such a large number of seats and formed the government. But before the party could get settled, an internal factional fight erupted. It lost power in 1998 as one of the contenders, Shankarsinh Vaghela, defected from the party and formed the government. Again elections took place in 1998 and the BJP won 117 seats with 44 percent votes and the Congess won 53 seats with 35 percent votes. But within three years a reversal started. The party experienced spectacular defeat in the September–October 2000 elections to the local governments. It lost in all the district *panchayat*s and 80 percent of the *taluka panchayat*s. BJP secured only 27 percent of the *zilla panchayat* seats as against 82 percent in the 1995 elections. *Taluka panchayat* elections tell the same story. Its strength reduced from 67 percent to 33 percent of the seats. The reversal took place in all the districts though in different degree;

it was more in north and central Gujarat (Figure 6.1). Though the
BJP has lost its lead in all the districts, its defeat was marginal in
Saurashtra. It had still somewhat maintained its hold in Bharuch
district but lost heavily in central Gujarat—Kheda, Vadodara, and
Panchmahals districts—as also in Dangs and Surat. Its grip in its
traditional urban fort had loosened. The party lost power in five out
of six municipal corporations, including Rajkot, where it had been
in power for over two decades.

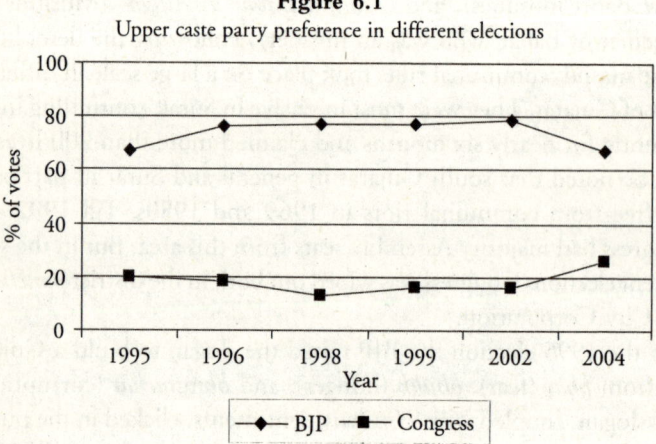

Figure 6.1
Upper caste party preference in different elections

Fearful of a further debacle, the government postponed many municipal and *nagar* as well as *gram panchayat* elections under one pretext
or another. The results sent a shock wave through the party. It is true
that even the Congress did not expect such a windfall. Haren Pandya,
the then Minister of State for Home, lamented that:

> We are shell-shocked, just as the Congress is by its victory, as are the poll
> pundits and media. We are surprised because nobody had expected such
> a rejection by the voters. We are also sad, for the punishment is too harsh
> given the intensity of the crime. The results are an eye-opener, because
> we had absolutely no idea of what was coming.[7]

The major contention within the party was between hard-liners and
so-called moderates on the issue of *Hindutva*. A number of leaders

criticized Bangaru Laxman for his pro-Muslim statement that 'displeased the Hindu voters'. Kishor Makawana, editor of *Sadhana,* the mouth organ of the RSS, believed that 'the workers of the party and the Parivar were displeased by Bangaru's statement that they should reach to Muslims. Gujarat was always sensitive on the issue of Hindutva.'[8] The people felt that BJP had given up the issue of Hindutva. Haren Pandya said, 'This was one election when we had no national favourable trend to help us, no Hindutva, no wave, just us.'[9] Pravin Togadia, VHP's International Secretary General observed,

> The BJP tried to woo Muslims. But neither the Muslims nor committed Hindu voters supported this time. They (BJP) have paid a heavy price for giving up the Hindutva plank. If they understand this soon they will be able to recover, if they do not, it will be disastrous for them. It would not take time before they return to the level they were between 1980 and 1984.[10]

However the moderates, though a small section, felt that the party could no longer win elections on the *Hindutva* card. It had been exhausted. Suryakant Acharya, the then Deputy Chairman of the Gujarat Planning Board said, 'When all the political parties talk about Hindutva, then how could you attract voters on that issue?'[11]

In April, the BJP again lost two by-elections to the state Assembly. One of them was the Sabarmati seat, a segment of Advani's parliamentary constituency. Keshubhai was unceremoniously removed and Narendra Modi, who was waiting in the wings, became the chief minister. After four months, with all resources and state machinery at his command, Modi won the Rajkot by-elections with a small margin of only 1,400 votes although the constituency was considered safe for the party for more than a decade. The BJP also lost two Assembly seats as well as one Lok Sabha seat. The CM had a loud and clear signal about the bleak future of the Party. Some of the BJP leaders assumed that the 'Hindu voter needs security first and not bread.'[12] By implication, insecurity was a favorable situation for mobilizing votes for the party. The Godhra incident facilitated their task.

The post-Godhra riots were concentrated in the *taluka*s and districts where the BJP lost heavily in the *panchayat* elections (Table 6.1).

Table 6.1

Zilla and *taluka panchayat* (direct) election results by party and district, 2000

District	Zilla Panchayat			Taluka Panchayat			Intensity of Communal Violence
	BJP % of Seats	Congress % of Seats	Total Seats	BJP % of Seats	Congress % of Seats	Total Seats	
Kutch	34	59	29	34	60	164	L
Surendranagar	26	74	27	40	54	156	L
Rajkot	32	68	37	38	60	236	M
Jamnagar	35	58	31	45	47	166	L
Junagadh	34	58	41	42	52	242	L
Porbandar	12	88	17	80	12	51	L
Amreli	45	52	31	44	44	183	L
Bhavanagar	31	69	39	36	57	203	M
Ahmedabad	27	73	33	35	55	187	H
Gandhinagar	24	76	25	35	62	65	M
Mehsana	22	73	37	29	59	181	M
Patan	33	63	27	40	53	136	M
Banaskantha	NA*	NA	NA	NA	NA	NA	N
Sabarkantha	24	76	41	35	60	235	H
Panchmahals	31	67	39	33	61	209	H
Dahod	15	85	33	24	68	151	H
Kheda	NA*	NA	NA	NA	NA	NA	M
Anand	3	97	35	20	73	162	M
Vadodara	6	94	47	15	79	244	H
Bharuch	34	52	29	37	51	144	M
Narmada	37	52	19	31	59	70	L
Surat	18	82	45	27	69	262	L
Navsari	37	63	27	29	68		L
Valsad	28	69	29	30	68	117	L
Dangs	12	88	17	21	79	19	L
Total	27	71	735	33	60	3,848	
Total (1995)	82	15	761	67	24	3,812	

Sources: Compiled on the basis of newspaper reports and data provided by *Communalism Combat*, Vol. 8, Nos 77–78, March–April 2002. Election data: *Report on Elections of Local Urban and Rural*, Gandhinagar, State Election Commission, Gujarat, 1997; and newspapers *Sandesh* and *Gujarat Samachar*, September–October 2002.

Notes: N = none or negligible; L = less than 5 persons killed or injured; M = moderate, more than 5 and less than 20 persons killed; H = high, more than 20 persons killed and arson to more than 100 shops and houses.
*Elections did not take place in 2002.

In places like Ahmedabad and Vadodara communal riots have become endemic, so they were the worst affected areas in the 2002 riots. However, communal violence was more extensive in central Gujarat— Kheda and Anand districts and the tribal belt of Panchamahals and Vadodara districts—where the BJP won few Assembly seats in 1998. In Kheda and Anand districts the BJP had captured only five as against 12 seats of the Congress. The situation was similar in Panchamahals. In the 2000 *panchayat* elections the BJP lost significantly in these districts.

Modi organized the *Gaurav Yatra* along the route where riots did not take place. It had the same logic of arousing *Hindutva* passions and reaping the harvest in the elections. The *Yatra* had been launched from Kheda district and began with the worship of the *Kshatriya* diety Bhathiji who, according to a legend, had saved cows from a Muslim. This was done with a view to counter Congress leaders Shankarsinh Vaghela's and Madhvasinh Solanki's base among the *Kshatriya*s in the district. Modi and the *Hindutva* machinery again and again magnified Godhra's carnage with all kinds of fabricated stories. Posters with pictures of the burning Sabarmati Express carrying *Ram Sevak*s and with the catchy questions: '*Aapanu Kon?*' 'Who is ours? Who provides security to us?' was widely exhibited. Implicitly, it suggested that Hindus were set on fire by 'others', and asked who could provide security to them. The VHP also used the Godhra incident to arouse emotions and fear of insecurity among the Hindus.

This helped the BJP to sweep the 2002 Assembly elections. It won 126 seats and nearly 50 percent of the votes. Its major gains were in the riot affected constituencies. The Congress on the other hand made gains in the areas where the riots were not intense (Table 6.2). Within a year's time, the impact of the propaganda had began to melt. In the 2004 Lok Sabha elections, the BJP captured 14 seats out of 26. In the 1999 elections it had 22 seats. Thus it lost eight seats to the Congress, which gained both in the districts affected and unaffected by the riots.

Table 6.2
Performance of the BJP and Congress in riot affected and unaffected
constituencies in the 2002 Assembly and 2004 Lok Sabha elections

	Total	BJP		Congress	
Areas	Seats	Seats Won	Gain/Loss	Seats Won	Gain/Loss
Assembly elections 2002					
Riot affected	65	52	+14*	13	–8
Unaffected	116	74	–4	38	+6
Lok Sabha elections 2004					
Riot affected	10	4	–2**	6	+2
Unaffected	16	10	–6	6	+6

Sources: Compiled on the basis of newspaper reports and *Communalism Combat*, Vol.
8, Nos 77–78, March–April 2002. Election results for 2004 are compiled from
various newspaper reports.
Notes: *Compared to 1998 elections
**Compared to 1999 elections

HINDU UNITY

BJP's ideology of Hindu *rashtra* and adherence to the *Chaturvarna*
system is based on Hindu culture. Such ideology is antithetical to the
interests of the lower castes who constitute a majority. *Hindutva* is a
political ideology conceived and dominated by members of the upper
castes to maintain harmony among various sections of society. V.D.
Savarkar, the author of the concept clarifies, 'The definition is not
consequently meant to be a definition of Hindu Dharma, or Hindu
religion. It is a definition of "Hinduness". It is essentially national in
its outlook and comprehends the Hindu people as a Hindu nation.'[13]
Accordingly, Hindu is a race and its civilization is superior to others.
The *Chaturvarna* system, the four-fold division of the Hindu hierarchical social order, is a basis of nationality. It is believed that 'the
land where the system of four *varnas* (division) does not exist should
be known as the *mlechcha* (impure) country.'[14] The *Chaturvarna*
system 'draws a line of demarcation between us and foreigners.'[15]
All those whose 'holy land' is outside this country—Christians,
Muslims, Jews, etc., whose gods and angels were born elsewhere—are
not and cannot be 'true' patriots of India and hence not part of the
nation. 'Hindutva has little to do with agnosticism, or for the matter

of that, atheism.'[16] This ideology legitimizes a hierarchical social order in which the Other Backward Castes (OBCs), Dalits, and Adivasis are at the bottom of the ladder.

However, an electoral system that grants equality of vote to all adults irrespective of social status poses a threat to the ideology of ascribed hierarchy. A quest for equality in the form of upward mobility has emerged among the deprived strata thanks to the forces of 'modernity' and mass political mobilization of the last several decades. No political party can ignore this process. The challenge before the parties is to either accelerate the process, or camouflage it with rhetoric, or ignore it or divert the process by arousing identity politics.

In terms of socio-economic status in contemporary Gujarat, the traditionally deprived castes are OBCs (36 percent), ex-Untouchables or Scheduled Castes, called Dalits (8 percent), and tribals or Scheduled Tribes called Adivasis (14 percent). Among the OBCs the Kolis, now called Kshatriyas, form the largest caste cluster with 24 percent population. All of them together constitute 58 percent of the state's population. On the whole, the deprived communities are economically poor. In rural areas the dominant land-owning caste is Patidar. Nearly 45 percent of Patidar families own at least 10 acres of land. A landless, laborer household is an exception among Patidars. Urban-dwelling Patidars are professionals, white-collar workers or traders. A few are blue-collar workers and fewer are casual laborers. The same pattern is found among the other upper castes, whereas among the deprived communities, the majority, except the Adivasis, are landless or poor peasants. In the urban areas a vast majority of the deprived communities are casual laborers. There is hardly any household among the upper castes—particularly Brahmins and Vanias—with illiteracy. On the other hand, only 40 percent of the households of the deprived communities are literate.

The process of sanskritization of some kind among all the lower castes, including Dalits and Adivasis, has a very long history extending into the pre-British period. The process is not uniform, varying from caste to caste and time to time, depending upon their power relationship with the dominant castes. In the 20th century, those who improve their material conditions by availing themselves of new opportunities in agriculture, trade and white-collar sectors, strive for higher status and a new identity. One of the ways of acquiring higher position has been to follow the lifestyle of the dominant caste. This process had been encouraged, facilitated and legitimized not only by the British colonial rulers, but also by social and religious reformers and liberal leaders. It has continued in post-Independence India, with some differences. It is no longer a sanskritization confined to rituals and construction of myths regarding the past. Their quest is for 'modernization' which involves competition for economic and political opportunities and higher social status. Both the processes intermingle and continue together. For instance, a section of the Kolis, particularly from central and north Gujarat, claim Kshatriya status but not so with the Kolis of south Gujarat and Saurashtra. The latter continue to be known as Kolis. Both, however, want respect and dignity.

The process of Hinduization and sanskritization however does not resolve their conflict with the dominant strata. Adivasis of the Panchmahals and north Gujarat, following the path of sanskritization, launched several struggles in the early 20th century, and soon after Independence against caste Hindus—the Vanias and Patidars—who grabbed their land. The same is true for the Kolis who claim to be Kshatriyas. The Gujarat Kshatriya Sabha also launched struggles against forced labor practice by land-owning castes of Rajputs and Patidars. In central and north Gujarat, the Koli Kshatriyas had several battles with the Patidars on the issue of land tenancy, land rights and use of common village resources.[17] It may be mentioned here that in order to win the elections in 1962 and 1967 the Gujarat Swatantra Party, dominated by the Patidars, won over some of the leaders of the Gujarat Kshatriya Sabha. The Party evolved a strategy referred to by the acronym PKASH; that is the 'party of Patidars and Kshatriyas.' It nominated a large number of the Kshatriyas as party candidates and also gave them positions within the party organization. But that alliance did not last. The party and the Kshatriya Sabha's leaders could not resolve ground-level conflicts between the poor Kolis and well-off Patidar peasants.

Take the case of the Dalits. During the 1920s and 1930s, the majority of them followed Gandhi's concept of the *Chaturvarna* system and did not follow Dr Ambedkar. But at the same time their urge to fight against discrimination was not reduced despite Gandhi's advice for self-improvement, patience, social reform and tolerance. Going against Gandhi's advice they forcibly entered temples and restaurants, took water from public sources and destroyed the cups and saucers kept separately for them in tea stalls and other eating-places. They openly and violently protested against the practice of discrimination or humiliation in public areas. In short, adherence to Hinduism or sanskritization does not always necessarily mean forgoing economic and social interests.

Though the Congress, as a mass-based party, tried to win over all social groups, it could not satisfy everyone when it began to follow some pro-poor policies and postures. A large section of the upper castes were in search of an alternative to the Congress. The Swatantra Party provided the first major political platform that attracted them, particularly the landed (ex-*zamindars*) Rajputs and Patidars. They opposed the Congress because of its land reform legislation and its plea for a socialistic pattern of society. The Patidars of Saurashtra who had benefited by the land reforms and were strong Congress supporters, also gradually shifted to the Swatantra Party. After its demise, the landed gentry slowly shifted their support first to the Janata Party and then to the Jana Sangh. The reservation policy for OBCs and SC/STs added fuel to the fire, particularly when the Congress openly adopted a strategy of KHAM (Kshatriya, Harijan, Adivasi, and Muslim) alliance in the late 1970s. Since then the upper and middle castes have constituted a major support base of the BJP (Figure 6.1). Among the upper castes, Patidars are the BJP's backbone, but that is not sufficient for survival in electoral politics.

For the BJP, support of the deprived communities who constitute a majority is *sine qua non* not only to win elections but also to defeat 'others', that is Muslims and Christians. Hence, after winning a foot-hold in the urban middle class through riots, agitations and coalition politics, the BJP followed the Congress strategy of KHAM— mobilization of the lower strata, with a difference. The first task for the BJP with regard to its ideology was to isolate Muslims as 'others' from the deprived communities. In fact, at several places government functionaries excluded poor Muslims from welfare programs of the state.[18] While doing this, unlike the Congress, the BJP was careful not to address internal conflicts among various upper-caste Hindus over the distribution of economic and political resources. Hegemony of the upper castes was maintained and social reforms and the abolition of untouchability were never the priority of the Sangh Parivar. The upper castes were advised that they 'should now become alert and not widen the gap between the castes, they must compromise with Dalits and not continue to remain selfish.'[19]

In order to penetrate the Koli Kshatriya base of the Congress, the BJP under the leadership of Shankarsinh Vaghela formed the Kshatriya Sabha in the 1980s, parallel to the Gujarat Kshatriya Sabha. Several Kshatriyas and other OBCs were given positions in the organization. The party nominated a large number of OBCs as the candidates in the 1985 elections. But the party could not sustain their support. Because of the internal power conflict in the BJP, Vaghela left the party and later joined the Congress.[20] Like the Swatantra Party, the BJP also could not reconcile conflicting interests of the OBCs and Patidars. Hence one finds vacillation in OBC support between the Congress and BJP (Figure 6.2). Local factors swing the balance one way or another. The Sangh Parivar successfully mobilized them in central Gujarat against the Muslims in riots, *rath yatras* and also during the 2002 elections. The BJP secured a majority of the Assembly seats from Kheda and Anand districts, which were riot-affected areas. But the OBCs' support to the BJP receded in the 2004 elections. Both the Lok Sabha seats from these districts went to the Congress.

Figure 6.2
OBC party preference in different elections

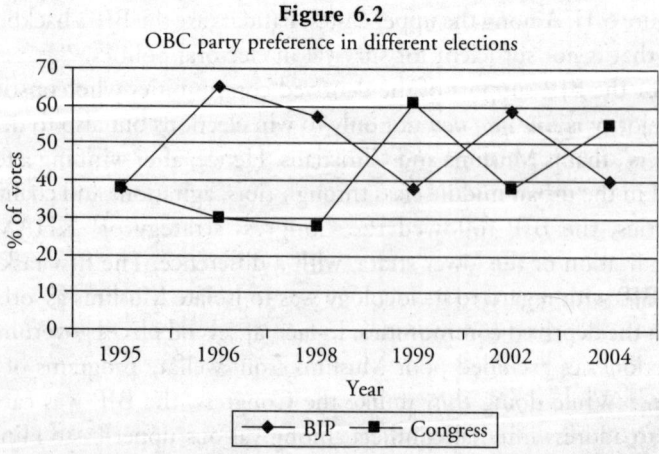

The major challenge before the BJP is to win over Dalits and also to retain the support of caste Hindus. The latter continue to treat Dalits as 'untouchables' and resent their assertion for equality. In 1980, the BJP formed Harijan and Vanvasi (Adivasi/tribal) cells to take up various activities for them. Using the buzzword 'justice', the party organized a *nyaya yatra* (pilgrimage for justice) in 1985–86. Significantly the *yatra* began on Ambedkar's birthday, December 6, and ended on Vivekanand's birthday, January 12, linking the Dalit leader with the champion of Hinduism. During the *yatra*, Dalits were mobilized but nowhere were caste Hindus confronted for not allowing Dalits to take water from village wells or enter temples, or protesting against other forms of 'atrocities' against them. Concurrently, RSS floated the organization, Samajik Sam-Rasata Manch (SSM), or 'Social Assimilation Platform,' to attract Ambedkarists and other Dalits for the purpose of developing Hindu unity. The organization was launched on April 14, 1983, the birth anniversary of Dr Ambedkar, and Dr Hedgewar, founder of the RSS, again associating the former with the ideologue of *Hindutva*. 'We are one', Dr Hedgewar emphasizes. 'We all are Hindus, where is untouchability? All of us are Hindus and nothing else .... There is no *varna* of the *Chaturvarna* or of caste. Today we have only one *varna* and *jati* (caste)—that is Hindu.'[21] He stressed the inculcation of brotherhood among all Hindus. A strategy to expropriate Ambedkar was also floated. According to the proponents of the SSM, the central thrust of Ambedkar's ideology was *dharma* (religion). He was a strong critic of the Brahmin caste who exploited society in the name of religion.

According to RSS leader Dattopant Dhengadi, however, it was the fault of the Brahmins and not of religion. Giving a twist to Ambedkar's decision to adopt Buddhism, it was asserted that Dr Ambedkar did not accept Islam or Christianity because he feared those religions would make people anti-national. With such assertions, the RSS supports its position that the Indian nationalist is one whose *punya bhumi* (holy land) is India. To strengthen its position further, the RSS 'quotes' Ambedkar thus, 'I would support a movement for the saffron flag.'[22] Ambedkar's *Thoughts on Pakistan* were highlighted to show that he was anti-Muslim. According to RSS interpretation, Ambedkar believed that so long as a Muslim clung to his faith, he couldn't become an integral part of Hindustan; and that aggressiveness was part and parcel of Muslims who misused the weakness of the Hindu *samaj* (society).[23] It is an objective of the SSM to assimilate Dalits with the mainstream, thereby strengthening Hindu society and the nation. RSS also published a book, translated from Marathi by a Maharashtrian Dalit volunteer, entitled *Hau, Manu and Sangh* (I, Manu [the author of the *Manusmurati*] and RSS), narrating his experience within the RSS to show that he had never experienced discrimination in the organization. In fact, he argued that it was the Congressmen who practised untouchability and not the BJP members.[24] The book was widely circulated among middle-class Dalits. The Sangh Parivar successfully converted the anti-reservation agitation to communal riots involving Dalits against the Muslims in Ahmedabad.[25] Notwithstanding, except in 1996, it failed to get larger support from the Dalits (Figure 6.3). Soon after the Godhra incident, the BJP could win over a section of urban Dalits. But it could not sustain their support in 2004. In fact, more and more Dalits are withdrawing their support from the BJP though they do not see the Congress as an alternative.

Figure 6.3

Scheduled Castes' party preference in different elections

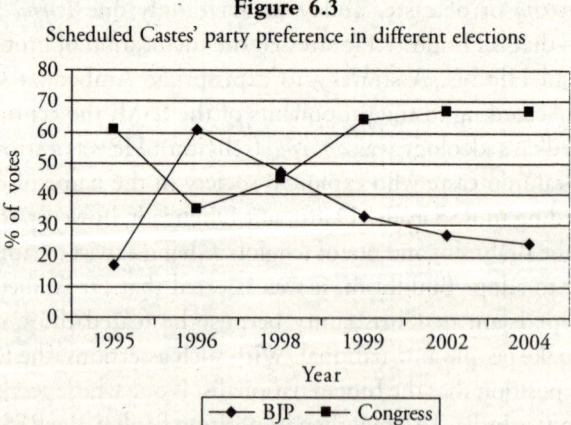

Penetration of dominant regional Hindu culture among the Adivasis has a long history. The process accelerated with the expansion of British interests in forests, to maintain law and order in the region and the spread of a market economy, though in an incipient stage. The freedom movement encouraged some Gandhians to launch constructive programs to uplift the Adivasis (then called Kali Paraj, i.e., black or backward people) and mobilize them in the freedom struggle. Schools and *ashrams* were started with the objective of teaching 'good culture and behavior' on the model of the reformed upper castes. Social values such as cleanliness, teetotalism, vegetarianism, and non-violence were inculcated. Hindu sects also spread their activities. After Independence, there were two schools of thought among the Gandhian constructive workers. One section, was the moralists who kept away from politics as they considered it 'dirty' and an obstacle in constructive activities. In the process they were either marginalized or reduced to managerial functionaries running schools and *ashramshalas*; and willy-nilly became a nut in the government machinery irrespective of the party in power. The other faction openly supported the Congress party with a hope to uplift the Adivasis. In the 1950s, a few member of this faction launched struggles for the implementation of land reforms giving land rights to the tribal cultivators. Later, in the 1960s, they started voluntary associations to carry out welfare programs of the government for Adivasis. During the elections they were actively involved in mobilizing the tribals in favor of the Congress. Jinabhai Darjee has emerged as their leader since the late 1960s. New Adivasi Congress leaders also came up, one of them being Amarsinh Chaudhari who was also the chief minister from 1985 to 1990.

However, the situation began to change in the late 1980s. The Congress stronghold in the Adivasis vote-bank began to crumble. The party which won all the 26 ST reserved seats in 1985 lost as many as 19 seats in the 1990 Assembly elections. Several factors were responsible for the decline of the Congress. First, factional fights among the Adivasi Congress leaders sharpened. Second, because of his strong pro-poor stance, Jinabhai Darjee was alienated from the party. In fact, in the mid-1990s he almost left active politics. Third, a sizeable number of Congress leaders left the Congress and joined the Janata Dal (United) under the leadership of Chimanbhai Patel who had no ideological or moral scruples. Fourth, Gandhian constructive institutions gradually became defunct. Finally, Advani's *rath yatra* en route to the tribal belt mobilized tribals against the Congress.

For the Sangh Parivar, the term Adivasi (original inhabitants) has been problematic. It counters their ideology, which asserts that Aryans are the original inhabitants of the land. According to them, tribals are an integral part of the Hindu *samaj*. The Sangh Parivar has set up a plethora of organizations that focus on tribal areas. Some of the prominent ones are the Vanvasi Kalyan Ashram, Ekalaya Vidyalaya, Sewa Bharati, Vivekananda Kendra, Bharat Kalyan, and Pratishthan Friends of Tribal Society. The objectives of these organizations are to 'uplift' the tribals, 'bring them back' to the Hindu faith and also to 'check' conversions to Christianity. The Vanvasi Kalyan Ashram, started in Gujarat in 1978, functions as the center of various religious, cultural and social activities. It runs health programs, schools and hostels and Hindu consciousness camps.

By 1998, its activities had spread to 245 locations with eight hostels, one school and 243 sports, gymnastics and discourse centers.[26] Non-resident Indians generously supports these activities. For instance, a number of children in Narwad's hostel in south Gujarat are supported through the VHP of America's 'adopt-a-child' program. These hostels organize *bhajan*s and *kirtan*s at the homes of Vanvasis as well as upper-caste Hindu festivals. They also distribute pictures of Hindu gods and goddesses. One unit of the *ashram* in Dharmapur reports that in one year they distributed 30,000 pictures of *Hanumanji* and the *Hanuman Chalisa* (a short and handy booklet of Hindu religious verse). The tribals were told that 'Guha Raja who helped Lord Rama was also a Vanvasi.'[27]

BJP's inroad in the tribal constituencies took off with Advani's *rath yatra* in the late 1980s. Till 1985 it did not win any Assembly seats from ST reserved constituencies; the candidates they fielded lost deposits in 1980 and 1985. In 1989, the BJP and other outfits of the Parivar, particularly the VHP and Bajrang Dals, intensified the Ram Janmabhumi campaign in the tribal villages of Bharuch and Vadodara districts. They collected bricks for the construction of the Ram temple in Ayodhya. In some places, each household was persuaded to contribute Rs 1.25 towards the construction of the temple. RSS and Bajrang Dal activists asked the people: 'Are you a Hindu? If you are, then prove it by contributing Rs 1.25 for the *Ramshila pujan*. If you do not contribute, you prove that you are from a Muslim womb!' Later, volunteers were recruited for the *kar seva*. In 1990, the party won six out of the 26 ST reserved seats. The Congress did not do better either in terms of seats though it secured 36 percent of votes. Janata Dal (United), consisting of dissident Congressmen and Janata Dal members, won a majority of the seats. BJP had seat adjustments with it. Two seats had gone to former Congressmen who contested as Independent candidates. The party reaped the advantage of the post-1992 riots in south Gujarat by intensifying its recruitment drive and propaganda.

The BJP won 14 seats with 36 percent votes in the 1995 elections (Table 6.3). Its main success was in south Gujarat where the party secured 11 seats out of 16. However, in terms of votes, the Congress was not lagging behind the BJP. It regained its position with 15 seats and 44 percent votes in the 1998 elections. The BJP secured only eight seats. The Sangh Parivar, with the support of the government, intensified its anti-Christian campaign in south Gujarat. Christians and their institutions were attacked in the Dangs.[28] A series of programs were organized by the VHP and Bajrang Dal for distributing *trishul*s among the tribals. A number of unemployed tribal youths were recruited to spread their activities. In the post- Godhra riots, tribal youths in central Gujarat—Dahod, Godhra, and Vadodara districts—were mobilized against the Muslims, particularly traders

Table 6.3

Performance of the BJP and Congress in
ST reserved constituencies in different elections

	Congress				BJP				Others			
Years	South*	Central	Total	% Votes	South	Central	Total	% Votes	South	Central	Total	% Votes
1990	5	2	7	36	4	2	6	20	8	5	13	
1995	3	5	8	36	11	3	14	39	3	1	4	
1998	7	8	15	44	7	1	8	37	3	–	3	
2002	10	1	11	38	5	8	13	41	2	–	2	

Source: Election Commission Reports.
Notes: * South region includes Bharuch, Surat, Navsari, Valsad, and Dangs districts.
Central region includes Vadodara, Godhra, Dahod, and Sabarkantha districts.

and contractors, whose numbers in the tribal region is substantial.[29] Muslims were projected as exploiters and intruders in tribal social life, and as abductors of tribal women. Consequently, the BJP captured all the Assembly seats in Vadodara, Dahod and the Pachmahals districts. But the party could not do as well in other Scheduled Tribe reserved constituencies in south Gujarat. It won 13 out of 26 ST reserved seats. Though the BJP continued to garner tribal support in the 2004 Lok Sabha elections (Figure 6.4), the Congress succeeded in capturing two of the three Lok Sabha reserved seats.

Figure 6.4

Scheduled Tribes' party preference in different elections

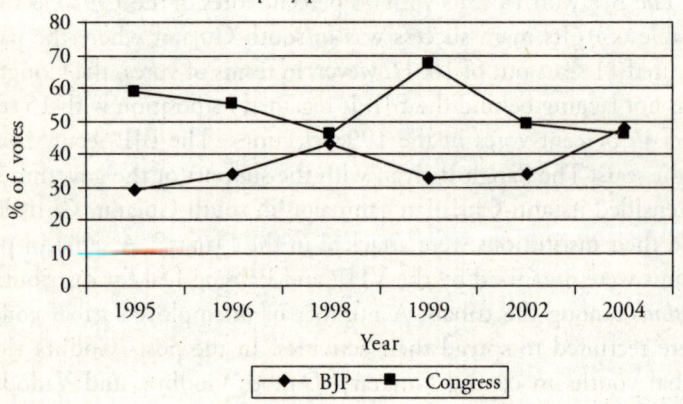

The BJP has accommodated several local leaders of the deprived communities but so far it does not have any leader with a regional stature who can project the interests of the downtrodden. If some one tries to do so he/she is discouraged by the dominant leadership, asserting that there is no difference in the interests of the deprived and others. Some BJP leaders do admit that it was a Herculean task for the BJP to win over and continue to maintain the support of the lower strata of society because of the dominance of the upper castes and Patidars in the party.[30] It may be mentioned here that a study of the 1995 elections showed that only one-tenth of the BJP voters in the sample explicitly preferred the party because it was pro-Hindu. The majority of BJP's supporters had far more mixed considerations. The party's oft-repeated promise to curb corruption and prices, and

its public image, of course at that time, of being a disciplined party—
different from others—attracted nearly one-third of its voters.[31]

After the 1998 elections, as Table 6.4 shows, the Congress has
been slowly winning back the support of OBCs, Dalits, and Adivasis.
This was evident in the 1999 Lok Sabha elections. The process has
continued in the local body elections in 2000 and in the 2004 Lok
Sabha elections. The BJP's support base among the upper castes and
Patidars continues to remain more or less the same. It gained a base
among the tribals but now a reversal has begun. So is the case with
the OBCs. Dalits by and large continue to support the Congress.

Table 6.4
Trend of party preference by various castes/communities

Caste/Community	BJP					
	1995	1996	1998	1999	2002	2004
Upper castes	67	76	77	77	79	67
OBCs	38	65	57	38	59	40
SCs	17	61	47	33	27	24
STs	29	34	43	33	34	48
Muslims	7	33	38	10	10	20
	Congress					
	1995	1996	1998	1999	2002	2004
Upper castes	20	18	13	16	16	26
OBCs	38	30	28	61	38	55
SCs	61	35	45	64	67	67
STs	59	55	46	67	49	46
Muslims	47	68	62	90	69	60

Source: The election survey of 1996 was conducted by CSS, Surat and confined to
rural areas. The other surveys were conducted by CSDS, Delhi, 1996.
Notes: N = 484; 1998 N = 340; 1999 N = 381, 2002 N = 1853, 2004 N = 914
(N = number of respondents).

POLARIZATION, SYNCRETIC CULTURE,
AND THE MODERN STATE

The concentrated process of planned intervention on the part of the
Hindutva forces to fracture Gujarati society on communal lines has

been going on since the 1960s. Their efforts yielded a dividend when they gained power in the 1990s. Since then the process has accelerated through state patronage. To some extent, the architects of the post-Godhra communal riots have succeded in their mission. Several, but not all, popular Hindu sects that were competing among themselves have forged some kind of unity by addressing the issue of *Rashtra* and patriotism which were never on their agenda. Attempts have been made in hijacking some sects rooted in a syncretic culture with an agenda to reconstruct them exclusively on the basis of a Hindu or Muslim sect. But all of them have not yet fallen in line. The minorities in a few cities and towns have been marginalized, not only physically but also culturally and socially. Wherever the diehard members of the Parivar are involved in violence and have state backing, the victims are still not able to go back to their houses and resume their occupations.

Culprits, particularly of the upper strata of society and associated with the BJP or VHP/Bajrang Dal, continue to threaten the minority communities as well as secular organizations engaged in building harmony and providing relief, with dire consequences for their activities. Their vandalism continues unabated. Though there is no remorse in a large section of the vocal urban middle class for the violence of 2002, many have begun to distance themselves from the VHP and Bajrang Dal's programs. Godhra and post-Godhra experiences and memories continue to haunt Gujarat public life. The non-BJP parties also started talking openly about Hindus and their rights. The chief campaigner of the Congress party in the 2002 elections asserted that only the Congress, not the BJP, can protect the Hindus.[32]

It is over-simplification to say that the *Hindutva* ideology of the Sangh Parivar brand has completely captured the space of public life in Gujarat. It needs to be mentioned that a large part of Gujarat, despite all efforts of the communal forces, kept away from communal violence. There are many examples where Hindus and Muslims, both in rural and urban areas, maintained harmony in the midst of provocation. There are also cases where one participated in rioting at the spur of the moment in an emotional outburst, but later repented their act; in fact in, some cases, the same person later rescued Muslims.[33] Roy Burban, in his study, has given several instances both of urban and rural Gujarat where both the communities protected each other.

The survey carried out by Cfore in April[34] found that only 37 percent of the people in riot-affected areas justified the riots that followed Godhra.[35]

Figure 6.5
Muslims' party preference in different elections

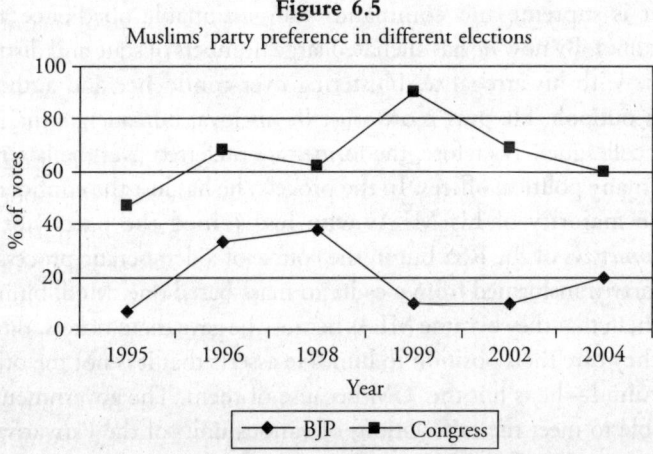

Another survey in December 2002 covering all of Gujarat conducted by CSDS shows that as many as 72.5 percent of the respondents believed that the post-Godhra riots were absolutely wrong. Only 5.7 percent stated that they were 'inevitable and necessary.' A section of Dalits who were not members of the Parivar, but got involved in the riots in the emotionally surcharged situation, now feel that they were used as an instrument in the rioting. In some places where diehard Parivar members are either absent or have lost credibility, the victims and accused are involved in a process of compromise of forgiving and forgetting. In Gomtipur, Ahmedabad, a Dalit-Muslim locality, Abdul Razzak, a rickshaw driver said, 'My house and shop was burnt by the rioters in April 2002. I lodged a complaint in the matter and police subsequently arrested some persons. But, now I want to forget all that and live peacefully. I am willing to withdraw my complaint.'[36]

During the post-Godhra riots and thereafter, the state machinery has blatantly eliminated or side-tracked all somewhat 'independent' officers from the mainstream administration. Their fault was that they acted 'objectively' and gave their personal observations and views on policy matters. Chief Minister Narendra Modi allows no discussion even in the advisory bodies after his speech or remarks. The chief minister treats the rank and file of the party and government functionaries as his *swayamsevak*s of the *shakha* (RSS units where the leader is supreme and commands unquestionable obedience and discipline). By now he has alienated large numbers of state and district leaders with his arrogance, blustering over-confidence and authoritarian outlook. He puts more trust in his loyal bureaucrats than in party colleagues. Therefore, the former are preferred over the latter to head many political offices. In the process, he has lost the confidence of the majority of his MLAs who had joined the party not as *swayamsevak*s of the RSS but in the course of a democratic process as the party transformed from a cadre to mass-based one. Modi bluntly tells them that they became MLAs because he gave them tickets, therefore they owe their position to him. He asserts that it is not the other way round—he is not the CM because of them. The government is not able to meet the expectations of various units of the Parivar who also have political ambitions.

Despite BJP's power and the spread of *Hindutva*, the RSS is not booming with trained and committed *swayamsevak*s. In fact, the number of *shakha*s and committed *karyakarta*s (workers) had stagnated in the preceeding five years. On the whole, the youth have become more overtly *Hindutva*-minded and more involved in religious rituals. But at the same time they are more consumerist and 'western' in their lifestyle than before. The VHP and Bajrang Dal do recruit youths for certain campaigns but they cannot sustain their enthusiasm and participation. Most of their activists are lumpens rather than disciplined and committed to any ideology or dream for society. The Parivar had not been able to mobilize a large number when the Shankaracharya was arrested or when Modi was denied a US visa. Even their well published Ram *mahotsava* in April 2005 could not attract large crowds in Ahmedabad and elsewhere. Ram Madhav, an RSS spokesperson concedes that 'modernization poses its own challenges to cadre based organization. But I feel that despite the onslaught of mindless entertainment and individual aspirations, which do pose a challenge in enlisting cadre for public service, the Indian youth is still very much rooted in our reality.'[37]

The local RSS cadre is not happy with Modi who belongs to their lineage. Modi did not follow their advice in all matters, as he has to satisfy the middle class and industrialists—local and foreign—for 'growth' to show that Gujarat was 'shining'. He has to meet deficit finance as also the terms and conditions of multinationals for aid and loans. The leaders of the Bharatiya Kisan Sangh, a BJP peasant organization, is at war with the chief minister because of his pro-industrial position and because he raised electricity charges. Modi could not prevent the Supreme Court from giving a verdict to re-open nearly 2000 cases related to the communal carnage. Despite his own preference, he could not prevent the arrest of some VHP and Bajrang Dal activists in riot-related cases. Hence they feel frustrated in the way the local administration treat them. One of the leading VHP members from central Gujarat, popularly known as 'Chhote Togadia,' committed suicide out of frustration. The Parivar does not have a formula to resolve the contradictions of their making and also of a modern, 'open' society. The BJP high command is caught in a dilemma. If it succumbs to the pressure of the dissidents it would mean the acceptance of the 'authoritarian' style of the chief minister who, according to a few BJP MLAs, was the mastermind in perpetuating riots. But if he is allowed to continue, a large number of party workers would become inactive. Modi cannot invigorate the party with a few loyalists and bureaucrats.

OVERVIEW

The post-Godhra communal violence was not sudden and abrupt. It is a part of the process developed over the last three decades of constructing *Hindutva* ideology and action. The process has been accelerated with the BJP's coming to power and then getting signals of losing power. The post-Godhra events helped the BJP to sweep the 2002 Assembly elections. The Parivar has also, to some extent, succeeded in polarizing a Gujarati society already fractured on communal lines. But the polarization is not total. There was and still is resistance against the agenda of *Hindutva*. A large part of the state did not experience direct communal violence. In several places people from both communities maintained harmony against provocation. The BJP has penetrated the deprived communities but could not get the sustained support that it got from the upper castes. Its major challenge in post-Godhra Gujarat is to resolve its contradictions so as to build unity among all castes and classes and accelerate economic growth with its *Swadeshi* model. On the other hand, the BJP no longer enjoys the image of being a disciplined and morally upright party that is different from the others.

NOTES

1. Justice Krishna Iyer, Justice P.B. Jaswant, Justice Hosbet Suresh, K.G. Kannabiran, Aruna Roy, Ghanshyam Shah, K.S. Subramaniam, and Tanika Sarkar, *Crime Against Humanity, Concerned Citizens Tribunal* (Bombay: Citizens for Justice and Peace, 2002).
2. Ghanshyam Shah, 'Communal Riots in Gujarat: Report of a Preliminary Investigation', *Economic and Political Weekly*, Vol. 5. Nos 3–5, Annual Number (1970). Under the Emergency, the RSS was banned. However Bala Saheb Deoras, head of the RSS, in his letter to Mrs Gandhi dated August 22, 1975 asked her to utilize the 'power of the Sangh for the upliftment of our country'. Its journal *Panchajanya* welcomed in December 1975 the emergence of Sanjay Gandhi as youth leader. See Madhu Limaye, *Janata Party Experiment: An Insider's Account of Opposition Politics* (Delhi, 1994).
3. Narendra Modi, *Aapaatkaal Mein Gujarat* (Hindi) (New Delhi: Prabhat Prakashan, 2004).
4. Ghanshyam Shah, *Protest Movements in Two Indian States* (Delhi: Ajanta Publications, 1977).
5. Ghanshyam Shah, 'Under-Privileged and Communal Carnage: A Case of Gujarat' (Amsterdam: The Werthem Lecture 2004, CASA and ASSR, 2004). Also see Ornit Shani, *The Making of Ethno Hinduism in India* (Tel Aviv: Tel Aviv University, 2003).
6. Ghanshyam Shah, 'Tenth Lok Sabha Elections: BJP's Victory in Gujarat', *Economic and Political Weekly*, Vol. 26, No. 51 (December 21, 1991).
7. *Indian Express*, October 9, 2002.
8. Personal interview, November 2000.
9. *Times of India*, October 9, 2000.
10. Ibid., October 11, 2000.
11. Personal interview, November 2000.
12. Ibid.
13. V.D. Savarkar, *Hindutva: Who is a Hindu* (Mumbai: Swatantryaveer Savarkar Rashtriya Smarak, 1999), p. xvii.

14. Ibid., pp. 17, 24.

15. Ibid., p. 17.

16. Ibid., p. 80.

17. Ghanshyam Shah and D.C. Sah (eds), *Land Reforms in India, Vol. 8. Transform-ance and Challenges in Gujarat and Maharashtra* (New Delhi: Sage Publications, 2002).

18. Nikita Sud, 'Acting on Development: Exploring the Interface between Policy and its Stakeholders' (M.Phil. Dissertation in Development Studies. Oxford: International Development Center, St. Antony's College, Oxford University, 2003).

19. Ghanshyam Shah, 'The BJP and Backward Castes in Gujarat', *South Asian Bulletin*, Vol. 14, No. 1 (1994). See also, Swami Atmanand, 'Hindu Samaj Samanvaya', p. 63 (Ahmedabad: Bharat Sewashram Sangh, 1982) (Gujarati).

20. Ghanshyam Shah, 'The BJP's Riddle in Gujarat: Caste, Factionalism and Hindutva', in Thomas Hansen and Christophe Jaffrelot (eds), *The BJP and the Compulsion of Politics in India* (New Delhi: Oxford University Press, 1998).

21. Quoted by Dattopat Dhengadi, *Samajik Samrasta* (New Delhi: Kartavati Samajik Samrasta 1992), p. 18.

22. Ibid., p. 21.

23. Dattopat Dhengadi, *Samajik Samrasta* (New Delhi: Karnavati Samajik Samarast Manch, 1993) (Gujarati).

24. Ramesh Patange, *Hau, Manu Ane Sangh* (in Gujarati) (Karnavati: Sadhana Pustask Prakashan, undated).

25. Shah, 'Under-Privileged and Communal Carnage', op. cit.

26. Gajendra Shukla, *Bhartiya Janta Party* (in Gujarati) (Ahmedabad: Atul Prakashan, 2000).

27. VHP plans schools in border areas to counter infiltration, *Hindustan Times*, May 9, 2001. http://www.hvk.org/articles/0501/139.html.

28. Ghanshyam Shah, 'Conversion, Reconversion and the State: Recent Events in the Dangs', *Economic and Political Weekly*, Vol. 34. No. 6 (February 6, 1999).

29. Chandan Sengupta, Anil Kumar, and Katy Gandevia, *Communal Riots in Gujarat, 2002: A Study of Contextual Factors* (Mimeo) (Mumbai: Tata Institute of Social Sciences, 2003).

30. Ghanshyam Shah, 'Contestation and Negotiations: Hindutva Sentiments and Temporal Interests in Gujarat Elections', *Economic and Political Weekly*, Vol. 37, No. 48 (November 30, 2002).

31. Ghanshyam Shah, 'BJP's Rise to Power', *Economic and Political Weekly*, Vol. 31, Nos 2–3 (January 1996).

32. Shah, 'Contestation and Negotiations, op. cit.

33. Ghanshyam Shah, 'Caste, Hindutva and Hideousness', *Economic and Political Weekly*, Vol. 37. No. 15 (April 13, 2002).

34. Center for Forecasting and Advisory Research, 2002.

35. *Outlook*, April 15, 2002.

36. *Indian Express*, April 18, 2005.

37. *Tehelka*, April 30, 2005.

CHAPTER 7

Political Articulation and Policy Discourse in the 2004 Elections in Andhra Pradesh

Karli Srinivasulu

The electoral defeat of the Telugu Desam (TD) government in Andhra Pradesh (AP) has been interpreted as a verdict on its economic reforms agenda pursued since mid-1990s.[1] TDP's strength has been reduced from 180 members in the earlier House to its all time low of 47 and Congress has been enhanced its position from 91 seats to 186.[2] An examination of this situation is important because of the serious implications it is likely to have to the political discourse and actual process of macro reforms in the state. The crucial questions are: can such a sweeping inference be drawn from the electoral outcome? How was the electoral agenda framed and what were the positions of different political parties on economic reforms in the electoral discourse?

Electoral performance of political parties involves a complex process and a multivariate analysis is required to understand it. The factors that are decisive in the making of an electoral outcome are the organizational strength of parties, structure of party competition, nature of political alliances, forms of political discourse and appeal, strategies of mobilization and their impact on alignment of social forces and support bases of parties. Thus, political and policy discourse forms one of the determining factors of electoral outcome. The AP elections provide a useful vantage point to reflect on the relationship between elections and policy issues that have wider political significance and implications,[3] for, AP under the TDP regime had been in the forefront of the economic reforms.

This chapter seeks to examine the significance of policy issues and position of different parties vis-à-vis the marginalized social groups in the policy discourse in the 2004 elections in AP. The analysis here is presented in four sections. The first section discusses the theoretical concerns and perspective of this chapter. Section Two briefly reviews the shifts in the policy framework of the TDP regimes with a view to contextualize the subsequent developments. The third section analyzes the policy discourse during the 2004 elections and the last section concludes the chapter.

Theoretical Concerns and Perspective

Discourse, defined as 'an ensemble of ideas, concepts and categories through which meaning is given to phenomena,'[4] helps us in appreciating how problems or issues are perceived and framed, and how certain problems are prioritized vis-à-vis others. If ideological perception is an important aspect of political activity and mobilization, discourse analysis helps us in analyzing the ideas that are crucial to the making of representations of social phenomena and giving political meaning and priority to a particular perception and representation vis-à-vis others.

The dominant model in the field of policy studies is the linear model in which the policy process is viewed in terms of stages—agenda setting, policy formulation and decision-making, implementation and impact evaluation placed in a linear sequence. This model, viewing policy-making as a rational process, privileges the place and position of the so-called experts in policy processes. The intricate technicalities in policy analysis and formulation are assumed to be incomprehensible to ordinary people, therefore the latter's participation could only be very minor and limited. In this model, policy-making is assumed to be an objective and value–neutral exercise and, by implication, policy experts become the bearers of objectivity.

Discourse theory, however, assumes that policy making is an intense political process involving various social groups with different perceptions and interests. Policy decision processes are influenced by the competition among different groups; and their capacities and relative strengths and weaknesses are critical to it. But these groups, more often than not, do not act individually. To be effective, they make attempts to gather wider support by identifying commonality in interests—long-term and short-term—in argument and narratives and forge what can be called discourse coalitions. This is possible only through discursive deliberations involving inclusions/exclusions and contestations over ideas, interests and truth claims. The discourse analysis makes us sensitive to contestation and conflict between different discourse groups in a diversity of situations, sites and spaces.

Discourse analysis also helps us in overcoming the economistic-reductionist limitations of orthodox Marxism that attributes causal primacy to categories of class and class interests. Two central issues that are rendered rather simplistic by a large corpus of Marxist analyses are the categories of truth and power.[5] Discourse analysis, instead of assuming truth, claims to be springing exclusively from class positions. It views truth as socially constructed and thus open to contestation and challenge. Therefore one can only talk about regimes of truth rather than a truth. Similarly, the grand notion of power as being vested in one location—a class or institution—and flowing in a top-down manner is contested. Discourse theory highlighting the 'micro-physics of power'[6] emphasizes the significance of local and micro contexts, institutions, networks, strategies and practices in policy analysis.

There is a tendency in a society like ours to view policy making as an official arena where only the bureaucracy, political élite and certain influential sections of the industrial and business class play a key role. It is true that the élite have clear advantage in terms of influence and access to policy processes involving agenda setting, networking, lobbying, information channeling, and decision-making arenas. The concerns of marginalized sections of society go unrepresented because of weak civil society, lack of information and inaccessibility to the channels of communication with the policy-making bodies.

For the above reasons, the electoral arena assumes significance. Elections provide important spaces for a debate on policy issues that tend to draw clear and sharp distinctions between political parties, different policy options and popular choices. The emergence of the states as distinct political theatres in the post-Emergency period and increasing electoral competition has compelled political parties and the political élite to expand the possibilities for their engagement with marginalized groups and their social networks, which are mostly informal.

With this perspective, we seek to examine the structure of policy discourse in the 2004 elections in AP with a focus on the concerns of the marginalized groups, their articulation, their reflection in the discourses of the contending political parties and discursive aspects of electoral agenda setting. Elections are an occasion when political parties engage with marginalized groups for their support and provide an opportunity to articulate their interests. The dominant perspectives in electoral studies tend to focus on political parties rather than investigating how these groups perceive themselves and are perceived by the political élite, how their concern are shaped and received and what spaces become available to them during the elections to articulate their interests. An examination of these aspects helps us in furthering the expansion of the democratic space and scope of this interaction so that better democratic and pro-people policies can be made possible.

TDP POLICY SHIFTS

The emergence of the TDP[7] as a major force in AP politics brought about a distinct policy orientation in the political discourse in the state. The policy initiatives by the N.T. Rama Rao (NTR) government pertaining to the administrative and welfare arenas marked this. The abolition of the traditional Village Officer system and the introduction of the *mandal*s in place of the *panchayat samithi*s were meant to strike at the support base of the Congress and expand the opportunities for the ambitious backward class political élite to accommodate them.[8] Welfare policies played a major role in shaping the popular perception of and support to the TDP. It acquired a pro-poor and pro-farmer image mainly because of its populist policies like the Rs 2 a kilo rice scheme,[9] Janata cloth scheme and subsidized power supply to the farm sector. The weaker section-housing scheme also visibly contributed to the government's popularity.

The Naidu regime made a decisive departure from this legacy of NTR by reformulating and replacing them with alternative policies in its drive towards the liberalization of the state economy. The much-publicized *janmabhumi* program, launched by the Naidu government with the twin objectives of facilitating grassroots involvement in the developmental process and making the administrative machinery accountable to the people, was supposed to reflect the shift. This program was meant to take the administration nearer to the people (*Prajalavaddaku Palana*) and evolve micro-plans by identifying their needs, assessing the availability and requirements of resources. The execution of the plans thus chalked out were to be implemented by actively involving the local people through *shramadanam* (voluntary work) and mobilization of resources by the people themselves.

In tune with the economic reforms, the Naidu regime launched a number of programs to promote need-based self-help among different target groups. Thus Water Users' Associations were formed to take care of water management, school committees were entrusted with the responsibility of maintenance and supervision of schools, *Vana Samrakshana Samithis* (forest protection committees) were formed for the protection and management of forests. Apart from these, women self-help groups were encouraged. The more visible and successful among them are those formed under the DWCRA (Development of Women and Children in Rural Areas) program. The Naidu government gave it the form of a movement, activating the existing groups and encouraging the formation of new ones. As part of this campaign, DWCRA *bazaar*s were held in Hyderabad and also in different towns in the state. The TDP government, including the local administrative machinery, gave it a high priority.

Further, the government introduced a series of schemes purportedly for the development of marginalized social groups with an emphasis on skill development and marketing support. The 'Deepam' scheme, under which the members of the DWCRA were provided with cooking stoves and gas cylinders, meant to encourage women's self-help groups, became quite popular with the womenfolk. Also popular was the 'Adarana' scheme under which tool kits were provided to the artisans and occupational communities to enhance their productivity. 'Roshini' scheme for the Muslims, under which financial provision was made for the construction of *shadikhana*s (marriage halls) and renovation of old mosques, and the 'Cheyutha' scheme meant for the handicapped were all launched prior to the 1999 elections.[10] Underlining these community-identity specific schemes and subsidies is the political strategy aiming to co-opt the marginalized caste-communities by re-articulating the identity political agenda, brought on to the center of political discourse of the state by the BSP, some CPI(ML) groups and the Dalit and backward caste organizations during the 1990s.[11]

POLICY DISCOURSE DURING THE 2004 ELECTIONS

The following developments form the context of the 2004 Assembly elections and are therefore relevant to the electoral discourse.

1. There has been a sharp polarization of the political spectrum between the TDP–BJP alliance on the one hand and the Congress–Telangana Rashtriya Samity (TRS)–Left alliance on the other. This has obviously led to the sharpening of the discursive contestation in the electoral campaign.
2. This election has seen the marginalization of small parties like the BSP, Maha Jana Front,[12] etc., which had significant discursive presence earlier.
3. The intensity of political competition and the compulsions to co-opt identity politics facilitated and expanded the space for policy issues in the electoral discourse and participation.

The discourse in the 2004 election is built around the performance of the TDP regime during its nine-year tenure. The TDP, as is well known, is a highly personalized party resulting in an overt and excessive focus on the persona of Naidu. In fact, he assumed an iconic status with regard to the state-level economic reforms in the international and national press and in the eyes of international donors and captains of domestic big businesses.

The Naidu regime sought to cultivate a pro-reform image for itself with all the hype.[13] What distinguished it from the other pro-reform state governments was not only its open commitment to the reforms agenda but more importantly its effort to justify reforms in a larger ideological framework. In this narrative, the 'global' was a strategic point of reference to judge the state of AP's economy and the accompanying criteria of the neo-liberal agenda, that is, efficiency, competitiveness, and good governance. Accordingly, the development of the state is premised on the tapping of the opportunities opened up by globalization. Emphasis on information technology and biotechnology as the priority sectors is informed by the above perspective. Further, it is this preoccupation with the global which underlines the regime's political criticism of the Left as redundant on the context of globalization.[14]

Governance reforms thus were identified as an important precondition for the development of the state. The term SMART (Simple, Moral, Accountable, Responsive, and Transparent) was popularized to send across the message that the government was serious about governance reforms to simplify procedures, to speed up decisions and to create an efficient and transparent service delivery mechanism. The TDP regime thus built up a discourse based on reform-development, good governance, and a global integration narrative.[15]

The 2004 elections in AP display a plebiscitary character. Conducted in the aftermath of the assassination attempt by the CPI(ML) (People's War) on Naidu at Alipiri near Tirupati, the electoral campaign became centered on him. Naidu facilitated this focus by declaring the election as a referendum on his nine-year rule. The TDP thus invested all its resources on Naidu. Within the above pro-liberalization framework, the election agenda was set by the TDP in sharply polarized terms of law and order versus violence and anarchy, separatism versus integration of the state and stability versus instability.

LAW AND ORDER VS. ANARCHY

This election, nine months early, was prompted by the expectation of a sympathy wave following the assassination attempt. It brought the question of Naxalite violence in the state onto the political agenda in the form of a debate on law and order versus backwardness and deprivation. The law and order perspective largely has informed TDP's approach to this issue. The number of so-called encounter deaths during the Naidu regime and absence of any comprehensive socio-economic program to tackle the issue of regional disparities and socio-economic deprivation are the pointers. Violence and counter-violence in the state by the People's War Group (PWG) and the police has reached almost maniac proportions. Responding to this violence, a forum—*Poura Spandana Vedika*—comprising civil rights activists and journalists and formed at the initiative of a former civil servant, advocated and pushed for a dialog between the government and PWG. Its premise is that the Naxalite problem should be viewed as a serious socio-economic issue. The recalcitrant attitudes created serious hurdles and led to the eventual failure of this attempt to initiate a dialogue.

In the post-Alipiri period, with the TDP going aggressively against PWG, the Congress and the TRS along with the parliamentary Left opted to view it as a social issue. The initiative by the citizens' forum could be seen as echoing the larger sentiment in the Naxalite influential areas. It is fairly well known that the people, especially the youth, in the Naxalite-dominated villages of Telangana are subjected to tremendous hardship. Unlawful detentions, torture, extortions and fake encounters are reported by civil liberties organizations and the media. If perennial drought and unemployment have been serious concerns of people here then the police repression has only added to their woes. The citizens' forum has been instrumental in bringing forth these concerns on to the political discourse and policy arena. The impact of this on the Congress and TRS's stated position on the process of dialog with the PWG is unmistakable.

By posing the Naxalite issue in extremely negative and hostile terms, the TDP could only sharpen the polarization of the discourse in terms of development versus anarchy. Accordingly, the TDP projected itself as a party that stood for development and the Congress and the TRS as against it and in favor of anarchy. As the electoral campaign progressed, with its top leadership as well as its grass-roots cadres subjected to threats and actual killings and its organizational network virtually paralyzed by the PWG, the TDP sharpened its criticism of and hostility towards the PWG. Thus the TDP lost its maneuverability, which is crucial to the shaping of the discourse.

SEPARATISM VS. INTEGRATION OF THE STATE

Another contentious issue in this election was the demand for a Telangana state. The Telangana issue re-emerged as an electoral issue after more than three decades. The TRS, formed in 2001 by a former TDP leader, K. Chandrasekhar Rao (KCR), championed the cause. If the performance of the TRS in the Panchayat Raj elections[16] held in 2001 was an indication of its growing popularity, then the popular response to its rallies and meetings further demonstrated it. This obviously had an impact on the TDP's support base. To further compound the problems of the TDP, the Telangana issue came to symbolize the condensation of serious policy concerns pertaining to agriculture, drought, irrigation and of course Naxalism, as large pockets of Telangana are perennially drought prone and have a Naxalite presence. By raising the Telangana question, the TRS sought to reflect all the above concerns.

The Telangana issue also posed a challenge to the Congress as well as. A section of Congressmen from Telangana forming the Telangana Congress Forum, have been raising the issue of statehood. This voice in the Congress grew in prominence as the TRS expanded its network and social base. With the demand for the Telangana state both inside and outside the Congress gaining prominence, the Congress High Command was forced to respond by promising to constitute a second States' Reorganization Committee (SRC).[17] With this the ground was prepared for electoral realignments in the state.

The Congress always contested elections in AP on its own, while from the beginning the TDP forged an alliance with one or the other of the non-Congress forces. With the change in the Congress national policy in favor of forging electoral alliances[18] to confront the NDA, the ground was cleared for an alliance with the TRS and the Left. What brought these parties together was obviously the main goal of defeating the TDP–BJP alliance. But differences among them on Telangana statehood, along with other issues, have been equally important. While the Congress continuously harped on the need for a second SRC, the

Left disagreed. Differences with the Left are reflected in the TRS putting up its candidates against the Left in some places.

On the other side of the political spectrum, while the TDP's stand has been against a separate state of Telangana, the state unit of the BJP, on the contrary, had taken a pro-Telangana stand with its slogan of 'one vote, two States' in the Kakinada conference in 1998. But since its alliance with the TDP in 1999, it was forced to keep it in abeyance. Since the BJP has greater presence and influence in Telangana compared to coastal Andhra, it is a risk that the state unit of the BJP was to take with a view to improving the prospects of the NDA government at the Center. Thus the BJP argued that though in principle it was in favor of small states, in the context of alliance politics it was forced to confine itself to the NDA agenda.

The discourse on Telangana therefore is marked by the internal dynamics and tensions of alliance politics. Given the fact that Telangana has been an emotive issue, the parties—even when they are opposed to the idea of a Telangana state—had to exercise caution. Though the terms of this discourse have been clearly spelt out and battle lines clearly drawn, a perceptible difference existed in the political stands of the parties in the two election phases. The first phase held on April 20, covered the Telangana region and parts of northern Andhra, while the second phase of polling held on April 26, covered the remaining coastal Andhra and Rayalaseema regions. During the first phase, the TDP's chief campaigner, Naidu, emphasized the need for an integrated AP and reeled out what the TDP had done and promised to do, if elected, for Telangana. In the second phase of polling in coastal Andhra, he sought to rake up Andhra sentiment by suggesting how a separate state of Telangana would lead to a water war as Telangana would demand a share of river water resources[19] and fertile and irrigated coastal Andhra would be forced to suffer.

Stability vs. Instability

The third theme that dominated the TDP's electoral campaign was the question of political stability. The TDP, as it has done continuously in its two decade-long history, equated Congress rule with political instability. The Congress's track record of frequent change of chief ministers, internal factional fighting, and interference of the party High Command in state affairs were emphasized by the TDP leadership. Congress and its allies countered this discourse by pointing to the 'real' instability in the AP economy and society under TDP rule. The destabilization of the agriculture and handloom sectors, which constitute the main sources of employment, reflected the gross neglect of these sectors during the TDP's nine-year rule, according to the Congress campaign. Holding the TDP responsible for the suicides of farmers and artisans, the Congress and its allies put the TDP regime and its *Supremo* on a public trial.

These broad positions on the questions of law and order, integration and stability have informed the TDP's position on specific policy issues like agriculture, handlooms, power, etc., in the fiercely fought elections. The TDP, by going in for early polls, apparently aimed at seizing the initiative and setting the agenda for the electoral debate. This initial advantage could not be sustained and in fact turned negative as it sought to define the electoral discourse in terms of sharp polarities. If the closed structure and implicit negativity in the TDP's electoral campaign were striking, then the Congress displayed a greater openness and inclusiveness in terms of agenda. This made the Congress party look more responsive to newer issues and demands from below.

FRAMING AND NAMING: CONGRESS POLICY DISCOURSE

Policy discourse can be compared with story telling. It should have a beginning, a story line, a narrative structure and an ending. The entry point in the Congress campaign in AP was the suicide of farmers and accordingly it built up a narrative that identified the phenomenon of farmers' suicides with TDP rule. The crisis in the agrarian sector and the absence of any effective intervention by the state government was projected as a clear instance of insensitivity. A serious public debate was sustained by the media,[20] farmers' organizations and the Left parties. In spite of the prolonged public debate on this issue there was no viable action. The only visible government response was one of denial. Suicides, if any, were attributed to personal, family or health reasons.

The following could be identified as the causes of the agricultural crisis, the brunt of which is borne by the small and marginal farmers, mostly belonging to the backward castes:[21]

1. failure to control the spread of low quality and spurious seeds, fertilizers and pesticides by fly-by-night companies;
2. near total collapse of agricultural extension services which would have helped the farmers with timely and necessary advice;
3. failure of the agricultural credit system, forcing farmers to go borrow from private moneylenders at high interest rates;
4. high rise in cost of agricultural inputs, especially power, impacting dry land cultivation in Telangana and Rayalaseema regions;
5. decline of marketing support for farm products leading to huge losses;
6. decline of irrigation facilities as a result of receding water tables in dry land areas and drought conditions in large parts of the state.

The most important line in this story, given the TDP's firm stand on power sector reforms, is the galvanizing of the agitation against the hike in power tariff in 2000. Immediately after the 1999 elections, the incumbent TDP government hiked power tariffs by claiming its victory as a popular approval of its reforms package, which included the power sector. An agitation in Hyderabad was quelled by the TDP resulting in the death of two protestors and injuries to 26. This was meant to be a signal to stop protests. The government's resolve was further made clear through its refusal to roll back the tariff hike.

Critical to the intensification of the public discourse on these issues was the *Praja Prasthana Padayatra* undertaken by Y. Rajasekhar Reddy (YSR) as the leader of the Opposition, during the summer of 2003. Covering 1,500 km on foot, YSR brought about a critical shift in state politics. First, he emerged as a charismatic leader of the party. Dressed in white shirt, *dhoti*, and a turban,[22] YSR could easily establish rapport with the simple and poor rural folks. His self-projection and image was in sharp contrast to that of Naidu clad in shirt and trousers and guarded by heavy security.

Second, through the *padayatra*, YSR enhanced his public image and sympathy, while activating the Congress cadre by boosting their morale. Third, the *padayatra* gave an opportunity to local groups and activists to present their problems to the leader of the Opposition, and by rallying the elements critical of the Naidu regime, YSR could bring grass roots issues pertaining to agriculture into the public gaze and sustain a critical debate on government priorities like IT, BT, and Formula One car racing and the subsequent neglect of issues of employment and livelihood. The *padayatra*, all along, provided for impromptu discussions on a one-to-one basis with YSR asking the village folk about their problems and consoling them. The *rachchabanda* or *adda*[23] participation reduced the gap between the political élite and the popular classes. It compares favorably in comparison with the nature of participation in the TDP's high profile *Janmabhumi*. *Janmabhumi* started promisingly but lost its voluntary participatory character and became a formality as the party cadre and local bureaucracy came to dominate it.

By undertaking a *Jaithra yatra* on the eve of elections held almost a year after his initial *padayatra*, YSR renewed his popular contact and pledge to ameliorate the condition of farmers, artisans, and other rural classes. Such *yatra*s were a famous mode of popular contact by NTR in state politics with all the dramatics and glamour associated with it. Naidu had a big disadvantage in this respect. Traveling in a helicopter and protected by a security cover, he could not counter the populist image gained by YSR. On the contrary, he ended up reinforcing the image of being hi-tech and IT savvy.

If *padayatra* was education for YSR (as he could learn about the problems at the grass roots), the *Jaithra yatra* was as a means to come back with promises based on feedback on the *padayatra*. These *yatra*s were seen as reminiscent of the ones NTR[24] was famous for and reminded the voters how far the TDP under Naidu had moved away from the founder's policies.[25] This had come to be a very important and effective strategy of communication for the Congress to establish rapport with the popular classes and for the latter to have informal dialog with the political élite.

Women and DWCRA

It is well known that women have been strong and reliable supporters of the TDP government. If NTR resorted to populist *adapaduchulu* (sisters) rhetoric to consolidate the TDP base among women, Naidu—following the poor performance of his party in the 1996 parliamentary elections—found in DWCRA[26] an instrument to strengthen women's vote for the TDP. He extended overwhelming patronage to the DWCRA and it became the major factor behind the TDP victory in the 1999 elections. This constituency continued to be relied upon for victory in the 2004 elections as well. It is precisely for this reason that the Congress had to make a special attempt to address women organized through the DWCRA program.

The Congress discourse with regard to the DWCRA groups can be described as one based on a dual strategy. First, the party tried to address the TDP's projection of women as a monolithic group in which the DWCRA was a major instrument by referring to their internal differences. Congress appealed to women who were dependent on agriculture and suffering due to TDP's policies. This strategy sought the demythification of women as an autonomous social group based on a coherent identity. Apart from this, Congress outbid the Naidu regime's liberal allocation of funds to the DWCRA. It promised loans to the DWCRA groups at 3 percent—far below the interest rate under the TDP government.

Congress-led Discourse Coalition

What is involved in the Congress' campaign, which following Hajer,[27] could be called the 'mobilization of bias.' By making suicides of farmers and weavers a signifier of a deep crisis and making TDP's policies responsible for this, a political judgment in the form of popular verdict was sought. The narrative contains multiple storylines that include Telangana's backwardness (justifying the demand for a separate state) drought and TDP's alleged surrender to the World Bank. The condensation of the discourse in the term 'crisis' is noteworthy. In other words, crisis had become a short-hand expression of what was rotten in the state. It is true that the crisis during the TDP regime is not as simple as stated by the adversaries, but simplification of the problem is a rhetorical device that is often used to convey clear political messages.

The concept of discourse coalition defined as an 'ensemble of a set of storylines, the actors that utter these storylines, and the practices that conform to these storylines, all organized around a discourse,'[28] is useful in this context. The electoral discourse pursued by the Congress and its allies is characterized by differences in terms of storylines or rathers, versions of story, narrative styles and rhetoric. What is common to them all is that the chief antagonist in the story is Naidu. These different versions of the same story begin, and in fact substantially revolve, around Naidu and his reforms. In all of them the narrative on agrarian crisis occupies major space. But in each of them the narrative assumes different twists and turns and the finale is explicitly different. As we shall see, despite these differences there is an underlying political necessity recognized by all of them that the TDP must be defeated and the premise on which that is possible is to accept the Congress as the leader of the alliance.

The acute perception of the crisis and an unprecedented sense of insecurity felt by a majority of social groups like farmers, weavers, unemployed youth and NGOs during TDP rule led to the swelling of the Congress ranks. Thus farmers and workers organizations, student and youth organizations,[29] and teachers and employees associations[30] overwhelmingly identified with the Congress coalition—sharing its narrative topography in spirit, if not in detail.

The TRS, the Left and other groups pursued storylines that are different from each other's and distinct from that of the Congress. Sometimes their narrative structures, and especially the closures, they aimed at were not compatible with each other. The TDP's counterstrategy was to highlight these differences and contradictions and draw the attention of the voters to how these differences, camouflaged by the alliance partners, could play havoc in state politics.

TRS AND TELANGANA DEMAND

To illustrate the above argument, let us look at the discursive persuasions of the TRS and the Left. The narrative on Telangana built by the TRS and the different discursive groups, even when they have serious differences with the former,[31] has an almost predictable story-line. It maintains that the Telangana region is backward while the coastal region has developed phenomenally at the cost of the Telangana region. Its backwardness is the logical outcome of the policy pursued by Andhra's political élite. This is evident in almost all sectors: irrigation, education, health, and so on. According to this narrative, the regional unevenness has increased during TDP rule.

In this narrative, there is silence on the Congress party's role. But it cannot be said that the Congress has been exonerated. What is significant here is not the factual veracity of the above construction but how, through the deployment of rhetorical devices and powerful imagery, it is sought to be imprinted on popular memory as an irrefutable 'fact'.[32] The backwardness of Telangana and innocence of its people become emotive devices with which mobilization is attempted. What is noticeable about the present discourse on Telangana, in contrast to that of the 1969 movement, is the deliberate underplaying of the anti-coastal Andhra sentiment.[33] The choice of target has been the TDP and its policies. Such a critique has a positive correlation, if not conformity, with the critique of the TDP by other parties in the coalition.

But there are also serious differences and curious convergences among the coalition partners. While the state unit of the Congress maintained a studied silence on the Telangana issue—giving credence to the TRS claim that it has reached an agreement on the issue with the AICC (All India Congress Committee)—the Left, especially the CPI(M) sticking to its linguistic nationality thesis, has taken a firm stand to oppose the demand. The Left instead proposed a special package for the development of the backward regions. There has been a strong convergence between the Left and the TDP on their stand on Telangana.[34] But the points of divergence and disagreement that occupied the larger discursive space overshadowed this common ground.

THE LEFT AND THE ECONOMIC REFORMS

The Left's discourse covers a wider policy space and situates the TDP regime in the macro-policy context. Thus the conditionalities of the

World Bank and the accumulation of external borrowings during Naidu's tenure became hotly-debated issues in this election. The Left, during its six years of separation from the TDP, virtually conducted a public trial on this issue through pamphlets, booklets, public meetings and agitations. Along with the Left parties, a number of citizens' initiatives, like the Forum Against Globalization (FAG), comprising activists, academics and journalists, have played a key role by bringing out booklets and informative pamphlets with analyses of the implications of liberalization to the vulnerable and marginalized communities.

It is true that Naidu's regime has seen a whopping increase in loans amounting to Rs 5,008.40 million. But the fact of the matter is that the external loans amounted to only Rs 1536.40 million of which the World Bank's share was Rs 892.20 million. The Bank has become a short-hand expression of the reforms face of the regime and that too with a stigma attached to it. The ground was thus prepared for the populist discourse. Not lagging behind the Left, the Congress also made it an election issue. Thus YSR asked in his road shows and public meetings: 'Where has this huge money gone? What did the farmers get? How many irrigation projects were built?' The answer was obviously in the negative. This rhetoric went down well—especially with the rural electorate.[35]

In the same refrain, the standard claim by Naidu that his government enhanced the stature of the state among international donors and brought huge funds for the development of the state has been clearly turned upside down. The Congress's response to this claim is simple: all the borrowings made in the name of development have gone into the pockets of *pacha chokkalu* (yellow shirts), the TDP cadre who, like 'bandicoots', have not only swallowed up the developmental funds but also the rice allotted by the Central government for the Food for Work Program (FFW). Related to these allegations is the major change in the TDP's organizational structure under Naidu's leadership. While NTR ran the party on the strength of his charisma and popularity, Naidu, lacking in both, sought to build his organizational base on managerial lines through an elaborate network based on distribution of spoils. Thus the organizational base of the TDP at different levels began to comprise people belonging to the class of contractors, builders and even speculators. This, needless to say, is in sharp contrast to the Congress, which relied on the traditional dominant caste élite and professional *pyravikaars* (power brokers). This contractor class, for whom politics is primarily a business proposition, developmental work and even the FFW program have become a 'feeding channel.'

The TDP's image in fact took a clear beating with the surfacing of scams involving pilfering of rice meant for the FFW program. The state government was allotted 0.55 million tons of rice estimated to be worth Rs 550 million by the center for drought relief work. YSR commented on the scam of rice 'recycling'[36] when he declared that 'while the farmers grew emaciated the TDP men became fatter by eating away government funds meant for development and drought relief like bandicoots.'[37] Thus, when the Congress and the Left raised the issue of 'disappearance' of the loans meant for development, the political message was loud and clear.

This put the TDP clearly on the defensive. The already present voter fatigue with Naidu was further intensified when he made it a point to paint a picture of *Swarnandhra* (Golden Andhra) through a series of live telecasts of the review of the performance of different governmental departments on the private TV channels.[38] The numbers that were reeled out during these reviews not only failed to make sense to the everyday life experiences of large sections of population but also increased their distrust of the TDP regime.

CLOSURES

Every story must have an ending, preferably an optimistic one. The party discourses suggest happy endings. In this sense the TDP is clearly at a disadvantage, for after being in power for nine long years its closure has nothing to offer except promises to continue its earlier policies with a different accent.

The Congress's discursive diagnosis suggests a series of solutions, the most significant of them being the promise of free power supply to agriculture. It may be recollected that the Congress had promised free power supply to the agriculture sector during the 1999 elections as well, but due to the low credibility of the party at that time it could not make any gains out of this promise. Subsequently, by keeping the debate on agriculture alive in the Assembly and other fora, the Congress gradually gained a pro-people image for itself.

Like in 1999, the TDP tried to neutralize the Opposition campaign with all the resources at its command. Naidu, through TV advertisements and in his speeches, sought to convey the message that the Congress's promise of free electricity was impractical and irresponsible. For, free electricity would only mean no electricity, as there would be nothing left to supply. Thus he warned, 'We will end up using transmission lines for drying clothes.'[39]

Electricity is crucial to farmers in the dry land areas in Telangana and Rayalaseema. There are an estimated 2.28 million pump sets in these two regions. The increase in power tariffs has been disastrous for the poor and marginal farmers. The power subsidy is justified on the ground that it would cost the state exchequer only Rs 30 million whereas the expenditure incurred on the publicity by the TDP government was estimated to be above Rs 35 million. This is the reason why this promise went well with the farmers and the poor households.[40]

The electoral discourse in the state has historically shown a high proclivity for populism, resulting from the sharp political polarization and intense electoral competition since the early 1980s. But none of the elections have ever seen any informed debate on the desirability and viability of populism as the basis of public policy. Thus the populist promise of free electricity treats the entire farming community as undifferentiated, whereas the strata that have suffered as a result of governmental negligence and apathy are the small and medium farmers.

The discourse on free electric power also raises certain other important issues. The most important one pertains to the propriety of the promise of free given the fact that the crisis of dry land farming is to a large extent due to the decline in groundwater levels, which in turn is a result of unchecked bore-well digging. Free power supply would only worsen the situation for the poor and marginal farmers and play ecological havoc, as there would be much more intensive exploitation of water by the big landowners. Perhaps a comprehensive debate is required on groundwater usage and regulation of cropping patterns in tune with the agrarian ecological conditions of different regions. However, these issues found no place in the electoral debate. TDP's argument against free electricity was also largely in the nature of a techno-economic objection based on its non-viability rather than on the invocation of a larger perspective.

The narrative of the Congress-led alliance was woven around the theme of evil and anti-people rule under which all sections of society had suffered. In the speeches of YSR and KCR, the TDP rule is referred to as *Dusta* and/or *Narakasura*[41] *palana*. There are interesting sub-plots or narratives in the storyline of the Congress which are basically meant to expand its social base. If the promise of free electricity to the agriculture sector was meant to stabilize its support base among the farmers, then the promises to weavers of regulation of yarn supply, creation of credit and marketing facilities, removing harassment[42] and creation of employment opportunities for the educated youth were meant to expand the Congress's base.[43] Thus, the social unrest and discontent against TDP rule was sought to be tuned by the Congress to forge a social base with the promise of specific packages for each of them.

The discourses of the TRS and the Left have predictable closures. Though they differ with the Congress in matters of detail and final goals, the immediate objective, which is the defeat of the TDP, weighed over them. Since the TRS has built up its political image on the demand of statehood to Telangana, its narrative of the major issues— crisis in dry land agriculture, suicide of farmers, unemployment and insecurity in the Telangana countryside—are argued to be due to neglect of the region by a regime dominated by the coastal Andhra élite. A solution to the problems of the Telangana region is considered to be possible only through statehood. The alliance with the Congress is premised on the recognition of the need of a Telangana state. Despite the multiple voices in the Congress on this issue, there was an attempt by the TRS to project acceptance of its demand by the Congress High Command.[44]

The parliamentary Left, which built up a sustained critique of the TDP's economic reform agenda, had their own issues against Naidu: the conditionalities of the World Bank, the 'surrender' of the TDP government to the Bank, the neglect of the agriculture sector leading to the agrarian crisis and farmers' suicides and unemployment. The review of the reform agenda and re-prioritization of sectors, interests and subsidies are the main demands of the Left. The discourse coalition forged by the Congress, as suggested earlier, combined these issues in its macro-narrative. The closure of the Left thus coincided with that of the Congress. The electoral alliance forged by the Congress therefore was also substantially a coalition of discourses, narrative and storylines, and closures.

CONCLUSION

The policy discourse in the 2004 elections in AP displayed a plebiscitary character. This was because of the dominance of the TDP by the persona of Naidu and political investment of the party in terms of its image, resources, choices and risks in him. For this reason the defeat of Naidu's regime, which gained an iconic status with regard to state-level economic reforms, has been interpreted as a 'vote against anti-people reforms.'[45] The discourse analysis of the election campaign of different parties clearly shows that except for the Left, no mainstream party made this election a contest on reforms.

The dominant discourses of the Congress and the TDP are framed in terms of crisis versus development. While the TDP's development centric discourse in view of the multiplier effects of demand for demonstration of proof hypothetically remained a closed option, the crisis-centric discourse of the Congress campaign displayed possibilities for new discursive coalitions and political alliances. Because of the discursive centrality of crisis, the concerns of the marginalized groups gained prominence in the electoral campaign of the Congress and its allies. Through a continuous focus on the suicides of the farmers and weavers to demonstrate the TDP's insensitivity to the people's anguish, the Congress sought to deepen the legitimacy crisis of the TDP regime.

Popular initiatives and grass-root organizations can play a crucial role in policy discourse. The more dynamic these organizations are the more pressure they exert on political parties to respond to their issues. If any party fails to do that it can only do so at its own risk and loss of legitimacy. We find such organizations playing a catalytic role in discursive terms in this election—against the TDP for its closed discourse and in favor of the Congress because of its discursive openness. The presence of these initiatives is evident in the three crucial issues of rural crisis, the Naxalite question and the Telangana demand that dominated the electoral debate this time. All the above issues have been shaped and presented as social questions pertaining to the marginalized sections and have been inclusively presented as part of the discourse of crisis.

Generally, reference to historical personalities and legacies is a strong element in the political discourses. In this respect the TDP clearly had a disadvantage. While the Congress invoked the legacy of Indira Gandhi and promised Indiramma *rajyam*[46] (Indira Gandhi's rule) the TDP could not draw on the popular image of NTR because of its move away from his legacy.

It is necessary to distinguish between the co-option of the subaltern concerns by the dominant structures for electoral gains and providing of spaces to marginalized groups so that they can participate in policy discourses. The 2004 election in AP has shown a certain degree of convergence of these two processes. The sustained activities of the subaltern organizations played a key role in making the crisis a central issue in the electoral discourse. Further they could be seen expanding the spaces in the policy discourse as these organizations were accorded visibility and promised a role in the policy making in the form of consultations and involvement in the deliberations.

The Congress's promise of involvement of the farmers' and weavers' organizations in the formulation of policies for agricultural and hand-loom sectors and the *Poura Spandana Vedika* with regard to the Naxalite issue are important indications of expansion of policy spaces for the marginalized and their concerns. (An earlier version of this chapter was published in the *Economic and Political Weekly*.)

NOTES

1. The interpretation that the election results are a rejection of the economic reforms and World Bank loans is put forward by the Left and not by the Congress.

2. While the Congress–Telangana Rastra Samithi–Left alliance gained 48.37 percent vote, the TDP–BJP alliance still retained 39.66 percent vote. Despite its poor performance, the TDP continues to be a formidable political force with a strong electoral support and organizational structure.

3. Just to cite one example of the wider impact and larger political and policy implications of the Congress victory in AP, the promise of free power to agriculture sector, which is considered to be the major factor for the defeat of the TDP, prompted the AIADMK government in Tamil Nadu to implement free power for agriculture sector. Similar demands are voiced in other states as well.

4. Des Gasper and Raymond Apthorpe, 'Introduction: Discourse Analysis and Policy Discourse,' in Raymond Apthorpe and Des Gasper (eds), *Arguing Development Policy: Frames and Discourses* (London: Frank Cass, 1996).

5. Stuart Hall, 'Foucault: Power, Knowledge and Discourse,' in Margaret Wetherell, Stephanie Taylor, and Simeon J Yates (eds), *Discourse Theory and Practice* (London: Sage Publications, 2001).

6. Ibid.

7. K. Srinivasulu and P. Sarangi, 'Political Realignments in Post-NTR Andhra Pradesh,' in *Economic and Political Weekly*, Vol. XXXIV, Nos 34–35 (1999).

8. K. Srinivasulu, 'Telugu Desam Party and the Restructuring of the Panchayat Raj System: Certain Considerations in Political Interpretations', in M. Kistaiah (ed.), *Administrative Reforms in a Developing Society* (New Delhi: Sterling, 1990).

9. Wendy K. Olsen, 'Eat Now and Pay Later: Impact of Rice Subsidy Scheme', in *Economic and Political Weekly*, Vol. XXIV, No. 28 (1989).

10. K. Srinivasulu, 'Party Competition and Strategies of Mobilisation: An Analysis of Social Coalitions in Andhra Pradesh,' in Paul Wallace and Ramashray Roy (eds), *India's 1999 Elections and 20th Century Politics* (New Delhi: Sage Publications, 2003).

11. K. Srinivasulu, 'Caste, Class and Social Articulation in Andhra Pradesh, India: Mapping Differential Regional Trajectories', Working Paper 179 (London: Overseas Developing Institute, 2002).

12. The Maha Jana Front (MJF) is a conglomerate of the backward caste and Dalit organizations with grass roots support base.

13. Jos Mooij, 'Hype, Skill and Class: A Comparative Analysis of the Politics of Reforms in Andhra Pradesh, India' (Mimeo, 2003).

14. This shift has serious political implications and import in view of the fact that the TDP had been a highly populist policy regime under NTR. A pro-development image highlights the departure by Naidu from NTR's legacy.

15. N. Chandrababu Naidu and Sevanti Nina, *Plain Speaking* (New Delhi: Viking, 2000).

16. The TRS won 1,043 MPTCs and 84 ZPTCs. See, Suri (2001).

17. The first SRC headed by Justice Fazal Ali recommended formation of the Hyderabad state comprising the Telugu speaking districts of the Telangana region, 'along with Bidar district, and the Munagala enclave in the Nalgonda district belonging to the Krishna district.' See, *Report of the States Reorganisation Commission*, 1955, p. 257.

18. The Congress party in its Shimla resolution in 2003, recognizing BJP success through its electoral alliances with anti-Congress parties, decided to forge its own electoral alliances against the BJP-led NDA.

19. *The Hindu* (Hyderabad edition), March 3, 2004.

20. The role of *Vaartha*, the Telugu daily is noteworthy in this regard.

21. Reports of Farmers' Commission of Experts on Agriculture in Andhra Pradesh and *Vyavasayaranga Parirakshana Aikya Porata Vedika*, Hyderabad, 2002.

22. The generation of politicians wearing *dhoti*s across the parties is fast disappearing. YSR is perhaps the only very well known *dhoti* clad politician in his age group in the state.

23. A Dalit activist insightfully characterized it as emphasizing the informality and personalized nature of the dialog.

24. YSR's *padayatra* and *Jaithra yatra* were reminiscent of what NTR did after he established the TDP in 1982. This is a channel Naidu could not afford to use because of a high security threat. While in the case of Naidu the distinction between the leader and the people was quite conspicuous, YSR could effectively blur such demarcations for the time being and create a space for the people to interact with him freely.

25. It is instructive to note that NTR continues to be remembered as a pro-poor CM for his Rs 2 kilo rice and housing for the poor schemes. Interviews by *TV 9*, a Telugu news channel, with the rural poor during the elections brought this out. Curiously enough there were instances when people compared YSR with NTR.

26. DWCRA is a Central government program meant for the development of rural women and children started in 1980. The Naidu regime hit upon and activated these groups since 1997 following its disappointing performance in the 1996 elections. The DWCRA almost assumed the dimension of a movement with its network of 0.37 milion groups in the state. The social significance of this program, apart from its stated objective of economic empowerment, lies in building up their self-confidence and making them visible in the public sphere.

27. Maarten A. Hajer, 'Discourse Coalitions and the Institutionalization of Practice: The Case of Acid Rain in Britain', in Frank Fisher and John Forrester (eds), *The Argumentative Turn in Political Analysis and Planning* (Durham and London: Duke University Press, 1993).

28. Ibid., p. 47.

29. There is wide spread disgruntlement among unemployed youth because of the ban on recruitment in the government sector. The only departments that continued to recruit were the police and to some extent school education as *vidya* volunteers thanks to the DFID funding under the District Primary Education Program (DPEP).

30. A general perception among employees was that if returned to power the TDP would would wind up the pension scheme and lower the retirement age apart from a vigorous implementation of the voluntary retirement policy.

31. The Telangana Aikya Vedika, a non-election front, has emerged as a major voice since the late 1990s striving to educate popular classes through a variety of activities. Telangana Jana Sabha of the CPI(ML) (People's War) and Telangana Jana Sanghatan of the CPI(ML) (Janashakti) and Telangana Maha Sabha are the CPI(ML) wings that actively advocate the Telangana issue. TRS is an electoral beneficiary of the groundwork done by these organizations.

32. There has been a proliferation of propaganda literature on Telangana in the form of booklets and pamphlets. Most of them have *dagapadda*, *vanchita* (meaning 'deceived', 'duped' emphasising the conspiracy factor in the Telangana backwardness). For instance, *Vanchita Telangana* by D. Sangameswar Rao (Hyderabad: Nymisha Publications, 2004).

33. The TRS leadership has repeatedly clarified this aspect. The argument thus runs that TRS is only for the state of Telangana and is not against the migrants who have come here for livelihood. It is this non-hostile approach that is the reason for the absence of pro-Andhra backlash, despite the attempts by certain interests during the elections.

34. The parliamentary Left's position on Telangana in terms of rigidity equals that of the TDP. It is an evidence of the sharpness of the differences that they not only surfaced into the open but also led to the fielding of TRS candidates in the constituencies allotted to the Left as part of the pre-electoral understanding.

35. Discussions with journalists, field notes, April 2004.

36. The process by which, the food grain allocated for the 'Food for Work' program instead of reaching the poor, gets back into the open market is called recycling. There was reported to be a widespread practice of such recycling and in most cases it is the local TDP men who benefited.

37. *Eenadu* (Hyderabad), April 19, 2004.

38. These programs tried to project an 'Andhra shining' image in correspondence with Vajpayee's 'India shining.'

39. *The Hindu* (Hyderabad edition), March 20, 2004.

40. Free power was also promised to single bulb households. 'Power bills have equaled the house rents' has become a common middle class refrain.

41. Interestingly it echoes the slogan of NTR in the 1994 Assembly elections that he would kill *Sarasura* (the demon of arrack) by putting his first signature on the prohibition order immediately after taking oath of office. YSR made a similar promise with regard to the free power order and kept it by signing the

order immediately after assuming the office of CM in the huge public presence in the Lal Bahadur Stadium in the capital city.

42. It is interesting to note that the *Janmabhumi*, considered to be highly prestigious by the Naidu regime, was seen as a major source of inconvenience and harassment by the subaltern ranks or the 'street-level bureaucracy' (Lipsky, 1980). The bureaucracy was kept on their toes through regular and close monitoring. The teachers were subjected to humiliation by being made to undertake 'all kinds of surveys.' Field notes.

43. The list of promises includes completion of irrigation projects, supply of quality seeds, subsidized fertilizer and pesticides, loans at a low interest rate, revival of extension services, the revival of Public Sector Enterprises, etc.

44. KCR sharing platform with Sonia Gandhi during the election campaign in Telangana districts is shown as suggestive of the Congress High Command's sympathy to the TRS' demand.

45. Interviews with Left parties' activists, June 2004.

46. Indiramma *rajyam* signified *garibi hatao*, land reforms and rural welfare. There are tensions between the legacy and populist styles of Indira Gandhi and NTR (for instance, NTR marginalized the land reforms question), the Congress was careful not to refer to them. In fact it may even be suggested contextually that the Congress could benefit from the Naidu regime's distance from NTR by repeatedly highlighting it.

CHAPTER 8

The New Alliance Made
the Difference in Bihar

SANJAY KUMAR

Bihar's three elections in the last two years witnessed very different results. First, in the 2004 Lok Sabha elections the Rashtriya Janata Dal (RJD) and its allies managed to register a convincing victory, though the people of Bihar negatively rated the performance of the government. Less than a year later, in February 2005, they lost in the Assembly elections. What changed between the 2004 Lok Sabha elections and February 2005 Assembly elections to occasion such different results? The third election in October 2005 resulted in the RJD's worst ever electoral defeat. A Janata Dal (United) (JD[U])-led coalition gov-ernment, with the Bharatiya Janata Party (BJP) as its ally, came to power with Nitish Kumar as the new chief minister.

The answer to the RJD's loss of power requires little explanation. The decline of the RJD and its allies during the February 2005 Assembly elections, and subsequently its defeat in the October 2005 Assembly elections can be credited to the poor performance of the RJD gov-ernment during the 15 years of its rule. If we look back, its performance was not rated positively even during the 2004 Lok Sabha elections, but still the RJD, with its allies, managed to register a massive victory. This is the real puzzle that needs to be examined. What explains the emphatic victory of the RJD and its allies in the Lok Sabha election? Did the caste arithmetic add up differently in that election as compared to the subsequent two Assembly elections? Did the alliance of the RJD with Ram Vilas Paswan contribute to the its Lok Sabha victory? Were the voting considerations in the Lok Sabha and Assembly elections different? Before examining the Lok Sabha victory of the RJD and its allies in 2004, it will be useful to review the two Assembly elections in 2005.

The results of the February 2005 Assembly election indicated the decline of the RJD, and the results of the October 2005 Assembly elections confirmed that it no longer controlled the state government. Not only was RJD defeated, but it also came in third with only 54 seats. JD(U) led with 88 Assembly seats and the BJP won 55. The RJD, which had won 75 seats barely eight months earlier during the February 2005 Assembly elections, won 21 fewer seats and polled only 23.5 percent votes. Clearly, there had been a decline in its support base. RJD's alliance with the Congress helped very little. Results clearly indicated disenchantment with the RJD and its supremo, Laloo Yadav.

A paradox however remains. How could the RJD and its allies register such an emphatic victory in the preceding Lok Sabha elections even with the poor rating of the state government's performance? This chapter also examines another paradox which goes beyond mere politics. It relates to the overall development of the state. Why has Bihar, which used to be one of the more prosperous states in India, become a poor and backward state?

It may be incorrect to say that Bihar's steep decline began during the last decade rather than much earlier. The decline relates to several factors, but the past decade is particularly important because state politics took a complete U-turn in the early 1990s and fully bloomed in the mid 1990s. The Mandal agitation[1] changed the whole course of politics as it enabled leaders belonging to the Other Backward Castes (OBC) to come to power—previously dominated largely by upper caste leaders. Dalits[2] and Muslims[3] also had increased expectations. These three categories—OBCs, Dalits, and Muslims—are poorer than the upper castes. With this change in the social profile of the leadership, there was hope that social and political change would bring about improvement in their economic situation as well. But did the new leadership in Bihar bring about the desired change? Change has occurred, but it has been negative rather than positive. The poor have become poorer, and Bihar has plunged to the bottom of the scale of economic development.

During the 1990 Assembly elections, the Janata Dal (JD) (now RJD) contested the Assembly elections in alliance with the Communist Party of India (CPI) and the Communist Party of India (Marxist) (CPI[M]). Though the JD won only 122 of the 276 Assembly seats contested and fell short of the majority, it managed to form the government in alliance with the CPI and the CPI(M). The split in the Janata Dal before the 1995 Assembly elections led to the formation of the Samata Party, with Nitish Kumar as its leader. JD again contested the 1995 Assembly elections in alliance with two Left parties. Anticipated competition from the three opposition parties—Congress, Samata Party, and the BJP—fell far short of expectations. JD not only managed to win the elections, but also won a majority on its own. Contesting only 265 Assembly seats, the Janata Dal won 167 seats in a house of 324. From 25.6 percent votes in 1990, it won 28 percent votes in 1995. The Samata Party, which was seen as a possible alternative to JD, lost badly with only seven of the 310 Assembly seats it contested and polled only 7.1 percent votes. The BJP won 41 seats while the Congress won 29 Assembly seats. The 1995 Assembly elections should be considered as the high mark for the JD.

It became more or less clear that a divided opposition could hardly defeat the JD. Realising this, the BJP and the Samata Party entered into an alliance to contest the 1998 Lok Sabha elections. In addition to the alliance, the split in the JD also gave Laloo Yadav a jolt. Prior to the 1998 Lok Sabha elections, RJD under the leadership of Laloo Yadav split from the JD, which remained as a party under the leadership of Sharad Yadav. The Lok Sabha election of 1998 was the first one in which the RJD contested with its new lantern symbol. The BJP–Samata alliance managed to put up a strong contest and the RJD suffered some setbacks during this election. The RJD managed to win only 17 of the 38 Lok Sabha seats it contested.

The merger of JD and the Samata Party into Janata Dal (United) before the 1999 Lok Sabha elections led to the emergence of a formidable opposition to the RJD. The BJP–JD(U) alliance registered an impressive victory, winning 41 of the 54 Lok Sabha seats during that election. But the story of the success of the BJP–JD(U) alliance could not be repeated in the Assembly elections in 2000 when just before the Assembly elections, the JD(U) again split into JD(U) and

Samata Party. Though the BJP–Samata combine and JD(U) came together for the 2000 Assembly elections, they also contested against each other in various Assembly constituencies. The RJD, contesting the 2000 Assembly elections in alliance with the CPI and the Marxist Coordination Committee (MCC), won 124 Assembly seats and formed the third government in succession in alliance with the Congress party.

The puzzle remained. Before every election, analysts firmly believe Laloo Prasad will meet his waterloo because of the lack of development in the state and the unhappiness of the people with the ruling party. But after each election, the party emerges victorious. How does the RJD manage to get the support of voters who seem disillusioned with the state government? Are there no alternative political choices, or are people simply not bothered about economic development in the state? If development is not the key word for politics in Bihar, what mobilizes the people in support of the ruling RJD? Alternative explanations attribute the RJD election victories to booth capturing and other electoral malpractices, or a clever act of election management. Like elections in most states, elections in Bihar do witness some electoral malpractices, but this cannot be the sole reason for RJD's success. Survey data is used in this chapter to provide more detailed explanation.

THE 2004 LOK SABHA ELECTIONS:
RESULT AND SIGNIFICANCE

The result of the 2004 Lok Sabha elections in Bihar is significant mainly due to two factors. First, it re-established the political dominance of the RJD in the state. Second, it played a very important role in the formation of a non-NDA government at the centre, which had seemed a distant dream before the Lok Sabha elections. Winning 22 of the 26 seats contested, the RJD turned out to be the biggest coalition partner in the Congress-led UPA government at the center. Moreover, the Congress won three of the four Lok Sabha seats it contested in Bihar. Had these parties not entered into an alliance, both the Congress and the RJD would not have been so successful. It is important to note here that the Dravida Munnetra Kazhagam (DMK), with 16 Lok Sabha seats, is the third biggest coalition partner in the new national alliance, which formed the government after the election. The BJP–JD(U) alliance managed to win only 11 Lok Sabha seats, a loss of 19 compared to the 1999 Lok Sabha elections and 6 percent fewer votes.

Bihar has a history of playing an important role in most of the alternative political transformations that have taken place at the national level. Going back to the formation of the Janata government in 1977, Bihar played an important role, when the Janata Party won all the 54 Lok Sabha seats. Again during the 1989 Lok Sabha election which witnessed the formation of another non-Congress government under Prime Minister V.P. Singh, large numbers of non-Congress MPs were elected from Bihar while the Congress managed to win only four Lok Sabha seats. A few years later, the 1996 Lok Sabha election resulted in the formation of another non-Congress government led by H.D. Deve Gowda, and Bihar played an important role in electing many non-BJP MPs. Figure for SMT for years 1996 and 1998, JD(U) for 1999 and 2004 JD for 1996, and RJD for 1998, 1999, and 2004 (see Table 8.1).

Table 8.1
Bihar: Results of Lok Sabha elections, 1996–2004

Year	Total Seats	Turnout (%)	INC C/W	%	BJP C/W	%	JD(U)/ SMT C/W	%	JD/ RJD C/W	%	Others C/W	%
1996	54	59.5	54/2	13.0	32/18	20.5	20/6	14.5	44/22	31.9	1,298/6	20.1
1998	54	64.6	21/5	7.3	32/20	24.0	21/10	15.7	38/17	26.6	357/2	26.4
1999	54	61.5	16/4	8.8	29/23	23.0	23/18	20.8	36/7	28.3	393/2	19.1
2004	40	58.0	4/3	4.5	16/5	14.6	24/6	22.7	26/22	30.7	380/4	27.5

Source: CSDS Data Unit.
Notes: C = Seats contested, W = Seats won.

A similar drama had been enacted during the 2004 Lok Sabha election, but with minor differences. Previously, Bihar voters opposed the Congress party. But during the 1996 and 2004 Lok Sabha elections, NDA–JD(UF) came to be seen as the enemy by the voters of Bihar. That is to say that the actors had changed, from the Congress earlier to the NDA in recent years. The RJD–Congress alliance registered an impressive victory in Bihar. As Table 8.2 shows, of the total of 40 Lok Sabha seats, the alliance won 29 seats and polled 46.6 percent votes, 9.6 percent more than the votes polled by the BJP allies in the state. Not only did the RJD alliance perform much better than the BJP alliance, but individually it was the RJD which performed much better compared to all other political parties in the state. Of the 26 Lok Sabha seats it contested, the RJD managed to win 22 and polled 30.7 percent votes, while its alliance partner, the Lok Jan Shakti Party (LJNSP) won only four of the eight Lok Sabha seats contested and polled 8.2 percent votes. The Congress won three of the four seats contested and polled 4.5 percent votes. In terms of the percentage of votes polled per seat contested by the three alliance partners, the RJD polled 48.6 percent, the Congress 46.3 percent, and LJNSP 42.3 percent.

Both of the NDA alliance partners suffered losses in terms of votes polled and seats won as compared to the 1999 Lok Sabha elections. Among the two alliance partners, it is the JD(U), which suffered a greater loss. While the BJP suffered a loss of seven seats and polled 2.3 percent votes less than the 1999 Lok Sabha election, the JD(U) suffered a loss of 12 seats and 6.23 percent votes. In terms of votes polled per seat contested, the BJP polled 37 percent and JD(U) polled 35.5 percent votes.

Table 8.2

Lok Sabha elections, 2004: Seats won and votes polled by alliances and parties

Alliances	Parties	Seats Contested	Seats Won	% of Votes
BJP and allies	Total	40	11	37.0
	BJP	17	5	14.2
	JD(U)	23	6	22.9
Congress and allies	Total	40	29	46.6
	Congress	4	3	4.8
	RJD	26	22	29.8
	LJNSP	8	4	8.7
	NCP	1	0	1.0
	CPI(M)	1	0	0.8
Left	Total	5	0	1.1
	CPI	5	0	1.1

Source: CSDS Data Unit.

THE REGIONAL PATTERNS

The results of the Lok Sabha elections of 2004 are clearly a setback for both the BJP and the JD(U). Compared to the 1999 Lok Sabha elections, these two political parties lost both in terms of number of seats and percentage of votes polled. The net gainer had been the RJD and its alliance partners. But the question is: did BJP and its allies suffer equally in all regions of the state or has there been gains for the NDA alliance in some regions, while they lost in some other.

For a meaningful regional analysis of the results, I have divided Bihar into five different regions: Tirhut, Mithila, Magadh, East, and Bhojpur (see Table 8.3). While Tirhut and Magadh are the two biggest regional divisions accounting for 12 and 10 Lok Sabha seats respectively, the other three regions, Mithila (seven Lok Sabha seats), East (seven Lok Sabha seats), and Bhojpur (four Lok Sabha seats) are relatively small.[4] The results from different regions indicate that in terms of the votes polled, both the BJP and the JD(U) suffered a loss in all the regions. There is no region where any of these two political parties could improve upon its performance in the 1999 Lok Sabha election. In terms of the number of seats won, the BJP did manage to improve its performance in the East, the region with a high concentration of Muslim population, where it won four of the seven Lok Sabha constituencies compared to two in 1999. It is also in this region that the BJP polled its highest percentage of votes (26.96 percent), nearly twice the votes polled by the party throughout the state.

Though the JD(U) won three of the six Lok Sabha seats won by the party from Tirhut region during the 2004 Lok Sabha elections, it is in this region that the party suffered a loss of 11.4 percent votes, the biggest loss among all the five regions. The party had won six Lok Sabha seats from this region during the 1999 Lok Sabha elections and had polled nearly 34 percent votes. In the Mithila region also, the party suffered a loss of 9.31 percent votes. Of the seven Lok Sabha seats, the JD(U) won five during the 1999 Lok Sabha elections, but in 2004 it drew a blank. The party suffered in the other three regions as well.

Table 8.3

Region-wise analysis of Lok Sabha 2004 election results

Regions	Total Seats	Turn Out 2004	Ch from 1999	Congress				BJP				JD(U)				RJD				Left				Others			
				Won 2004	Ch 1999	Vt(%) 2004	Ch 1999	Won 2004	Ch 1999	Vt(%) 2004	Ch 1999	Won 2004	Ch 1999	Vt(%) 2004	Ch 1999	Won 2004	Ch 1999	Vt(%) 2004	Ch 1999	Won 2004	Ch 1999	Vt(%) 2004	Ch 1999	Won 2004	Ch 1999	Vt(%) 2004	Ch 1999
Tirhut	12	55.24	-12.32	0	0	0.00	-3.46	0	-3	10.55	-2.04	3	-3	22.58	-11.42	8	5	38.24	-2.69	0	0	0.60	0.33	1	1	28.02	19.27
Mithila	7	58.03	-8.72	1	1	6.44	1.15	0	-2	10.31	-4.10	0	-5	28.24	-9.31	4	4	29.34	-6.86	0	0	2.13	0.15	2	2	23.54	18.97
Magadh	10	61.36	-2.49	1	-1	6.82	-2.01	0	-3	14.22	-1.79	2	-3	27.09	-3.76	6	6	32.17	2.17	0	0	2.08	-4.84	1	1	17.63	10.23
East	7	58.45	-3.26	0	0	0.00	-3.05	4	2	26.96	-1.15	0	-2	11.75	0.42	3	2	21.54	0.45	0	-1	4.52	-4.58	0	-1	35.23	7.91
Bhojpur	4	55.45	-5.66	1	1	14.53	14.53	1	-1	12.71	-5.74	1	1	15.79	-2.29	1	-1	23.69	-16.47	0	0	0.41	-2.13	0	0	32.87	12.10
Total	40	57.94	-6.85	3	1	4.49	-0.28	5	-7	14.58	-2.34	6	-12	22.33	-6.23	22	16	30.67	-3.25	0	-1	1.94	-2.02	4	3	25.98	14.11

Source: CSDS Data Unit.

In terms of number of seats, except for the Bhojpur region where they suffered a loss of one Lok Sabha seat, the RJD gained in all the regions of the state. One would expect that the party might have increased its support base throughout the state, but the results indicate that this is not what seems to have happened. Despite a gain of 16 Lok Sabha seats (increasing its tally from six seats during the 1999 Lok Sabha to 22 seats in 2004), the RJD suffered a loss in terms of votes polled in three of the five regions. The increase in votes polled by the party had been only 2.17 percent in Magadh and marginal 0.42 percent, in the East. Clearly the victory of the RJD is credited more to its alliance with other parties than to its improved performance. The alliance of the RJD with the LJNSP and the Congress not only prevented the splitting of the anti-NDA vote, but also ensured transferability of votes from one party to the other. This contributed enormously to the victory of the RJD and its allies.

WHAT LED TO THIS MASSIVE VICTORY FOR THE CONGRESS AND ITS ALLIES?

There is some unease about the results in Bihar. The RJD had been in power in the state for nearly 15 years. The party had won three successive Assembly elections—in 1990, 1995, and 2000. But the party had not performed well during the Lok Sabha elections held during this period. If one looks at the results of the last three Lok Sabha elections held in 1996, 1998, and 1999, one can see the deteriorating performance of the RJD. It is believed that people were generally unhappy with the functioning of the state government and it seemed this election might seal the fate of the RJD for some time. But to the contrary, the RJD with its alliance partners, Congress, LJNSP, Nationalist Congress Party (NCP), and the Marxist Communist Party (CPI[M]) registered an impressive victory in the state. Does this indicate that people are not unhappy with the performance of the state government? Can one assume that this is a positive vote in favor of the state government and the ruling party, the RJD? One cannot have a definite answer, but certainly the findings of the survey (which will be discussed later) suggest that people are not happy with the general performance of the state government. Then what contributes to the victory for the RJD and its alliance in successive elections?

It is the alliance arithmetic which seems to have worked in favor of the RJD and its allies. There had been a significant change in electoral alliances in Bihar between the 1999 and 2004 Lok Sabha elections. In 1999, Ram Vilas Paswan was elected as a JD(U) candidate in the Lok Sabha, but a few months after the formation of the government, he resigned from the government and formed his own party, the LJNSP. Just before the 2004 Lok Sabha elections he entered into an alliance with the RJD and contested eight of the 40 Lok Sabha seats in Bihar. It is generally believed that the success story of RJD lies in the pre-poll alliance they formed.

It is true that the alliance with Paswan's LJNSP brought some new voters into the RJD fold and both parties benefited from this move. It is equally important to note that more than the RJD, it is the LJNSP that benefited. If there had been no alliance between these two parties, both would have suffered electoral losses. Even LJNSP leader Ram Vilas Paswan might have faced a very tough contest. The findings of the NES 2004 survey confirmed that voters of both the alliance partners managed to transfer their votes to each other. During the survey, the voters were asked which party they would have voted for if there were no alliance. Among those who identified themselves as RJD supporters, 89 percent, and among those identified themselves as LJNSP supporters, 88 percent confirmed voting for the RJD alliance. Therefore, the alliance did contribute to the success of the Congress alliance in Bihar to a great extent.

HOW DID THE NEW ALLIANCE MAKE ALL THE DIFFERENCE IN THE ELECTORAL OUTCOME?

The new alliance brought a new social coalition of voters from different social strata. The RJD had a strong presence among the Yadavs and Muslims, according to surveys conducted about support during the last decade. Similarly, Ram Vilas Paswan seems to enjoy support among the Dalits, and especially among the voters belonging to Dushad community. There is no official source about the population figures for people belonging to different castes, but the NES survey estimates that while in undivided Bihar the Yadavs were nearly 12 percent of the population, in divided Bihar their proportion in the population has gone up to to nearly 14 percent. Similarly, the Muslims constitute 16.5 percent of the population and are the deciding factor in a large number of constituencies. Though Dushads are numerically not very large, yet they are about 5 percent of the total population. The three castes together are nearly one-third of the total population of Bihar. Such an unbeatable social formation certainly had an electoral strength capable of upsetting the calculations of any political opposition. The electoral success of the RJD–Congress alliance in Bihar during the 2004 Lok Sabha elections is a reflection of this arithmetic.

LALOO'S CHARISMA GAVE ADDITIONAL ADVANTAGE TO THE RJD

The results indicate that the Congress alliance stood way ahead of the NDA alliance in Bihar both in terms of the number of seats won and percentage of votes polled. There are indications that the new electoral alliance did magic for the ruling RJD, but there is something more, which contributed to the success of the RJD and its alliance partners. In fact, the results of the 2004 Lok Sabha elections indicate that besides the alliance, it is the charisma of the RJD leader Laloo Prasad Yadav, which also contributed to the landslide victory of the alliance.

It may not be correct to say that the people of Bihar hardly care about development. In fact, the government has been negatively evaluated on various developmental issues. Nonetheless, RJD leader Laloo Yadav still remains popular among some sections of voters; enough to give RJD a winnable advantage. Though Laloo does not carry the same image among voters belonging to all social communities, he still holds a positive image among voters belonging to the Dalit and backward communities. The general belief is that no government can ensure food for the poor people, but Laloo at least provided dignity to them, and it is during his tenure that the poor could live with a sense of pride. This social empowerment of the poor and the backward seems to be having an over-riding impact on the ills associated with underdevelopment which plagues the state.

The findings of the NES 2004 survey indicate that, as on various other issues, the opinion of the people about Laloo Prasad is also divided. Large numbers of people from socially marginalized segments, especially the Dalits and OBCs, consider him as the messiah of the poor despite his non-performance. To the contrary, only a few among the upper castes show a similar faith in Laloo. The backward castes constitute a large section of the population in Bihar. In spite of numerical minority, the upper castes have had a firm control over political power in Bihar for a long time. When Laloo Yadav became the chief minister, those belonging to the OBCs saw new hope for themselves. Even though nothing much has changed for them, a large number among them continue to see Laloo as the leader who will get them justice. This opinion is more prevalent among those belonging to the Yadav caste.

What adds to the strength of the RJD is the absence of any formidable leader who could challenge Laloo Prasad. Being in power for so long, Laloo has emerged not only as a leader of the RJD, but as a strong OBC leader in the state. It is true that not all OBC voters accept him as the leader of the OBCs but he still remains the tallest leader among them. The leadership of the Congress still remains in the hand of upper-caste leaders. The BJP is in alliance with the JD(U) in the state, but the party is also plagued by the problem of a mainly upper-caste leadership. Though the JD(U) (earlier Samata Party) portrayed Nitish Kumar, a member of a backward caste, as the leader of the party, different warring groups within the party did not allow undisputed OBC leadership to emerge. On the other hand, Laloo Prasad has remained the uncontested leader of the RJD for more than 15 years, as shown in Tables 8.4 and 8.5. No doubt, a majority of the people, especially those belonging to the OBCs, see Laloo as the undeniable leader.

Table 8.4
Community-wise opinion of Laloo Prasad Yadav

Caste/ Community	There is no Alternative for Laloo Yadav in Bihar			Only Laloo Yadav Can Give Justice to the Poor and the Backward			Laloo Yadav is the Messiah of the Poor		
	Agree	Disagree	No Opinion	Agree	Disagree	No Opinion	Agree	Disagree	No Opinion
All voters	36	45	19	34	53	13	45	49	6
Yadavs	60	22	18	63	29	8	70	26	4
Other OBC	32	41	27	32	49	19	45	46	9
Kurmi+Koeri	29	56	15	22	66	12	30	69	1
Upper castes	32	58	10	18	73	9	25	71	4
Dalits	31	37	32	41	36	23	51	41	8
Muslims	38	47	15	40	52	8	66	27	6

Source: NES 2004, CSDS Data Unit. All figures are in percent.

Table 8.5
Class-wise opinion of Laloo Prasad Yadav

Economic Class	There is no Alternative for Laloo Yadav in Bihar			Only Laloo Yadav Can Give Justice to the Poor and the Backward			Laloo Yadav is the Messiah of the Poor		
	Agree	Disagree	No Opinion	Agree	Disagree	No Opinion	Agree	Disagree	No Opinion
Very poor	34	37	29	33	46	21	49	41	10
Poor	38	43	19	36	53	11	47	49	4
Middle class	31	58	11	35	57	8	39	56	5
Rich	40	59	1	29	68	3	35	65	0

Source: NES 2004, CSDS Data Unit. All figures are in percent.

DOUBTS ABOUT THE PERFORMANCE
OF THE STATE GOVERNMENT

While the victory of the RJD and its alliance in 2004 is an indicator of popular public support for the party, it would be too simplistic to conclude that everything is working well in the state. The overall performance of the state government is more or less satisfactory, but people have shown a great deal of dissatisfaction about various civic amenities. There seems to be no improvement of any sort during the last four years. As can be seen from Table 8.6, people feel that there has been a deterioration in the condition of hospitals and other medical facilities, while only 10 percent think otherwise. They expressed similar opinions on the issue of electricity and condition of roads. Unemployment has increased over the years and the situation of law and order has deteriorated. People also hold a similar negative opinion on the issue of supply of drinking water, though the proportion may be a little less.

Table 8.6
State of civic amenities and social conditions

Issues	Deteriorated	Improved	No Change	No Opinion
Medical facilities	55	10	27	8
Electricity supply	55	10	23	12
Condition of roads	55	23	18	4
Employment opportunities	43	23	18	16
Law and order	42	24	24	10
Supply of drinking water	33	22	26	19
Hindu–Muslim brotherhood	20	44	20	16

Source: NES 2004, CSDS Data Unit. All figures are in percent.

What explains the victory of the RJD alliance is that voters in Bihar were hardly concerned about economic development. With increasing poverty and immense hardships faced by the people, one would have expected the people to vote against the RJD alliance. But that this does not seem to have happened in the 2004 Lok Sabha elections. During the survey, voters were asked to express their opinion about changes in their economic condition during the past five years. Opinion seems to be greatly divided on this question. There were 48 percent who believed that there had been no change in their economic condition during the last five years. The rest were equally divided; while half of them believed that their economic condition has improved, a similar proportion mentioned that it had deteriorated. The findings of the survey as seen in Tables 8.7 and 8.8, indicate that voting preferences were hardly influenced by their general economic condition. Among those who believed that their economic condition had either worsened, or that there had been no significant change during the last five years, a large number voted for the RJD alliance, while among those who felt that their economic condition had improved, a majority voted for the BJP and its allies. For the rich and the middle class, development might mean only economic gains, but the poor in the state seemed to have either ignored the notion of development or have interpreted it in their own way. But whatever may be the case, the findings of the survey indicate that economic development was hardly a concern among large numbers of voters in Bihar.

Table 8.7

Changes in economic condition during 1999–2004

| Economic Condition | Voted for | | | |
	Congress & Allies	BJP & Allies	Other Parties	Proportion in Sample
Worsened	47	29	24	25
Improved	36	51	13	25
No change	46	34	20	48

Source: NES 2004, CSDS Data Unit. All figures are in percent.

Table 8.8

Level of satisfaction with present economic conditions

| Level of Satisfaction | Voted for | | | |
	Congress & Allies	BJP & Allies	Other Parties	Proportion in Sample
Fully satisfied	41	49	10	18
Somewhat satisfied	42	37	21	47
Somewhat dissatisfied	32	44	24	11
Fully dissatisfied	53	26	21	22

Source: NES 2004, CSDS Data Unit. All figures are in percent.

People have also raised questions about the performance of the members of Parliament (MPs as shown in Table 8.9). The level of dissatisfaction with the performance of the MPs is generally high. Nearly 34 percent of the people are completely dissatisfied with their MPs, while only 20 percent were fully satisfied with the performance of their representatives in Parliament. But there is also variation in terms of MPs belonging to different political parties. The level of dissatisfaction of the people with the MPs belonging to the RJD was much higher compared to that of MPs of other political parties, such as the BJP and the JD(U).

Table 8.9
Level of satisfaction with MPs of different political parties

Party	Fully Satisfied	Somewhat Satisfied	Somewhat Dissatisfied	Fully Dissatisfied	No Opinion
All	20	33	5	34	8
BJP	16	37	5	32	10
JD(U)	27	31	5	29	8
RJD	11	31	7	46	5

Source: NES 2004, CSDS Data Unit. All figures are in percent.

Hopes Still Alive

From the discussion in the previous sections, it is very clear that though the RJD and its allies registered a big victory in 2004, in no way is this any reflection of the performance of the general functioning of the state government. There has been deterioration in the services of a large number of civic amenities and large numbers of people were dissatisfied with their economic condition. Nonetheless, nearly one-third of the people believed that their economic condition would improve in the coming years, while only 10 percent thought that their economic condition would deteriorate. A large number of people did not express their views on this issue. The RJD alliance may have had high expectations for this group (see Table 8.10).

Similarly, the figures in Table 8.11 make it clear that a majority of the people think that there has been some development in the country, and that the security situation of the country has also improved. It is not surprising that there are large numbers of people who think that the image of the country in the world has also improved. People tend to believe that though there is corruption, there is better control on it in the country today. Findings of the survey also suggest that during the last five years, there has been an improvement in the Hindu–Muslim relationship in Bihar. These findings suggest that though there has been very little development in the state, people still believe that there would be some development in the coming years.

Table 8.10
Future expectations about economic conditions

	Voted for			
	Congress–RJD	BJP–JD(U)	Other Parties	Proportion in Sample
Improved	34	51	15	32
Remain same	43	39	18	14
Worsened	48	25	26	10
No opinion	51	29	20	44

Source: NES 2004, CSDS Data Unit. All figures are in percent.

Table 8.11
Opinion regarding the country's image

	Improved	Deteriorated	No Change	No Opinion
Development of the country	51	14	16	19
Security of the country	44	19	18	19
Image of India in the world	44	19	18	19
Control on corruption	32	28	23	17

Source: NES 2004, CSDS Data Unit. All figures are in percent.

SOCIAL PATTERNS OF VOTING

The results of the 2004 Lok Sabha elections indicate that the BJP and its allies, the JD(U), suffered a major setback, while the RJD and its allies made most of the gains. But despite a major defeat, the BJP remained popular among urban voters (see Table 8.12). While the lead for the BJP alliance over the RJD alliance in the cities was very narrow, the RJD alliance remained very popular among the rural voters. What added to the advantage of the RJD was that only about 25 percent of the voters live in towns and cities, while a vast majority live in villages. Being popular only among the urban voters was good enough for the BJP alliance.

Table 8.12
Popularity of the various political alliances

Locality	Congress & Allies	BJP & Allies	Others	N
Rural	45	36	19	840
Urban	44	45	11	132

Source: NES 2004, CSDS Data Unit. All figures are in percent.
Note: *N* = Number of samples.

What added to the success of the RJD alliance were the sharply polarized voters belonging to the Yadav and Muslim community, who also are numerically very large. The findings of the NES 2004 survey, as shown in Table 8.13, indicate that despite the poor performance of the BJP and its alliance partner, the JD(U), the alliance had not lost its upper caste support. Due to its alliance with the Congress, the RJD managed to get some upper caste votes, though essentially upper caste voters stood firmly behind the BJP–JD(U) alliance. The OBC voters seemed to be divided in their support for the two alliances. While a majority of the Yadavs voted for the RJD allies, one could see a similar kind of support for the BJP–JD(U) alliance among the other two dominant OBCs—the Kurmis and the Koeris. Besides these three dominant OBC voters, the other OBCs seemed to be more or less equally divided between the two alliances. One would have expected the Dalits to have voted for the RJD alliance in large numbers, but in reality they seemed to be only marginally in their favor.

Table 8.13
Yadav and Muslim support for RJD alliance

Caste	Congress+	BJP+	Others	N
Upper caste	25	64	11	214
Yadav	77	16	7	126
Kurmi and Koeri	19	65	17	97
Other OBC	39	36	25	226
Schedule Castes	44	28	28	124
Muslim	79	9	12	150

Source: NES 2004, CSDS Data Unit. All figures are in percent.
Note: *N* = Number of samples.

Economic class provided another category for distinction between the two major competitors in 2004. The Congress alliance remained the popular choice of voters belonging to all economic classes, but support for the BJP alliance was much higher among the rich voters. Table 8.14 shows that while 31 percent among the very poor voted for the BJP alliance, among the middle class (read rich) voters, 43 percent voted for them.

Table 8.14

Voting pattern by economic class

Economic Class	Congress–RJD	BJP–JD(U)	Others	N
Very poor	48	31	22	349
Poor	42	40	17	390
Lower middle	43	40	17	123
Middle	49	43	8	110

Source: NES 2004, CSDS Data Unit. All figures are in percent.
Note: N = Number of samples.

Similar voting patterns could be seen among voters belonging to different educational levels (see Table 8.15). Among large numbers of illiterate voters, the Congress alliance remained the popular choice, but among the educated voters, support for the BJP alliance was higher than for the Congress alliance.

Table 8.15

Voting pattern by level of education

Level of Education	Congress–RJD	BJP–JD(U)	Others	N
Non-literate	49	29	23	344
Up to primary	43	36	21	146
Up to matric	42	42	16	281
College and above	45	46	9	195

Source: NES 2004, CSDS Data Unit. All figures are in percent.
Note: N = Number of samples.

There is very little variation in voting patterns among voters belonging to different age groups (see Table 8.16). But the survey seems to suggest that the young in Bihar voted more in favor of the Congress alliance (read RJD). The support for the Congress alliance is higher compared to the support for the BJP alliance among voters of all age groups, but voters between in the age group of 36–55 years seem to be somewhat in favour of the BJP alliance.

Table 8.16
Voting pattern by age

Age Group (in years)	Congress–RJD	BJP–JD(U)	Others	N
Up to 25	48	36	16	196
26–35	47	36	18	314
36–45	43	41	16	207
46–55	41	40	20	138
Above 55	45	34	22	119

Source: NES 2004, CSDS Data Unit. All figures are in percent.
Note: N = Number of samples.

CONCLUSION

The first four decades of politics in Bihar have been marked by the dominance of the Congress party, led mainly by Brahmin leaders. The 1990s not only marked the decline of the Congress, but also the diminishing hold of the upper castes in the politics of Bihar. With the implementation of a new reservation policy for Central government jobs for members of the OBCs, there has been a radical shift and upsurge of OBCs in the politics of the state. The new emerging social forces were mobilized under the banner of a political party, the JD. The upper caste voters, who opposed the new reservation policy, were mobilized by the BJP. In this competition, the support base of the Congress was eroded since both the upper caste and the OBC voters deserted the Congress and aligned with other political forces.

The experiment of mobilizing all the OBCs under one banner did not last long. Cracks soon appeared which ultimately led to the formation of the Samata Party before the 1995 Assembly elections, with its support base predominantly from two OBC castes, the Kurmis and the Koeris. The triangular contest of the 1995 Assembly elections did not change the politics of the state and the JD remained the dominant force. It was clear that the upper castes alone could not provide any challenge to the dominant political position which the JD enjoyed under the leadership of Laloo Yadav. This resulted in a re-alignment of the social forces in which the Kurmis and the Koeris tried to form a social coalition with upper caste voters. This resulted in the two parties—the Samata/JD(U) and the BJP—forming an alliance in 1996 to oppose the JD under the leadership of Laloo Yadav.

What started as a struggle for social and political dominance in the state between the upper caste and the OBCs very soon shifted to the struggle among the dominant OBC castes, namely the Yadavs, the Kurmis, and the Koeris. This struggle for political dominance among the backward castes had at least two major consequences. First, this struggle led to the marginalization of the upper castes in the politics of Bihar. The upper castes still identified themselves with the BJP and looked to it to challenge the ruling JD/RJD in Bihar. Second, in the struggle for political and social dominance among the backward castes, the Dalits and Muslims remained the biggest sufferers. While there has been very little development for them, they still lived on the hopes and promises made by the ruling RJD in the state.

This struggle for political dominance resulted in total neglect of the issue of development in Bihar. There has hardly been any development in the state during the 15 years of RJD rule. Realizing that the issue of development could result in the defeat of the ruling party, Laloo successfully diverted the attention of the voters from development to *izzat* (respect) and security. While he has been able to play his *izzat* card successfully among the Dalits and large numbers of OBCs, he has been equally clever in reminding the Muslims of the security of their life and property during RJD rule. This seems to have again worked in favour of Laloo during the 2004 Lok Sabha elections. An important element of the popularity of the party is its solid support base among the numerous Yadavs in the state. Though they might complain of the lack development, yet they still tend to support the RJD, since with Laloo Prasad Yadav they felt much closer to political power.

The division of Bihar also strengthened RJDs political position. The creation of the new state of Jharkhand separated the Adivasi-dominated districts from Bihar. The settlement pattern of people had been such that the present Bihar had the largest concentration of the

Yadavs, Muslims, and Dalits while few lived in districts of present Jharkhand. Their proportion in the population of Bihar went up by about 2–3 percent. As per the 2001 Census, the proportion of Dalits and Muslims in present Bihar has gone up from 14 percent and 14.8 percent to 17.1 percent and 16.5 percent, respectively. Acording to unofficial estimates, Yadavs comprise nearly 17 percent of the population in present Bihar, an increase of about 4 percent. This added to the political strength of the RJD. This also explains why Laloo performed much better in 2004 as compared to the 1999 Lok Sabha elections. There are reasons to believe that Laloo, who once claimed that Bihar would be divided over his dead body would like to forget that earlier statement. With RJD seemingly much stronger with the division of Bihar, Laloo could afford to use his political skills, and echo the issue of *izzat* and security to the section of voters who support his party.

In spite of his dominant position, doubts were raised about how long the two magic words—*izzat* and security—could win votes for the RJD. The doubts turned into reality with the defeat of the RJD in the October 2005 Assembly elections, the results of which clearly indicated that Laloo's charisma no longer seemed to be working. After 15 years of RJD rule, they do want some development to take place in the state.

But does the new JD(U)–BJP government in Bihar indicate the return of upper-caste dominance in Bihar politics? It is true that the coalition of the JD(U) with the BJP does enable upper-caste leadership to play a greater role in Bihar politics than during the Laloo regime, but it may be an over-statement to say that the new government signifies the return of upper-caste dominance. The new Chief Minister, Nitish Kumar, represents the other dominant OBC caste, the Kurmis. Power still remains largely in the hands of a numerically large OBC caste. The acceptance of Nitish Kumar as the leader of the alliance certainly added to the success of the JD(U)–BJP alliance during the latest Assembly elections. The BJP leadership, with exceptions, accepted this social reality. A key to success in Bihar is to give adequate share to OBC leadership. The social churning that took place in the 1990s marked a radical shift in Bihar politics, from the dominance of the upper castes to the dominance of the OBCs. It seems likely that in the next few decades governments will come and go, political parties will win and lose elections, but the dominance of the OBCs in Bihar politics is likely to remain. The key to success for any political party in Bihar will remain in accommodating the aspirations of the people belonging to the numerically dominant OBCs. The party that masters this art is destined to rule the state in the coming years.

NOTES

1. The Mandal Commission report of August 1990, which recommended reservation of government jobs for people belonging to the Other Backward Castes in the Central government, sparked a nation-wide agitation, mainly of youths, against its implementation.
2. The Dalits and OBCs combined, constitute a majority of the population. The 2001 Census estimates that Dalits are about 15.7 percent of the population (divided Bihar). There are no official estimates for the number of people belonging to the OBCs, but the National Election Study 2004 (NES 2004) estimates that the OBC population is about 52 percent of the total population in the state.
3. As per the 2001 Census, Muslims are 16.5 percent of the total population.
4. Parliamentary constituencies in

> Tirhut: Bagha (SC), Bettiah, Motihari, Gopalganj, Siwan, Maharajganj, Chapra, Hajipur (SC), Vaishali, Muzaffarpur, Sitamarhi, and Sheohar
> Mithila: Madhubani, Jhanjharpur, Darbhanga, Rosera (SC), Samastipur, Saharsa, and Madhupura
> Magadh: Barh, Balia, Monghyr, Begusarai, Nalanda, Patna, Aurangabad, Jahanabad, Nawada (SC), and Gaya (SC)
> East: Araria (SC), Kishanganj, Purnea, Katihar, Banka, Bhagalpur, and Khagaria
> Bhojpur: Arrah, Buxar, Sasaram (SC), and Bikramganj.

CHAPTER 9

Politics of Separatism in Assam

SANDHYA GOSWAMI AND MONOJ KUMAR NATH

Ethnicity based on tribal identity is an important political issue in contemporary Assam. The identity formation is a historical process, the character of which is determined by time and space. Primordial elements such as language, race and religion provide an institutional frame, while the cultural perception of the community towards other groups leads to crystallization of identity. In a multi-ethnic society, the reaction to challenges arising out of attempts by the dominant groups towards assimilation, growing economic competition among different ethnic groups and political and developmental processes enforced by the state, reinforce identity formation. Moreover, the whole process gets fillip when emergent middle classes politicize the issues of language, culture, ethnicity, and even religion to their advantage.[1] This chapter examines the issue of tribal identity vis-à-vis electoral politics in the context of the 2004 Lok Sabha election.

TRIBAL POPULATION

Assam's tribal population forms an important component of its demography and socio-political process. The Scheduled Tribes (STs), usually called tribal people, mostly belong to the Tibeto-Burman ethno-linguistic group. Besides this major group, another group called Austro-Asiatic (Mon Khemer-speaking Khasis and Mundari-speaking Munda, Santhal, Ho Aron, etc.) forms a small segment of the state's tribal population. The total population of Assam as per the 2001 Census is 26,655,528, of which the ST population is 3,308,570 (12.41 percent). Among the various tribal communities of Assam, Bodo-Boro Kachari, Mishing, Kachari including Sonowal, Karbi, Dimasa, Rabha, Deoris, and Tiwa are the major tribes in terms of numerical strength. With regard to distribution pattern of tribal people, except for the Karbi and Dimasa (hill tribes) living mostly in the Karbi Anlong district, the rest live in the plains and are concentrated in distinct areas of the state. Assam has two hill districts, Karbi Anlong and North Cachar, inhabited mainly by the Karbis and Dimasa Kacharis, respectively. These two districts have their own Autonomous District Council which comes under the provisions of the Sixth Schedule of the Constitution. This provision has provided the hill tribes with some autonomy in managing their own tribal society. This pri-vilege however was not extended to the plains tribals of Assam.

The presence of ethnic diversity in Assam leaves tremendous scope for political polarization on ethnic lines. From among a total of 14 Lok Sabha constituencies, Kokrajhar and the Autonomous District are re-served as ST constituencies. The present analysis is confined to these constituencies which had been a bastion of the Congress party until the 1985 election. However the Congress appears to have lost its elect-oral significance. High voter turnouts (Table 9.1) in these constituencies in the last decade, including 2004, indicate the prevailing assertive behavior of tribal voters in support of their ethnic identity. And quite clearly, in these areas, specific issues like Bodoland for Bodos and the autonomous state demand of the Karbis succeeded in mobilizing the tribal voters in support of their ethnic identity. However, after many rounds of ethnic clashes and military operations affecting a great num-ber of people, the demand for an autonomous state seems to have lost steam largely due to recurring splits within the movement and obfuscation of issues under electoral politics.[2]

The Kokrajhar Lok Sabha constituency is mostly dominated by Bodos, the largest group of plains tribes of Assam. Historically, major sections of the Bodo people have merged into an Assamese sub-national formation. The recent Bodo upsurge is undoubtedly a deter-mination to reverse the process. Actually, Bodo nationalism in Assam emerges through a multifaceted contestation. It is against the Indian state, against the dominance of an Assamese national identity and

Table 9.1

Voter turnout in Lok Sabha elections, 1991–2004

(figures in %)

Constituencies	1991	1996	1998	1999	2004
Karimganj	73.76	80.24	77.12	73.74	68.60
Silchar	71.67	78.64	75.34	73.51	69.18
Autonomous district (ST)	67.45	79.85	73.09	74.00	69.41
Barpeta	77.18	79.38	61.09	73.69	70.89
Guwahati	66.60	83.47	43.81	63.30	61.18
Mangaldai	71.57	75.06	59.90	72.74	70.10
Tezpur	70.49	74.72	69.44	69.71	71.60
Nowgaon	70.84	75.11	59.42	68.40	68.39
Kaliabor	70.67	83.40	59.85	68.25	66.21
Jorhat	62.43	76.77	34.53	62.85	61.99
Dibrugarh	60.26	76.19	40.31	58.96	65.11
Lakhimpur	67.40	72.64	63.45	70.12	71.04
Kokrajhar (ST)	81.02	82.62	64.55	77.96	79.48

Source: *Report on The General Election to the 14th Lok Sabha, 2004*, Assam Government
Press, 2005.

clashes with other peripheral and dominant identities.[3] Bodos feel
that they have been subjected to neglect and poverty over the years.
Although their demand for community rights dates back to 1929,
their first demand for a separate state for the plains tribals of Assam
was made by the Plains Tribal Council in 1967. Since the early 1960s
they have been trying to revive their culture and distinct identity on
the plank of ethnicity. However, over time, the Plains Tribal Council
has become part of mainstream politics and has lost its grip over the new
generation of Bodos. Developments since 1961, such as welfare
schemes, educational facilities and employment in state services, have
somewhat contributed to the emergence of a middle class among them.

It is this younger generation which is articulating a resurgence
among the tribal communities. The formation of the All Assam Tribal
Students Union (AATSU) in the late 1970s marks a departure point
in this resurgence. By the end of the 1980s practically every group had
its own distinct representative organization.[4] This process is intensified
by the policies pursued by the state. The discontent increasingly has
to do with the Centre's policy of neglect and its alleged unconcern
for the people, coupled with its manipulation of the different ethnic

groups inhabiting Assam. Even during the Asom Gana Parishad's (AGP) first year in office, as a regional party it displayed an insensivity towards tribal feelings in the choice of policies despite the fact that the All Bodo Student Union had thrown its full support to the Assam Movement.[5] As the assertion of the Assamese sub-nationalism became vocal and politically overbearing, the tribal people were reminded of their own distinctive socio-cultural identity . They too began to assert themselves politically by demanding a distinct homeland for themselves through sub-regional parties like the All Bodo Student Union (ABSU), People's Democratic Front (PDF), Plains Tribal Council of India (PTCA), and United Reservation Movement Council of Assam (URMCA). At times they compromised their ethnic character by merging with national mainstream parties such as the BJP or the Congress party, which are known for their integrationist positions.

The movement for a separate Bodo homeland began in 1987 by dividing Assam on the basis of what they called 'fifty-fifty'. Ultimately the leadership gave up the demand for a separate state and agreed to accept autonomy instead, under the provisions of the Bodo Accord in 1993. The constitution of the Bodoland Autonomous Council (BAC) promised to provide the Bodo population with control over development affairs. But the lack of a clear-cut boundary and presence of a significant number of non-Bodos in the proposed Bodoland area created a problem and has complicated the question of autonomy, the future of BAC and the relationship between ethnic and non-Bodos living in the BAC areas. The state failed to reciprocate the confidence of the Bodo leaders in federalising institutions for autonomy within the state. Vital provisions of the Accord were violated. Hopes of an election to choose members of an Autonomous Council that could have gone a long way in removing Bodo discontent have been belied time and again.

The pending interim elections of BAC in 1993 intensified factional and individual competition for leadership positions in the council among the younger generation of leaders involved in the Bodo movement. The state also fostered the sharpening of factional rivalry among the leadership so as to further weaken the movement.[6] On February 10, 2003, the Central government signed a new Bodo Accord for the creation of a Bodoland Territorial Council (BTC) on the north bank of the Brahmaputra, under modified provisions of the Sixth Schedule of the Constitution. The BTC would have control over 10 major socio-political areas. This includes land, any forests other than reserved forests, any canal or water course for the purpose of agriculture, any form of shifting cultivation, establishment of village and town committees, all matters relating to village and town administration, etc. The BTC would have legislative, executive, administrative, and financial powers with respect to the subjects transferred to it. It was also decided during the accord that initially the BTC would comprise 3,082 villages where the Bodos are in majority, and that within three months all surrounding villages where the Bodos account for at least 50 percent of the total population would be included in the new council.

But the Congress-led state government failed to implement the accord until the elections of 2004. Though an interim BTC was created, no power was transferred to it by the state government. Funds were also not properly allocated to run the business of the newly born Bodoland Territorial Autonomous District (BTAD). No appointment rights were given to BTAD authorities. The question of additional villages, which was to be settled within three months after the Accord was signed, was also not solved even after one year. Funds were not sanctioned to build new administrative buildings in the newly created districts, Baska and Siring. Simply put, the state government showed a benign negligence towards the Bodo Accord of 2003. This negligence towards the Accord became the main election issue of the opposition parties against the Congress party. ABSU and former BLT leaders threatened the Congress that the state government's negligence towards the BTC Accord could again result in a violent movement in Assam.

ABSU and other Bodo organizations supported S.K. Bwiswmuthiary, the then sitting Lok Sabha MP as their consensus candidate from the Kokrajhar constituency. Bwiswmuthiary, who fought the election as an independent candidate, had two main election issues: success of the Bodo movement and negligence of the Congress state government towards the Accord. For Bwiswmuthiary, the BTC accord of 2003 was a victory resulting from the decades-long Bodo movement as it gave constitutional recognition to a virtual Bodo homeland in Assam. The BJP-led National Democratic Alliance (NDA) government at the Center focused on building its organizational base in the Kokrajhar constituency in the 2004 Lok Sabha election. Therefore, it did not nominate its own candidate for this SC constituency but supported the consensus Bodo candidate. The BJP thus looked ahead to the forthcoming 2006 Assembly elections.

The state government's agreement to constitute the BTC generated considerable resentment in the lower Assam area. Eighteen non-Bodo organizations formed the Sanmilita Janagosthiya Sangram Samiti (SJSS) to oppose the Accord. The main argument of these non-Bodo organizations against the BTC Accord is that Bodos constitute only 20 percent of the total population in the proposed BTC area and hence should not be given the right to rule over the total population. The statewide 2004 post-poll survey undertaken by the Center for the Study of Developing Societies (CSDS) confirms this fact. When asked about the approval of the special provisions given to the Bodos within the BTC Accord areas, 24 percent replied negatively, 26 percent did not have an opinion, and only 17 percent seemed to have approved it. This time, non-Bodo groups from the proposed BTC area did not rally behind the AGP because of the party's moral support to the BTC Accord. The SJSS supported the independent candidate Mr Sabda Rabha in the name of safeguarding the interest of the non-Bodo people. The dominant issue for the SJSS was its opposition to the 2003 BTC Accord. They demanded the cancellation of the Accord for safeguarding the rights and interests of the majority, non-Bodo population.

Thus, in the Kokrajhar parliamentary constituency, competition between Bodos and non-Bodos, and their respective positions toward BTC emerged as the dominant issue. The only related issue that could emerge significantly was the demand for ST status by the Adivasis living within the constituency. Unemployment, economic under-development, good governance and other issues important in other elections in India were of little or no importance in the 2004 election. Since Bwiswmuthiary was nominated as the consensus candidate he could retain his seat with the highest margin in the state. The Congress appeared to have lost its electoral significance in this constituency (see Table 9.2). Even during the poll boycott call given by an insurgent group during the 1998 Lok Sabha election, a massive turnout took place in this constituency. However, it appears from the election results that the winning margins were not very high because no dominant tribal party had emerged. Tribal votes thus seemed to have become divided and they went against the Congress (INC). The limited direct evidence available from the post-poll survey data of the CSDS on the dimension of voting behavior clearly reveals this fact (see Table 9.3).

Table 9.2

Lok Sabha elections, Assam: Voting pattern within ST communities

(*figures in %*)

Year	INC	BJP	AGP & Allies	Others
1996	38.1	19.0	33.3	9.5
1998	25.0	37.5	25.0	12.5
1999	16.2	37.1	27.3	12.9

Source: Based on Assam sample of post-poll surveys of the National Election Studies, 1996, 1998, and 1999, conducted by CSDS.

The other tribal-dominated Lok Sabha constituency in Assam is an autonomous district that covers two hill districts of Assam—North Cachar and Karbi Anglong. These two are autonomous districts, enjoying this status from the very beginning of the constitution. The Karbis, earlier known as Mikir, are the prominant population of Karbi Anglong District. Unlike the Karbis in Karbi Anglong, the Dimasas, the majority in North Cachar Hills district, have not had as clear a dominant position vis-à-vis the other people inhabiting the district. There is a long-standing agitation in both the districts for their elevation to an autonomous state, including the existing District Council, under the provisions of Article 244A.[7]

These two hill districts have experienced violence in recent years. There have been clashes between Kukis and Karbis, and between Dimasas and Hmars. The Assam Movement of 1979–85 brought considerable changes in the support structure and political articulation of political parties in Assam by triggering various sub-regional and ethnic aspirations. In 1986, the Autonomous State Demand Committee (ASDC)—an ethnic party from the two hill districts emerged,

Table 9.3
Voting pattern in Lok Sabha elections in Kokrajhar, 1991–2004

Name of Candidate	Party	Percentage of Votes Polled
1991		
Satyendra Nath Brahmo Chaudhury	IND	53.20
Louis Islary	INC	20.39
Birendra Chandra Boro	AGP	17.55
Samar Brahma Choudhury	PTCA	08.96
1996		
Louis Islary	IND	24.36
Rabi Ram Brahma	IND	20.22
Pani Ram Rava	AGP	20.15
Lahendra Basumatary	INC	16.93
Charan Narzary	BJP	16.09
Amritlal Basumatary	IC(S)	02.25
1998		
Sansuma Khunggur Bwiswmuthiary	IND	25.55
Theodore Kisku Rapaz	URMCA	20.07
Binod Gayary	IND	18.60
Charan Narzary	BJP	15.34
Premsing Brahma	INC	11.85
Louis Islary	AGP	06.34
Thaneswar Boro	PTCA	01.72
Jamini Mohan Basumatary	IND	00.55
1999		
Sansuma Khunggur Bwiswmuthiary	IND	37.57
Theodore Kisku Rapaz	URMCA	27.75
Gangadhar Ramchiary	PDF	19.37
Premsing Brahma	INC	07.33
Anil Murma	IND	07.13
Kanakeswar Narzary	UBNLF	00.85
2004		
Sansuma Khunggur Bwismuthiary	IND	71.32
Sabda Ram Rabha	IND	21.25
Derbagra Mochabary	INC	06.35
Rajendra Mushahary	IND	01.08

Source: *Assam Election Report*, Government of Assam.

articulating the interests of these communities. In 1986, it spearheaded the movement for a separate state that led, in 1995, to a memorandum of understanding with the state government that granted greater powers to the hill councils in both districts in accordance with theSixth Schedule. Demands for statehood were put forward for two distinct and autonomous ethnic homelands, which gained momentum with the support of the United People's Democratic Solidarity (UPDS) of the Karbis and Dima Halam Daogah (DHD) of the Dimasas.

Such issues acquired urgency in the poll process. During elections, ASDC consistently raised the issue of separate statehood for Karbis, and it became the most sensitive issue in the election in this constituency. But after the division within ASDC, this demand seemed to have lost its past significance. Peace and corruption emerged as the major issues in the 2004 elections in this constituency. In addition, continuous Karbi–Kuki and Hmar–Dimasa clashes also had an impact on the elections. Though the people of Karbi Anglong and North Cachar acquired significant 'autonomy' in the past, no major change took place in the lives of the people. Both districts remain economically backward as compared to the other districts of Assam. Rampant corruption by the district council members is said to be the main cause of their backwardness.

Ever since its emergence, the ASDC party made its presence felt in the state's electoral politics (see Table 9.4). The ASDC candidate, Dr Jayanta Rongpi, won this seat four consecutive times with a high percentage of votes. But in 1999, he contested as the CPI(ML) candidate, and won by polling 53.98 percent of the votes against 38.5 percent by the Congress candidate. There was no candidate from ASDC. In 2000, the ASDC split into two groups, one of which, under Rongpi's leadership, joined the CPI(ML). As a CPI(ML) candidate in the 2004 elections, he managed to poll only 18.54 percent of the votes and the ASDC candidate fielded against him polled 25.36 percent of the votes. Dividing the vote in this manner enabled the Congress candidate to win this seat by polling 31.38 percent. The AGP did not put up a candidate in the 1998 and 1999 elections, but in the 2004 Lok Sabha elections its candidate lost with a very low 0.93 percent of votes. On the other hand the BJP, which had never before been a significant force, made inroads into these areas by increasing its share to 14.35 percent of the votes polled.

Table 9.4
Voting pattern in Lok Sabha elections in the Autonomous districts, 1991–2004

Name of Candidate	Party	Percentage of Votes Polled
1991		
Dr Jayanta Rongpi	ASDC	47.12
Biren Singh Engti	INC	27.53
Nigamananda Maithar	AGP	15.03
Brojen Langthasa	IND	04.80
Bapuram Singnar	BJP	05.41
1996		
Dr Jayanta Rongpi	ASDC	52.68
Elwin Teron	IND	22.50
Gakul Chandra Hojai	IND	21.86
Gujar Teron	BJP	03.06
James Hanse	IND	00.50
Kaban Timungpi	IND	00.20
1998		
Dr Jayanta Rongpi	ASDC	47.08
Biren Singh Engti	INC	20.28
Elwin Teran	IND	18.18
Pabindra Kr. Kemprai	BJP	12.00
Augelus Terang	IND	02.46
1999		
Dr Jayanta Rongpi	CPI(ML)	53.98
Biren Singh Engti	INC	38.50
Elwin Teran	IND	07.08
Kaban Tamungpi	IND	00.44
2004		
Biren Singh Engti	INC	31.38
Elwin Teran	ASDC	25.36
Dr Jayanta Rongpi	CPI(ML)	18.54
Ratan Teron	BJP	14.35
Sanmoni Kemprai	IND	06.66
Chember G. Momin	IND	01.99
Sailendra Hasnu	AGP	00.93
Harsing Teron	SAP	00.79

Source: CSDS Data Unit.

CONCLUSION

The 2004 electoral verdict in Assam presents a mixed scenario.[8] Electoral competition led to the mobilization of votes on the basis of ethnic identity. The processes of ethnicization of politics and political fragmentation had started with the Assam Movement, 1979–85. Two fundamental changes become evident in the electoral politics of Assam in the last two decades. These are the fragmentation of the party political space and explosion of ethnicities in the arena of politics. Competitive politics creates and recreates imagined communities. The rise of a large number of hitherto unknown tribal groups illustrates this process. Electoral competition has mobilized many formerly passive socio-economic groups and brought them into the political arena. This period in the politics of Assam also illustrates a realignment in the relationship among various kinds of pre-existing social cleavages. The simultaneous operation of these alignments has made contemporary Assam into a virtual laboratory of the politics of ethnicities.

NOTES

1. M.N. Karna, 'Ethnic Identity and Socio Economic Processes in North-Eastern India', in Kailash S. Aggarwal (ed.), *Dynamics of Identity and Inter-group Relations in North East India* (Shimla: Indian Institute of Advanced Study, 1999), pp. 29–38.
2. S. Barbora, *Autonomy in the North East-The Frontiers of Centralised Politics*, Chapter 8. Accessed from www.uta.fi/laitokset/isss/6B.htm.
3. S. Roy, 'Conflicting Nations in North East India', *Economic and Political Weekly*, Vol. XL, No. 21 (May 21–27, 2005), pp. 2178–79.
4. S. Goswami, 'Assam: Ethnic Conflict in Assam', *Indian Journal of Political Science*, Vol. 6, No. 1 (March 2001), pp. 124–26.
5. S. Hazarika, *Strangers of the Mist* (New Delhi: Penguin, 1994), pp. 75–80.
6. Goswami, op cit., pp. 134–37.
7. M.S. Prabhakara, 'Reinventing Identities', *Frontline*, Vol. 21 (June 4, 2004), pp. 38–42.
8. S. Goswami, 'Assam: Multiple Realignments and Fragmentation of Party System', *Journal of Indian School of Political Economy*, Vol. 15 (January–June 2003), pp. 221–47.

CHAPTER 10

Ethno-Regional Identity and Political Mobilization in Meghalaya

Democratic Discourse in a Tribal State

RAJESH DEV

INTRODUCTION

Any attempt to understand the nature of competitive politics and the obligatory political mobilization in the north-eastern states of India is a daunting exercise. This is not because of the complexity of social relations and almost non-liberal mode of organizing social and political life, but because the standard 'assumptions that go into scholarly analysis'[1] of competitive politics in India is least applicable to the societies of the region. Most of these states were carved out of Assam at different moments of post-Independence history in deference to claims for ethnic autonomy and other differences.[2] These states usually are collectively referred to as the North-East region of India. However, they don't have intrinsic comparable markers either in terms of a common cultural history, demographic composition or even common political consciousness so as to be referred to collectively as the 'North-East'. But as Sanjib Baruah puts its, 'such generic locational place names are attractive to political engineers *because* they evoke no historical memory or collective consciousness'[3] yet they recursively justify the potential of such a collective category to be someday incorporated as an oppositional political project.[4]

This chapter considers that such a generic designation is simply not the outcome of a deliberate political engineering but is the upshot of a common wavering and sense of alienation that the region experiences in its relationship with the Indian state. The political units that comprise the region—Assam, Tripura, Arunachal Pradesh, Manipur, Nagaland, Mizoram, and Meghalaya—at least, at some niche of popular imagination, experience a collective sense of estrangement from the Indian state. Though the source of this can be traced to the political strategy of integration in the post-Independence phase along with the geo-strategic and cultural linkages of this region with neighboring nations, contemporarily this sense of estrangement is employed more as a politico-cultural capital for bargaining with the Indian state.

This region, additionally, experiences a dense frequency of ethnic groups that are at different stages of political development organizing their social and political life through political organizations that are habitually referred to as 'traditional political authority structures.'[5] Several of these structures are recognized in numerous legal instruments including the Constitution[6] that accords them with a 'strategic legitimacy' alongside the institutions of the modern state. It is argued that these mechanisms endorsed the autonomy of 'collective life-worlds' of many of the ethnic communities residing in the region,[7] simultaneously allowing them the space to participate in the broader democratic mechanisms of the modern state. Indeed, it is the region's ethnic pluralism that is also its provocation for cascading political claims and assertions that are also invariably crystallized into 'ethnic insurgencies' seeking independent 'homelands' that frequently overlap similar claims by 'others'.[8] Briefly put, the region encounters escalating assertions by ethnic groups to reclaim their purported distinctiveness through 'nativist movements,' as such political mobilization and competitive politics frequently operate and are shaped by the margins established by the dynamics of these contestations.[9]

THE STATE

Though the people inhabiting the present state of Meghalaya were initiated into modern constitutional governance in the late 19th century,[10] their encounter with full-fledged competitive electoral politics began with the granting of statehood on January 21, 1972 vide the North Eastern Area (Reorganization) Act 1971, where a single-tier legislature with 60 members were to perform the political tasks of the new state. This process, of course, ensued from the interim political arrangement made earlier when 'autonomous statehood' within Assam was approved as a 'Christmas gift'[11] to the hills people in 1969 (*Assam Reorganisation [Meghalaya] Act 1969*). In fact during the autonomous state phase a provisional Legislative Assembly of 41 members was established, where 38 members were elected and three members were nominated.[12] However, elections to this provisional Assembly were not based on universal franchise since only an electoral college consisting of the representatives in the three hill districts autonomous councils of Khasis, Jaintias, and Garos could cast their votes. In this provisional Assembly, 34 members were from the All Peoples Hills Leaders Conference (APHLC), a group leading the Hills state movement; four members were from the Congress, who later aligned with the APHLC, and three nominated members who also later joined the APHLC.[13]

Interestingly, Chaube reflects significantly on the process of democratization in the state in his comments that the lasting contribution of the APHLC to the politics of the region in general, and the state in particular, is the perfection it achieved in conducting constitutional politics in one of the most sensitive regions of India.[14] This assessment resonates prophetically if placed in the context of contemporary discourses and methods of expressing political protests in the region where disregard for democratic norms are *élan vital*.

This party-wise break-up of the composition of the provisional Assembly may not be useful in terms of the electoral statistics of the state but is important in the context that it provides us a preliminary glimpse of the nature of political recruitment and ideological commitment of political parties in the emerging state. The nature of political alignments—pre and post poll—and the concurrent failure of any formidable opposition to develop, had a telling effect on the stability of future governments in the state. This pattern is evinced by the twists of political alignments in the provisional Assembly. As Pakem[15] observes, governments in the state of Meghalaya were to always function as a coalition with no opposition, and where all 60 members were to become ministers at some point in the five-year history of the Assembly.

BACKGROUND OBSERVATIONS

The state is dominated by three major tribal communities—the Khasis, the Jaintias (also referred to as the Pnars), and the Garos—who together constitute 80 percent of the total population of the state. Besides, other smaller tribal congeries of Bodos-Kacharis, Hajongs, Rabhas, Dimasas-Kacharis, Hmars, along with Mikir and a number of Kuki tribes inhabit the margins of the political landscape. The state also has a small section of 'non-tribes' who constituted only 14.5 percent in the 1990s. The non-tribes include the Bengalis, Marwaris, Nepalis, and a small group of communities from other parts of India engaged in professional jobs, trading activities and petty services.

The distribution of seats for the 60-member Assembly is made in relation to the relative demographic dominance of the ethnic groups residing in the state. As such, the Khasis who constitute 77.37 percent of the total population in the Khasi hills are represented in 26 seats, while the Jaintias who constitute 95.09 percent of the total population in the Jaintia hills are represented through seven seats. The Khasis and the Jaintias, who assert a common ethnic identity and origin myth, collectively share 33 seats among themselves. This contiguity of ethnic identity between the Khasis and the Jaintias is also shared in asserting a common set of political claims that often gets reflected and was recently made in their demand for a common Khasi-Jaintia state.[16]

The Khasis and the Jaintias are said to be of Paleo-Mongoloid origin, speaking an Austric language of the Mon-Khmer group; Garos are Indo-Mongoloid, speaking a Tibeto-Burman language.[17] The Garos are predominant in the Garo hills and represented through 22 seats. The remaining five seats are technically 'open' seats where 'others' can contest. Three of these seats are in the Shillong region of East Khasi Hills district, while the remaining two are from the West Garo Hills district. The 'non-tribes' who are legally eligible for electoral candidature from these seats are predominant in these 'open' areas.

The state is represented in the Lok Sabha by two seats, one from the Khasi-Jaintia hills and the other from the Garo hills, and is represented in the Rajya Sabha by one seat. Though the people began sending their representatives to the Parliament as members, especially, from the autonomous united Khasi-Jaintia districts, the turning point of this representation came after the 1976 split in the APHLC, after the formation of the new state in 1972.[18] As Chaube states, it was only from the 1977 elections that 'local issues crept in' the electoral agenda of political parties contesting the parliamentary elections. In fact it was from these elections that the contest between regional agenda and national identity received political articulation and internal schisms between the regional parties also began to get revealed.[19]

But of course the interesting question would be how does one explain this simultaneous loyalty for 'localism' and preference for 'national' linkage? This can partly be explained by the analysis of the discourse and rhetoric of 'culture in politics'[20] that utilizes culture as a resource for 'transactional' goals and partly by the historical conditions[21] of the region. The circumstances become a little escalating and complex when the grammar and principles of competitive politics compel home-grown political forces to adopt these cultural symbols in an aggressive bid to recapture lost or losing political space to 'national' political forces. Besides, as Chaube[22] has expressed in a different context, the simultaneous swings between 'localism' and preference for 'national allegiance' is the outcome of a 'fairly middle-order choice' by an emerging middle class that adopts the strategy for 'convenient bargaining' motivated by rational electoral exigencies.

As a natural corollary to what we have already said about the political perception of the region in general towards the state of India, it follows that competitive politics is also perceived in many parts of the North-East as a subtle oblique system of introducing the legitimacy of the Indian state into these 'disputed'[23] areas. Nonetheless, it is also true that such a perception does not hold the fort when weighed against the degree of popular participation in elections to the state assemblies, at least statistically.[24] Though compared to its more virulent regional neighbors, Meghalaya is a relatively peaceful state; a nascent insurgency engaged in by sections of the indigenous groups is experienced to the extent that reports of insurgent groups having influenced the outcome of electoral politics have dominated popular discourse in the state.[25] Nonetheless, the participation level of the electorate has often been above 50 percent in Meghalaya.

Another issue that has dominated competitive political experiences in Meghalaya, which is similar in most of the states of the region, is the concern for the preservation of indigenous identity given the popular perception about the 'sustained exodus and influence of non-indigenous communities' upon the fragile socio-economic and cultural fabric of the state. As such, all parties including 'national' ones like the Congress, the Bharatiya Janata Party or the nascent Nationalist Congress Party along with the 'regional' parties have emphasized issues like 'preservation of tribal culture,' 'preservation of local self-governing institutions' and more 'rights for the indigenous communities in determining their destiny.'[26]

This central feature of balancing regional aspirations with national demands by the parties in the state encouraged Sengupta [27] to observe that in Meghalaya a 'national' party like the Congress calls itself a 'national party with a regional outlook,' while regional parties call themselves, 'a regional party with national outlook.' However, besides the Congress and the BJP (prior to 1998), other 'national' parties like the Communist Party of India, that have been contesting elections since the inception of the state, could not build a social base in the state. This, Sengupta[28] believes, is due to their adherence to a classical Marxist model, which seeks the presence of an organized working class as a ground for the initiation of class-consciousness complemented by the absence of an 'exploited class' in an un-stratified tribal society.

The state has, however, experienced a plethora of regional parties, especially prior to an election to the Legislative Assembly. Beginning with the All Peoples Hill Leaders Conference (1970), the most prominent have been the Hill State Peoples Democratic Party (HSPDP) (1971), the Hill Peoples Union (HPU) (1988), the Public Demands Implementation Convention (PDIC) (1983), the United Democratic Party (UDP) (1998), the Youth Democratic Front (YDF) (1993), the Peoples Democratic Movement (PDM) (1998), and the Meghalaya Democratic Party (MDP) (2002). The regional parties have often expressed the claims of the dominant tribal groups of the state to the extent that some of the radically pro-tribal groups have demanded the exclusion of non-dominant groups from any political participation and social rights.[29]

Nonetheless, most of the regional parties have often merged with national parties like the Congress after winning a few seats or even after receiving electoral setbacks. Besides, as we had stated, regional parties have often entered into a 'strategic alliance' with the Congress to form governments. We say this alliance is 'strategic' because the regional parties and the Congress have perceptively different political constituencies. Where the Congress down-plays issues that have regional and ethnic significance, the regional parties are vociferous in their assertion of the same, and as such they cater to divergent political constituencies and interests.

Yet it would not be proper for us to establish a clear polarization of the social base of the Congress and the regional parties, keeping in mind the general outlook of the 'national' and 'regional' parties we explained earlier. This becomes apparent if we also explore some 'pre-electoral maneuvers, of these parties. For instance, during the 1977 parliamentary elections, the Congress 'issued a press note reminding the people that unauthorised transfer of land ... from tribals to non-tribals and from non-tribals to *other*[30] non-tribals ... was illegal, void and punishable under the Meghalaya Transfer of Land Act 1971.' Moreover, it is the Congress-led coalition government that today (2005) seeks to promulgate the amended Meghalaya Transfer of Land Act 1971, wherein provisions for including a few more tribes as 'indigenous' to the state to enable them to purchase and sell landed property within the state and stop all sorts of sale and transfer of land from non-tribals to non-tribals, are to be prohibited.[31] The press note of 1977, Chaube claims, was 'directed to get tribal support for the Congress candidates countering the opposition campaign' being built predominantly around 'regional' issues[32] and the amendment sought in 2005 is merely a reflection of the consolidation of vested interests initiated during the early phase of 'state building.' Furthermore, it was a national party like the Congress that had opposed land reforms in the state on the plea that the concept was alien to Khasi culture,[33] while to the contrary, the APHLC had been planning some kind of land reform.[34]

The tenuous nature of the 'balancing act' between the Congress and the regional forces was also evident during the 2004 Lok Sabha elections. During these elections, the regional parties silently denied the call by the Congress for a common candidate for the parliamentary seats, by the coalition partners. This refusal by the regional forces was partly dictated by the distrust among the regional forces that any such direct electoral alliance would lead to a categorical appropriation by the Congress, which has been the dominant partner in the ruling coalition in the state, and would lead to the forfeiting of political space to the Congress.

Like other states of the region, in Meghalaya too, students and student bodies have had a very prominent role in configuring the politics of the state. They have often floated regional fronts during elections, though many of them have not been able to continue as a party after their electoral defeats, except for a few like the Khun Hynniewtrep National Awakening Movement (KHNAM) formed by members of the Khasi Students Union (KSU) in 2003, though their future prospects cannot be foretold. The other fronts floated by students or their supporters during various phases of the state's electoral history included the Hynniewtrep National Front (HNF) (1978), the Democratic Hills Movement (DHM) (1984), the Alliance for the Reconstruction of Meghalaya (ARM) (1988) and even the already mentioned PDM. Students' organizations like the KSU have often tacitly backed these fronts since student bodies, especially the KSU, always had a 'soft corner for the regional political parties.'[35]

What's more, irrespective of the partial successes by regional forces backed by the emerging intelligentsia, students have been at the forefront of political movements that set the agenda for numerous political leaders and parties. They have for instance led the anti-foreigners agitation in 1979 and 1987, which in a sense initiated the ethnocentric divide between the dominant communities and the assortment of minorities residing in the state and which continues to determine the dynamics of not only electoral outcomes but also popular democratic mobilizations.[36] The students have also demanded the non-extension of railway head to the state; 100 percent job reservation and seats in the Assembly; implementation of the inner-line regulation, revision of electoral rolls to eliminate alleged 'foreigners', and implementation of work permits for non-indigenous workers. Public representatives in Parliament have often pleaded for similar demands on behalf of the students when arguments for the extension of the inner-line regulation to check the entry of 'outsiders' into the state and 100 percent reservation of seats in the Legislative Assembly for the indigenous tribes,[37] were made by them.

In fact, student bodies like the KSU are so hegemonic that parallel 'secular' students bodies like the National Students Union of India (NSUI) are denied any role or legitimacy in the affairs of the state through categorical assertions that 'there is no student union other than the KSU in the Khasi Hills.'[38] Even when other pan-regional platforms of students were established in the state, for example the All Khasi–Jaintia Students Union (AKJSU) in 1987, the North Eastern Hills Students Association (NEHSA) in 1970, the North East Region Students Union (NERSU) in 1979 or the North Eastern Region Indigenous Students Federation (NERISF) in 1985, the president of the KSU presided over them.[39] These student bodies have also often defied traditional authorities, whose legal recognition and institutionalization have often been demanded by them,[40] obtained the resignation of ministers[41] and influenced the formation of post-electoral political alliances in the state.[42] These instances highlight the importance and influence of students and student bodies not only on political alignments and political decision-making but also on the organizing of socio-political discourse in the state.

Another feature that needs emphasis in any analysis of political mobilization in Meghalaya is the influence and role of 'traditional political authorities' and a 'tradition-guided' society on the nature and outcome of modern liberal multiparty democracy. The traditional political authorities that have in the recent past been vocal on the granting of legal recognition to their systems of governance have received political backing for their assertions. For instance the Nationalist Congress Party (NCP) that came into being after P.A. Sangma parted ways with the Sonia-led Congress, became a staunch supporter for the granting of constitutional recognition to the traditional bodies, whereby a quasi rational-legal legitimacy could be accorded to these bodies.

Though the issue of constitutional recognition to traditional authorities had gathered momentum after the 73rd Amendment to the Indian Constitution, the issue was further politicized by the NCP.[43] We can attribute this action on the part of the NCP to the political compulsions it encountered, since being a new political competitor in the state it had to carve out a separate segment of the state's social base. To do so, it adopted a cultural–political discourse to distinguish itself from the other players that had already patented political issues and social bases. It, thus, effectively provided political expression to an already familiar and popular social belief that traditional authorities require constitutional recognition to be legally able to exert their already existing comprehensive authority over the people without interference from modern state structures and institutions.

This issue has been so highly politicized that the Federation of Khasi States, a body of traditional authorities, pleaded to all parties to support its candidate to the Lok Sabha in the parliamentary elections of 2004. However, the adaptable nature of the relationship between the institutions and processes of liberal democracy and the traditional sources of political authority prevented any political party, even the regional ones, from extending any such direct political support. It is important to stress here that the relationship between the traditional authorities and the liberal democratic authorities is complicated and dense—at times the traditional authorities act as appendages to the state institutions and at times they contest its legitimacy.[44] In fact, many of the legislators are often themselves traditional authorities or members of these institutions and the popular view has also been that these institutions are apertures to political aspirations in the institutions of the modern state. Nonetheless, despite this tenuous relationship between institutions of modern government and the traditional authorities, the issue of 'recognizing' the traditional authorities has a wide cultural and political appeal among a section of the people, though skeptic voices question their role in a modern political setting.[45] The silent refusal of support by political parties to this proposal of the traditional authorities during the 2004 elections reveals that current political entrepreneurs are unwilling to wholly accord legitimacy to cultural symbols that might induce a new set of actors into the political arena but, nonetheless, they are willing to adopt these symbols only to the extent that they provide them with some 'transactional' benefits in everyday politics.

The candidate proposed by the traditional institutions had to ultimately refrain from contesting since it was evident that the political constituency of the traditional authorities was insecure and unreliable even though they could evoke an effective (cultural) political interest through such demands. Needless to emphasize that though traditional institutions serve as 'mobilizing structures' for collective actions laced with ethnic rituals and cultural symbolism in a discursive space where 'culture is politics,'[46] they continue to occupy the fringes of contemporary political discourse without any significant and homogenous political base.

Another significant feature of the political culture of the state is that despite being a matrilocal and matrilineal society (among the Khasi, Jaintia, and Garos), the participation and visibility of women in politics is negligible. Very few women have played any significant role in politics so as to represent the people in the state legislature or in Parliament. They also play an insignificant role in the traditional political institutions.[47] An explanation of such a failure is presented by Baruah and Sharma,[48] who argue that this society pursues matrilineal traditions but operates through rules of patriarchy. Effective power, thus, remains with male members of the society who hold negative images about the capability of women in decision-making roles.[49] But this analysis does little to explain why there is the emergence of a growing dissonance among a section of the Khasi men folk against the matrilocal and matrilineal form of society.[50]

DYNAMICS OF POLITICAL MOBILIZATION

As we have already indicated, like the other states of the region, Meghalaya too is in a state of political transition where democratic mobilization and competitive politics is a recent and modern phenomenon. Its initiation into modern political mobilization began with the formation of the Eastern India Tribal Union (EITU), which was formed by a group of tribal leaders in the state of Assam to seek more autonomy for the tribals within the state.[51] The opening elections to the Legislative Assembly were held in March 1972 when a new state was established vide the North Eastern Area (Reorganization) Act 1971. It would be useful to recall here that the new Assembly was to be composed of 60 seats, 50 to be 'reserved' while 10 were 'open' seats. The number of 'open' seats was subsequently reduced to five seats[52] from which, technically, non-dominant 'non-tribes' could contest. This democratic limitation to non-dominant groups in the state must nevertheless be assessed in the context of the social transformation the state is experiencing where an increasing assertion of 'indigenity'[53] and ethnic identity has placed effective limitations upon the political empowerment of non-dominant groups and, as such, their participation in any form of democratic mobilization is tangential to actual political decision-making.[54]

During these elections, the regional parties together secured a majority in the Assembly, while the Congress contesting in 12 seats, secured nine. The remaining seats were captured by the Independents (see Table 10.1). A crucial feature of Meghalaya previously noted is that the politics of defections and coalitions began immediately after the 1972 elections. A faction of the APHLC led by Captain Williamson A. Sangma merged with the Congress after the APHLC's Mendipather conference in 1976.[55] The other group led by B.B. Lyngdoh was to remain the guiding light and hub of regional forces in the state, though the taxonomy and nature of political alignments of the party was to undergo alterations time and again. This merger provided the Congress with a strong footing in the new state, which it further consolidated, especially in the Garo and east Khasi hills. The political history of the Congress in the state has passed through assorted trajectories, where it has often received more votes than the regional parties separately, but could never form a government on its own. It always had to engage in the politics of defections from, and coalition arrangements with, the regional parties to form governments in the state. Even in the case of parliamentary elections, the history of the Congress is a series of swings and slides. For instance, from an all-time high of 74.3 percent of the vote-share in 1980, it received only 53.6 percent of the total vote-share in 1996.[56]

Table 10.1

Party-wise seats share in the Meghalaya Assembly, 1972–2003

Year	National Parties				Regional Parties												Total
	INC	NCP	BJP	CPI	APHLC	PDIC	MPPP	APHLC(A)	UDP	MDP	GNC	HSPDP	KHNAM	PDM	HPU	IND	
1972	9	–	–	Nil	32	0	–	–	–	–	–	8	–	–	–	11	60
1978	20	–	–	Nil	16	0	–	–	–	–	–	14	–	–	–	8	60
1983	25	–	–	Nil	15	2	–	–	–	–	–	15	–	–	–	3	60
1988	22	–	–	Nil	–	2	2	2	–	–	–	6	–	–	19	9	60
1993	24	–	0	Nil	–	2	2	3	–	–	–	8	–	–	11	10	60
1998	25	0	3	Nil	–	–	–	–	20	0	1	3	0	3	–	5	60
2003	22	14	2	Nil	–	–	–	–	9	4	0	2	2	0	–	5	60

Source: *Election Handbooks/Statistical Records*, Election Commission of Meghalaya, Election Commission of India.

Nonetheless, the Congress is generally perceived by a majority of the dominant tribal groups as a 'national' party that sponsors[57] the interests of the non-tribes—the cultural and political 'other'. As such, the Congress is seen with distrust by a significant section of the tribal population, especially in the Khasi and Jaintia hills. This distrust is evident in the low number of seats won by the Congress in these areas.

The regional parties, on the other hand, are seen as sponsors of tribal interests, and if we view their membership profile we find that it is overwhelmingly composed of indigenous tribes. Besides, the issues that have often been flagged by the regional parties are those that the dominant tribal groups perceive as securing their protection from 'outside' influence and intervention.

This estimation of the social base of the Congress as well as the regional parties can also be made from an analysis of the vote-share of these parties in the 'non-tribal' pockets of the state. The regional parties invariably receive a lower share of the votes compared to the Congress in areas of 'non-tribal' dominance. Often, the support of 'non-tribal' electors for the regional forces is strategic to their survival needs and is relative to their thin demographic distribution in areas of overwhelming 'tribal' concentration. This is evidenced in the support for the KHNAM candidate during the 2003 Assembly elections in the Jaiaw constituency, which is a predominantly 'tribal' constituency, with a sparse 'non-tribal' presence.

This assessment of the social base of the Congress and the regional parties, however, is applicable in a limited sense in the case of the Garo hills, where the Congress has had a strong support base among the tribal population. This difference in the social base of the Congress in respect to the Khasi and the Garo hills has been attributed by Baruah,[58] taking an imperfect cue from a more nuanced argument provided by Brass,[59] to the degree of political consciousness and consolidation of an emerging educated middle class. Baruah believes that when an educated élite or middle class begins to emerge in a less developed community it ensures its benefits by remaining close to more powerful and hegemonic forces, but when it gains strength it uses regional or ethnic politics as a bargaining strategy.[60] This is partially true since the nascent élite in the Garo hills have not desisted from

introducing ethnic politics or regional issues during political mobilization in the areas dominated by them.

Moreover, it must be emphasized that personalities, rather than
ideological polarization, matter more in electoral politics in the Garo
hills in particular, and in the state as a whole in general. The influence
of W.A. Sangma and P.A. Sangma has been almost all-embracing in
the political milieu of the area and their relations with the Congress
had been responsible, to a great extent, for the influence of the Congress
in the area. Only in 1972 and 1988 did the regional forces secure
17 and 12 seats, respectively from the Garo areas. This can be explained
by the fact that during 1972, the regional forces had just achieved
statehood—but under the leadership of W.A. Sangma. In 1988, it
can be attributed to the pre-election tribal–non-tribal ethnic clashes
that shook the entire state, including several parts of the Garo hills,
which generally remain unaffected by ethnic clashes that occur in other
parts of the state. These ethnic clashes that made the tribal people
more defensive, helped shift the allegiance of the people towards the
regional forces who argued for more protection to the tribes. Besides,
during these elections, W.A. Sangma experienced personal problems
that affected his leadership.[61] In 1988, the Hill Peoples Union (HPU),
which was formed with the partial amalgamation of the APHLC and
the HSPDP during the parliamentary elections in 1984,[62] secured a
total of 19 seats in the Assembly. Ten of these were[63] from the Garo
hills, the highest for any regional party from the area after the dissolution of the APHLC.

In 1978, the elections to the Legislative Assembly took place in the
backdrop of this merger of a section of the regional élite with the
Congress, which resulted in the strengthening of the Congress's position (in the total seats won) after the elections. The Congress contested
57 seats and won 20 of them, 11 of which were from the Garo hills.
HSPDP and APHLC, regional parties, won 14 and 16 seats, respectively especially from the Khasi and Jaintia hill areas, while the remaining 10 seats were won by independents. The combined strength of
the regional parties was more than that of the Congress and close to
a majority, but personality and ego clashes between the leaders of the

regional forces made it difficult for them to join hands against the Congress. It required pressure from a tribal body, the Meghalaya Tribal Youth Organization (MTYO), for the regional parties to come together and form the first 'non-Congress coalition' in which the leadership issue was solved by the toss of a coin, thus teasingly referred to by the Congress as the 'first lottery government.' The pressure of the 'tribal body' upon the nature of political alignments in the state reflected the growing influence of a nascent tribal élite who were to utilize 'ethnic identity' and 'regional demands' simply as political capital for self-serving motivations. This assessment can be made from the fact that most of these social bodies and 'regional parties' had an ephemeral existence in the political landscape of the state before their dissolution, alignment or merger with the Congress.

This assertion of 'indigenous identity' and 'regional aspirations' reached its culmination in 1979, when a student-led movement and the regional forces backed a gory 'anti-foreigners movement' that polarized political interests and claims along ethnic lines. The movement fractured the polity in terms of 'tribes' and 'non-tribes'—two opposing poles of the political spectrum whose claims and interests were considered contradictory. The subsequent consolidation of the communities, especially the non-tribes, in 'ethnic enclaves' as a psychological defense mechanism against perceived threat from dominant groups, initiated their disenchantment with politics. It may be said to have initiated a form of 'confessional politics'[64] that found expression initially in the support for Congress candidates from the 'non-tribal' areas and later in 1998, the election of BJP candidates from the same areas.

However, the nature of this 'confessional politics' is that it is neither motivated nor processed simply by religion but also by the idea of ethnic difference, where ethnicity became a source of political disempowerment. As such, the hint of scepticism that we perceive among the 'non-tribes' for the regional parties initially vis-à-vis the Congress and then, with the arrival of the BJP, vis-à-vis the regional parties as well as the Congress, can be attributed to this politics of confession. Many scholars have hinted that this scepticism for the regional forces among the non-dominant 'non-tribes' of the state was inherent in

the birth of the state since measures for the protection of 'tribal' interests in the new state would, they perceived, affect their interests.[65]

The election to the Legislative Assembly in 1983 was thus held in
the backdrop of this sustained 'anti-foreigners' assertion by regional
forces throughout the state. Even though the regional parties
collectively secured a majority in the elections (see Table 10.1), because
of 'disunity, defections and differences' among the regional forces,
they could not unite under a regional coalition to form the government. The opposition split with an ensuing drama[66] under the leadership of the veteran leader of the Opposition B.B. Lyngdoh, and the
Congress formed a United Meghalaya Parliamentary Forum (UMPF)
government under P.A. Sangma with the HPU (BB), APHLC (A)
and Independents. In the early 1990s, this Congress-led forum was
reduced to a minority because of a split that led to the establishment
of B.B. Lyngdoh as the chief minister heading a combined government of the regional parties, labeled the Meghalaya United Parliamentary Party (MUPP). But dissidence was a perennial 'ideology' in
Meghalaya politics and ultimately President's Rule was imposed in
October 1991,[67] which was revoked and a Congress government came
to power in 1992. Even if subsequently the Supreme Court gave a
ruling favoring the regional combine, MUPP, it had no political impact
since by then another election had taken place and a coalition government was in power after the 1993 elections.

This coalition government called the Meghalaya United Front
(MUF), formed by the Congress along with a splinter group of the
HSPDP (L) and the APHLC (A) and some Independents, happened
to be the only 'United Front' government in the political history of
Meghalaya to complete its five-year term.[68] In the 1998 elections, the
efforts of the regional parties to constitute a pre-poll alliance achieved
partial success, with a regional combine called the United Democratic
Party (UDP) resulting from the amalgamation of the HPU, PDIC,
and a section of the HSPDP. Nonetheless, the drama concerning government formation continued with efforts by the Congress to foist
a government lasting a proverbial 12 days when the 'coalition' government resigned without facing a trust vote. Later a coalition government was formed under B.B. Lyngdoh, but ultimately dissidence
forced him to pave the way for another chief minister from the regional

parties—E.K. Mawlong. Some significant aspects of this election are that the BJP secured three seats in the Assembly, thereby making its presence felt in a predominantly Christian state,[69] while the UDP secured all the seven seats in the Jaintia hills, the most ever by a regional party in the state.[70] However, 'splits' in the regional parties continued and the UDP reconciled to a group breaking from it to form the Meghalaya Democratic Party (MDP). This government for the first time faced a strong coalition of civil society organizations, called the People's Rally Against Corruption (PRAC), that rallied together to force the resignation of the government on charges of corruption.

Elections to the Assembly in 2003 was held amidst a severe division in the social base of the regional parties because of 'splits' in the regional parties and the entry of newer regional fronts like the KHNAM. This possibly allowed 'national' parties like the Congress and the BJP to collectively secure their highest ever seats in the Khasi-Jaintia hills areas[71] (Table 10.2).

Table 10.2

Party-wise performance in the Garo and Khasi-Jaintia areas, 1972–2003

Year	Garo Hills				Khasi-Jaintia Hills			
	Regional	National	Independent	Total	Regional	National	Independent	Total
1972	17	05	2	24	23	4	9	36
1978	08	11	5	24	24	9	3	36
1983	05	18	1	24	27	7	2	36
1988	12	07	5	24	17	15	4	36
1993	02	14	8	24	24	10	2	36
1998	03	18	3	24	24	10	2	36
2003	02	19	3	24	15	19	2	36

Source: *Election Handbooks/Statistical Records*, Election Commission of Meghalaya, Election Commission of India (courtesy: Baruah and Malngiang).

The history of elections to Parliament also saw similar vacillations on the part of the regional parties and more often than not the Congress won the parliamentary constituencies.[72] Pre-poll alliances and mergers between regional parties were merely temporary as they often could not be sustained after the defeat of candidates. In the 2004 general elections to Parliament, the Congress as the dominant partner in a

coalition government formed after the 2003 state elections in association with regional parties, made an appeal for a common candidate
but it was rejected by the regional parties. Therefore, during these
elections, there were three candidates from the Shillong constituency
and two from the Tura constituency. Paty Ripple Kyndiah of the Indian
National Congress, Sanbor Swell Lyngdoh of the Bharatiya Janata
Party and S. Loniak Marbaniang as a joint representative of the
regional forces contested the elections from the Shillong constituency. P.A. Sangma of the All India Trinamool Congress (AITC) and
Dr Mukul Sangma of the Congress contested the elections from the
Tura constituency.

If we consider the pattern of voting during these elections we
will appreciate the ethnic polarization we had tried to examine earlier in the case of elections to the State Assembly. During these elections, the BJP candidate received the highest number of votes in the
Pynthorumkhrah, Laban, and Mawprem constituencies as compared
to the Congress and the Independent candidates.[73] These three constituencies have the highest number of 'non-tribal' voters than any
other constituency in Shillong, besides the Pynthorumkhrah and
Laban constituencies which have sitting BJP MLAs. Likewise, the
Congress candidate received a significant portion of votes from the
Jaintia-dominated constituencies of Rymbai, Raliang, and Jowai. In
the case of the Congress candidate, it is possibly ethnic kinship that
influenced electoral outcomes, while in the case of the BJP candidate
it is more due to party-based support. This can, as we have indicated
earlier, be attributed to the nature of the politics of confession pursued
by the disempowered 'non-tribes'. The BJP provides this group, who
are restricted by the dynamics of ethnic demography and politics
from contesting parliamentary elections, with an immediate 'national
kinship' by exploiting their sense of disempowerment released by the
dynamics of ethnic polarization.

The political contest was between the Congress and the Independent candidates put up by the regional parties combine. While the
Congress candidate secured majorities in 26 out of 36 Assembly constituencies under the Shillong constituency, the regional party candidates won in seven Assembly segments. The BJP candidate secured

a majority in only three Assembly segments. Between the BJP and the regional parties' candidate, the BJP could take a lead in only five Assembly segments that includes the three 'non-tribal'—dominated segments.

In the Tura constituency, the veteran Purno A. Sangma, an AITC candidate, was pitted against his one-time political ally and apprentice Dr Mukul Sangma, the Congress candidate. Surprisingly, the regional parties of Meghalaya put up no candidates and some, like the UDP, tacitly supported P.A. Sangma. Ethnic polarization was also visible in the Tura constituency where Mukul Sangma received overwhelming support of the 'non-Garo' voters, especially in the Phulbari and Mahendraganj Assembly segments where significant sections of the electorate are 'non-Garos' and many of the voters looked upon Mukul Sangma as a person with multiple ethnic identity and, possibly, loyalty.

The dominant influence of P.A. Sangma in the Garo hills led to his securing majorities in 21 Assembly segments out of the total of 24 in the Tura constituency. Mukul Sangma could secure majorities in only three Assembly segments, which also have a large concentration of 'non-Garos'.

The major issues during these elections, especially in the Garo hills, i.e., the Tura constituency, had been the need for development and peace. The concern for development is in fact another issue that divides the perceptions of the Garos and Khasi-Jaintias. Garos often express the view that the Garo hills is the most neglected segment of Meghalaya, despite a large number of Garos holding powerful positions in the political hierarchy. The Khasis view the Garos as having always dominated the political hierarchy in the state. In the Khasi hills, the issues were very adaptable since all parties, except the BJP were part of a coalition government. Both the Congress and the regional parties' candidate harped on the successes of the coalition government and promised more from the same. It was only the BJP which highlighted the issue of corruption and lack of accountability on the part of the state government. The final election results favored the Congress candidate in the Shillong constituency with 52.68 percent of the total vote share, while in the Tura constituency the AITC candidate, receiving 61.69 percent of the vote share, trounced his Congress rival.

Table 10.3

Candidates returned to Parliament, 1977–2004

	Tura Constituency			Shillong Constituency		
Year	Party	Candidate	Vote Share (%)	Year	Party	Candidate	Vote Share (%)
1977	INC	Purno A. Sangma	57.64	1977	IND	H.S. Lyngdoh	30.27
1980	INC	Purno A. Sangma	74.31	1980	–	Not Held	NA
1984	INC	Purno A. Sangma	74.30	1984	INC	G.G. Swell	55.75
1989	INC	S. Marak	62.70	1989	INC	P.G. Marbaniang	50.77
1991	INC	Purno A. Sangma	68.31	1991	INC	P.G. Marbaniang	48.75
1996	INC	Purno A. Sangma	78.47	1996	IND	G.G. Swell	56.18
1998	INC	Purno A. Sangma	67.27	1998	INC	P.R. Kyndiah	35.10
1999	NCP	Purno A. Sangma	63.18	1999	INC	P.R. Kyndiah	39.75
2004	AITC	Purno A. Sangma	61.69	2004	INC	P.R. Kyndiah	51.68

Source: www.eci.gov.in.

We can argue that the characteristics and dynamics of political mobilization in the state remain almost similar for the elections to both the Legislative Assembly and Parliament, with only subtle differences in the degree of emphasis.

IN LIEU OF CONCLUSION

This synoptic analysis of the conditions and dynamics of politics in a predominantly tribal state exposes certain issues that require more sustained engagement by scholars and policy framers alike if we are to understand the agency for 'political discontinuities and social upheavals' in many of the states of this region euphemistically referred to as the 'North-East'. The overwhelming concern for identity and ethnic difference that unite groups against a 'common' adversary often fail to coalesce the groups making such claims towards any common agenda for political justice and emancipation. Groups and clusters that emerge as a result of the cascading politicization of ethnic identities have merely resulted in the shallow ethnicization of politics where justification of claims and their legitimization can take place only on ethnic terms. The shrinkage in the representative voice of the non-dominant groups[74] occupying the margins of political decision-making have only served to undermine democratic dispensations resulting in social tensions and ethnic rivalry.

Besides, the emergence of regional parties as a logical corollary to the growing consciousness of exploitation by the 'majority/outsiders' have not in any sense been able to establish themselves as an alternative to the non-indigenous bias exhibited by 'national' parties. On the contrary, the regional forces have often been censured for elevating 'pure materialism and self-aggrandisement as the ultimate in political idealism.'[75] Even authorities that seek constitutional legitimacy for being the 'authentic cultural inheritors' like the traditional authorities, have been condemned for 'exploiting the ... wealth of the state.'[76] All these emerging social and political dilemmas are said to have 'manifested themselves into an identity syndrome'[77] in the state, indeed the entire region, where insular defensive political slogans and regional sentiments seem to be the only genuine political idioms.

However, it may be worth noting that a nascent but alert and inclusive civil society is emerging in the state. The emergence of such 'a site where public opinion is formed through discourse in which private individuals forge a common understanding about public goals and exercise scrutiny over the state'[78] could possibly allow the space for a 'public' unanointed by primordial loyalties. The formation of the PRAC, which for the first time forced a chief minister to resign, indicates the possibility of a transformation of the social and political agenda in the state in a manner where ethnic solidarity may not remain the major base for political mobilization. Such a development would possibly ensure that greater democratic visibility and political accountability is a strategy still worth being pursued in an ethnically fashioned society.

NOTES

1. See Subrata Mitra, *Culture and Rationality: The Politics of Social Change in Post-colonial India* (New Delhi: Sage Publications, 1999), pp. 70–71.
2. Rajesh Dev. 'Human Rights, Minorities and Relativism in the North-East', *Economic and Political Weekly*, Vol. 39, No. 43 (October 23, 2004), pp. 4747–52.
3. Sanjib Baruah, *Durable Disorder* (New Delhi: Oxford University Press, 2005), pp. 4–5. Emphasis mine.
4. Ibid.
5. See J.N. Sarkar and B. Datta Ray (eds), *Social and Political Institutions of the Hills People of North East India* (Calcutta: Anthropological Survey of India, 1990).
6. For example, the Fifth and Sixth Schedules of the Indian Constitution or Article 371 grants special status to the state of Nagaland. Also relevant is Abhijit Choudhury, 'The Contextual Dimensions of the Sixth Schedule', *Contemporary India*, Vol. 1, No. 4 (October–December 2002).
7. Dev, op. cit.
8. For instance, the Dimasa, a tribe predominantly from Assam, claim Dimapur a city in the neighboring state of Nagaland as part of their homeland, or the more publicized claims of '*Nagalim*' by the Naga separatists that include parts of Assam, Manipur, and Arunachal Pradesh.
9. For instance, in the state of Nagaland, political parties are alleged to be frequently guided by the interests of various factions of Naga insurgents combating the forces of the Indian state for a separate homeland. For details, see Rajesh Dev, 'Nagaland: More Space for Democratic Politics', *Economic and Political Weekly*, Vol. 38, No. 17 (April 26, 2003).

10. See S.K. Chaube, *Hill Politics in Northeast India* (Hyderabad: Orient Longman Ltd., 1999 reprint), pp. 13–15.

11. *The Implanter*, Shillong, December 28, 1969.

12. For details, see B. Pakem, *Coalition Politics in North-East India* (New Delhi: Regency Publications, 1999), and R.S. Lyngdoh, *Government and Politics in Meghalaya* (New Delhi: Sanchar Publishing House, 1996).

13. Pakem, op. cit., p. 97.

14. S.K. Chaube, *Electoral Politics in North East India* (Madras: Universities Press, 1985), p. 8.

15. Ibid., p. 98

16. 'H.S. Lyngdoh Leaves for Delhi Today', *The Shillong Times*, August 30, 2004.

17. See P.S. Datta, 'Ideological Bases of Regional Political Parties in Meghalaya', in B. Pakem (ed.), *Regionalism in India* (New Delhi: Har-Anand Publishers, 1993), p. 91.

18. S.K. Chaube, op. cit., pp. 137–62.

19. See ibid., pp. 139–40.

20. See Subrata Mitra, op. cit., p. 207.

21. For a delineation of these conditions, see Chaube, op. cit., pp. 7–14.

22. Chaube, op. cit., p. ix.

23. I have used 'disputed' since many of these states are experiencing movements that base their resentment on the questionable nature of their accession to India. In Manipur and Meghalaya, for example, groups engaged in contesting the legitimacy of the Indian state often argue that the Instruments of Accession signed by the respective rulers with the Government of India have not been honoured in letter and spirit and numerous legal ambiguities remain.

24. See Statistical Records, www.eci.gov.in.

25. See Avirook Sen, 'Tightrope Triumph', *India Today*, March 23, 1998.

26. Election manifestoes of the parties convey these themes.

27. See Susmita Sengupta, 'Regionalism in Meghalaya', Unpublished Ph.D. thesis submitted to the North Eastern Hill University, Shillong, 1997.

28. See Susmita Sengupta, 'Communist Party of India in Meghalaya', Unpublished M. Phil Thesis, North Eastern Hill University, 1988.

29. For instance, the HSPDP has been asserting 'no person who is not a member of the Scheduled Tribes of the Autonomous District has the right to represent or contest elections from the autonomous districts of Meghalaya'. See *The Shillong Times*, December 12, 1987. Besides, parties like the KHNAM have been exclusively formed to assert the rights of the indigenous groups. (See manifestoes of regional parties.)

30. Italics mine. The 'other' expresses the contestation evident in Meghalaya since the formation of the new state between groups who are considered indigenous and groups considered non-indigenous. It is widely believed that since the state was formed in deference to the avowed claims of the Khasis, Jaintias, and the Garos—three dominant tribes of the state—the principle of 'indigenity'

as the justification of rights and claims must always be in their favor and tribes, or even non-tribes, who have been residing in areas that became part of Meghalaya cannot be assigned the 'indigenous' status.

31. See, 'House to Study Land Transfer Bill', *The Shillong Times*, April 19, 2005.
32. See Chaube, 1985, pp. 144–47.
33. Ibid., p. 24.
34. Ibid.
35. *The Statesman*, May 11, 1968, quoted in Chaube, op. cit., p. 144.
36. For elaboration, see Dev, op. cit.
37. Malngiang, op. cit.
38. *The Implanter*, November 28, 1983.
39. Malngiang, op. cit., p. 17.
40. 'KSU—Admn Heading for a Showdown', *The Shillong Times*, September 12, 2001.
41. Mr D.D. Lapang resigned as Home Minister in 1987. See 'Resignation Letter of State Home Minister Accepted', *The Shillong Times*, June 24, 1987.
42. In 1978, the student-backed Meghalaya Tribal Youth Organization called all regional parties to align together to form the first non-Congress coalition of the state. See. B. Pakem, op. cit.
43. Public opinion regarding the granting of constitutional recognition is sharply divided and many observers feel that such a move would encourage 'tribalism' in a heterogeneous state. For details, see Abhijit Choudhury, 'The Contextual Dimensions of the Sixth Schedule', *Contemporary India*, Nehru Memorial Museum and Library, Vol. 1, No. 4 (October–December 2002), p. 33.
44. For a more elaborate assessment of this relationship, see Rajesh Dev et al., 'Liberal Democracy, Traditional Institutions and Politics of Representation', A.K. Baruah, et al., 'Tribal Traditions and Crisis of Governance in North East India'. www.crisisstates.com.
45. Patricia Mukhim, 'Importance of the Smit Summit', *The Telegraph*, January 20, 2004. Also see T. Blah, 'Fifteen Years of Back Pedaling–II', *The Shillong Times*, October 10, 1987.
46. See Subrata Mitra, op. cit., p. 207.
47. See Pascal Malgniang, 'Women and Elections in Meghalaya', *Proceedings of the North East India Political Science Association* (1996).
48. A.K. Baruah and Manorama Sharma, 'Matriliny, Land Rights and Political Power in Khasi Society', *Indian Journal of Human Rights*, Vol. 3, Nos 1 and 2 (January–December 1999), pp. 210–28.
49. This was revealed in a survey conducted for the Crisis States Programme of LSE conducted by a group of scholars, including this writer, for parts of Meghalaya. See www.crisisstates.com.
50. For details on the debate, see Purabi Shridhar, 'Report on Threat to Matrilineal System in Meghalaya', *Femina*, December 1, 2000.

51. See Diren Bhagawati, 'Meghalaya: The struggle of the three sisters to have a place in the sun', in Girin Phukon (ed.), *Political Dynamics of North East India* (New Delhi: South Asian Publishers, 2000), pp. 175–86.

52. See 'Election Commission declares 5 "general" seats for Meghalaya', *The Shillong Times*, December 28, 1987.

53. Indigenity is a term that has a fuzzy and imprecise connotation since it is open to myriad interpretations according to the social and political proclivities of the agents seeking to define it. It is meant to refer to a collective consciousness among members of groups who are 'recognized' or even seek recognition, by the state and its institutions and perceive themselves to be the 'first' peoples of a territorial region. In the North-East it can refer to a 'social organizational system' through which members share a cognitive perception of 'peoplehood' in relation to a specific territory. Frequently, members of the same ethnic group contest each others' claims on the basis of 'indigenity' rather than 'ethnicity'.

54. See Dev, op. cit. See also, an open letter to the chief minister by five non-tribal members of the Legislative Assembly entitled, 'Non-tribals are being used as Scapegoats', *The Shillong Times*, November 9, 1987.

55. See Pakem, op. cit., pp. 98–99.

56. Calculated from the Election Commission of Meghalaya sources.

57. This support for the Congress has its roots in the state's history with Congress opposing the Land Transfer Act as being discriminatory to non-tribals or slow-pedaling issues that concerned the non-tribals. For elaboration, see *The Meghalaya Legislative Assembly Debates*, Vol. V, No. 1 (1971).

58. A.K. Baruah, 'Middle Class Hegemony and the National Question in Assam', in Milton Sangma (ed.), *Essays on the North East India* (New Delhi: Indus Publishing House, 1994).

59. See Paul R. Brass, *Ethnicity and Nationalism* (New Delhi/Newbury Park/London: Sage Publications, 1991), pp. 22–26.

60. Ibid.

61. See 'CM Capt. Sangma defends move for Inner-line regulation', *The Shillong Times*, May 16, 1987, 'CM admits Lapses in protection of Non-tribals', *The Shillong Times*, October 5, 1987.

62. See Pakem, op. cit., p. 102.

63. Calculated from Election Commission of India, *Statistical Reports*. www.eci.gov.in.

64. For a discussion on 'Confessional Politics', see Susanne Rudolph and Lloyd Rudolph, *In Pursuit of Lakshmi: The Political Economy of the Indian State* (Chicago: University of Chicago Press, 1987).

65. See Diren Bhagawati, 'Ethnic Conflict in Meghalaya: An Epitome of Northeast India', in Girin Phukon (ed.), *Ethnicity and Polity in South Asia* (New Delhi: South Asian Publishers, 2002), p. 246.

66. See *The Shillong Times*, February 21, 1988.

67. For a detailed historical note, see Pakem, op. cit.

68. See Pakem, op. cit., for more details.

69. The state has around 85 percent Christians according to the Census Reports of 1991.

70. Pakem, op. cit., p. 105.

71. See Election Results of Meghalaya, 2003. www.ceomeghalaya.nic.in.

72. See *Statistical Records*, www.eci.gov.in.

73. www.ceomeghalaya.nic.in.

74. See 'Four Rebel Ministers oppose Non-tribal representation in Meghalaya Assembly', *The Shillong Times*, November 7, 1987.

75. T. Blah, 'Meghalaya—15 years of back pedalling–I', *The Shillong Times*, October 9, 1987.

76. Ibid.

77. Ibid.

78. See Carolyn M. Elliot, *Civil Society and Democracy: A Reader* (New Delhi: Oxford University Press, 2003), p. 7.

CHAPTER 11

Validating Status Quo and Local Narratives in Orissa

MOHAMMED BADRUL ALAM

Orissa's election results deviated from the national trend in 2004. The Biju Janata Dal (BJD) and the Bharatiya Janata Party (BJP) achieved remarkable success in both the Lok Sabha and Assembly elections. By contrast, the nationally victorious Congress party won just two out of 21 seats in the Lok Sabha election. Congress, however, did increase its vote percentage and marginally increased its seats in the Assembly. In the bi-polar nature of electoral competition in Orissa, the BJD–BJP coalition team repeated its success in the 1999 Lok Sabha and 2000 Assembly elections. It soundly defeated the Congress-led front that consisted of the Jharkhand Mukti Morcha (JMM) and other smaller regional parties such as the Orissa Gana Parishad (OGP).

How did the BJD–BJP coalition partners turn the anti-incumbency factor common to all parties in India, into one of electoral advantage? Why did Congress lose the parliamentary and Assembly elections for the second consecutive time? How could a third party or front evolve or enlarge its political space in Orissa? The primary factors for this are:

- intra-party squabbles within the Congress party,
- the active co-ordination among BJP's various organizational wings as well as between BJD and BJP,
- and the successful public relation campaigns unleashed by the ruling BJD–BJP coalition government.

This chapter will attempt to explain these factors.

In the Shadow of the 2004 Election: Analyzing Orissa Politics

Orissa politics, for the most part, has been dominated by coalitions. Barring Biju Patnaik's victory in 1961 and 1990 and J.B. Patnaik's victories in 1980, 1985, and 1995, all other state ministries in Orissa have been coalitions either at the formal or informal level. In 2004, the Naveen Patnaik-led BJD–BJP coalition is the only coalition ministry in Orissa to have won an absolute majority back-to-back in the 2000 as well 2004 state Assembly elections. The BJD–BJP duo also won 19 of the 21 Lok Sabha seats from Orissa in both the 1999 and 2004 parliamentary elections.

From the Ganatantra Parishad in the 1950s to the Jana Congress in the 1970s, Orissa has been a happy hunting ground for the provincial political parties. BJD, formed in 1997 by Naveen Patnaik, son of ex-Chief Minister late Biju Patnaik, had been in the ascendance since 1999 and scored spectacular victories in the 1999 and 2004 Lok Sabha elections as well as in the 2000 and 2004 state Assembly polls.

Intra-provincialism is also an emerging feature of Orissa politics. The two important focuses of such conflicts are: (*a*) the rivalry between the highland districts of Orissa and the coastal plains and (*b*) the demand for a separate state by the tribals of Orissa on ethnic grounds, with the former being the most dominant forces of regionalism. The hills versus the plains friction has emerged as a major contentious issue with demands for equality of opportunity and social justice for the people residing in the highland region of the state. In its virulent form, it is a protest against exploitation and a manifestation of a separatist tendency.[1]

Factionalism is yet another salient feature of Orissa politics. It has been more rampant in the politics of the Congress party. As Ramashray Roy (1999) has commented,

each of the factions seeks to outbid rival factions in getting tickets. At different levels of party organization, struggle for power goes on unabated in which the relative power position determines which faction gets how many nominations, which, in turn, confirms a particular faction's relative power position in the party. The widespread factional struggle for superiority in the Congress, especially the struggle for party tickets, creates bad blood among party workers, attenuates party loyalty, encourages defections, and adversely affects the electoral fortunes of the party.[2]

In the 1960s, it was a troika consisting of Harekrushna Mahatab, Biju Patnaik, and Biren Mitra who used to run the state's affairs. Each of them had their own constituencies among the student union leaders, labor groups and civil service personnel. However, factionalism forced Nabakrishna Choudhury, Biren Mitra, and Nandini Satpathy to resign from their offices. The J.B. Patnaik ministry also faced serious discontentment within his Congress party in the 1980s and in 1995, when he again became the chief minister. Similarly, Naveen Patnaik who became chief minister in 2000 following his father's, Biju Patnaik, legacy, had to contend with intra-party squabbles within the BJD. This included cross-voting in the Rajya Sabha election in 2002 resulting in the unexpected victory of Dilip Ray, Naveen Patnaik's political detractor who contested as a rebel candidate against the official BJD nominee.

Orissa, for the most part, has not been able to provide strong mass-based or cadre-based political parties. Most of the political parties which have been successful so far have based their program on populist slogans and demagoguery. Unlike West Bengal and Kerala, where CPI and CPI(M) have developed strong cadres of support, in Orissa these parties have support bases in select constituencies. The western parts of the state are still dominated by feudal elements, whereas in the coastal belt, parties fight it out using personality-based politics. Of late, BJP with its grass-roots organizational support from the Rashtriya Swayamsevak Sangh (RSS), Vishwa Hindu Parishad (VHP), and the Bajrang Dal has been able to build a cadre of its own on a limited basis.

The state of Orissa has a number of prominent Oriya language dailies, and four of these with wide circulations had their editors as contestants in the 2004 Lok Sabha election. While two of these four newspaper editors contested from the BJD, the other two were Congress candidates.[3] Tathagat Satpathy, who defeated K.P. Singh Deo of the Congress party from the Dhenkanal Lok Sabha constituency, has been the editor of *Dharitri* for over a decade. Similarly, Bhatruhari Mahtab, the BJD candidate and editor of the Cuttack city-based *Prajatantra*, won the Cuttack Lok Sabha seat by defeating Jayanti Patnaik of the Congress. (Bhatruhari Mahtab's father, late Harekrushna Mahtab, an ex-chief minister of Orissa, founded the *Prajatantra*.)

Soumya Ranjan Patnaik of the Congress and editor of the Bhubaneswar-based *Sambad*, contested the Bhubaneswar Lok Sabha seat in 2004 which he had earlier won in 1996. However in 2004, he lost to BJD's Prasanna Kumar Patsani, who had defeated Patnaik in 1998 as well. BJP candidate Kharavela Swain, editor of the Oriya daily *Bidesh Khabar*, won from Balasore Lok Sabha constituency three consecutive times in 1998, 1999, and 2004. In Jagatsinghpur Lok Sabha constituency, Ranjiv Biswal, the Congress candidate and editor of the Bhubaneswar-based *The Samay*, lost to Brahmananda Panda of BJD in the 2004 Lok Sabha election. Biswal had won this seat in 1996 and 1998.

The most prominent Oriya daily, *The Samaj*, although apolitical at present, also had as a long-time editor, the late Radhanath Rath, who was a minister in an earlier Orissa cabinet. He had contested and won as an independent candidate from Athgarh assembly constituency with the help of national level parties at different times. *Pragativadi*, another Oriya daily, had as its editor, the late Pradyumna Bal. He won a Lok Sabha seat as a Janata candidate in the 1977 Lok Sabha election from Jagatsinghpur constituency. Most of these newspapers are financed by politicians, and in some cases industrialists, who want to influence the electorate.

SPECIAL SOCIAL CATEGORIES

ROLE OF THE ERSTWHILE ROYALS

Although the princely states merged their territories with the Indian union soon after Independence, the royals, although bereft of power and glory, have played a major role in Orissa elections. In this context, the 2004 election was no exception. Bolangir, in western Orissa, is from where ex-royal Rajendra Narayan Singh Deo rose to become the state's chief minister in 1967. It had four royal candidates for the 2004 poll and each of them won.[4] State Steel and Tourism minister A.U. Singh Deo, son of late Rajendra Narayan Singh Deo, was the BJD candidate from the Bolangir Assembly constituency. His son, K.N. Singh Deo, was BJD's candidate from the Saintala constituency, whereas his daughter-in-law Sangeeta Singh Deo was BJP's candidate from the Bolangir Lok Sabha seat. Sangeeta Singh Deo's husband, Kanak Bardhan Singh Deo, sought re-election from Patnagarh Assembly seat on a BJP ticket. In Kalahandi district, BJP had Bikram Keshari Deo as its Lok Sabha candidate, while his son, Anant Pratap Deo, was contesting on a Congress ticket for the Junagarh seat. In Dhenkanal, K.P. Singh Deo was the candidate for the Lok Sabha while his son, Amarjyoti Singh Deo, was the Congress candidate from Gondia Assembly constituency. They were defeated by BJD candidates in their respective constituencies. BJD, in particular, had a record number of nine royals in its list of candidates including Sugyani Kumari Deo (Khalikote), Pratap Keshari Deo (Aul), Usha Devi (Chikti), Pushpendra Singh Deo (Koksara), Rajnikant Singh (Anugul), Bijay Singh Baria (Padmapur), and Kishore Chandra Singh Deo (Sorada). All the royals who contested as BJD–BJP candidates won, while all such contestants from the Congress lost in the 2004 Lok Sabha and Assembly elections.

WOMEN REPRESENTATION FROM ORISSA

Women comprise 48.5 percent of Orissa's population. After assuming office for the first time in March 2000 as head of the BJD–BJP coalition ministry, Chief Minister Naveen Patnaik launched Mission Shakti, a scheme aimed at empowering women through the formation of self-help groups.[5] By 2004, around 100,070 women Self-help Groups (SHG) involving 1.4 million women had been formed in the state. In Naveen Patnaik's own Ganjam district, there are around 11,000 SHGs with 15–25 members in each of these groups aimed at self-employment and related *sanchyaika* (savings) groups. For the BJD, the women's self-help groups have proved beneficial in courting women voters. Like his father, the late Biju Patnaik who was chief minister in the 1960s and again from 1990–95, Naveen Patnaik continued the policy of reservation of 33 percent of seats for women in village *panchayat*s and urban bodies in order to wean away women voters from the Congress party.

Nonetheless, few women candidates contested in the 2004 Orissa state Assembly election, and just 11 got elected, thus showing a wide gender gap. Out of a total of 802 candidates, only 55 were women. BJD fielded four and its BJP ally had five, while there were nine Congress candidates with the rest being Independents. In terms of percentage, women Assembly members constituted 7.48 percent in 2004—as opposed to 10 percent of the total strength of the Orissa Assembly in 2000. Of the 11 women candidates who won the 2004 Orissa state Assembly election, Pramila Giri (Baisinga), Sanchita Mohanty (Korei), Surama Padhy (Ranapur), Ajayanti Pradhan (Udaygiri), and Hema Gamang (Gunupur) were first-timers, whereas Draupadi Murmu (Rairangpur), Anjali Behera (Hindol), and Bijaylaxmi Patnaik (Khandapra) were elected for the second time. Pramila Mallick (Binjharpur) and Usha Devi (Chikti) won their third term in the state Assembly, and Sugyani Kumari Deo won for the sixth time. In the 2004 Lok Sabha election, only two women were elected—Sangeeta Singh Deo and Archana Nayak from the Bolangir and Kendrapara constituencies, respectively. In the 1999 Lok Sabha elec-tion, three women candidates, Sangeeta Singh Deo, Hema Gamang, and Kumuduni Patnaik were elected.

ROLE OF TRIBAL POPULATION IN ORISSA ELECTIONS

Orissa has the largest variety of tribal communities in the entire coun-try. Koraput, Mayurbhanj, Phulbani, and Sundargarh districts are where most of the tribals reside. Out of 427 Scheduled Tribes in all of India, 62 live in Orissa. The Kondhs alone are the seventh largest tribal group in India and they are twice as large as the Naga tribes of northeastern India. The Scheduled Tribes constitute 24.07 percent of the total population of Orissa and 14.2 percent of the tribal popu-lation of India.[6]

Tribal solidarity was clearly displayed in the 2004 election. On March 10, 2004, just a few weeks prior to the election, hundreds of tribals formed a human chain in Bhubaneswar to mark the 'Tribal Sur-vival and Self-Respect Day,' demanding the establishment of a Tribal

Autonomous District Council (TADC) and re-introduction of subsidies for tribes. The human chain organized, under the banner of
Orissa Nari Samaj, an apex body of 53 tribal organizations, submitted
a memorandum to Chief Minister Naveen Patnaik highlighting their
six-point charter of demands. The memorandum stated that till the
formation of TADC, water, land and forest resources—key to the
survival of tribes—be handed over to the Area Local Tribal Village
Council (ALTVC).

Among their demands geared toward empowerment of tribals was
that ALTVC should be legally empowered to carry out forestation,
regeneration and protection of the forests, as well as its use for subsistence. This involves all developmental works. Other demands included
that welfare programs for tribals should be allowed under ALTVC
supervision to keep the poorest section free from money-lenders, and
that they should be given interestfree loans. Also, non-tribals should
not be allowed to carry out economic activities like mining, industry,
and other business enterprises by acquiring tribal lands.

At the local level, tribal groups formed strategic alliances with
various political parties. In Dhenkanal district, the Adivashi Kranti
Sangathan decided to support the BJD Lok Sabha candidate, Tathagat
Satpathy, after securing a firm commitment that if elected he would
insure tribal interests in the reserve forest and work for the general
improvement of the area. Satpathy's resounding victory in the 2004
Lok Sabha election reflected tribal support.

The Congress maintained its tribal-dominated Koraput stronghold
in western Orissa. Former Chief Minister Giridhari Gamang and his
wife Hema Gamang won the Koraput Lok Sabha seat and Gunupur
Assembly constituency respectively. In Mayurbhanj, where the
Jharkhand Mukti Morcha (JMM), has made serious inroads, the state
has not seen any tribal–non-tribal divide. In the 2004 elections, JMM
received 37.43 percent of the votes and its candidate, Sudam Marandi,
won. Earlier, JMM had received only 10.37 percent of the votes in
1991 and 16.33 percent in the 1999 Lok Sabha elections. Unlike
its counterpart in the state of Bihar that relentlessly pursued and
eventually succeeded in having a separate state in recognition of
Jharkhandi identity, the Orissa wing of the JMM looked at the issue
of developmental imbalance in the context of tribal population residing in Orissa alone.[7]

In the tribal dominated Phulbani Lok Sabha constituency, BJD's nominee Sugrib Singh won 42.9 percent votes and defeated Congress', Abhimanyu Behera who received 40.4 percent of the votes polled. One of the main reasons for BJD's victory was the support it received from the highly influential Kondh tribal groups who used the well-crafted *Muthadari* system. A *Mutha* consists of a group of villages, usually between seven and 10, but may go up to 20. In each *Mutha*, there is a tribal head called *Muthadar* or *Patra*, and under them are one or two sub-*Muthadar*s following a hierarchical pattern down to the foot soldiers. Furthermore, in spite of their ethnic rivalry, the Kondhs in Phulbani made a strategic alliance with the Pana community. Although the Kondhs are clan based, the three main sub-groups, Dongaria Kondh, Kutia Kondh, and Desia Kondh, constitute a population of over 11 million and constitute about 16.5 percent of the overall tribal population in Orissa.[8] The *Muthadar* acting as the hierarchical head and a strategic, tactical coalition strategy between the Kondhs and Panas, the core support titled the scale favor of the BJP candidate.

Important tribes in Orissa also took advantage of the institutional incentives offered by the Union and state governments. Provisions have been made under Article 164 of the Constitution for a ministry for Tribal Welfare in the states as well as at the Center. Article 338 provides for a National Commission to investigate and monitor all matters relating to the safeguards provided for the Scheduled Tribes. This includes the planning process for socio-economic development and inquiring into specific complaints about rights and safeguards of Scheduled Tribes. Empowerment of tribals had its origin in the Fifth Five-Year Plan, 1977–82, that was hailed as a landmark in the history of tribal development. The Tribal Sub Plan approach contained the following features:[9]

- Identification of states with tribal majority blocks into the Integrated Tribal Development Projects (ITDP), with a view to adopting and implementing an integrated approach for development.
- Preparation of an integrated pilot project report for each ITDP, keeping in view the natural resources of the regions as well as the skills, aptitudes and needs of the tribal population.

- Creation of a relevant administrative structure in tribal areas and adoption of appropriate personnel policies.
- Quantification of financial resources from out of the state and Central plans for tribal areas and tribal peoples broadly corresponding to the tribal population percentage in the total population of the state.

At the time of elections, whether for the state Assembly or Lok Sabha, the tribes in Orissa, despite their heterogeneous character, can unite and successfully bring tribal welfare issues to the forefront.

LACK OF ÉLITE

The dominant social and political élite of Orissa have not come forward to take up the mantle of leadership. In this connection, the *kendu* leaf traders, one of the most highly visible interest groups in Orissa politics, must be blamed for corrupting the entire political system of the state. The traders obtains leases of reserved forest land for growing *kendu* by bribing politicians of the ruling party. Also, political defections based on personal considerations have been so frequent that, barring a few, all major political leaders have resorted to defections at some time or another.[10] It is an unfortunate aspect of Orissa politics that leading politicians of the state have been associated with the game of '*Aya* Ram, *Gaya* Ram,' a term coined for frequent defections in the state of Haryana. On the positive side, the emergence of the middle class is likely to consolidate the regional political arena in Orissa in the absence of a powerful bourgeois class and the decline of feudal influence in the state.[11]

DYNASTY AND ITS MEANING IN ORISSA POLITICS

Dynastic representation in the 2004 Lok Sabha and Assembly elections capitalized recognition and mass appeal of their family names. Former congress chief minister J.B. Patnaik won his Begunia Assembly seat while his wife Jayanti Patnaik and son-in-law Soumya Ranjan Patnaik lost. From the Cuttack Lok Sabha seat, it was Bhatruhari Mahtab, son of ex-chief minister Dr Harekrushna Mahtab, who defeated Jayanti Patnaik of the Congress party. Despite an internal family feud, Giridhari Gamang, a former chief minister, and his wife Hema Gamang—both from the Congress party, won their respective Lok Sabha and Assembly seats from Koraput district.

Chiranjiv Biswal, son of former deputy chief minister Basant Biswal, won the Assembly election from Tirtol constituency as a Congress nominee while his brother Ranjiv Biswal lost the Jagatsinghpur Lok Sabha seat to the BJD candidate. At Dhenkanal, Tathagat Satpathy, a BJD candidate and son of former chief minister Nandini Satpathy, defeated K.P. Singh Deo, for its Lok Sabha seat. Senior BJD minister, Bijoyshree Routray, son of former chief minister Nilamani Routray, was elected as the BJD candidate from the Basudevpur Assembly constituency. The incumbent chief minister, Naveen Patnaik of BJD, son of former chief minister Biju Patnaik, was re-elected from the Hinjli Assembly constituency. From the BJP, former Union minister Debendra Pradhan lost in the Pallalhara Assembly constituency, while his son, Dharmendra Pradhan won the Deogarh Lok Sabha seat.

EMERGENCE OF BJP IN ORISSA POLITICS

The Bharatiya Janata Party was formed in 1980 following its earlier version—the Jan Sangh. BJP won one seat in the Orissa state Assembly in 1985, and lost all of the six Lok Sabha seats it contested in 1989 with only 1.5 percent of votes polled. Its vote percentage went up to 3.56 percent for the Assembly in 1990 with two seats won.[12] In the 1991 Lok Sabha election, BJP did not win any Lok Sabha seats, but the vote total received went to 9.50 percent. In the 1995 Assembly election, BJP won nine seats.

In the 1996 Lok Sabha election, although the party did not win any of the 21 Lok Sabha seats, yet BJP candidates were able to get more than 100,000, or 13.2 percent, votes in 10 constituencies. In the subsequent election for *Zilla Parishads* (district council) in 1997, BJP improved its profile further by winning as many as 118 seats, mainly in western Orissa. The 1998 Lok Sabha election was a golden phase for the BJP where, along with its pre-election partner BJD, they won 16 out of the 21 Lok Sabha seats from Orissa. From among the newly-elected BJP MPs, Debendra Pradhan and Joel Oram were appointed as ministers in Vajpayee's Cabinet. In the 1999 Lok Sabha election, BJP made a clean sweep by winning all of the nine seats it contested.

The growth of the BJP in Orissa can be attributed to the overt and covert support extended to it by the Sangh Parivar: the Viswa Hindu Parishad, the Bajrang Dal, the RSS, the ABVP, and related saffron affiliates. While the Hindu plank was consolidated through Advani's *rath yatra* in 1992, concerted efforts were made in the tribal belt to break the monopoly of the JMM's influence by re-converting the Christian converts—the core of support for the Jharkhand party. The Banabasi Kalyan Ashram, a Sangh tribal outfit, also took up populist measures in western Orissa which in turn enhanced BJP support among the tribal population. One can also argue that strategic alliances with popular regional leaders played a crucial role in the BJP's 1999 electoral successes in Orissa.

Another factor can be BJP's adjustment with the 'fragmented and increasingly de-centered structure of India's party system.'[13] However, its number was reduced to seven in the 2004 Lok Sabha election. Similarly, in the Assembly election, its number was reduced from 38 in 2000 to 32 in 2004. Part of the reason can be ascribed to a section among the electorate opposing the RSS and VHP call for a blanket ban on cow slaughter and a legislative curb on conversion by Christian missionaries. The loss of support to some sitting BJP MLAs was another contributing factor. However, with its coalition partner BJD which got 61 seats on its own, both parties came back to power in the state in 2004 with a combined 93 seats out of a total of 147 seats, compared to 106 seats in the 2000 Assembly. In terms of voting per-centage, while BJP polled 18.2 percent in the 2000 Assembly election, it secured 17.1 percent in 2004, as shown in Tables 11.1 and 11.2.

One of the key reasons as to why BJP could not replicate its earlier success in the tribal belt in western Orissa in 2004 was its ambiguous

Table 11.1

Orissa Assembly elections, 2000 and 2004

Party	Seats Won in 2000	Seats Won in 2004
BJP	38	32
BSP	–	–
CPI	1	1
CPI(M)	1	1
Congress	26	38
JD(S)	1	–
BJD	68	61
OGP	–	2
JMM	3	4
AITC	1	–
Independents	8	8

Source: Election Records, Home (Election) Department, Government of Orissa, 2000 and 2004.

Table 11.2

Orissa Lok Sabha elections, 1999 and 2004

Party	Seats Contested (1999/2004)	Seats Won (1999/2004)	% of Votes (1999/2004)
BJD	12 (12)	10 (11)	33.00 (30.20)
BJP	9 (9)	9 (7)	24.63 (19.30)
Congress	20 (21)	2 (2)	36.94 (40.43)
JMM	7 (1)	0 (1)	1.70 (1.54)
Independents	33 (26)	0 (0)	1.31 (4.50)

Source: Election Commission of India, official Website, www.eci.gov.in.

stand on the Western Orissa Development Council (WODC) and the BJP's inability to overcome the necessary legislative limitations that were imposed on the council.[14] As a result, instead of being an autonomous body, WODC was reduced to the status of a local board with virtually no fiscal or administrative power. The same was the case with the ambitious KBK (Kalahandi–Bolangir–Koraput) project, which disillusioned many tribals. The demand for a separate Koshala state by a section of local leaders from Bolangir, Kalahandi, and Sundargarh in western Orissa, further diminished the BJP's popularity.

NAVEEN PATNAIK: WAS IT CHARISMA OR TEFLON?

In the 2004 Lok Sabha and Assembly elections, Orissa was one of the few states that withstood the Congress resurgence as well the anti-incumbency factor.[15] The BJD–BJP retained power in spite of a reduced vote percentage—47 percent as compared to 58 percent in 2000. One can argue that the only visible sign of development in Orissa under Naveen Patnaik in the period 2000–2004 is the 520 km newly built stretch of National Highway 5 connecting Kolkata to Chennai and part of Vajpayee's popular Golden Quadrilateral Project. So how did Naveen Patnaik retain his support in 2004?

First, it needs to be understood that Orissa is one of the few states that has not seen Mandalization or any class-based mobilization. This low level of politicization may have created a context that enabled Naveen Patnaik to survive without doing anything spectacular.[16] Second, Naveen Patnaik distanced himself and his party from the politics of the previous Congress regime by crafting a message of clean and transparent governance. It was reinforced through his first term in office from 2000 to 2004 by undertaking various anti-corruption drives, including a few of his own Cabinet colleagues and long-time Assembly members. In the 2004 election, Naveen Patnaik brought in 29 new faces to contest the Assembly election. The Congress welcomed some of these expelled leaders such as the Speaker of the State Assembly, Sarat Kar, Cabinet Minister Ramakrishna Patnaik and his wife Kumudini Patnaik. Congress election prospects were not helped by these actions.

Third, Naveen Patnaik cultivated a personal image built around probity in public life. He characterized his bachelor status and being born in a rich family to his advantage, by portraying an image of himself as not having any desire for wealth. Although his detractors dubbed him as a non-resident Oriya and a person who could not even read or write Oriya, he was widely seen as a leader determined to curb corruption in the state. Finally, under Naveen Patnaik's stewardship the BJD–BJP alliance strengthened its organizational base throughout the state. As a result, the BJD was stronger in the coastal region while

the BJP was stronger in western and in interior parts. Similarly, there
was a neat fit between BJP's traditional appeal to upper-caste voters
and BJD's support for the OBCs (other backward castes).

In their joint election manifesto that was released on April 8, 2004,
BJD–BJP made several populist planks.[17] Among these were creation
of employment and self-employment opportunities for more than
2.4 million youth in the state and establishing a KBK development
authority. This manifesto also included setting up a foreign investment
forum, providing free cycles to all high school-going tribal girls, electricity for all villages, no hike in power tariff, and expansion of irrigation facilities. It also demanded special category status for Orissa
by the Central government, to establish special courts to expedite trial
of corruption cases, exploitation of mineral resources of the state and
development of industrial and tourism potential. Although most of
the election promises made in 2000 were yet to be implemented,
Naveen Patnaik's ministry is perceived to be a lesser evil than its counterpart in the Congress party. In the 2004 poll, the Congress party
under J.B. Patnaik's leadership had a less-than-favorable image before
the Oriya electorate due to the numerous acts of corruption and nepo-
tism committed in the state during the 1980s and mid-1990s.

VOTING TRENDS AND LESSONS LEARNT IN SELECT LOK SABHA CONSTITUENCIES

Analysing a few select Lok Sabha constituencies across various regions
of Orissa illustrates why the BJD–BJP alliance maintained its electoral
strength in the 2004 Lok Sabha election, as it had done in 1999,
securing 19 out of 21 seats.

EASTERN ORISSA: DHENKANAL, SAMBALPUR, SUNDARGARH, KEONJHAR, DEOGARH

In eastern Orissa, BJD–BJP won in all five constituencies. In Dhenkanal
constituency, the BJD nominee Tathagat Satpathy won in all seven

Assembly segments under it. The Congress won the Dhenkanal Assembly seat, yet the BJD won it in the Lok Sabha poll. A number of reasons can be ascribed to BJD's victory. First, in the earlier 1999 Lok Sabha election, Satpathy narrowly lost to Congress nominee K.P. Singh Deo by only 3,674 votes, which was 0.61 percent of the total valid votes. Second, Satpathy had a strong organizational base in Dhenkanal city and its suburbs as he had won the 1998 Lok Sabha poll and the 1990 state Assembly election. K.P. Singh Deo was also a veteran of Dhenkanal politics by virtue of being an ex-royal and one who had won from this constituency several times—both as a Swatantra Party candidate and later as a Congress party candidate. Yet the high voltage campaign unleashed by Satpathy, with strong support from Chief Minister Naveen Patnaik and the rank and file of the BJD and BJP, resulted in a resounding victory for the BJD candidate. Furthermore, Satpathy was assisted by the fond memory of his mother Nandini Satpathy. She was the chief minister in the mid-1970s and a long-time MLA from both Dhenkanal and Gondia Assembly constituencies who had undertaken a number of notable developmental projects in the district. A two-way contest also helped in 2004. In the 1999 election, the Independent candidate, Rudra Narayan Pani, acted as a spoiler who diverted a large chunk of votes from Satpathy's vote bank as the former was an influential BJP leader of the region who wanted a ticket for himself.

COASTAL ORISSA: CUTTACK, JAGATSINGHPUR, KENDRAPARA, BHUBANESWAR, JAJPUR, BHADRAKH, PURI

The BJD–BJP coalition won all seven parliamentary seats in the coastal belt of Orissa in 2004 thus repeating their success in the 1999 election. For the Jagatsinghpur seat, BJD candidate Brahmnanda Panda defeated Congress nominee Ranjiv Biswal who had won in 1996 and 1998. Unlike the Cuttack Lok Sabha seat, it was a close contest. Congress candidate Biswal received more votes than his BJD rival in Tirtol and Balikuda Assembly segments. Coincidentally, the Congress MLA from Tirtol is Chiranjeeb Biswal who is the younger brother of Ranjiv Biswal. Both Ranjiv and Chiranjiv are sons of late Basant Biswal, who was the deputy chief minister during the 1980s. Basant Biswal and later his son, Chiranjiv, had represented Tirtol Assembly constituency in the past. However, what made BJD's Panda the overall winner was by garnering sufficient votes in the Nimpora Assembly belt where the Assembly seat was won by the coalition government's BJP MLA, Baidhar Mullick. Through these surplus votes, Panda compensated for the deficit he had in other Assembly segments of Jagatsinghpur Lok Sabha constituency. Similarly, in the Kakatpur Assembly constituency, where the state agriculture minister and BJD's Surendra Nath Nayak was re-elected, the BJD candidate for the Lok Sabha received more votes than his Congress counterpart. In Ersama Assembly constituency too, Damodar Rout, a cabinet member of the Naveen Patnaik ministry and BJD Assembly candidate, helped BJD's Lok Sabha candidate Panda with his direct supervision in of the relief work after the 1999 super cyclone that had ravaged Ersama constituency.

SOUTHERN ORISSA: BERHAMPUR, ASKA

There are two Lok Sabha seats in southern Orissa which BJD and Congress party shared in Aska and Berhampur constituencies, respectively. In Berhampur, it was the Congress party that avenged its defeat in the 1999 election when its nominee Chandra Sekhar Sahu defeated the BJP candidate Anadi Sahu, winner of the 1999 election. Chandra Sekhar Sahu received 49.48 percent of the total votes polled while Anadi Sahu got 42.3 percent. What was remarkable about Congress' victory was that its candidate led in six of the seven Assembly segments. What tilted the scale for the Congress candidate for the Lok Sabha poll was a result of various factors. First, Chandra Mohan Sahu himself was a party veteran who had earlier contested against Naveen Patnaik in the adjacent Aska Lok Sabha seat. Second, the Berhampur seat has traditionally been a Congress stronghold with BJP winning the seat only in the 1999 election. Even former Prime Minister P. V. Narasimha Rao had contested and won this seat in 1996 as the constituency was considered to be safe for him.

Western Orissa: Koraput, Nowrangpur, Phulbani, Bolangir, Kalahandi

This backward region consists primarily of tribal populations such as the Sabars, Doruas, Parajas, Kondhs, and Bhumias. Except Koraput, where Congress party retained the seat, BJD–BJP coalition won the remaining four seats in the western region. In Koraput Lok Sabha constituency, nearly 70 percent of the voters live in and around 4,000 villages. The politics of Koraput in many ways is the story of the Gamangs. Although the BJD nominee, Mutika Papanna, gained more votes in two Assembly segments, Pottangi and Jeypore, it was not enough to overcome Gamang's electoral advantage that was helped by his long association with the constituency. He had set up tribal development agencies during his tenure as a Union minister and later as the state's chief minister in 1999. He also benefited from Congress chief Sonia Gandhi's campaign and from dissatisfaction among BJD's rank and file for not giving the BJD ticket to party veteran Jayaram Pangi.

Northern Orissa: Balasore, Mayurbhanj

In north Orissa, the Balasore Lok Sabha seat was won by the BJP, while the JMM candidate won the Mayurbhanj seat by defeating the BJP. Balasore constituency consisted of seven Assembly segments. In the 2004 Lok Sabha election, BJP candidate M.A.K. Swain defeated his Congress rival Niranjan Panda by a wide margin of 236,955 votes. In fact, the percentage of votes received by the BJP candidate was the highest in the three consecutive elections—2004 (58.37 percent), 1999 (55.68 percent), and 1998 (53.17 percent). Swain's victory can be attributed to:

- Dissatisfaction in Bhograi constituency with Kamla Das switching from BJD to Congress.
- Denial of tickets to either of the Patra couple (Kartikeswar and Umarani) who had won the Bhograi Assembly seat and the Balasore Lok Sabha seat several times in the past.

- BJP's organizational skills resulting in the BJP MLA's victory in the traditional Congress seat of Jaleswar constituency. This also helped Swain in the Lok Sabha poll.
- Development work: Swain's adroitly disbursed MPLAD (Member of Parliament Local Area Development) funds for a few select projects across the Balasore Lok Sabha constituency and his tireless efforts succeeded in getting more central assistance for road construction and bridge repair work between Jaleswar and Bhograi.
- Holding meetings with the people of his constituency on a regular basis paid handsome dividends at the poll.

Concluding Observations

The Congress Party is no Longer the Epi-Center of the Power Game

Although the Congress party recovered some ground in the 2004 Assembly election due to the selection of strong candidates and local factors, in the Lok Sabha poll, it could not improve its 1999 margin of two seats. The only aspect common between the 1999 and 2004 election was in the Koraput constituency where Hema Gamang won in 1999, and her husband Giridhari Gamang who had won this seat since 1971(except the 1999 election) won it in the 2004 election as well. In Dhenkanal, Congress candidate K.P. Singh Deo (who squeezed by in 1999), lost to the same BJD candidate, Tathagat Satpathy, by a larger margin in the 2004 poll. In the Berhampur Lok Sabha constituency, Chandra Mohan Sahu of the Congress re-asserted his party's sway over this constituency in southern Orissa by wresting the seat from the BJP which had won it in the 1999 election.

What is conspicuous about the Congress party's decline is the party's inability to hold on to its edge in the tribal belt of northern and western Orissa—its support base in the 1980s. The unpopularity of J.B. Patnaik and the corruption charge against him during his tenure as the state's chief minister that lasted for much of the 1980s and part of the 1990s, turned out to be a serious liability for the party. Congress party also lost in an institutional sense as the segmental brand of politics was taking increasing hold in Orissa with single-cleavage parties such as BJD in Orissa undercutting the Congress' self-serving 'catch-all' politics.[18]

Except Koraput where BJD had fielded a greenhorn, Muttika Papanna, against veteran Giridhari Gamang, the 2004 election from the BJD standpoint surpassed 1999 with 11 seats compared to 10. In 2004, BJD wrested the Dhenkanal Lok Sabha seat from the Congress who had won it in 1999. Similarly, In the 2004 Assembly election, BJD secured 61 out of the 84 seats contested. Although BJD had late Biju Patnaik as its lucky election mascot that was presented to the electorate through a carefully orchestrated media blitz, BJD's organizational wing was, between 1999 and 2004, able to build a strong network from the bloc to the district level and was also successful in forming co-ordinating committees with the BJP, its coalition partner, in most of the 147 Assembly constituencies of the state.

Several BJD candidates who had won in the 1999 Lok Sabha poll and 2000 Assembly elections were denied tickets for neglecting their constituencies. For example, the selection of Brahmanand Panda in place of Trilochan Kanungo for the Jagatsinghpur, and Mohan Jena in place of Jagannath Mullick in the Jajpur Lok Sabha seats, were based on their winnability factor as determined by the BJD party high command.

BJP's GRASS-ROOT ORGANIZATION PAID GOOD DIVIDENDS

In the 2004 Lok Sabha election, the BJP lost two seats, Mayurbhanj and Berhampur, but the party was able to maintain its overall strength so as to win seven of the nine seats it contested. One of the main reasons for BJP's continuing strength was due to its Sangh Parivar support group—the VHP, the RSS, and the Bajrang Dal. In the run up to the 2004 election, L.K. Advani, Deputy Prime Minister in the NDA government, made a well publicized and well attended 'Bharat Uday Yatra' across key Lok Sabha constituencies of western, eastern, and coastal Orissa. His message was a rallying call to BJP activists and cadres that made a significant electoral impact. On the issue of conversion of tribals to Christianity and subsequent re-conversions to Hinduism, the BJP succeeded in dividing JMM support. BJP state-level leaders from the neighboring states of Bihar, West Bengal, and Andhra Pradesh also played key roles in several constituencies.

One important aspect of their successful publicity was the display-ing of the then Prime Minister Atal Behari Vajpayee's pictures at strategic junctions in coastal Orissa along the national highways that were being expanded under his ambitious plan to connect the four metropolitan cities of the country in a single network. The scheduling of the Lok Sabha poll in two phases also enabled BJP's top leadership to use its resources most effectively. The BJP's ascendance in Orissa could also be due to its particular brand of Hindu nationalism. In Orissa, the BJP sought to exploit the state's linguistic and regional diversity by highlighting the grievances of discrete segments of the population at the local level and also by taking advantage of the pol-itical space created by the endemic rivalries and sense of apathy within the Congress party.

POLITICS OF DEFECTION IS NEUTRALIZED BY THE NAVEEN FACTOR

The 2004 Lok Sabha election witnessed several defections on the eve of the polls. While some changed sides because they were not sure of getting their party's nomination, others were expelled due to their anti-party activities. As for the BJD, thanks to the charisma and the aura of relative corruption-free image of Chief Minister Naveen Patnaik, defections were minimal. When Ramakrishna Patnaik, a senior BJD member and cabinet minister in the BJD–BJP coalition ministry, was expelled for anti-party activities by Naveen Patnaik, he contested as a Congress candidate from the Aska Lok Sabha seat and lost by a huge margin. His wife, Kumuduni Patnaik, was also expelled from BJD and later contested as a Congress MLA candidate from Kodala constituency, faced a similar fate. Ironically, the winner of the Aska Lok Sabba seat in 2004 was Harihara Swain, previously of the Con-gress party. Earlier, in 1998 and 1999, Naveen Patnaik had won this southern Orissa seat.

Similarly, in coastal Kendrapara Lok Sabha constituency, Archana Nayak, defeated as the Congress candidate in 1996 and 1998, won in 2004 as a BJD candidate against the former, Union Minister, Srikanta Jena. In the prestigious Bhubaneswar Assembly seat, the Assembly Speaker and expelled BJD leader Sarat Kar who was given a Congress ticket, lost to BJP's Bishwa Bhusan Harichandan.

Erstwhile Royals Win by being on the BJD–BJP Coalition Bandwagon

Several former maharajas contested the 2004 Lok Sabha poll in Orissa, providing color and pageantry to the elections. It was again due to BJD–BJP's repeat success in 2004 that enabled Bolangir Lok Sabha candidate Sangeeta Kumari Singh Deo and Kalahandi's Bikram Keshari Deo to win from their respective constituencies. In the Assembly election, too, several members of won from the royal families former princely states of Bolangir, Kalahandi, and Ganjam. Although the BJD–BJP campaign co-ordination team provided valuable feedback to their candidates well ahead of the election, in the case of Sangeeta Singh Deo and Bikram Singh Deo, both were well versed and familiar with their constituencies as they had won in 1998 and 1999 as well. Apart from their earlier victories, they had also allocated a good chunk of their MPLAD fund for the development of infrastructure in their respective constituencies. In Bolangir Lok Sabha constituency, Sangeeta Singh Deo was also assisted by her husband, state industry affairs minister Kanak Bardhan Singh Deo, and son, Kalikesh Narayan Singh Deo, who won the Patnagarh and Saintla Assembly seats in the Bolangir Lok Sabha constituency. Another close relative of Sangeeta Singh Deo, an ex-royal and minister in Orissa's BJD–BJP coalition government, Ananga Udaya Singh Deo, won the Bolangir Assembly seat, thus insuring an easy electoral victory for Sangeeta Singh Deo from the district's sole Lok Sabha seat.

NICHE PARTIES LOSE THEIR SHINE

In the 2004 election, the race was bi-polar in almost all the constituencies except Mayurbhanj where in a friendly contest for this Lok Sabha seat, the Congress party provided a stiff challenge to both the

JMM and BJP paving the way for an eventual victory for JMM. As per the pre-election pact between the BJD and BJP, the former contested 12 Lok Sabha seats whereas the latter fielded nine candidates for the state's total number of 21 Lok Sabha seats. As for Congress, it contested all the 21 seats, including Mayurbhanj, despite its pre-election arrangement with JMM for all seats, and for the purpose of not splitting the tribal votes among these two parties.

The fringe parties in Orissa politics such as the BSP, SP, and TC, could not make their presence felt as their candidates did not have enough resources to match the campaigns of BJD–BJP or the Congress. These candidates were relatively unknown in the constituencies they contested from and also lacked a focused campaign. Furthermore, the major issue of some of these niche parties were co-opted by the major parties. For example, for the Bhadrakh Lok Sabha poll, the BSP could not make any headway as its minority and Dalit plank was usurped by the Congress and the BJD–BJP coalition resulting in the victory of their candidates in both the Lok Sabha and Assembly constituencies.

TRIBALS ARE BEING PROACTIVE IN ASSERTING THEIR RIGHTS

The 2004 election also resulted in the pro-tribal JMM winning the Mayurbhanj Lok Sabha seat (won by the BJP in 1998 and 1999) with Sudam Marandi defeating the BJP candidate. Apart from its Lok Sabha win, JMM also won the key Assembly constituencies of Bahalda, Baripada, Biramitrapur, and Raghunathpalli spread across northern and eastern Orissa, in the 2004 election. It gained support through a sustained campaign, including an agitation against eviction from the tribal lands, coupled with political rallies in various parts of the state.

Chief Minister Naveen Patnaik and the BJD–BJP coalition made concerted efforts to address issues important to the tribal population resulting in small yet significant support from the tribal bloc. However, tribals remained united in their demands for a major say in the policies that were germane to their land and livelihood. If the BJP was able to tap into some pockets of tribal votes, credit must go to Union Tribal

Welfare Minister Joel Oram. He provided funding for various tribal development projects and other related initiatives in both his own Sundargarh Lok Sabha constituency as well as in other adjoining constituencies.

CONCLUSION

To sum up, the study and analysis of electoral outcomes in the 2004 Lok Sabha polls in Orissa must emphasize Naveen Patnaik's personal popularity. In spite of being criticized as a person who lacked proficiency in Oriya language, the incumbent chief minister deftly silenced his critics by a careful prioritizing of populist programs such as Operation Mission Shakti for women and strategic implementation of the Tribal Sub Plan for the welfare of the state's tribal population. Second, the 2004 election showed effective co-ordination among BJP's various organizational outfits as well as between BJD and the BJP at all levels, with successful public campaigns resulting in a decisive victory for the coalition partners. In this context, the Sangh Parivar, consisting of the VHP, Bajrang Dal, ABVP, RSS, and Banabasi Kalyan Ashram, provided both overt and covert support to BJP candidates in a consolidated manner. These efforts resulted in retaining for the most part the political space the BJP had created for itself since 1999. On the other hand, the Congress party lacked a unified approach and suffered from infighting and selection of weak candidates for various Lok Sabha constituencies. Leadership struggles among Congress élites over the possibility of becoming chief minister further sent mixed signals to the party's core constituency across the state, resulting in a lower morale.

NOTES

1. R.N. Mishra, *Regionalism and State Politics in India* (Delhi: Ashish Publishers, 1984).
2. Ramashray Roy, 'Orissa: The Fall of the Congress Fortress', in Paul Wallace and Ramashray Roy (eds), *Indian Politics and the 1998 Election* (New Delhi: Sage Pubications, 1999).

3. 'From the newsroom to the poll arena', *The Hindu* (Chennai), April 15, 2004.
4. 'Orissa going royal all the way', *The Times of India* (New Delhi), March 28, 2004 and 'Orissa Polls: Royals add a dash of colour', *The Pioneer* (Delhi), March 24, 2004.
5. 'BJD woos women with self-help groups', *The Statesman* (Kolkata), April 23, 2004 and 'Orissa's bachelor CM out to woo women', *The Times of India*, April 4, 2004.
6. Tara Dutt, *Tribal Development in India* (New Delhi: Gyan Publishing House, 2001). See 'Tribals want BJD to fulfill their demands'; available on www.OrissaIndia.com, accessed on April 12, 2004, and 'Navin promises development package for tribals', *The Pragativadi*, Oriya language newspaper, March 25, 2004, available on www.pragativadi.com.
7. Amit Prakash, *Jharkhand: Politics of Development and Identity* (Delhi: Orient Longman, 2001), p. 356.
8. Sukant Chaudhury, *Tribal Identity* (New Delhi: Rawat Publications, 2004), pp. 137–45. Dutt, op. cit., p. 11.
9. Dutt, ibid.
10. Babulal Fadia, *State Politics in India* (New Delhi: Radiant Publishers, 1984), p. 148.
11. Bishnu Mohapatra, 'Orissa—Elections and Everyday Politics: Local Narratives of a National Event', *Economic and Political Weekly*, January 22, 2000, vol. 35, No. 4, pp. 170–73. Bishnu Mohapatra, 'Complex Scene', *Frontline* (Chennai), July 12, 1996.
13. John Echeverri-Gent, 'Politics in India's Decentred Polity', in Alyssa Ayres and Philip Oldebnburg (eds), *India Briefing: Quickening the Pace of Change* (New York: M.E. Sharpe, 2002).
14. 'Naveen springs surprises, brings in 29 new faces', *The Pioneer* (New Delhi), March 23, 2004.
15. 'The One Who Stayed', *Outlook India*, May 31, 2004; 'A Chief Minister's Victory', *Frontline*, Vol. 21, No. 11, May 22–June 4, 2004; *The Hindu* (Chennai), May 20, 2004.
16. 'Naveen Patnaik's popularity was the key', *The Hindu* (Chennai), May 20, 2004.
17. 'BJD–BJP releases its joint manifesto', available on www.orissaindia.com, accessed on April 13, 2004.
18. 'Catch-All Party' is a term first used by Otto Kircheimer in reference to changes post World War II. See, Otto Kirscheimer, 'The Transformation of the Western European Party Systems', in Joseph La Palombara and Myron Weiner (eds), *Political Parties and Political Development* (Princeton, NJ: Princeton Uni-versity Press, 1966), pp. 177–200. Also see, Paul Wallace and Ramashrary Roy (eds), *India's 1999 Elections and 20th Century Politics* (New Delhi: Sage Publications, 2003), p. 2.

CHAPTER 12

CPI(M) Dominance and 'Other' Parties in West Bengal

Amiya K. Chaudhuri

The post-Emergency Assembly election in 1977 served as the watershed in the politics of West Bengal both in its electoral and political processes. The Jyoti Basu-led coalition government that came to power in 1977 continues with only a change of chief minister in 2000. The Communist Party of India, Marxist (CPI[M]), has been the predominant partner; however, other coalition partners have assumed more importance since the 2001 Assembly election, and the coalition continued to dominate in the 2004 parliamentary elections (Table 12.1). The three major coalition partners—the Forward Bloc (FB), the Revolutionary Socialist Party (RSP), and the Communist Party of India (CPI)—now have, theoretically, more bargaining power in the system but governmental stability has never become an issue. By contrast, the Congress party appears to be almost decimated in the emergent socio-political scenario, although it registered small gains in the 2004 parliamentary elections.

A number of factors contribute to the unique stability of the Left Front régime in West Bengal. History has taught the CPI(M) and other Front partners the lesson of accommodation with people of different persuasions. All the Left parties, particularly the CPI(M), have acquired power through a series of political movements that brought them closer to the people. Important components of leftist politics in the state include substantial measures of land reforms,

Table 12.1

Percentage of seats won by the Left Front in *Panchayat* elections, 1978–2003

Year	Gram Panchayat	Panchayat Samiti	Zilla Parishad
1978	70.28	76.95	71.51
1983	61.20	66.27	62.15
1988	72.32	78.79	73.45
1993	64.35	72.75	65.67
1998	56.09	67.08	58.08
2003	65.75	74.05	67.21

Source: Compiled; *Paschim Banger Panchayat Nirvachan Tathya o Samiksha (1978–2003)*, Bharater Communist Party, Pachim Banga Rajya Committee (Bengali).

the reviving of the system of rural self-governance with a view to getting nearer to the base of real power, and taking some genuine policy decisions of a populist nature. They also limited inter-party rivalries, remained alert against the opposition and built formidable party organizations. Party networks spread to grass-roots levels so as to nurse their electoral bases and create a congenial environment for a coalition culture.

The Left Front régime has continuously stayed in power for about three decades by winning six consecutive elections. One of the principal reasons is the predominant position of the CPI(M) in the coalition structure. What accounts for its dominance is its capacity for 'direct and mediated'[1] social mobilization. It has held a majority of the Assembly seats from 1977 to 1996. Its share of Assembly seats began declining from 1996, yet its percentage share of votes remained about the same. The Left parties learnt from experience that the voters favored politics that was basically anti-establishment in its thrust. They also came to realize that the voters for were, various reasons, inclined towards Left parties. It was clear that a coalition between Left social forces was in the offing and would eventually emerge as a major political force. This was a favorable mandate for the Left Front with the CPI(M) at its head.[2]

Earlier, other partners of the Left Front quarreled with the CPI(M) regarding the sharing of portfolios and other offices and minor partners do clash with local CPI(M) leaders in some rural areas. There is a tendency in the CPI(M) to spread horizontally, particularly in the electoral bastions of the minor partners. However, they suppress their tendency to quarrel during elections since the survival of the minor parties is rooted in the support of the CPI(M). The party organization of the CPI(M) includes ancillary organizations of peasants, trade unions, women's associations, student unions, registered teacher associations at all levels, 'democratic writers and performing artistes forum' and ambitious middle-class intellectuals. They have become formidable since the second LF government was firmly saddled in 1982.

Elections for the CPI(M), at all levels, is a serious and continuous affair. While the party is in a position to provide logistic support in all the 48,500 and more polling stations in the state, the opposition parties together fail to man even half of them. This is one of the major reasons for the electoral stability of the CPI(M)-led government, and despite some internal differences, junior partners like the FB, RSP, and CPI realize the electoral importance, to them, of the CPI(M) and its allied organizations. This is evident from the statements of the secretary of the state committee of the FB who emphasizes that they are to guard the 'unity of the Left Front as the apple of the eye.'[3]

The Left parties did not repeat their mistakes of the late 1960s when they casually attempted to put together a coalition. Ideological differences stood in the way, and they were not at all convinced of the efficacy of the Western type of parliamentary democracy. Before 1977, they doubted their ability to form a government of only the Left parties.[4] The combination itself is the outcome of a series of past economic and political movements.[5] Ideologically they shared leftist views, but before 1977 they could not put a coalition together.

The question of why the West Bengal Left Front is unique with outstanding stability and electoral successes has many answers. The most commonly accepted and important one is that the opposition parties failed to forge a dependable alternative coalition. All the opposition parties—Congress, Trinamul Congress (AITC), BJP, and the other smaller Marxist local parties all declaim against the 'electoral fraud and authoritarianism'[6] of the CPI(M) in the LF coalition. But they fail to earn the trust of the voters as they are too individualistic to come closer together and have not been able to provide a viable alternative.

In all other Indian states, including Kerala, political instability, social fragmentation in terms of caste and religion, crisis of governance and electoral reverses are endemic, and turnover in the ruling coalition is frequent. The Left Front government in West Bengal was firmly established in 1977, and the total Left Front vote has been above 50 percent till the1998 parliamentary elections. They pit the state against New Delhi with their politics of anti-Centrism. It could successfully preserve its societal bases among the rural masses despite differences of caste, communities and economic class divisions. Caste and communal animosities do not usually play a significant role in West Bengal as it does elsewhere in India. Millions of refugees following Partition in 1947 and thereafter, extended support to the Left parties. Earlier, they focused on the Nehru government's alleged discrimination against West Bengal in regard to refugee rehabilitation as compared to Punjab, and later against other policies perceived as discriminatory to West Bengal—including the freight equalization and industrial licensing policies.

The influx of displaced persons, both Hindu and Muslim, during the Bangladesh War in 1971, supported the Congress party governments at the Center and in the state under the chief ministership of Siddhartha Shankar Ray. Some of them, mostly Muslims, returned to Bangladesh after its liberation in 1971. Those who remained in West Bengal subsequently began to side with the Left parties. Initially the Bengali Muslim community[7] supported the established Congress governments at the Center and the state. With the rise of the Bharatiya Janata Party (BJP) in Indian politics, the Muslim population's support shifted to the Left Front in West Bengal.[8] They now constitute an important support base of the Left Front.[9]

Several scholars have provided incisive analyses from different perspectives,[10] particularly of the earlier period of West Bengal. Nossiter, for example, points out

the CPI(M) and the Left Front have succeeded in identifying themselves with Bengali resentment at what is perceived to be a chronic Central government neglect of the State,… whatever deficiencies there have been in the performance of the Left Front, it is perceived as having a mission, discipline and leadership …. The CPI(M) and its partners have shown a capacity to learn from past mistakes.[11]

Foreign scholars are highly impressed by the remarkable achievements of the Marxist regime that has been working within the framework of a parliamentary democratic system.

The Left Front government initially took very politically prudent decisions and sincerely sought to implement them. These policies involved land reforms programs and their implementation through 'Operation Barga.' The government overhauled the moribund *panchayat* system. Following the recommendations of the Ashok Mehta Committee Report, the three-tier *Panchayati Raj* system of rural self-government was introduced with the first elections in 1978. It was a massive exercise and people began participating in the process of local governance. It was, in fact, the first determined effort on the part of the resurgent leftist regime to spread its politico-electoral net in the rural areas. The last election to all the three tiers was held in 2003 with the LF in general, and the CPI(M) in particular, winning their largest ever majorities.[12] The initial programs of land reforms, distribution of surplus lands through 'Operation Barga' and capturing of the *Panchayat* bodies at the grass roots during mid-1980s are possibly the two other major factors that contributed to the exceptional stability of the LF régime in this state.

In respect of land reforms, the LF government did not commit the same mistake of alienating the rich and middle peasants as it had done during United Front (UF) regimes in the late 1960s. The LF government acquired more than 1.30 million acres of *benami* (registered in fake names) land and distributed them to landless *barga* laborers and marginal peasants. According to Pranab Bardhan and Dilip Mookherjee, the LF government appears to have the political will to undertake such land reform measures. They comment:

> intrinsic policy preferences of elected officials may derive from the partisan interests of their electoral constituencies, and additionally be subject to moral hazard wherein implementation requires effort on the part of the officials. Second, the electoral competition or populism can matter; land reforms may be motivated by the need to expand vote shares.[13]

However, the claim to the efficacy and sincerity in the implementation of land policy was contested later in the 1990s.

The urban and semi-urban middle classes were already sympathetic to the politics of the Left parties. From the failures of its earlier United Front experience, the CPI(M) learned an important lesson: it involved the packing of the administrative system with persons sympathetic to the party. It created a situation in which general personnel as well as police administration could work in favor of leftist organizations. To make its policies and objectives more acceptable, the CPI(M) attempted to woo large numbers of middle-class employees in different organizations and professions. It allowed, unofficially, the registered Left-oriented Government Employees Co-ordination Committee to exercise supervision not only over ordinary employees but also over the officers. Most of the employees in the government and semi-government institutions, like government undertakings, co-operative societies, factories, schools, colleges, and even universities financially aided by the government were won over by the LF government. They changed their service manuals, enacted laws for their security of service and increased salary packets.[14]

Even non-gazetted police personnel were allowed to form associations of their own and function as a trade union.[15] All these policies brought about enormous electoral dividends to the Left Front regime making it increasingly stable. The LF government even allowed its employees to go on strike to press their demands[16] and it supported the politics of *Banglabandh* (All Bengal strike) or *Bharatbandh* (All India strike) and *Chakkajam* (stopping rail movements) against the alleged 'anti-people policies' of the 'inconvenient' Central governments. The Left Front regime undertook a large number of populist measures at an economic cost that threatened a near fiscal collapse in the 1990s. This prompted the LF government, headed by the new Chief Minister Buddhadeb Bhattacharya, to consider rolling back some of their earlier political decisions after the 2001 Assembly election.

In the late 1970s, the Finance Minister, Asok Mitra announced unemployment benefits without going into the long-term question of their feasibility. The government also established a large number of primary schools, and later colleges and even universities, in the state. Salary hikes were given to government employees, teachers of all categories and employees of the *panchayat* bodies and municipalities. The scheme of free education sought to reduce the number of drop-outs in schools, and it abolished the tradition of teaching English in government-aided schools up to Class VI. Because of this policy decision, nearly two generations of students had to suffer in the competitive employment market. Ultimately this policy had to be discarded.

After the *panchayat* elections, the middle and rich peasants shifted their allegiances to the new government. The rural poor and a large section of the peasants were already supporting the Left Front. Regular municipal elections began to be held from 1981 onward. Thus, the Left Front consolidated its political base in both rural and urban areas. The main opposition parties were in a shambles. The Janata Party government at the Center collapsed in the middle of 1979. The state unit of the party was split into factions, with many joining the Left Front.

The Congress party was almost decimated till it gained a little in the 1996 Assembly election. Then, Mamata Banerjee vertically split the party by forming her AITC. The Congress and AITC, however, came closer with their seat adjustment before the 2001 Assembly elections. Allegations were made that the CPI(M) manipulated some of the Congress leaders. This was intended to make the Congress–AITC seat adjustment less workable.[17] Those who were disenchanted with the CPI(M) are yet to find a powerful opposition party or an acceptable and viable alternative coalition of parties. Moreover, the organizational strength of the CPI(M) continues to be visibly powerful. The front organizations[18] of the CPI(M), as discussed above, continuously work for the party, while the Opposition parties charge the CPI(M) with electoral malpractices. This allegation seems to be gaining some credibility with even the Election Commission and some external political analysts noting the allegations.

The politics of a state is the product of a combination of several factors like history, geography, density of population and cultural differences within a varied social system. Historically, West Bengal can be called a truncated state with problems peculiar to it. It is a densely populated border state. The border is porous and infiltration is difficult to check. The state has a very large Muslim population of 25.25 percent.[19] The Scheduled Castes and Scheduled Tribes constitute 23.02 percent and 5.5 percent of the total population, respectively. The cultural attributes of the population in different regions of the state are varied. The state of economic development, occupational engagements and idioms of politics as observed in the past also vary even within a region. In recent years, since the statewide rise of Left politics, attempts have been made to initiate a process of modernization and secularization.

Glyn Williams' observations emphasize the ethnographic approach in the analysis of West Bengal's Left politics. He refers extensively to the works of Atul Kohli, Suzanne and Lloyd Rudolph, Partha Chatterjee, and others. Atul Kohli emphasizes West Bengal's Left politics as succeeding in reversing the 'crisis of governability' prevailing in several Indian states as well as at the Center since 1989. The LF's style of political management, the prevalence of peace and the absence of caste and communal conflicts in the state have been important factors in the stability of the regime. Ruud's research is 'anthropological' and use 'oral history' for detailed analysis and ethnographic discourse of village politics and its changes under the auspices of Left politics in Bengal.[20] A number of scholars in their field of studies have used survey data so as to highlight politico-economic developments within a liberal democratic framework of politics.[21]

The Left coalition is credited with success in changing the face of rural society by introducing effective politico-administrative decentralization. Consequently, the changes are reflected in the economic life and relations among the rural people. All these changes have gradually diluted the earlier Marxist theoretical framework of 'democratic centralism' within a liberal democratic paradigm of politics. Bardhan and Mookerjee observe the following about the 80 *panchayat* bodies that they surveyed: 'Land reform and implementation was highest in villages where local governments were more evenly contested between the Left and Rightist parties.'[22] These *panchayat* bodies successfully engaged in rural development during the 1980s. The Left Front still sported its ideological slogan of 'people's democratic revolution' but in a much-diluted form. The CPI(M) too underwent a subtle change with substantial increase in the number of local party leaders.

The consequences of this shift are many, including the spread of centralized control by the party. In the process, a paradoxical reversal took shape in rural governance. The local satraps of the party took over control of *panchayat*s at the *gram* and *samiti* levels. This made it possible for the influential rich and middle peasants to ally with those in power in village politics. In addition, in the last two decades many CPI(M) leaders at the local level were seen to become the 'party unto them.' This phenomenon was especially operative in the disjointed belt of under-developed districts of North Bengal and in the western belts of Purulia, Bankura, Hooghly, and Midnapore (Table 12.1). At all levels of the three-tier *Panchayati Raj* system, the LF won more than two-thirds of the total number of seats.

The Left Front's massive presence in rural areas might have ushered in a 'democratic socialist system' and brought about 'redistributive justice' alleviating extreme rural poverty. But the real picture is entirely different. The story of death by hunger in Amlasole,[23] southwest of Midnapore, and in some tribal villages of Cooch Bihar, Purulia, Nadia, and eastern parts of Murshidabad might be contested by the CPI(M), but the facts are undeniable. To redress abject poverty in tribal areas and the poorer sections of the people, the Central government floated the scheme of supplying food for those with Below Poverty Line (BPL) cards which were to be issued by the local governing authorities. The Central funds allotted for this purpose were supposed to be utilized by the state government through its chain of local governments. But in many tribal areas, local leaders did not distribute the BPL cards to the genuinely poor and the Minister for Tribal Affairs, Maheswar Murmu, spoke out frankly to the press that the money meant for tribal development was being misused.[24]

The government admits that 4,612 villages have been identified as 'underdeveloped.' It is reported that 4.6 million people are living below the poverty line in West Bengal.[25] The *West Bengal Human Development Report 2004* states that the poorest sections in several districts are underfed for want of work in agriculture and related sectors.[26] But despite this, the Left Front won nearly 85–90 percent of Assembly seats from this poorest western belt of the state as also from North Bengal.

The phenomenal growth of the CPI(M) along with its frontal organizations in the state has become both its strength and weakness. In electoral politics, opposition parties like AITC, Congress and BJP, or smaller parties like the Socialist Unity Center (SUC) and others, either separately or combined, are no match for the CPI(M). Under the circumstances, it has become easier for the CPI(M) to politically manage any situation as no viable alternative coalitions are in sight.

But the long stay in power has led to sowing seeds of disaffection among the partners because of the continuance of the CPI(M)'s style of politics. Dissatisfaction is marked by the growth of the Maoists and People's War Group (PWG), with the Naxalites actively engaging in the western belt of Purulia, Bankura, Birbhum, and the southwestern part of Midnapore, which appears to be disconcerting. Other so-called 'secessionist' forces include the 'Kamtapur movement' by the Rajbanshis in 'clandestine understanding' with the Kamtapur Liberation Organization (KLO), the Gorkha National Liberation Front (GNLF) of Subhas Ghising and the more recent movements for 'Greater Cooch Bihar Demand' led by Banshibadan Burman and the indigenous people (Rajbanshis) of Cooch Bihar.

Also noteworthy is the divergence between the politico-electoral management by the party organization and the governmental management of the economy in the state. Recession in industries like jute, coal and iron mining, smaller iron factories, manufacturing and engineering industries and tea-processing units of North Bengal is alarming. Near absence of agro-industries and moribund village industries are plaguing the state. There are few running small-scale industries to provide alternative opportunities for employment. Retrenchment of workers, even very low-paid ones, coupled with unemployment in other sectors is increasing. Among the unemployed, more than 7.2 million, are a large number of educated unemployed. As the *India Development Report 2004–05* shows, this tops the list of unemployed among the Indian states. A government survey regarding poverty and unemployment found that poverty stricken villages were spread across the state.[27] Despite the unique political stability of the regime and political management skills of the Left Front, the inference that the government often failed to redeem its pledges, is quite apparent.

However, this attitude of the LF government and its lackadaisical approach to development (as at present) may antagonize the poorest sections of the population of West Bengal which include the Schedule Castes, Scheduled Tribes, and the Muslim community. The *West Bengal*

Human Development Report 2004 observes that 'these three categories ... together account for more than half the population, and these are also the three poorest groups in rural Bengal.'[28] Thus, they constitute a formidable electoral base, and any party or coalition of parties that obtains the majority support of these three groups are most likely to form the government in this state.[29] Given the neglect of the poor sections of society under Left Front rule, the question of why they continue to succeed needs a satisfactory answer. This answer is perhaps contained in its political past. It is, therefore, necessary to take a closer look at some of the political developments that led to the establishment of the LF government in the state.

Protest movements by radical groups like the Marxists during the dominant Congress party regime in the past, the fallout of Partition and other popular activities mobilizing the people both 'directly' and 'indirectly' by several of party frontal organizations helped the Left parties enormously. The political mobilization of the Congress was in a sense 'indirect' and consequently unstable. It depended on caste and community leaders as well as on big landholders and the moneyed trader and business communities. The party did not try to build up other stable ancillary organizations as the Left parties did for mobilizing popular support. After Partition, the Muslims supported the Congress, as did many of the millions of Hindu refugees. The Left parties mounted massive protest movements against the Congress government led by B.C. Roy against its policy of rehabilitating the uprooted to Dandakaranya and Andaman and Nicobar Islands. In the face of continuous movements launched by the Left parties, the Congress government gave in. In the process, the Leftists won the hearts and support of the refugees.

The chief minister did, however, attempt to build up an industrial infrastructure in the Durgapur–Asansol belt, and hydro-electricity and thermal power plants in selected locations with natural advantages. It also built river barrages to prevent floods and help agriculture, and established new satellite townships at Durgapur, Kalyani, and Salt Lake. The Roy government created the State Transport Corporation that created job opportunities for unemployed refugee youths.[30] Several regions of West Bengal have been drought and flood prone. It was due mainly to the lack of the application of modern technology. The crop patterns of the cultivated areas, poor irrigation facilities, sub-standard quality of seeds and poor storage facilities were other problem areas. Opposition Left parties launched political actions, including food movements, in 1957, 1959, 1965, and 1966.[31]

The Congress became identified as a party of the 'bourgeoisie,' 'the feudal landowners,' and 'rich and middle peasants.' In the mid-1960s the Congress party was split. Ajoy Mukherjee formed a new party, the Bangla Congress (B. Cong.) and fought the 1967 election against the Congress and won enough seats to make it impossible for Congress to form the government on its own even though it won 127 seats and was the single largest party in the Assembly. The Left parties took full political advantage of this situation and made a post-election coalition of two Fronts to form the first United Front (UF) government in June 1967. This was the first coalition government in the state after 19 years of Congress dominance, with Ajoy Mukherjee as the leader of the new coalition.

The new United Left Front (ULF) government led by the CPI(M) comprised the Marxist Forward Bloc, Revolutionary Socialist Party, Workers' Party, Samyukta Socialist Party, Revolutionary Communist Party of India, and the Bolshevik Party. The other Progressive United Left Front (PULF) consisted of the Praja Socialist Party, Lok Sevak Sanga, Forward Bloc, Communist Party of India, and Bangla Congress (Table 12.2). Governor Dharma Vira aborted the 1967 UF experiment 'at the direction of the Central Congress government' as alleged by the leaders of the UF. The second UF experiment of 1969 involved a pre-election coalition of all the Left parties of the first UF goverment. Ajoy Mukherjee again headed the government and Jyoti Basu became the deputy chief minister. Basu, as leader of the largest Marxist party, was never happy with his chief minister's Congress party background.

The first United Front government lasted for a period of nine months and the second a little over 13 months. In fact, Jyoti Basu followed Marxist objectives to dominate both the UF coalitions from the very beginning. His twin objectives were to establish hegemony over the general and police administrations and to send a Marxian political message to the ordinary people. CPI(M) leaders were divided in both their subjective perception and objective assessment of the prevailing situations according to Marxist–Leninist ideology.

Table 12.2

Seats and percentage of votes won by political parties in Assembly elections, 1967–2001

Party	1967	1969	1971	1972	1977	1982	1987	1991	1996	2001
INC	127 (41.12)	55 (41.32)	105 (29.25)	216 (49.06)	20 (23.25)	49 (35.59)	40 (41.80)	44 (35.12)	83 (39.48)	26 (7.98)
B. Cong	34 (12.14)	33 (11.78)	5 (1.78)	–	–	–	–	–	–	–
CPI ('72–'77) with Cong	15 (6.17)	30 (6.99)	13 (8.42)	35 (8.33)	2 (2.62)	7 (1.81)	10 (1.72)	6 (1.75)	6 (1.75)	7 (1.79)
CPM	44 (18.27)	80 (19.97)	113 (32.81)	14 (27.46)	177 (35.32)	174 (38.47)	188* (39.48)	187* (36.64)	156* (37.92)	143 (36.59)
RSP	6 (1.38)	12 (2.80)	3 (2.19)	3 (2.14)	20 (3.75)	19 (4.01)	18 (3.94)	18 (3.47)	18 (3.72)	17 (3.43)
FB	13 (4.43)	21 (5.01)	3 (2.90)	– (2.49)	26 (5.32)	27 (5.75)	26 (5.84)	29 (5.51)	21 (5.20)	25 (5.65)
BJP						(0.61)	(0.51)	(11.37)	1 (0.34)	(5.19)
AITC										60 (30.66)
Ind. & Others	75 (26.78)	82 (29.28)	43 (15.45)	12 (4.28)	49 (16.66)	18 (6.12)	12 (4.08)	10 (3.40)	10 (3.40)	16 (5.44)
Total	280	280	280	280	294	294	294	294	294	294

Source: *Assembly Election in West Bengal (1952–2001)*, Chief Election Officer, West Bengal.

Note: *Indicates minor parties that fought elections on CPI(M)'s symbol. In the 1996 election, the CPI(M) alone won only 150 seats. Smaller LF partners contested on the CPI(M) symbol.

Hardliners believed that effective popular mobilization and movements were urgent to bring about socio-political revolution while wielding state power. Their programs were to eliminate the *jotedar*s (big landholders) in the rural areas and forcibly grab their cultivable lands. But the growing conflict between the hardliners in the CPI(M) and the more radical ultra-Left elements, later known as pro-Naxalites, in the party could not be resolved. A new Communist Party of India, (Marxist-Leninist), (CPI[ML]) was formed on May 1, 1969. The CPI(M) was branded by this party as 'social chauvinist' and a 'bourgeois party,' anxious to defend the existing system to serve the ruling classes.[32]

From the very beginning, Jyoti Basu sought to control the police force. In order to win the allegiance of the lower ranks, he allowed them almost trade union rights. The higher echelon of the state bureaucracy was seen to be more loyal to Deputy Chief Minister Jyoti Basu rather than to the chief minister. As a result of the inner contradictions within the government, some major partners of the second United Front became disillusioned. They came to realize that the Front was in danger of collapse, largely because of the CPI(M)'s 'sectarian move' that required a collective drive to protect the Front's interests.[33]

The period during which the United Front regimes ruled may be characterized as the period of political aggrandizement. In spite of having won the largest number of seats, 43 in the first UF and 80 in the second UF coalitions in 1967 and 1969 respectively, the CPI(M) had to concede the leadership of the governments both times to Mukherjee of the Bangla Congress. The Naxalite movements were mounting and indiscriminate killings of ordinary policemen and political activists of other parties[34] took place. Law and order deteriorated. Industrial strikes and *gherao*s (illegal confinement) as legitimate weapons of the trade union movements became increasingly common and frequent. Many public undertakings, big companies and industrial houses found it difficult to continue operations. Industrial unemployment was rising, agricultural production, particularly of rice, was low and inflation ran high.

After the 1971 mid-term poll, another non-Marxist coalition government, with Ajoy Mukherjee as the leader, emerged. It assumed office with only a thin margin of seats. The CPI(M) had won 113 seats as the largest party, but it was not invited by the Governor to form the government and Jyoti Basu warned, 'CPI(M) would seek to dislodge the reactionary government'[35] from within and without. The Mukherjee-led coalition, with the support of Congress, had 105 seats was short-lived. But it seemed that the Congress party was electorally gaining ground when compared with its loss in 1969 and gain in 1971 (Table 12.2). The Bangladesh war in 1971 strained the state's economy and greatly changed the demographic characteristics of the border areas of the state. Under the leadership of Siddhartha Shankar Ray, a large number of Youth Congress activists came to play a significant political role. The CPI, the FB and a few other political players were already beginning to distance themselves from the politics of the CPI(M).

But then a macabre incident took place at Burdwan, reported as the 'Sain brothers' murder, allegedly perpetrated by CPI(M) activists.'[36] Such violence was unprecedented in the state. This politics of murder aroused a high degree of public anger. Chief Minister Mukherjee bitterly stated, 'under the circumstances clinging to office would have been treachery,' and described his own government as 'barbarous and uncivilized.'[37] It was a period of violence, and politics of retaliation and reciprocal decimation. For the first time, murders and elimination of political opponents came to be used as a political weapon. Intimidation also emerged as a potent political force.

The next Assembly election, held in 1972, saw the appearance of a Congress party with a new look. It formed the Progressive Democratic Alliance (PDA), a political coalition with the CPI on the basis of a seven-point program. The Alliance won the election with the Congress party capturing 216 seats and the CPI 35 seats. On the other side, the CPI(M) won only 14 seats (Table 12.2). The rise of the Youth Congress (Chhatra Parishad) was especially remarkable. The public mood, as usual, was influenced by the urbanites. The percentage of vote-share of the CPI(M) nosedived from 32.81 to 27.46. Political analysts saw the loss of 99 seats by the CPI(M) as a 'statistical aberration.' The defeated party dubbed the election as a 'fraud', and the 14 newly elected members refused, as a policy of the party, to participate in this Assembly (1972–77).

Law and order was reasonably restored and a few people-oriented policies were formulated. But due to rivalries among the ministers inducted from among the Youth Congress leaders and the consequent internal feuds in the Congress party, the government failed to deliver the goods and was plunged into a traumatic 'crisis of governance.' The major problem that the earlier coalition regimes faced was the nature of their 'political culture' in a broader sense of the term. The Marxist opposition political parties were yet to learn the political culture of coalition-making and forging a ruling coalition capable of providing a stable government and good governance. The strategy of mobilization of support, socially as well as politically, was flawed. A workable coalitional spirit seemed to prevail only during the Left Front regime beginning from the late 1970s. A unique experiment that was symptomatic of the willingness to abandon rigid ideological stances and crossing ideological boundaries signaled the beginning of a steady political process in the state. It was the beginning of a period of resurgent political culture of accommodation among the partners of the ruling Left Front.

The first Left Front government was formed with Jyoti Basu as the chief minister, on June 21, 1977. The Secretary of the state committee of the CPI(M) stated that 'the development paradigm adopted by the Congress party had failed to combine growth with equity.' The 'fruits of development have come to be enjoyed only by 10 per-cent of the country's population. The Left Front in West Bengal, however, has changed this development process.'[38] For them, the secretary further declared, 'economic growth and equity' were the goals of the successive LF governments. Chief Minister Jyoti Basu spoke in the same vein.[39]

To a great extent, the claims of the parties forming the government that they contextualized their earlier Marxist ideological stances, are justified. The power to run the state government cooled down the high political temperature of the CPI(M). This is reflected in the fact that although it was a single party majority victory for the CPI(M) (Table 12.2), it did not show an unwillingness to share substantial power with its weaker partners. A friendly Janata Party government at the Center compromised opposition by the Janata Party in the state. The Congress party, following their nation-wide electoral debacle after the 20-month Indira Gandhi-led Emergency, won only 20 seats, their lowest ever, and the leaders of the party appeared to be demoralized.

The LF could very well have implemented its commitment to what the Secretary of the state committee himself underlined as the 'Left Front aims at growth with equity.' It was expected that having ruled the state unhindered by any disrupting opposition movements in the social and political arenas, the Left Front could have done better in terms of realizing its twin objectives of 'growth and equity.' But economic indices with regard to growth in industry, 'health, sanitation, literacy and primary education, gender equality,'[40] as also insufficiency of potable water, and electricity in rural backyard and a road network in the state tell a different story. The failure of the coalition in attending to such basic problems is incomprehensible in view of the fact that it received ample Central funds for removing illiteracy, launching programs for gender equality, health and sanitation, rural housing schemes and alleviating rural poverty in the form of issuing BPL cards to the people living mostly in rural areas and in abject poverty.[41]

The Comptroller and Auditor General's (CAG's) reports show that the state government could not utilize the funds released by the Center because of it defaulted in providing necessary matching grants, which was perhaps due to the fact that the state government had been facing severe financial difficulties in the preceding years. The chief minister was expected to initiate a process of all-round development. One explanation is that the Left parties could not yet overcome their previous mind-set of the 'politics of opposition.' Even in the changed socio-economic and political scenario, Marxist political rhetoric always won over the logic of economics.

Basu relinquished office on November 6, 2000, a few months before the May 2001 elections. He was able to maintain unity among the Left Front partners by utilizing his skills in political management and persuasion; however, he occasionally had to deal with them with a heavy hand. Jatin Chakraborty, the minister in-charge of the Public Works Department (PWD), had to leave because he raised the question of the 'Bengal Lamp scam' that involved allegations of 'corruption' by Basu's son. As a result, Jyoti Basu 'strongly ... censured the PWD minister.'[42] Subsequently, there were difficulties with the press as well.[43]

Another incident involved Buddhadeb Bhattacharya leveling serious charges against some of his Party and Cabinet colleagues for their hobnobbing with the 'elements of the underworld.'[44] When the charge of corruption remained unexamined, he resigned from the Cabinet in a huff. The chief minister was embarrassed, but the Party leaders at the state and the Politburo backed Bhattacharya and would not consider dispensing with his services.[45] This was a rare phenomenon in a Marxist Communist Party. Bhattacharya was re-inducted into the Cabinet after a few years with the same portfolio. Moreover, a few months before Basu relinquished office, Bhattacharya was made deputy chief minister 'to help the old man having indifferent health in his late 1980s.'

Bhattacharya's appointment indicated that Basu was gradually losing his authority over the Party and the government. Bhattacharya was groomed and backed by the CPI(M)'s state committee Secretary Pramod Dasgupta, the main architect of the party's organizational structure.[46] The other young leaders he groomed in order to form a coherent team later were Biman Basu, presently the chairperson of the Left Front Committee, and Anil Biswas, the then state party Secretary who ultimately took over the rein of the party organization.[47] Basu was, in fact, the public as well as the administrative face of the Party till Pramod Dasgupta's death in 1983—after the second Left Front government was installed in 1982 election.

The LF government appears to project a popular image of a responsible and radical governing coalition that has attracted many political analysts to study this aspect of the regime.[48] Irrespective of the nature of Central governments, either strong or weak in the 1980s and the 1990s, the CPI(M)'s anti-Center politics helped the Left Front regime to maintain cohesion among the coalition partners. The leaders of the LF government were astute enough to divert popular discontent against the state government's policies to that of the Central government. A perennially weak Central government was what the Left Front always desired. With a view to de-stabilizing the Rajiv Gandhi regime, Basu and the CPI(M) joined hands with Atal Behari Vajpayee, the leader of the BJP, to prop up V.P. Singh in forming a very weak minority government at the Center after the parliamentary election in 1989.[49] In West Bengal, the BJP registered, for the first time, a respectable presence by obtaining a significant share of votes. The credit goes largely to CPI(M)'s tactical politics of confronting the 'stronger enemy' in collaboration with the 'lesser one.'

The Left Front coalition subsequently opposed the BJP-led alliance at the Center. During these years, West Bengal suffered from a lack of competitive politics. Political movements launched by the Opposition parties could not gather momentum. It was sporadic and mostly urban-centered. The Opposition parties were not in a position to clearly define their policy perspectives. The Congress as the main Opposition party lacked a coherent ideological alternative to the Marxist regime. Mamata Banerjee, the AITC supremo, started a rabid anti-CPI(M) campaign in her own distinctive style. But the Opposition parties offered no sustained movements against the policies of the LF and failed to articulate alternative policy choices. The people of the state thus could not find any dependable and viable alternative even after three decades of Marxist rule.

The inability of the LF regime, particularly since early 1990s, to perform is reflected in the industrial stagnation in the state. In order to overcome the industrial sickness and attract foreign and non-resident Indian (NRI) investors, Basu went to different countries, but few visible results were achieved. The CPI(M)-affiliated Center for Indian Trade Unions (CITU) kept quiet when workers of public undertakings, including several jute mills, industrial houses and tea industries in North Bengal, lost their jobs. Despite several lacunas in the education policy, the Students Federation of India (SFI) remained quiet in contrast to its past behavior as has the Kisan Sabha, the CPI(M)'s peasants' organization in regard to the party's recent thrust on land-related issues.

Meanwhile, groups of miscreants—under the patronage of some of the leaders—entered the Party organization. Businessmen, party-backed real-estate promoters, land grabbers, suppliers of building materials and contractors established close relations with the CPI(M) and other major partners. Watching the deteriorating situation, CPI(M) leader and former Minister of Land Revenue Benoy Chowdhury charged that 'It has become a contractors' raj.'[50]

Many party functionaries and office bearers of the *Panchayat* and urban civic bodies were allegedly involved in various corrupt activities. Many newspaper reports and even administrative reports referred to this. It evoked a negative reaction from voters in the 1996 elections, and the CPI(M) Assembly seats were drastically reduced to only 150, and the total number of seats gained by the Left Front as a whole was 203 as compared with 246 in 1991. But the 1996 parliamentary election could have proved to be a boon since Jyoti Basu was being considered as the next prime minister of India. He was willing, but his younger party colleagues prevented him from accepting the offer, and Basu commented that 'it was a historic blunder'[51] on the part of the Party. This is symptomatic of the fact that the younger generation of leaders began asserting themselves from this point of time, if not earlier when Bhattacharya had resigned.

Mamata Banerjee, a mass leader, initiated another phase of re-vival for the Congress party. But she left the Congress, founded the Trinamul Congress (AITC) in 1997 and joined the National Demo-cratic Alliance (NDA) at the Center. Her joining the NDA and ability to attract large crowds in both rural and urban areas sent a danger signal to the CPI(M) (Table 12.3), whose younger leaders already began thinking that Basu might prove to be a liability in the emerging context.

In the mid-term parliamentary polls in 1998 and 1999, the AITC had an agreement on seat adjustments with the BJP, its NDA partner. With her support, the BJP won one seat in 1998 and two seats in 1999 (Table 12.3). The Marxist parties could not gauge the public mood against them. Banerjee's popularity was at its peak between 1997 and 2001. She was able to raise people's 'courage to protest' but did not invest sufficient effort to organize her AITC to reach out to the grass-roots level. Subsequently, she alienated a large section of the urban middle class and intellectuals. Just before the 2001 Assembly election, she broke her alliance with the BJP, resigned from the Union Cabinet and entered into seat adjustments with the Congress. That was perhaps the unmaking of the AITC in the state.

Immediately after assuming office on November 7, 2000, the new chief minister promised to offer an 'improved Left Front Government'

Table 12.3

Seats and percentage of votes won by political parties in
Lok Sabha elections, 1996–2004

Party	1996	1998	1999	2004
CPM	21	24	21	26
	(34.50)	(35.61)	(35.59)	(38.56)
CPI	2	3	3	3
	(2.49)	(3.65)	(3.47)	(4.01)
FB	3	2	2	3
	(3.40)	(3.32)	(3.45)	(3.66)
RSP	4	4	3	3
	(4.74)	(4.51)	(4.25)	(4.49)
INC	11	1	3	6
	(40.66)	(15.24)	(13.29)	(14.56)
AITC	–	7	8	1
	–	(24.49)	(26.05)	(21.04)
BJP	–	1	2	–
		(10.23)	(11.14)	(8.06)
Ind. & Others	–	–	–	–
	(14.21)	(2.95)	(2.76)	(5.62)

Source: Compiled. Chief Election Officer's Reports, West Bengal.

to the state. He wanted to inject a dynamic work culture and raised the slogan of 'do it now.' He publicly declared that he would initiate a new phase of industrialization and bring in an improvement in trade, business, and service sectors. He had a clean image and fixed his priorities in terms of initiating a modernized and balanced growth process. Unlike his predecessor, he maintained a good rapport with the Central government. But he had to make compromises, whether it was on the question of economic welfare, *madrasa*-imparted religious education, infiltrations from Bangladesh or inviting foreign investors. It was politics as usual—involving accusations and then promises of building a good political order and initiating good governance.

The 2001 Assembly election was seen to be a breather for the Left Front (Table 12.3). But just before the election, Subhas Chakraborty, an important Minister in Basu's Cabinet, was rumored to be leaving the party with his followers to join the Opposition.[52] However, he backed out at the last moment. Buddhadeb Bhattacharya had actually pointed his guns at Chakraborty and his 'un-Marxist activities.'[53]

The election of 2001 became a contest between the highly organized LF and the tottering coalitions of the AITC, Congress and one or two minor local parties. The BJP fought the elections independently.

The result was a thumping victory for the Left Front for the sixth consecutive time. This was 'unexpected' even to the leaders of the Left Front who had to fight the 'toughest battle' with what they called their 'back against the wall.'[54] The Opposition parties and even most of the major vernacular dailies alleged that 'the secret of the CPI(M)'s success in elections depended on electoral malpractices' and sustained 'stick and carrot tactics.' There is evidence to support the allegation that CPI(M) candidates used to poll 99.9 percent of votes in several polling stations in Purulia, Bankura, Hooghly, and the western part of Midnapore.[55] Significantly, the percentage share of votes polled by the Left Front plummeted to an all time low in the 1999 election (Table 12.4). But it recovered substantially in 2001 and in all subsequent elections at different levels.

Table 12.4

Percentage of votes won by LF in Parliamentary, Assembly, and *panchayat* elections, 1998–2004

Year	Parliament	Assembly	Zilla Parishad	Panchayat Samiti	Gram Panchayat	Average/Three-tier Panchayat
1998	47.09	–	–	–	–	–
1999	46.76	–	–	–	–	–
2001	–	48.98	–	–	–	–
2003	–	–	86.82	74.05	65.75	75.54
2004	50.72	–	–	–	–	–

Source: Compiled from Official Reports, Government of West Bengal.

CONCLUSION

In conclusion, electoral figures shown in the tables indicate that the Left Front coalition has continued to be successful. The anti-incumbency factor has not operated in West Bengal as in the rest of India. The Left Front created a coalition culture of political accommodation, which it had earlier ignored. This resulted in governmental stability despite frequent differences among the partners. Initial measures of land reforms and the building up of local governing systems added to the stability of the regime. Setting up new co-operative societies and reviving the old ones made visible improvements in various sectors, especially agriculture. All these measures helped the LF initially to consolidate its power base. It was able to inculcate a sense of dignity and consciousness among the very low strata of working people and peasant communities. Through political movements and social penetration, the Left parties, despite occasional bitterness among themselves, had been able to reduce significantly the ideological distances among themselves.

But there is another side of the picture. For more than one-and-a-half decades, the LF government has been only half-heartedly inclined to improve the political economy of the state. It promised everything to everybody. As a consequence, it failed to do away with undesirable elements at the administrative level as well as within the ever-inflating party and frontal organizations. A huge wealth in terms of human resources or, as Robert Putnam's phrases it, 'social capital,' has been at the disposal of the different[56] social and other frontal organizations of the CPI(M). Using liberal guidance to the maximum, and shedding off its ideological baggage and outmoded way of practicing politics, the CPI(M) could have built bridges between the different levels of society. With the co-operation of the front organizations, it could politically control and mobilize their activists, their committed supporters and others at each level of society. Thus it could have helped increase productivity of the economy following the principles of 'equity and sustainability'[57] as the secretary of the Party had earlier promised.

Over the years, a political culture of accommodation among the partners of the LF coalition has taken shape in the state led by the pragmatism of the CPI(M). Even Basu had to alter his hegemonic style of politics in the new context. Bhattacharya is, therefore, in an advantageous position. But he is forced to always work under the lengthening shadow of his Party, and the more assertive partners of his promised 'improved Left Front government.' The chief minister is still in the habit of telling his officers and government employees to 'do it now.' From the very beginning the incumbent chief minister began putting emphasis on 'work culture' and cautioned the trade unions not to get into conflicts with industrial and business houses. CPI(M)'s pragmatism, as it has been developing over the years, is evidence of a political culture of accommodation among the several alliance partners.

Buddhadeb Bhattacharya, in a positive sense, is more political and very cautious about his utterances against political opponents. This is unlike his predecessor who publicly abused the NDA government led by the BJP as 'uncivilized and barbaric,' and called the main Opposition leader of his state, Mamata Banerjee, a 'fraud'.[58] Immediately after assuming office, Bhattacharya developed a better rapport with the NDA government at the Center, displaying an accommodative style. He promised to bring about a better government with a clean administration and is determined to create a favorable environment for industrial investments in the state. He is committed to creating the necessary infrastructures in terms of roads, communications, extensive irrigation facilities, canals and electricity. But even after four-and-a-half years of being in office, nearly one-third of the villages are still without electricity, and peasants lack sufficient irrigation facilities and roads. Agricultural production has increased, but because of the low development of agro-industries, rural unemployment is on the rise. The fruits of development, in terms of food, nutrition, health care, literacy, primary and higher education are not reaching the marginal people.

The political situation has changed after the 2004 parliamentary election. The minority United Progressive Alliance coalition government at the Center depends upon the Left Front, with its 61 Lok Sabha seats, for support. The LF has been opposing the policy of privatization and disinvestment of public sector undertakings fearing that a large number of workers may be retrenched or retired. But in West Bengal over 243 factories and industries have been shut down and the unemployed, whether factory labourers or tea garden workers, were either retrenched or forced to work with less than minimum wages. Many unemployed workers have been serving the real estate dealers and promoters in exchange for very low wages.

The educated but unemployed youth do not expect anything beyond getting even underpaid positions in the Left Front regime, but they have become docile and apolitical. There are two reasons for this: no Opposition parties are in a position to improve the prevailing situation and are unable to form a viable alternative coalition. Second, if they go against the government, particularly the CPI(M), their chances to advance may be permanently blocked. The Haldia Petrochemical project with a promise to set up down-stream units is still incomplete. The power plant project at Bakreswar with Japanese collaboration seems to have slowed down. The Opposition parties occasionally make noises but then become silent and opposition politics has been tortuously groping with finding its genuine political space in the state.

In order to invite foreign direct investments, Buddhadeb Bhattacharya offered hundreds of acres of land including cultivable tracts to the Salim Group of Indonesia and others to build industries. It appears that the CPI(M) has been maintaining two faces at two different points of time and place, opposing direct foreign investments at the Center and yearning for it in the state. The LF has been nursing two constituencies for two different purposes, one nationally and the other in their original bastion of power. In the name of industrialization, the government has been indulging in joint collaboration with local investors, foreign industrialists and Non-resident Indians for building satellite townships. In the process, the government will have to acquire thousands of acres from poor peasants. In its *Human Development Reports* the World Bank praises land reforms in West Bengal, but during the 1990s the land reform programs ceased due to a lack of enough cultivable land. Cultivable land, as it stands now, is only 62 percent while it was more than 70 percent in 1980. Further transfer of land from the peasants would aggravate unemployment and poverty without compensating gains from the proposed ventures.

Regarding the land transfer to the Salim Group, there are divisions within the ranks of the CPI(M) itself. Left Front partners CPI, FB, and RSP are opposing the proposal to acquire cultivable lands for the Salim Group. They argue, 'We are all in favour of industrialization but the Salim Group are coming to the state as multinational traders not industrialists.'[59] Building townships, gyms, health cities and shopping malls does not help the process of industrialization.

The arguments are put forward publicly by the state committee secretaries of major partners, the RSP, FB, and CPI.

The present main Opposition party and its leader Mamata Banerjee continue to engage in populist agitations against the CPI(M). The Congress party in West Bengal opposes the AITC, but is in a mixed situation against the CPI(M). It has to fight the CPI(M) in the state but engage in friendly co-operation with the same party nationally so as to maintain its minority coalition government at the Center. The CPI(M) and its front partners continue to politically dominate the key societal spaces in the state which include peasants, industrial workers, unemployed youth, students, the middle class, the Schedule Castes and Tribes, Muslims and other religious and ethnic minorities. It has used this social capital to maintain the Left Front in power since 1977. The government could have utilized this social capital and political power to improve the efficiency of the larger society, and facilitate co-ordination[60] among all sections of the people. Instead it has a mixed record.

To summarize: West Bengal is unique among India's states as anti-incumbency has not been a factor since 1977. No one factor provides the answer to the political longevity of the CPI(M)-led Left Front. Instead, all of the following appear to be important: initial programs of land reforms, introduction of local rural self-governance through *Panchayati Raj* institutions, the maintenance of law and order, electoral and political management, the absence of any viable alternative non-Marxist coalition and, above all, the formidable Party and frontal organizations of the CPI(M) are the main components of the stability of the LF governments since 1977.

Notes

1. Suzanne Rudolf and Lloyd Rudolf, *Determinants and Varieties of Agrarian Mobilization* (University of Chicago, 1979) quoted by Rakhahari Chatterji, 'Political Change in West Bengal', in Rakhahari Chatterji (ed.), *Politics in West Bengal: Institution, Processes and Problems* (Calcutta: World Press, 1985).
2. Electoral data substantiate the point.
3. Ashok Ghosh, secretary state committee, Forward Bloc, November 5, 2004.

4. Interview with Jyoti Basu, former Chief Minister (1977–2000), September 4, 2004.

5. Prafulla K. Chakrabarti, *The Marginal Men* (Kalyani: Lumiere Books, 1990), pp. 329–404; see *also*, Sankar Ghosh, *The Disinherited State: A Study of West Bengal 1967–70* (Calcutta: Orient Longman, 1971).

6. Prabir Ghosal, *CPM-er Rigging* (Bengali) (Kolkata: Mukherjee Publishing, 2005); Nazrul Islam, *Police Prasange* (Bengali) (Kolkata: Sahitya, 2006); Malay Chaudhuri and Arindam Chaudhuri, *The Great Indian Dream* (New Delhi: Macmillan India Ltd., 2003), p. 223; Manas Ghosh, 'Means to an End', *The Statesman* (Kolkata, April 1, 2006) and 'An Amanullah Recipe for Bengal's, *The Stateman* (Kolkata, April 4, 2006). Amanullah was the observor in West Bengal during the 2004 Parliamentary elections.

7. *Census Report 2001*. The Muslim Community constitutes 25.25 percent of the total population of West Bengal.

8. *Field Survey*, CSDS 1999 and 2001 elections; UPIASI Field Survey, 2004–05.

9. *The Statesman* (Kolkata), May–June 2005; *The Times of India* (Kolkata), May 15–20, 2005.

10. Myron Weiner, *The Politics of Scarcity* (Calcutta: Asia Publishing House, 1963); Marcus Franda, *Political Development and Political Decay in Bengal* (Calcutta: Firma K.L. Mukhapadhyay, 1971); Paul Brass, *Ethnicity and Nationalism* (New Delhi/Newbury Park/London: Sage Publications, 1991); Atul Kohli, *The State and Poverty in India* (Cambridge: Cambridge University Press, 1987); *Democracy and Discontent* (Cambridge: Cambridge University Press, 1991).

11. Nossiter, *Marxist State Governments in India: Politics, Economics and Society* (London and New York: Printer Publishers, 1988), pp. 138–39.

12. Out of more than 48,600 seats in three tiers, the LF won 6,800 seats uncontested. The major Opposition parties could not field candidates in 22,000 seats in the 2003 election. The local newspapers widely reported the allegations of opposition parties 'that the local leaders of the CPI(M) prevented the main opposition parties to file their nomination papers.'

13. Pranab Bardhan and Dilip Mookerjee, 'Political Economy of Land Reforms in West Bengal', *Journal of Political Economy*, Vol. 110, No. 2, pp. 239–89.

14. Ross Mallick, *Development Policy of a Communist Government: West Bengal since 1977* (Cambridge: Cambridge University Press, 1993), Chapter 5; *see also The Statesman* (Kolkata), February 10, 1998.

15. Interview with IPS officers (in service), January 15, 2004, and Amiya K. Samanta (retd. DG), August 17, 2005.

16. *The Statesman* (Calcutta), May 25, 1980 and *Ananda Bazar Patrika* (Kolkata), September 30, 2005, reporting on 'government sponsored strike and bandh.'

17. Interview, Jyoti Basu said: 'many of the Congress leaders used to come to Him, while in office, for some personal favours,' September 4, 2004.

18. *Sources*, Central Party office of the CPI(M), Kolkata. Number of members of the Party's frontal organizations: Student Federation of India—0.01 million,

Democratic Youth Federation of India—0.07 million, Krisak Sabha—0.13 million, CITU—0.01 million, and CPI(M) Party members—266,000 as of December 2004.

19. *Census Report 2001*, Government of India, New Delhi.
20. Arild Engelsen Ruud, *Poetics of Village Politics: The Making of West Bengal's Rural Communism* (New Delhi: Oxford University Press, 2003).
21. Neil Webster, *Panchayati Raj and the Decentralization of Development Planning in West Bengal* (Calcutta: K.P. Bagchi & Co., 1992); G.K. Lieten, *Development, Devolution and Democracy: Village Discourse in West Bengal* (New Delhi: Sage Publications, 1996).
22. Bardhan and Mookerjee, op. cit., p. 239.
23. *Ananda Bazar Patrika* (Kolkata), July 27, 2005.
24. *Dainik Statesman* (Bengali edition of *The Statesman*, Kolkata), July 30, 2005.
25. *Ananda Bazar Patrika* (Kolkata), August 8, 2005.
26. *India Development Report 2004–05* (New Delhi: Oxford University Press, 2005), p. 4.
27. *Ananda Bazar Patrika* (Kolkata), August 21, 2005.
28. *West Bengal Human Development Report 2004*, Government of West Bengal, op. cit.
29. *CSDS Survey*, 1999 and 2001 elections; *UPIASI field survey*, 2004–05.
30. *West Bengal: An Analytical Study* (New Delhi: Oxford and IBH Publishing Co., 1971).
31. S.N. Sen, *The City of Calcutta* (Calcutta: Book Land Private Ltd., 1960), p. 224.
32. Nossiter, *Marxist State Governments in India*, op. cit., p. 24.
33. *The Statesman* (Calcutta), November 10, 1969.
34. Sajal Basu, *Politics of Violence: A Case Study of West Bengal* (Calcutta: Minerva Associates, 1982).
35. *The Statesman* (Calcutta), May 16, 1971.
36. *The Statesman* (Calcutta), March 22–23, 1970.
37. The Chief Minister said this on the floor of the West Bengal Legislative Assembly. See *WBLA Proceedings*, Vol. 50, No. 1 (February 5, 1970).
38. Buddhadeb Bhattacharya et al. (eds), *People's Power in Practice: 20 years of Left Front in West Bengal* (Calcutta: National Book Agency Private Limited, 1997), pp. xvii–xx.
39. Ibid., p. xii.
40. *The Pratichi Health Report*, 2005 (Delhi: Pratichi [India] Trust, 2005).
41. Aloke Banerjee, 'Bengal tops the hunger list', *The Hindustan Times* (Kolkata), July 14, 2004.
42. *The Statesman* (Calcutta), February 23, 1991.
43. *The Statesman* (Calcutta), January 23, 1993.
44. *The Statesman* (Calcutta), August 30, 1993.
45. *The Statesman* (Calcutta), August 31 and September 4, 1993.

46. David Apter, *Introduction to Political System* (New Delhi: Prentice Hall of India, 1981), p. 158.

47. *The Statesman* (Calcutta), May 4, 1995.

48. John R. Wood (ed.), *State Politics in Contemporary India, Crisis or continuity?* (London: West View Press, 1984), pp. 81–102; Atul Kohli, 'From Élite Activism to Democratic Consolidation: The Rise of Reform Communism in West Bengal', in Francine R. Frankel and M.S.A. Rao (eds), *Dominance and State Power in India: Decline of a Social Order,* Vol. II (New Delhi: Oxford University Press, 1990), pp. 367–415.

49. *The Statesman* (Calcutta), November 12, 1989.

50. *The Statesman* (Calcutta), December 10 and 20, 1995.

51. *The Statesman* (Calcutta), January 2, 1997.

52. Interview with Samir Putatunda, Secretary, Party for Democratic Socialism (PDS), and CPI(M)'s former 24-Parganas (South) district committee secretary (expelled since), August 31, 2005.

53. Interview with Suman Chatterjee, Executive Director (till September 30, 2005) Star Anand TV, September 10, 2005.

54. *Ganasakti,* May 3, 2001 (CPI[M]'s party paper).

55. *The Statesman* (Kolkata), August 11, 2005; *Dainik Statesman* (Kolkata), July 26, August 11 and 12, 2005; Manas Ghosh on Election Observer's Reports, *The Statesman* (Kolkata), August 28, 2005.

56. Robert Putnam et al., *Making of Democracy Work: Civic Tradition in Modern Italy* (New Jersey: Princeton University Press, 1993).

57. Neela Mukherjee, 'Measuring Social Capital', *Economic and Political Weekly,* July 20–26, 2002, p. 2994.

58. Amiya K. Chaudhuri, 'Regime Changes in West Bengal and the 1999 Parliamentary Elections', in Paul Wallace and Ramashray Roy (eds), *India's 1999 Elections and 20th Century Politics* (New Delhi: Sage Publications, 2003), pp. 249–72.

59. *Gana Barta,* RSP Party paper, where the opinion of the Party was published, and quoted in *Dainik Statesman* (Bengali edition of *The Statesman,* Kolkata), September 15, 2005. Ashoke Ghosh, the Forward Bloc state committee secretary, issued a statement against land transfer to the Salim Group (same source, same date).

60. Putnam et al., *Making of Democracy Work,* op. cit.

About the Editors and Contributors

EDITORS

RAMASHRAY ROY is a founding-member and former director (1976–82) of the Center for the Study of Developing Societies, Delhi. He is currently a visiting Fellow at the G.B. Pant Social Science Institute, Allahabad. During a long and distinguished career, Professor Roy has taught at several prestigious universities including the University of Texas, Austin; the University of California at both Los Angeles and Berkeley; and the University of Missouri, Columbia. A recipient of Woodrow Wilson and Ford Foundation Fellowships, Professor Roy has also been a National Professor of the University Grants Commission (1987) and a National Fellow of the Indian Council of Social Science Research (1994–96). His areas of interest include political parties, bureaucracy, electoral behavior, Indian politics, development, Gandhian thought, and political philosophy. His most recent of over 20 books is *Democracy in India: Form and Substance* (2005). Recently, he also completed a research project on 'Development, Communalism and Insurgency: The Case of the Northeast Region of India.'

PAUL WALLACE is Professor Emeritus of Political Science at the University of Missouri, Columbia. He has been a consultant on South Asia to members of the US Senate Foreign Relations Committee, the US Attorney General's Office, defense lawyers, and other agencies in North America and has received five Smithsonian-funded awards for national election studies in India. His research in India also includes a Senior Fulbright Research Award, and funding from the Ford Foundation and American Institute of Indian Studies. Professor Wallace is the author or editor of seven books and 40 book chapters and articles. His last book, with Ramashray Roy, is *India's 1999 Elections and 20th Century Politics* (Sage Publications, 2003). His latest chapter publication is 'Counter-terrorism in India: Khalistan and Kashmir' for a

US Institute of Peace book, *Democracy and Counter-terrorism: Lessons From the Past* (2006). In September 2003, Professor Wallace served as the expert witness on Sikh violence at the Air India trial in Vancouver, Canada.

CONTRIBUTORS

MOHAMMED BADRUL ALAM is Professor of Political Science, Jamia Milia Islamia University, New Delhi. His two major books are *Constructing Nuclear Strategic Discourse: The South Asian Scene* (2005) and *Essays on Nuclear Proliferation* (1995). Some of his recent publications deal with state politics of India, US–India relations, Indo–Japanese relations, and security issues of northeast Asia.

SIKATA BANERJEE is Associate Professor of Women's Studies at the University of Victoria, Canada. Her two major books are *Warriors in Politics: Hindu Nationalism, Violence, and the Shiv Sena in India* (2000) and *Make Me A Man!: Masculinity, Hinduism, And Nationalism In India* (2005). She has also contributed articles to *Asian Survey and Women and Politics*.

AMIYA K. CHAUDHURI is a Fellow, Maulana Abul Kalam Azad Institute of Asian Studies, Kolkata; Visiting Lecturer at Calcutta University and also a member of the Lokniti network, Center for the Study of Developing Societies, Delhi. He has been associated with Vidyasagar University and Netaji Subhas Open University, Kolkata. He has authored *Legislative Control over Public Administration and Contemporary Indian Politics and Administrative Disorder* (in Bengali). He has written over 30 research papers in professional journals, 10 chapters in different edited volumes, and is a regular newspaper columnist, having contributed more than 200 articles. He authored the chapter on West Bengal in Paul Wallace and Ramashray Roy (eds), *India's 1999 Elections and 20th Century Politics* (Sage Publications, 2003).

JYOTIRINDRA DASGUPTA is Professor Emeritus of Political Science at the University of California, Berkeley, where he also served as

Chairman of the Program in Development Studies. His work has focused on development politics, language planning, ethnic mobilization, and socio-economic development both in India and in comparative perspective. His publications include *Language Conflict and National Development: Group Politics and National Language Policy in India* (1968) and *Authority, Priority, and Human Development* (1981). Some of his recent publications deal with different aspects of multicultural democratization and federal development processes.

RAJESH DEV is faculty member in the Department of Political Science at Women's College Shillong, and visiting faculty in political science in the Department of Law, North Eastern Hill University, Shillong. His research interests are in areas of political ethnography, identity politics and democratic discourse, as well as human rights and political ethnography. His recent co-edited books include *Ethnonarratives, Identity and Experience in Northeast India* and *Ethnic Identities and Democracy* (2006). He has also authored numerous articles and chapters. He is Executive Secretary of argueIndia, a re-search group based in Shillong.

SANDHYA GOSWAMI is Reader in the Department of Political Science, Guwahati University, Assam. Her M.A. and M.Phil degrees are from the Center of Political Studies, Jawaharlal Nehru University, and Ph.D. from Guwahati University. She has authored *Language Politics in Assam* and also published several research papers in prominent journals and edited books. She authored the chapter on Assam in Paul Wallace and Ramashray Roy (eds), *India's 1999 Elections and 20th Century Politics* (Sage Publications, 2003).

PRAMOD KUMAR is Director, Institute for Development and Communication (IDC), Chandigarh, and a recipient of the Homi Bhabha Fellowship in 1988. Among his published works are *Polluting Sacred Faith: A Study on Communalism and Violence* (1992), *Punjab Crisis: Context and Trends* (1984), *Victims of Militancy in Punjab* (co-author) (2001), and *Towards Understanding Communalism* (edited) (1992). He has written more than 24 articles and chapters, including the chapter on Punjab in Paul Wallace and Ramashray Roy (eds), *India's 1999 Elections and 20th Century Politics* (Sage Publications, 2003).

SANJAY KUMAR is Fellow at the Center for the Study of Developing Societies (CSDS), Delhi, specializing in survey research and electoral politics. He was their National Coordinator of National Election Studies for 1998, 1999, and 2004. He also directed various other CSDS national and state-level studies, and participated in a pioneering study on assessing election expenses during the 1999 Lok Sabha elections. He has contributed more than 125 articles to national dailies, news magazines, academic journals, and edited volumes.

MONOJ KUMAR NATH is in the Department of Political Science, Nowgong College, Guwahati University. He received his M.A. degree from Jawaharlal Nehru University, New Delhi, and is currently working towards his Ph.D. degree.

GHANSHYAM SHAH is Professor (Retired), Jawaharlal Nehru University, and former Director, Center for Social Studies, Surat. He is author and editor of several books, among them *Social Movements in India* (Sage Publications, 2004), *Caste and Democratic Politics in India* (2004), *Public Health and Urban Development: The Plague in Surat* (1997), and *Dalit Identity and Politics* (Sage Publications, 2001).

KARLI SRINIVASULU is Professor of Political Science at Osmania University, Hyderabad. He has been Visiting Fellow at Queen Elizabeth House, University of Oxford, and Senior Fellow of the Indian Council of Social Science Research. Dr Srinavasulu's research interests include political theory, agrarian and Dalit movements, electoral politics and public policy. He has numerous publications to his credit, including the chapter on Andhra Pradesh in Paul Wallace and Ramashray Roy (eds), *India's 1999 Elections and 20th Century Politics* (Sage Publications, 2003). His forthcoming book is *Karamchedu, Chunduru and Beyond: Dalit Movement in Andhra Pradesh*.

VIRGINIA VAN DYKE is an Affiliate Assistant Professor at the South Asia Center, Henry M. Jackson School of International Studies, University of Washington. She was formerly an Assistant Professor in Political Science at the University of Wisconsin-Milwaukee. Her research interests include religion and politics, religious mobilization and electoral politics in India. She has published on these topics, including in the Roy–Wallace Sage election books, as well as on communal violence.

Index

Acharya, Suryakant 159

Adivasis 163
  and Hindu culture 168
  vote-banks in Gujarat 169

Advani, L.K. 104, 159, 285
  in Gujarat 170
  rath yatra of 156, 169–70, 277

Adivashi Kranti Sangathan, Orissa 273

Ahilyabai 43

Akali Dal 65
  and Bharatiya Janata Party government in 128
  Communist Party of India (M) and Janata Party coalition in Punjab 127
  government in Punjab 127
  Jan Sangh support to 125

Akalis 128, 129

Akhil Bharatiya Vidyarthi Parishad (ABVP) 155, 277, 289

Al-Aqsa mosque, attack on, and protests by Muslims 154

Ali, Syed Amir 110n

Aligarh, educational movement in 91, 92
  religious nationalism in 92

All Assam Tribal Students Union (AATSU) 231, 232

All India Anna Dravida Munnetra Kazhagam (AIADMK), Tamil Nadu 11, 15

All India Catholic Congress, Kerala 137

All India Women's Conference 34

All Khasi–Jaintia Students Union (AKJSU) 248

All India Trinamul Congress (AITC), in Meghalaya 258, 259

All Peoples Hill Leaders Conference (APHLC) (1970) 242, 244, 245, 246, 251, 254, 256

Alliance for the Reconstruction of Meghalaya (ARM) 247

alliance politics 4

Alva, Margaret 51, 54

Ambedkar, B.R. 137, 164
  adoption to Buddhism by 167

Andaman and Nicobar Islands, rehabilitation of uprooted population in 301

Andhra Pradesh 4
  agricultural crisis in 191
  Adarana scheme in 184
  Assembly elections of 1994 and 2004 in 63, 64
  Cheyutha scheme in 185
  DWCRA program in 184, 193, 203n
  economy of 186
  elections and law and order and anarchy in 186–88
  electoral discourse in 201
  farmers' suicides in 190, 200
  issue of rural crisis in 201
  life conditions in 21–23
  mandals in 183
  Naxalite question in 201
  politics and policy discourse in 2004 elections in 180, 185–200
  Roshni scheme in 184

women and DWCRA in 193
World Bank loan to, 200
and conditionalities for 193,
195–96
Anthony, A.K. 138
anti-defection law 120
Area Local Tribal Village Council
(ALTVC), Orissa 273
Arunachal Pradesh 241
Arya Samaj 72, 101, 102, 110n, 114n
Ashok Mehta Committee Report 295
Asom Gana Parishad (AGP) 232, 234
Assam 241
 Cachar constituency in 235, 237
 Congress government in 233
 ethnic diversity in 229, 230
 Karbi Anglong constituency in
  235, 237
 Kokrajhar constituency in 230,
  233, 234, 235–36
 Lok Sabha elections of 1991–2004
  in 231
 politics of separatism in 229
 separatist politics in 4
 tribal population in 229–38
 tribal votes in 235
 voting patterns in Lok Sabha elec-
  tions in 238, 239
Assam Movement (1979–85) 235, 239
Atmiya Sabha 82
Austin, Granville 25
Autonomous District Council, Assam
 230, 242
Autonomous State Demand Committee (ASDC) 235, 237
Awami League 112n

Babri Masjid, campaign for demolition
 of 156
 demolition of 103, 157
backward castes, justice for 61
 mobilization of 68
 political dominance in Bihar 226

social empowerment of 217
support to Congress 15
Badal, Prakash Singh 126, 127, 128,
129
 Bharatiya Janata Party support to
  124
Bahujan Samaj Party (BSP) 69, 72–73,
128, 185
 Bharatiya Janata Party coalition in
  Uttar Pradesh 130–33
 manuwad ideology of 73
 in panchayat elections 130
 purity and pollution ideology of
  72, 73
Bajrang Dal 170, 174, 176, 277
 in Orissa 269, 285, 289
Bal, Pradyumna 270
Banabasi Kalyan Ashram, in Orissa
 277, 289
'Bande Mataram' 109n
Bangla Congress 302, 304
Banerjee, Mamata 11, 18, 35, 48, 54,
297, 314, 316
 anti-CPI(M) campaign of 309
 founding of Trinamul Congress
  (AITC) 310
Bangladesh, creation of 94, 112n
Bangladesh war, of 1971, 305
 and displaced persons 294
Baria, Bijay Singh 271
Barnala government, in Punjab 127
Baruah, Sanjib 240
Basu, Biman 308
Basu, Jyoti 308, 313
 -led coalition government in West
  Bengal 291, 302, 304–6
Behera, Abhimanyu 274
Bengal, development in language, edu-
 cation and communication in
 82–85
 Hindu and Muslim culture in 81
 Hindu religion and social reform
  movements in 80

leadership in 86
partition of 94, 98
popularization of patriotic songs in
    88–89
Bengali, media, and social reforms 84
    as official language in Pakistan 96
Behera, Anjali 272
Bharat Kalyan, Gujarat 170
Bharti, Kamlesh 44
Bharti, Uma 35, 43, 48, 51, 54
Bharatiya Janata Party (BJP) 1, 4, 14,
    58, 62, 103, 104, 118, 122, 165,
    166
    in Bihar 5, 208, 222–25
    Biju Janata Dal coalition in Orissa
        267, 268, 271, 277, 279–80,
        287, 288
    and *chaturvarna* system 162
    and CPI(M) in West Bengal 308,
        309
    Dalits' support to 167, 168
    defection from United Front gov-
        ernment 67–68
    formation of 102
    in Gujarat 69, 70, 155–56, 159–61,
        178
        in Assembly elections 69, 70,
            157–58, 161, 162
        in 2004 Lok Sabha elections
            161
        in ST reserved constituency
            elections 171–72
        and spread of *Hindutva* in 176
        upper caste support to 173
    Hindu *rashtra* ideology of 162
    'India Shining' campaign of 62
    and Janata Dal (U) alliance in
        Bihar 206–8, 210, 217, 226,
        227
    in Meghalaya Lok Sabha elections
        245, 258–59
    -led National Democratic Alliance
        (NDA) 128, 233–34
    in Orissa politics 5, 276–78,
        285–86, 289
    in Parliament elections of 1984–
        2004 2, 10, 68
    Patidars' support to 165
    in Punjab 129
    rise of 294
    and Samata Party alliance in Bihar
        208, 209, 226
    setback in 2004 Lok Sabha elec-
        tions 212
    Shiromani Akali Dal (SAD), sup-
        port to 124
    support base of 15
    on Telangana issue 189
    and Telugu Desam alliance in
        Andhra Pradesh 185
    in tribal constituencies 170
    tribals' support in Orissa 288–89
    in 2001 elections in West Bengal
        312
    in West Bengal 299
Bharatiya Kisan Sangh 177
Bhattacharya, Buddhadeb 296, 308,
    311, 313
    as Chief Minister of West Bengal
        314, 315
Bhindranwale, Sant Jarnail Singh,
    Congress support to 127
Bihar, alliance politics in Lok Sabha
    elections in 4
    Assembly elections of 1995 225
    of 2005 in 207
    backward castes dominance in
        politics in 226
    civic amenities and economic con-
        ditions in 219–22
    election alliances in 206, 215
    Janata Dal (U)-led coalition gov-
        ernment in 206
    Lok Sabha elections of 2004 in
        206, 210
    members of Parliament from 220

performance of governments in 218–21

social patterns of voting in 222–25

Biju Janata Dal (BJD) 11, 267, 285
and Naveen Patnaik 286
victory in Lok Sabha elections 274

Biswal, Basant 276, 281, 282

Biswal, Chiranjeeb 281, 282

Biswal, Ranjiv 270, 276, 281

Bodo Accord of 1993 232, 233

Bodo nationalism, in Assam 230

Bodo-Boro Kachari tribe, in Assam 230

Bodoland, demand for, by Bodos 230, 231, 232

Bodoland Territorial Autonomous District (BTAD) 233

Bodoland Territorial Council (BTC) 232, 233
Accord of 2003 233, 234

Bolshevik Party 302

Brahmo Samaj, in western and southern India 86

Brahmins, in Gujarat 163

Brahmo religious services 83

Brahmo Samaj 82, 85
reformers in Bengal 88
struggle against tradition and rituals 86

Burman, Banshibadan 300

Bwiswmuthiary, S.K. 233, 234

caste, and electoral politics 58, 67
evils of 83
groups, and voting pattern in 1999–2004 elections 14–15
as political capital 71–73

Center for Indian Trade Unions (CITU) 309

Central National Mohammedan Association (1877), Bengal 110n

Chakraborty, Jatin 307

Chakraborty, Subhas 311

Chandigarh, issue of status of 128

Chandra, Kanchan 28

Chandrasekhar 50

chastity, notion of 39–46, 48, 52, 54

Chatterjee, Bankimchandra 89, 109n, 110n

Chaturvarna system 162, 164, 167

Chaudhari, Amarsinh 169

Choudhury, Nabakrishna 269

Chowdhury, Benoy 309

Chief Election Commissioner 67

Christian missionaries 85
propaganda by 83

Christianity 81

Clinton, Bill 20

closed minimal range theories (CMRT) or policy 121

coalition governments, in India 58, 117, 118
and feudalism 123

Committee on the Status of Women, report of 35

communal monoliths, as vote banks 68–71

communal riots 156, 157
in Gujarat 154–55, 161
and electoral mobilization 153–62

Communist Party of India (CPI), 302
in Kerala 139
in Meghalaya 245
in West Bengal 291, 293, 305

Communist Party of India (Marxist) (CPI[M]) 313
and Akali Dal and Janata Party coalition in Punjab 127
and Bharatiya Janata Party (BJP) in West Bengal 308
in West Bengal 5, 291, 293, 298, 299, 306, 316

Communist Party of India (Marxist-Leninst) (CPI[ML]), formation of 304

communities, religion and cohesion 77–79

composite nationalism 98, 99, 101, 104

Comptroller and Auditor General's (CAG), reports of 307

Congress party 2, 4, 10, 13, 14, 58, 97, 98
    and allies victory in 2004 elections 214–15
    in Andhra Pradesh Lok Sabha elections of 2004 64, 187, 190–92, 197–99, 202n
        coalition discourse in 193–94, 200, 201
        government in 195
        Pourna Spandana Vedika program in Andhra Pradesh 201
    in Assam, government of 233
        support to 234–35
    Backward community support to 15
    in Bihar, support to 208, 223–34
    Brahmin leaders in Bihar 225
    and crisis of 1967 102
    defeat in 1977 parliament elections 11, 30n, 31n
    election manifesto of 62
    Emergency and defeat of 307
    in Gujarat Assembly elections 70, 71, 157, 158, 162, 165, 169, 171–73
    -led government in Kerala 138, 139
    Koli-Kshatriya base of 166
    Left parties support to, at Center 122, 138
    in Meghalaya Lok Sabha elections 245, 258, 259
        history in Meghalaya 251, 253, 254
        -led government in Meghalaya 246–47, 265n
        -led UMPF in Meghalaya 256

Members of Parliament 29
    in nationalist movement 99
    in Orissa Lok Sabha elections of 2004 267, 284–85, 287–89
    in Punjab 124–27, 129, 138
    and RJD alliance 211
    role in factional politics 139
    role in Khilafat movement 113n
    Scheduled Castes' support to 14
    Sonia Gandhi-led 248
    and Telangana issue 188
    and Telangana Rashtriya Samity (TRS) alliance in Andhra Pradesh 185, 202n
    -led UPA government at Center 2, 122, 138
        coalition with RJD, DMK, National Congress, and Left parties 11
    in Uttar Pradesh 138
    in West Bengal 293, 297, 299, 301, 302, 305

Congress (S), in Kerala 138

Constitution of India 25, 100
    73rd Amendment to 249

Dalit communities 61, 163, 167–68
    assertion in Punjab 72–73
    in Bihar 207, 216, 217, 226–27
    in Gujarat 167
    and 'pollution' 72
    social empowerment of 217

Dalit identity, concept of 71
    and political parties 72

Dalit politics 68–69

Dandakaranya, rehabilitation of uprooted population in 301

Dandavate, Pramila 50, 51

Darjee, Jinabhai 169

Das, Kamla 283

Dasgupta, Kamala 40

Dasgupta, Pramod 308

Datta, Aksay Kumar 83, 85

Debi, Sarala 39

Democracy 76
  and differential nationalism 100–105
  threat and need paradox of 66–67
Democratic Hills Movement (DHM) 247
Deo, Anant Pratap 271
Deo, Bikram Keshari 271
Deo, Bikram Singh 287
Deo, Pratap Keshari 271, 287
Deo, Sangeeta Singh 287
Deo, Sugyani Kumari 271, 272
Deoband school 92, 98
Deoras, Bal Saheb 178*n*
Deoris tribe, in Assam 230
depressed classes, campaign for rights by 87
Dharma Sabha 85, 108*n*
Dharma Vira 302
Dhengadi, Dattapant 167
Dhindsa 145*n*
differential nationalism, democracy and 100–105
Dima Halam Daogah (DHD), Assam 237
Dimsa tribe, in Assam 230
  in Nagaland 262*n*
discourse theory/analysis 181, 182
discourse coalition, concept of 194
Dravida Munnetra Kazagham (DMK), coalition with Congress-led UPA government 210

East Pakistan, killings in 95
Eastern India Tribal Union (EITU) 250
economic reforms 62
  under Rajiv Gandhi 61
education, development in 79
egalitarian universalism 86
Ekalaya Vidyalaya, Gujarat 170
electoral politics 1, 5, 53, 58
Emergency of 1975–77 30*n*, 66, 178*n*
  and defeat of Congress 11
  protests against 155

exclusive religious nationalism 97
exclusive representation, system of 93, 95
Ezhavas, in Kerala 136
  reservation for 137

factional politics 118, 120–23, 141, 197–99
federalism, in India 3, 100, 118, 141
  and coalition governments 123
  and factionalism 116
Federation of Khasi States 249
foeticide 35
Food for Work program, in Andhra Pradesh 196, 197
Forum Against Globalization (FAG) 196
Forward Bloc (FB), in Bengal 291, 293, 302, 305
freedom movement, and upliftment of Adivasis 169
fundamental rights, with social justice 25

Gamang, Giridhar 273, 276, 284
Gamang, Hema 272, 273, 276, 283, 284
Ganatantra Parishad/Jana Congress 268
Gandhi, Indira 30, 35, 46, 59, 66, 139, 201, 205*n*
  assassination of, and anti-Sikh riots 69
  'Garibi hatao' slogan of 59, 62, 155
  Internal Emergency of 11, 30*n*, 31*n*, 307
Gandhi, Mahatma 37, 40, 164–65
Gandhi, Rajiv 68, 308
  economic reforms under 61
  and Punjab Accord 127
Gandhi, Sonia 19, 48, 54, 57*n*, 283
Gandhian constructive workers, in Gujarat 169

Garos, in Meghalaya 243, 259
general elections *see* Lok Sabha elections
Ghising, Subhas 300
Ghosh, Shanti 40
Gill, Lachman Singh 121, 126
Giri, Pramila 272
globalization 71
Goa, governments in 117
Godhra incident 71, 151, 159, 161, 175
Gokhale, Gopal Krishna 88, 97
Golden Quadrilateral Project, of A.B. Vajpayee 279
Golwalkar, M.S. 154
Gore, Mrinal 54, 57*n*
Gorkha National Liberation Front (GNLF), in West Bengal 300
Government of India Act of 1935 111*n*
Gowda, H.D. Deve 210
'Greater Cooch Bihar Demand' 300
Grewal, Mahesh Inder Singh 129
Gujarat,
    Assembly elections in 159–61, 169
      of 1995 157
      of 2002 in 161, 162
    BJP victory in 2002 Assembly and 2004 Parliamentary elections 30*n*, 69, 70–71
    BJP and *Hindutva* in 176
    castes in 163–64
    Godhra incident and violence in 3, 69, 70, 104, 151–53, 161, 174, 177
    Jana Sangh and RSS in politics of 154
    panchayat elections in 157, 158, 160, 161
    riots in 159
    zilla panchayat elections in 160
Gujarat Kshatriya Sabha 164
Gujarat Swatantra Party 164

Haldia Petrochemical Project, in West Bengal 315

Hali (Urdu poet) 90
Haricharan, Bishwa Bhushan 287
Hedgewar 167
Hill Peoples Union (HPU) 245, 254, 256
Hill State Peoples Democratic Party (HSPDP) 245
Hindu cultural nationalism 102
Hindu Dharma, definition of 162
Hindu Dharma Raksha Samiti 154
Hindu Mahasabha 102
'*Hindu Rashtra*' 154
Hindu reform movement 82
Hindu vote bank 68
Hinduism 38
    and nationalism 3, 38, 76, 101–2, 103
    and social reform movements, in Bengal 80
    unity in 162–73
'Hinduness', notion of 101, 102, 162
Hindutva ideology 1, 3, 44, 70–71, 101, 102, 151–53, 156, 161, 162, 173, 174, 177
    in Gujarat 176
    issue of 103, 104, 158–59
Human Development Report 315
Hyderbad state, formation of 203*n*
Hynniewtrep National Front (HNF) 247

illiteracy 98
inclusive nationalism 91, 97
India, Pakistan war 154
    Partition of 99
'India Shining', BJP's slogan of 1, 21, 62
Indian National Congress 88, 97, 101
    founding of 90, 91
    Presidents' of 91
    see also Congress party
Indian Social Conference 86
industrialization 60

infanticide 35
Integrated Tribal Development Projects (ITDP) 274

Jaintia population, in Meghalaya 243
Jana Sangh 30*n*, 102
    alliance with Janata Morcha 155
    and Arya Samaj in Punjab 125
    in Gujarat 154–55
    and RSS in Gujarat politics 154
Janata Dal, in Gujarat elections 171
Janata Dal (U) 11, 15, 169
    in 2004 Lok Sabha elections 212
Janata Morcha, alliance with Jana Sangh 155
Janata Party 165
    and Akali Dal, CPI(M) coalition in Punjab 127
    government of in the Center 306
    collapse of 297
    in 1977 elections 210
Jayakar, M.R. 114*n*
Jayalalitha, J. 11, 18, 35, 48, 54, 57*n*
    withdrawal of support to Vajpayee government 19, 123
Jayaprakash Narayan 66
Jena, Mohan 285
Jena, Srikant 287
Jharkhand state 273
    creation of state of 226
Jharkhand Mukti Morcha (JMM) 266, 273, 277
    in Orissa 286
    victory in 2004 elections 288
Jijabai (Shivaji's mother) 37, 42–43, 46
Jinnah, Mohammed Ali 94, 95
Joshi, Manohar 10
Joshi, Murli Manohar 10
Jury Act of 1827 106
    petition against 81

Kamtapur Liberation Organization (KLO), in West Bengal 300
'Kamtapur movement', of Rajbanshis, in West Bengal 300

Kanungo, Trilochan 285
Kar, Sarat 279, 287
kar seva 156
Karbi tribe, in Assam 230
Kargil conflict 20, 21
Karnataka, coalition government in 143*n*
Karunakaran, K. 140
Kashikar, Sarojtai 47
Kashmir, secessionist insurgency in 103
Kerala,
    coalition government in 3, 116, 133–40
    and Center–state relations 138–40
    CPI and CPI(M) government in 139
    Congress-led government in 139
    Left Democratic Front (LDF) government in 134
    panchayat elections in 140
    President's Rule in 139
    two-front system in 118
    United Democratic Front (UDF), Congress-led government in 134
Kerala Congress 140
    Christian support to 136
Khan, Khan Abdul Gaffar 98
Khan, Prince Agha 93
Khan, Syed Ahmed 91–92
Khasi population, in Meghalaya 243, 259
Khasi Students' Union (KSU), Meghalaya 247, 248
Khilafat movement 113*n*
Khun Hynniewtrep National Awakening Movement (KHNAM) 247, 257
Kisan Sabha 99, 309
Kishwar, Madhu 47, 49
Koeris 225
    support to BJP–JD(U) alliance in Bihar 223

Koli caste, 163
   Kshatriya status of 164
Krishak Praja Party (KPP) 99
Kshatriya Sabha 166
Kshatriyas, in Gujarat 166
Kumar, Ashutosh 129
Kumar, Nitish 4, 208, 217, 227
Kurmis 225
   support to BJP–JD(U) alliance in
      Bihar 223
Kyndiah, Paty Ripple 258

Lakshmibai, of Jhansi 43
land reforms, implementation of 61
   in West Bengal 5
language reforms, and literary creations in Bengal 85
Lapang, D.D. 264n
Laxman, Bangaru 159
Left Democratic Front (LDF), in Kerala
   133, 140
Left Front, government in West Bengal
   13, 292–95, 306–9, 313, 316,
   317n
   Muslim support to 294
   in Parliamentary and Assembly
      elections in West Bengal 312
Left parties, in Andhra Pradesh 185,
   189, 200
   and economic reforms in Andhra
      Pradesh 195–97
literary works, impact of 89–90
Lok Jan Shakti Party (LJNSP) 211, 215
Lok Sabha elections, of 1952 10
   of 1971 155
   of 1977 11, 30n, 31n
   of 1989 10, 117
   of 1999 14, 19
   of 2004 1, 9, 11, 14, 15, 34, 161,
      173, 257–61
      regional patterns in 212–14
      significance of 209–11
   women's representation in 35, 36

Lok Sevak Sanga 302
Longowal, Sant 127
Lyngdoh, B.B. 251, 256
Lyngdoh, Sanbor Swell 258

Madhav, Ram 176
Madhok, Balraj 154
Maharashtra, panchayats in 47
   reform movements in 86
   women in panchayats in 49–51
Mahtab, Bhatruhari 269
Mahatab, Harekrushna 269, 276
Makawana, Kishor 159
Mallick, Pramila 272
Mandal agitation, and politics in Bihar
   207
Mandal Commission 61
Mandal–Masjid saga 68
Manipur 241
Maoists, in West Bengal 300
Mappila revolts, in Kerala 137
Marandi, Sudam 273, 288
Marbaniang, S. Loniak 258
Marxism 182
Marxist Forward Bloc 302
Marxist–Leninist ideology 302
Mawlong, E.K. 257
Mayawati 131, 133
   -led government 130
   withdrawal of support to BJP 132
Meghalaya, 'anti-foreigners movement'
   in 247, 248, 255, 256
   Assembly elections in 251, 252,
      254–57
   'confessional politics' in 255
   Congress-led government in
      246–47
   ethnic clashes in 254
   ethnicity in 255, 261
   ethno-regional identity and polit-
      ical mobilization 240
   Garos in 243
   Jaintias in 243

Khasis in 243
Land Transfer Act 246, 265*n*
Lok Sabha election of 2004 in 244, 257–61
matrilocal and matrilineal society in 250
political mobilization in 250–61
President's Rule in 256
regional parties in 245–46, 253
separatist politics in 4
statehood to 242
students and student bodies in political movement 247, 248
tribal culture in 245
women in politics, failure of 250
Meghalaya Democratic Party (MDP) 245, 257
Meghalaya Tribal Youth Organization (MTYO) 255
Meghalaya United Front, and Congress coalition in 256
Meghalaya United Parliamentary Party (MUPP) 256
Mehta, Balwantrai 154
'middle-class liberalism' 102
minimum winning coalition (MWC) 118, 120, 121
minorities 61
Mishing tribe, in Assam 230
Ministry of Tribal Welfare 274
Mishra, Brajesh 20
Mitra, Asok 296
Mitra, Biren 269
Mizoram 245
Modi, Narendra 159, 176, 177
    Gaurav Yatra of 161
    government in Gujarat 9
Mohanty, Sanchita 272
monotheism, politics of ideological 67–73
Mookherjee, Dilip 295
Mookerjee, Shyama Prasad 102, 104, 114*n*

motherhood 39
    notion of, in Hindu context 38, 39–46
Mukherjee, Ajoy 302
    government of 304–5
Mullick, Baidhar 282
multicultural secularism, politics of 67–73
Murmu, Draupadi 272
Musharraf, Pervez 71
Muslim population, in Bihar 207, 226–27
    élite 92
    electoral and popular politics 93
    in Gujarat 165
    in Kerala 137
    as minority community 91
    support to RJD in Bihar 222
    in West Bengal 294, 297, 301
Muslim League, in Kerala 136
    establishment of, in West Bengal 93
Muslim League, of undivided India, policy to divide India 94
Muslim nationalism 91, 92, 94–96
Muslim religious identity, politics of 93

Nagaland 241
    political parties in 262*n*
Naidu, Chandrababu 4, 64, 185–86, 189, 200
    defeat of 22
    government, on farmers 21–22
    janmabhumi program of 184
    reforms under 194
Naidu, Sarojini 37, 46, 52
    as President of All India Women's Council 34–35
Nair Service Society, Kerala 137
Naoroji, Dadabhai 97
nation building projects 59, 66, 67, 70
National Democratic Alliance (NDA) 2, 23, 62, 104, 145*n*, 188, 211
    Coalition government of 9, 18, 117

defeat of 11
formation of, in 1999 19
National Disinvestments 21
nationalism, religion and 3
Nationalist Congress Party (NCP)
214, 248, 249
nationalist formulations, and religion
79–83
nationalist movement 89, 90, 98
nationalization, policy of 60
Nav Nirman students, Gujarat move-
ment 155
Naxalites/Naxalism 188
problems in Andhra Pradesh 21,
187, 201
in West Bengal 300
Nayak, Archana 272, 287
Nayak, Surendra Nath 282
Nawab of Arcot 93
Nehru, Jawaharlal 100
social justice under 59
and secularism 67
Nivedita, Sister 39
North Eastern Area (Reorganization)
Act 1971 242, 251
North Eastern Hills Students Asso-
ciation (NEHSA) 248
North Eastern Region Indigenous
Students Federation (NERISF) 248
North Eastern Region Students Union
(NERSU) 248

one-party system, replacement/demise
of 5, 13
'Operation Barga', program in West
Bengal 294
Operation Blue Star 69, 127
Oram, Joel 277, 289
Orissa, Assembly elections of 2000 and
2004 278
Bharatiya Janata Party in 5
constituencies, voting trends in,
Aska 282
Balasore 283–84

Berhampur 282
Bhadrakh 281–82
Bhubaneswar 281–82
Bolangir 283
Cuttack 281–82
Dhenkanal 280–81
Deogarh 280–81
Jagatsinghpur 281–82
Jajpur 281–82
Kalahandi 283
Kendrapara 281–82
Keonjhar 280–81
Koraput 283
Mayurbhanj 283–84
Nowrangpur 283
Phulbani 283
Puri 281–82
Sambalpur 280–81
Sundargarh 280–81
dynasty/royals and, politics in
270–71, 275–76
factionalism in politics 268
Lok Sabha elections of 1999 and
2004 278, 279
Operation Mission Shakti program
in 271, 289
reservations for women 271–72
role of tribals in elections 272–75
voting trends in 280–84
women representatives from
271–72
Orissa Gana Parishad (OGP) 267
Other Backward Castes (OBCs) 163
in Bihar 217
in politics 225, 227
reservations for 225
and voting patterns in 223
and power in politics 207

Padhy, Surama 272
Padmanabhan, Mannath 139
Pakistan, creation of 1947 94
elections of 1970 96
military domination in 96

*panchayat*s, reservation for women in 49, 52
in West Bengal 298–99
women in Maharashtra 38, 49–51
Panda, Brahmanand 270, 281, 282, 285
Pandya, Haren 158, 159
Pani, Rudra Narayan 281
Panji, Jayaram 283
Papanna, Mutika 283, 285
partisan categories 88–94
Partition, politics of 94
Paswan, Ram Vilas 215, 216
alliance with Rashtriya Janata Dal (RJD) in Bihar 206
Patel, Chimanbhai 169
Patidars, in Gujarat 163, 164, 165
pativrata, notion of 37, 46, 48
Patnaik, Biju 269, 271, 285
Patnaik, Kumuduni 272, 279, 286
Patnaik, Jayanti 270, 276
Patnaik, J.B. 268, 269, 275, 280, 284
Patnaik, Naveen 5, 268, 273, 276, 279, 281, 282
government of 269, 271, 280
neutralization of defection in politics under 286–87
popularity of 289
Patnaik, Ramakrishna 279, 286
Patnaik, Soumya Ranjan 270, 276
Patra, Kartikeswar 283
Patra, Umarani 283
patronage, in politics 118, 120, 141
democracy 122
patron–client relationship 59, 65
Patsani, Prasanna Kumar 270
Patnaik, Bijaylaxmi 272
Pawar, Sharad 11
Peoples Democratic Front (PDF), Assam 232
Peoples Democratic Movement (PDM), Assam 245

Peoples' Rally Against Corruption (PRAC), in Meghalaya 257, 262
People's War Group (PWG), in Andhra Pradesh 187, 188
in West Bengal 300
Phule, Jotirao 87
Plains Tribal Council of Assam (PTCA) 231, 232
Poona Sarvajanik Sabha 86
political moblization, social preparation and 83–88
Popular United Front, coalition in Punjab 125–26
Power of Motherhood, The 44
Pradhan, Ajayanti 272
Pradhan, Debendra 276, 277
Pradhan, Dharmendra 276
Praja Socialist Party (PSP) 136, 302
Prarthana Samaj, in western India 86, 108*n*
Pratishthan Friends of Tribal Society, Gujarat 170
Premchand 101
Progressive Democratic Alliance (PDA), West Bengal 305
Progressive United Left Front (PULF), in West Bengal 302
Public Demands Implementation Convention (PDIC) 245
Pulaya Maha Sabha, Kerala 137
Punjab, Akali Dal–BJP government in 128
Akali Dal–Jan Sangh coalition government in 121, 126, 127
Assembly elections in 135
coalition government in 3, 116
and state–Center relations 124–29
CPI(M), Janata Party, and Akali coalition in 127
Congress victory in 2004 elections 64–65
division of, at Partition 94
factional politics in 138, 141

Lok Sabha elections of 2004 65
President's Rule in 126, 127
reorganization of boundaries 124, 125
Punjab Accord 127
purity, notion of 54

Rabha tribe, in Assam 230
Ragi, Darshan Singh 127
Ram Janambhumi movement, and Hindu vote bank 68
Ram *mandir*, controversy 156, 170
Ramakrishna Mission/order 39
Ranade, Madhav Govind 86–87, 88, 98
   approach to religion 87–88
Rani of Jhansi 39
Rao, K. Chandrasekhar 4, 23, 188
Rao, N.T. Rama 22, 192, 203n
   government of 183, 184
   popular image of 196, 201
Rao, P.V. Narasimha 282
Rao, Rajashekhar 32n
Rashtriya Janata Dal (RJD) 4 , 122, 206
   and backward castes mobilization 68
   coalition with Congress-led UPA government 209, 211
   CPI and CPI(M) alliance with 208, 209
   Congress alliance in Bihar 216
   Congress, Lok Jana Shakti Party alliances 206, 214
   defeat of, in 2005 Assembly elections in Bihar 206, 207
   gains in 2004 Lok Sabha elections 207, 212, 221
   political dominance in Bihar 209
   rural voters' support to 209, 222
   Yadavs and Muslim support to 215–16
Rashtriya Lok Dal (RLD) 131
Rashtriya Sevika Samiti 38, 40–43, 53

Rashtriya Swayamsewak Sangh (RSS) 9, 102, 103, 167–68, 277
   Emergency, and ban on 178n
   government in Bihar 226–27
   in Gujarat 155
   and *Hindutva* 71
   L.K. Advani faction 20
   in Orissa 269, 285, 289
   in Punjab 125
   *shakha*s in Kerala 136
   VHP combine 104
Rath, Radhanath 270
Ray, Dilip 269
Ray, Siddharth Shankar 294, 305
Rebellion of 1857 79
Reddy, Y. Rajasekhar 196
   Jaithra yatra of 192
   Padyatra by 191–92, 203n
religion/religious, conversion campaigns 103
   and electoral politics 58
   extremists 5
   and nationalism 3, 76, 95
   nationalist formulations and 79–83
   reforms 83
   symbols, and division of Bengal 98
representation, concept of 95, 97
   and constituencies 96–97
   right of 99
reservation policy, for OBCs and Scheduled Castes and Scheduled Tribes 165
Rongpi, Jayanta 237
Rout, Damodar 282
Routray, Nilamani 276
Revolutionary Communist Party of India (RCPI) 302
Revolutionary Socialist Party (RSP), in West Bengal 291, 293, 302
revolutionary terrorist movements, of 1920s and 1930s 40
Roy, B.C. 301

Roy, Rammohun 80–83, 106*n*
  attitude to Muslims 81
  reforms through Atmiya Sabha and
    Brahmo Samaj 82
Rudolph, Suzanne Huber 116

Savitri 46
Sabarmati ashram, chaste and celibacy
  members of 40
Sadhvi Rithambhara 35
Sadhvi Shakti Parishad 38, 40, 43–46,
  53
Sahu, Anadi 282
Sahu, Chandra Mohan 282, 284
Sahu, Chandra Sekhar 282
Shajanand, Swami, and peasant move-
  ment 98–99
Samata Party (SP) 208, 217, 225
  and backward caste mobilization 68
  and BJP alliance in Bihar 208, 209
Samajwadi Party, and backward mobil-
  ization 68
  BSP coalition 130
Sampradaya 84
Samyukta Socialist Party (SSP) 302
Sangh Parivar 5, 155, 156, 166, 168,
  170, 171, 174, 177, 277
  call for *Dharma Yudha* 157
  and *Hindutva* ideology 151
  in Orissa 285, 289
Sangma, Mukul 258, 259
Sangma, P.A. 248, 254, 256, 258, 259
Sangma, Williamson A. 251, 254
Sanmilita Janagosthiya Sangram Samiti
  (SJSS) 234
Sanskritization, process in Gujarat 163,
  164
Sarb Hind Shiromani Akal Dal, Punjab
  129
Satpathy, Nandini 269, 276, 281
Satpathy, Tathagat 269, 273, 276, 281,
  284
Savarkar, V.D. 162, 102
Scheduled Castes (SCs), support to

Congress 14, 141
  Population in West Bengal 297
Scheduled Tribes (STs) 15
  Constitution on safeguards to 274
  population in West Bengal 297
Scheler, Max 28
Scindia, Vijayraje 48, 54, 57*n*
secularism 99
Sen, Keshab Chandra 86
Sewa Bharati, Gujarat 170
Shah Bano, decision on 68
Shah Bano-Muslim Women's Act 67
Sharif, Nawaz 20
Shetkari Sangathana 47
Shiromani Akali Dal (SAD), Punjab
  11, 118
  BJP support to 124
  and Sikh nationalism 138
  see also Akali Dal
Shiromani Gurudwara Prabhadak
  Committee (SGPC), elections to
  126, 127
Shiv Sena 10
Shivaji 37, 42–43
Shree Narayana Dharma Paripalana
  Yogam (SNDPY), Kerala 137
Sikhism 72
Sikhs, atrocities against 67, 69
Singh, Ajit 131, 132
Singh, Amarinder 65
Singh, Bhai Ranjit 129
Singh, Charan 130
Singh, Giani Zail 127
Singh, Gurnam 126
Singh, Manjit 127
Singh, Manmohan 10, 11, 65
Singh, Raghuraj Pratap (Raja Bhaiya)
  130
Singh, Rajnikant 131, 271
Singh, Sant Fateh 126
Singh, Sugrib 274
Singh, V.P. 68, 210
  minority government of 308
Singh Deo, A.V. 271
Singh Deo, Amarjyoti 271

Singh Deo, Ananga Uday 287
Singh Deo, K.N. 271
Singh Deo, K.P. 269, 271, 276, 281, 284
Singh Deo, Kalikesh Narayan 287
Singh Deo, Kanak Bardhan 271, 287
Singh Deo, Kishor Chandra 271
Singh Deo, Pushpendra 271
Singh Deo, Rajendra Narayan 270, 271
Singh Deo, Sangeeta 271, 272, 287
Sinha, Yashwant 10
Social Conference 88
social justice 60
social preparation, and political mobilization 83–88
social revolutionary goals 25–27
socialism 60
Socialist Party 14
Socialist Unity Center of India (SUCI), in West Bengal 299
Socialists 99
Solanki, Madhavsinh 161
Sonwal tribe, in Assam 230
States' Reorganization Committee (SRC) 188
Students Federation of India (SFI) 309
Sudershan, K.S. 115n
Surat, communal riots in 157
swadeshi 62
Swadeshi movements 110n
Swain, Harihara 286
Swain, Kharavela 270
Swami, Subramanian 19, 20
Swain, M.A.K. 283, 284
Swatantra Party, Gujarat 165

Tagore, Debendranath 85
Tagore, Rabindranath 89, 108n, 109n
    'Bande Mataram' of 89
Taj Corridor scandal 132
Tandon, Balramji Dass 126
Tehelka 20

Telangana region, issue of 4, 23, 199, 204n
    demand for separate state 188–89, 194, 201
Telengana Aikya Vedika 204n
Telugu Desam Party (TDP), in Andhra Pradesh 15, 64, 188, 196–97, 201
    and BJP alliance 185
    and Chandrababu Naidu 186
    and economic reforms 200
    electoral campaign for 2004 elections 187, 189–90
    electoral defeat of 4, 180
    government of, and farmers' agitation 191
    Janmabhumi program of 192
    on Peoples' War Group 187–88
    policy shifts 183–85
    stand on Telangana 195
    women's vote for 193
Telugu Rashtra Samithi (TRS), Andhra Pradesh 23, 32n, 188, 189, 199, 204n
    Congress and Left parties alliances 185, 194
    and Telangana demand 194–95
Temple Entry Proclamation 137
Tiwa tribe, in Assam 230
Togadia, Pravin 159
Tohra, Gurucharan Singh 128, 129
Towards Equality Report 35, 53
tribal population, in Assam 229–38
    in Gujarat 169, 170
    and identity 229
    in Orissa 272–75, 288–89
    and politics 1, 4
    and solidarity, in Orissa 272
Tribal Sub Plan approach 274
Trinamul Congress (AITC), West Bengal 11, 293, 297, 299
    and Congress party 310
    joining NDA government 310

Tripura 241
TRMC 15

United Democratic Front (UDF), in
    Kerala 138
    Congress-led, government in Kerala
        134
United Democratic Party (UDP), in
    Meghalaya 245, 256
United Front, government in West
    Bengal 295, 302, 304
United Meghalaya Parliamentary
    Forum (UMPF), government in
    Meghalaya 256
United People's Democratic Solidarity
    (UPDS), in Assam 237
United Progressive Alliance (UPA),
    government at Center 2, 10, 30,
    209, 314
United Provinces 92–93
United Reservation Movement Coun-
    cil of Assam (URMCA) 232
Untouchables, temple entry for 137
upper castes, in Gujarat 165–66
Urdu, as state language in Pakistan 95,
    96
    symbolic value for Muslims 95
Usha Devi 271, 272
Uttar Pradesh, Assembly elections in
    135
    BJP–BSP coalition in 130–31
    coalitions in 3, 116, 130–31
    Congress in 122
    support of caste groups in 141

Vaghela, Shankarsinh 71, 157, 161, 166
Vajpayee, Atal Behari 1, 9, 10, 18, 19,
    20, 25, 104, 279, 286, 308
*Vana Samraksaha Samithi*s, in Andhra
    Pradesh 184
Vania caste, in Gujarat 163, 164
Vanvasi Kalyan Ashram, Gujarat 170

Verma, Saheb Singh 10
Vidyasagar, Iswar Chandra 80, 84–85,
    106*n*
    on Hindu widows 84
Vishwa Hindu Parishad (VHP) 9, 44,
    71, 159, 161, 174, 176, 277
    on construction of Ram *mandir* 157
    on Dalits 103
    in Orissa 269, 285, 289
    Sadhvi Shakti Parishad of 43
Vishwa Hindu Samachar 154
Vishwanathan, Shiva 22
Vivekananda, Swami 37, 39, 46
Vivekananda Kendra, Gujarat 170
Vokakkan, Father 139

Wadedar, Preetilata 40
Water Users' Associations, in Andhra
    Pradesh 184
Weiner, Myron 66
welfare programs 27
West Bengal, Assembly elections in
    291, 303, 305, 310, 311–12
    CPI(M) dominance in 5, 291
    development in 314
    industries in 300
    land reforms in 5, 315
    Left Front government in 292–95,
        297, 298 306–8
    Lok Sabha, elections of 1996 310,
        311
    elections of 2004 291
    Muslim population in 297
    support to Congress 301
    *panchayat*s in 292, 295, 298–99,
        316
    refugee rehabilitation in 294
    Scheduled Castes and Scheduled
        Tribe population in 297
    United Front government in 295,
        302, 304

West Bengal Human Development Report 2004 299, 300–301

Western Orissa Development Council (WODC) 278

wifehood, notions of 37–46

women, access to political power 2

disempowerment of 37

electoral participation by 3

Members of Parliament 53

movement in India 52

and *panchayat*s in Maharashtra 49–52

in politics 34, 51

and chastity 47–49

representatives from Orissa 271–72

right to education 42

status of 35

Workers' Party 302

World Bank 315

loan to Andhra Pradesh 200

Yadav, Laloo Prasad 4, 207, 209, 217, 225, 226

class and community opinion of, in Bihar 218

and victory of RJD 216–18

Yadav, Mulayam Singh 130, 145

Yadav, Sharad 208

Yadav, Yogendra 13

Yadav population, in Bihar 222, 223, 227

Youth Congress, in West Bengal 305, 306

Youth Democratic Front (YDF) 245